Academic Research in Business and the Social Sciences

George P. Moschis

Academic Research in Business and the Social Sciences

A Guidebook for Early Career Researchers

Springer

George P. Moschis
College of Management
Mahidol University
Bangkok, Thailand

ISBN 978-3-031-56547-2 ISBN 978-3-031-56548-9 (eBook)
https://doi.org/10.1007/978-3-031-56548-9

This Springer imprint is published by the registered company Springer Nature Switzerland AG
The registered company address is: Gewerbestrasse 11, 6330 Cham, Switzerland

Paper in this product is recyclable.

In memoriam
Nancy W. Moschis

Preface and Acknowledgments

Almost everyone who starts an academic journey aims for success. The level of success in academia is primarily determined by one's capacity to produce original research for scholarly journals. Mastering the art of conducting and publishing academic research is a prerequisite for academic success, which is why individuals preparing for an academic career typically undergo several years of training, often in doctoral programs. Therefore, the quality and quantity of academic research training that individuals receive play a crucial role in determining their chances of achieving a prosperous academic career.

The ability to publish in academic outlets hinges primarily on two distinct sets of skills: the capacity to conduct reliable research and the knack for articulating one's findings effectively in scholarly articles. In my experience, as well as that of many peers, doctoral programs primarily concentrate on honing the skills necessary for conducting trustworthy research. For instance, candidates pursuing a Ph.D. are typically mandated to enroll in courses covering both quantitative and qualitative research methods, and they gain practical experience applying these methodological skills to research projects, such as their dissertations. Doctoral students often receive minimal, if any, training in crafting research-based papers for academic publications like journals and conferences, unless such tasks are part of their degree requirements. Proficiency in writing and publishing academic work tends to develop gradually over time, drawing from a variety of formal and informal sources, such as journal guidelines, interactions with editors and reviewers, and collaboration with colleagues.

Early career researchers, especially those who have recently fulfilled the core requirements of their doctoral degree, are less likely to have acquired the essential abilities for crafting and publishing manuscripts when compared to more experienced researchers. Therefore, they face a significant disadvantage. In the realm of journal submissions, every paper competes for limited publication slots, and those who possess both the ability to conduct credible research and the necessary skills for effective publishing enjoy a distinct advantage in securing a spot in prestigious journals. Consequently, individuals who have not had the opportunity to undergo rigorous training and have yet to master the art of writing for academic journals are unlikely to publish in top-tier journals, or they will require more time to achieve this.

I was motivated to write this book with the aim of lessening the disparities in the essential skills needed for academic publishing. Since academic research preparation predominantly emphasizes training in conducting effective research, I recognized the necessity for a resource that could assist early career researchers in composing research papers suitable for academic journals. I initially recognized this need during my doctoral studies at the University of Wisconsin, where I realized that my education was primarily focused on research methodologies rather than the publication process. Several experiences further underscored the importance of being proficient in academic journal writing.

A few years later, during my initial year of employment at Georgia State University, I designed a doctoral research seminar in marketing that concentrated on both the execution and publication of academic research. As I continued to offer this seminar on an annual basis, I observed students from various departments within the College of Business, as well as from other colleges of my university and even from nearby universities, enrolling in the class. I frequently conveyed to my students that while they could acquire the skills for conducting solid academic research by studying the proper methodologies and applying scientific principles, the process of publishing was more of an art than a science. I would often express my apologies to them because what I was teaching about the publication process was drawn from my own experiences and those of others, and these experiences were not documented in any available books during that period.

I noticed similar disparities in the necessary skill sets for conducting research versus publishing research when I had the chance to instruct the same seminar, or condensed versions of it, to faculty members and doctoral students of universities in both developed and developing nations. The variations in research skills across these universities were primarily attributable to discrepancies in the quality and rigor of their doctoral programs. On the other hand, differences in the quality and quantity of publications within various departments and across universities tended to be a reflection of variations in experience when it came to publishing, particularly the number of years engaged in research activities.

Considering these disparities and the resulting demand for a book that aims to address them, I have chosen to undertake the task of writing this book, with the expectation that it will be especially helpful to early career researchers. Since many of the "skills" involved in publishing are akin to an art form that can evolve gradually, often randomly due to various situational factors, the book is intended to streamline and expedite the process of grasping the essentials of academic publication process. This, in turn, should contribute to narrowing the gaps in ability to conduct effective academic research, not only among early career researchers who had different levels of preparation, but between early career and seasoned researchers as well.

This project would not have been possible without the assistance of several individuals. First, I am indebted to several of my former doctoral students and later colleagues, including Andrew Baker, Euhun Lee, and Anil Mathur, who provided me with numerous opportunities to learn about several research topics for which I was not as informed. Their research projects made me aware of a wealth of information that helped me keep up with developments in several areas related to academic research and publishing, from new methodologies to technologies that have helped advance knowledge. Next, I thank many colleagues at Thailand's Mahidol University, especially Randall Shannon and Akkapot Preechai for their assistance at various stages of this project. The feedback I received from doctoral students and faculty members of universities where I presented some ideas related to several topics of this book were helpful in shaping my thinking. I am particularly thankful to doctoral students and colleagues of Georgia State University, Hellenic International University, St. Louis University, Florida Atlantic University, UCLA, University of Florida, Sejong University, University of Sydney, Thammasat University, University of Malaysia, University of London, German Institute for Japanese Studies, Universidade Presbiteriana Mackenzie, University of Maastricht, and Iowa State University.

I began developing materials that I have included in this book from the first year of my employment at Georgia State University, as I had to develop and teach a doctoral seminar on academic research. Because I was not aware of any book on the subject that I could assign to my students, quite frequently I had to share with them my notes and relevant materials, including research projects. Some of the initial feedback I received from them on these materials in the form of questions and criticism were helpful in shaping my views about topics covered in this book. As I was learning more about academic research and publishing from various sources (e.g., literature, colleagues, reviewers), I kept on developing and revising materials for this seminar; and I continued sharing materials and ideas with my students. And the information I kept on receiving about academic research and publishing would help me revise and crystalize my views. This process lasted during my entire academic career that I taught this course, at times in the form of a seminar. Therefore, I am indebted to the many of my doctoral students who challenged my ideas and views, and gave me reasons to change my thinking and learn from them. I am especially thankful to those Georgia State doctoral students who collaborated with me on various research projects, including Leah Bovell, Janee Burkhalter, Melany Chambers, Jodie Ferguson, Jeff Foreman, Monica Guillory, Jill Mosteller, David Nickell, Hung Vu Nguyen, Belgin Unal, and Todd Weaver. And, for the same reason, I am also thankful to my doctoral students at Thailand's Mahidol University, College of Management, including Yuanfeng Cai, Boonying Kongarchapatara, Varapa Rakrachakarn, Pattharanitcha Prakitsuwan, Sarinya Suttharattanagul, Thuckavadee Sthienrapapayut, Jul Thanasrivanitchai, and Preecha Yingwattanakul.

During my academic career, I was privileged to have the opportunity to work on numerous cross-national studies with dozens of colleagues in all five continents. I thank Masood Abessi, Zerrin Arslan. Maria Bacha, Betul Balikcioglu, Russ Belk, Sarah Benmoyal-Bouzaglo, Teresa Davis, Helen Duh, Salomao Farias, Vasso Grougiou, Gianluigi Guido, Ilias Kapoutsis, Hans Kasper, Florian Kohlbacher, Choong Kwai Fatt, Yuko Minowa, Roy Moore, Fon Sim Ong, Simone Pettigrew, Marco Pichierri, Cristiane Pizzutti, Ed Rigdon, Thorsten Teichert, Prakash Vel, and Takako Yamashita. The knowledge I gained by collaborating with them on these projects not only helped me improve my research skills but also better understand the landscape of cross-cultural inquiry that I have tried to include in some book chapters.

Finally, I want to thank those individuals who helped me write this book. The suggestions and drafts of materials brought to my attention by Kris Babicci, Carl Lindwall, and Murtaza Haider were extremely useful in developing some chapters of this book. I also appreciate the help of Ms. Thanaporn Panarmart, Pailin Natichai, and Jennifer Firoglanis-Moschis, who assisted me in the development of various sections of this project, including references and subject index.

Bangkok, Thailand George P. Moschis

Contents

About the Author

George P. Moschis (Ph.D., University of Wisconsin) is Professor of Marketing Emeritus at Georgia State University (GSU). After his formal retirement as the Alfred Bernhardt Research Professor of Marketing at GSU, he assumed the role of Professor of Management at Mahidol University, Thailand, where he established and leads the Consumer Life-course Studies Group (GLSG), a global network of academic researchers. Dr. Moschis is widely recognized as one of the foremost authorities in consumer behavior globally. A bibliometric assessment of the 42 most prolific authors in the *Journal of Consumer Research* during its initial 15 years, a period that overlaps with the first 10 years of his academic career, positions him as one of the most influential researchers and the most prominent figure in consumer research based on his contributions to understanding young consumers. Additionally, Dr. Moschis earned acclaim for his work on older consumers during the same 10-year period, earning him recognition in the esteemed *Journal of Marketing* as "...the most knowledgeable expert on marketing to the older consumer." And a 2023 analysis of all published researchers by Stanford University ranks him in the top 2% of the most cited in the world.As a member of Georgia State University's marketing and gerontology faculties for nearly four decades, Dr. Moschis developed and taught courses and seminars on academic research for 45 years worldwide. He also developed and taught the first-of-its-kind graduate course, "Marketing to Older Adults," and authored ten groundbreaking books, including *Consumer Socialization*, *Marketing to Older Consumers*, and *Consumer Behavior over the Life Course* (published in 1986, 1992, and 2019, respectively). These publications have been widely utilized by universities and practitioners alike. In 1986, he founded the Center for Mature Consumer Studies (CMCS), where he conducted numerous studies and disseminated information to thousands of companies, media, and trade publications through reports, newsletters, articles, interviews, and advisory services. Recognizing its excellence, *American Demographics* magazine acknowledged CMCS for five consecutive years during the early 1990s as one of the best sources of marketing information, distinguishing it as the only university-based center.Dr. Moschis is well-known among both academics and practitioners. He has been invited by numerous universities, government agencies, and companies to travel globally and share his expertise. Additionally, he has worked as a consultant for major corporations and has served as an expert witness in high-profile litigation cases. This book serves as a compilation of his extensive knowledge in academic research, acquired through various channels during his lengthy academic career. The primary aim of the book is to assist early career researchers in acquiring insights that are often gained through years of experience in academic publishing, rather than through conventional doctoral programs.

1 Overview

This book presents my views on how to conduct and publish effectual academic research. These views rely primarily on personal experiences and anecdotal evidence. I rely upon my own academic journey and the experiences of others that I have encountered throughout my lengthy career to construct narratives and provide rationale for my views on conducting and publishing successful academic research. Given the limited literature on the subject, mainly because effective academic research rooted in scientific methodology and published in scholarly journals, is still often considered more of an art than science, there is a divergence in viewpoints regarding how to effectively produce and publish impactful academic research. Therefore, I fully anticipate that not all readers will share my viewpoints, and many may strongly disagree with various aspects of them. Some might even perceive some of these ideas as conventional wisdom. Nonetheless, I hope that readers will find some of my suggestions worthy of contemplation.

In this chapter, I delve into the definitions and distinctions between various research types and their respective objectives. I underscore the significance of academic research and elucidate the essential components of research that contributes to the advancement of a field. Following that, I provide insights for individuals aspiring to embark on an academic career, shedding light on the research requirements and expectations within this path. Lastly, this chapter imparts knowledge about the essential elements for conducting effective academic research, encompassing the necessary skills and the requisite research-oriented mindset.

G. P. Moschis, *Academic Research in Business and the Social Sciences*,
https://doi.org/10.1007/978-3-031-56548-9_1

1.1 Research in Context

1.1.1 Definition and Types of Research

While there exists considerable disagreement regarding the definition of research, a common perspective tends to restrict research to the creation of new knowledge. This conception confines research to a primary category and establishes the criteria for its classification. In essence, research is seen as effective when it contributes to the expansion of existing knowledge, with experts in the field being the arbiters who assess whether the contribution significantly advances knowledge. Consequently, publications in peer-reviewed channels are recognized as research for "knowledge creation," while non-peer-reviewed publications in outlets like trade journals and textbooks are categorized as "knowledge dissemination." It is important to note that this distinction does not diminish the significance of the latter category, as it can be argued that research that cannot be effectively utilized by, or communicated to, those who could potentially benefit from it holds little value.

Research typically yields knowledge in either quantitative or nonnumerical forms. Quantitative research, focused on the collection and analysis of numerical data, deals with objective, measurable phenomena that can be expressed in quantitative terms like counts, percentages, or scores. Conversely, qualitative research concentrates on comprehending and interpreting nonnumerical data, addressing subjective, intricate, and context-dependent phenomena that are often challenging to quantify.

Excluding research dedicated to methodology development, we can generally classify knowledge-producing research into two categories: applied and theoretical. Applied research is typically problem-specific and commences with the identification of a particular problem, often framed as a research question, and seeks solutions for it, for instance, questions like "Do online food product advertisements influence consumers more than television ads?" or "Do older consumers exhibit greater loyalty to grocery stores than their younger counterparts?" The pursuit of answers to these questions often involves the employment of empirical or quantitative research methods. Applied research tends to be context-specific, nongeneralizable, and aids in comprehending the relationships between variables within specific scenarios or contexts.

On the other hand, theoretical research aims to establish broader principles, essentially developing theories that facilitate our comprehension of various phenomena. It goes beyond applied research by attempting to provide explanations for observed phenomena or correlations. It delves into theoretical inquiries, such as "Why are online ads more effective than TV ads?" or "What are the reasons behind the higher loyalty of older consumers compared to younger ones?" Theoretical research can take the form of empirical investigations designed to test theory-based hypotheses concerning variable relationships, often exploring "cause-and-effect" connections. Alternatively, it can involve qualitative research that seeks to gain insights into observed phenomena, enhancing our understanding across diverse contexts.

It is worth noting that these two types of research are not mutually exclusive. Applied research, particularly when it involves empirical observations of variable relationships, can serve as the foundation for theory development. Furthermore, as a robust theory should encompass the "what" (the nature of variable relationships), the "why" (explanations for observed relationships), and the "how" (the mechanisms leading to observed relationships), both quantitative and qualitative research approaches are valuable for comprehending and elucidating phenomena.

This book places its emphasis on both forms of knowledge-generating research that result in publications relevant to academia, such as those found in Scopus and ISI journals, for several compelling reasons. First, this type of research is more likely to capture the interest of peer-reviewed journals, which hold substantial importance in the context of faculty promotion, tenure decisions, and merit increases. Second, academic research experiences a greater demand, as evidenced by the acceptance rates of peer-reviewed journals, compared to research in nonacademic or practitioner-oriented publications. Third, a department's Ph.D. program quality, its graduates, and its overall reputation are directly linked to the quantity and quality of academic research produced by its faculty. Last, based on my own experiences, conducting effective academic research necessitates a broader skill set than is required for conducting various forms of applied research, especially commercial research.

1.1.2 Research in Academic Career

For individuals in the early stages of their academic journey or those contemplating an academic career but uncertain about its advantages, requirements, and overall nature, it is important to understand that an academic career can offer significant rewards, but it also presents specific challenges and expectations. The paragraphs below present a general overview of what you can anticipate in such a career:

- *Research.* Research is the core of an academic career. You will spend a significant amount of time conducting research, which includes designing experiments or studies, collecting and analyzing data, and writing research papers. Collaboration with other researchers is common.
- *Publishing.* A major part of academia is publishing your research findings in reputable academic journals. Expect the process to be rigorous, with peer reviews and revisions. Publishing is how you contribute to the body of knowledge in your field.
- *Teaching.* Many academic positions involve teaching undergraduate and/or graduate students. This can be highly fulfilling but also time-consuming. You will be responsible for developing course materials, delivering lectures, and grading assignments.
- *Service and administration.* In addition to research and teaching, academics often participate in university committees, serve as department chairs or program directors, and contribute to the broader academic community through service.

- *Continuous learning*. Academia is all about learning and staying updated. Expect to engage in ongoing education, whether it is through formal coursework, attending conferences, or self-directed learning. Keeping up with the latest developments in your field is crucial.
- *Mentoring*. As you progress in your career, you may have the opportunity to mentor graduate students and postdoctoral researchers. This involves guiding them in their research and helping them develop their own academic careers.
- *Networking*. Building a network of colleagues and collaborators is essential in academia. You will be attending conferences, seminars, and workshops and engaging in professional organizations to connect with others in your field.
- *Tenure track*. If you are on a tenure track, be prepared for a rigorous evaluation process that usually takes several years. Tenure offers job security and academic freedom, but it also comes with high expectations for research, teaching, and service.
- *Work-life balance*. Achieving a work-life balance can be challenging in academia due to the demands of research, teaching, and administrative responsibilities. Time management and self-care are crucial for maintaining well-being.
- *Research funding*. Securing research funding can be competitive, and it often determines the scope and scale of your research projects. Expect to spend time writing grant proposals and justifying the importance of your work.
- *Impact and recognition*. Your work's impact on your field and society is a key measure of success. Recognition may come in the form of awards, invitations to speak at conferences, or appointments to prestigious committees.
- *Interdisciplinary collaboration*. As research becomes increasingly interdisciplinary, expect to collaborate with researchers from other fields to address complex problems.
- *Job market variability*. The job market for academics can be competitive and variable. Positions may be limited in your specific field or geographic location, so flexibility may be required.
- *Public relations (PR)*. You will be expected to use various communication channels, such as media, social media, press releases, speeches, and events, to convey information to the public to help create a favorable image and reputation of your institution.
- *Community service*. Your research and teaching expertise can be of value to different groups of practitioners, who may request your paid or unpaid assistances in various forms, such as consulting, speaking at events, and expert witness in litigation cases.

Remember that the specific expectations and experiences can vary widely depending on your field, the institution you work at, and your career stage. An academic career can be intellectually stimulating and fulfilling for those passionate about their subject matter and dedicated to advancing knowledge in their field. However, it also demands resilience, determination, and adaptability to succeed in the long term.

1.2 Requirements for a Successful Academic Career

1.2.1 The Ph.D. Degree

If you aspire to pursue an academic career, a Ph.D. is typically a requirement because this degree prepares one for academic research that is a major expectation in universities. Doctoral programs are generally designed to produce academic researchers. Readers of this book who are either planning to purse an academic career or are at early stages of their academic career should reassess their career goals. It is not uncommon for persons who wish to pursue a doctoral degree to invest many years and resources in preparation for an academic career, only to find out later that they had made the wrong decision. Nor is it unusual for some of those committed to pursuing an academic career to decide that their choice of the doctoral program or university was not the best. Outcomes of these decisions are usually the result of inadequate or incorrect information that was used for their decision.

It has been my experience that many of those who decide to pursue a Ph.D. degree are not fully aware of its requirements, expectations, and demands. They do not know what a Ph.D. program is about, and many think it is an extension of a Master's program they finished by taking courses and keeping a full-time job. Pursuing a Ph.D. degree is a significant academic and personal undertaking, and it is important to consider your motivations and goals before committing to this path. Below are several compelling reasons why you might want to consider pursuing a Ph.D. degree:

- *Expertise in your field.* A Ph.D. program allows you to become an expert in a specific area of study. You will have the opportunity to dive deep into your chosen field and make a meaningful contribution to the body of knowledge in that area.
- *Research skills.* Ph.D. programs are research-intensive. You will learn valuable research skills, including data collection, analysis, and interpretation. These skills are transferable and can be applied in various professions.
- *Intellectual challenge.* If you have a strong passion for learning and problem-solving, a Ph.D. program offers an intellectually stimulating environment. You will be surrounded by like-minded individuals and engaged in stimulating academic discussions.
- *Career opportunities.* While academia is a common career path for Ph.D. graduates, these degrees are valuable in other sectors as well. Many industries value the research, critical thinking, and project management skills that Ph.D. holders possess.
- *Contribution to knowledge.* A Ph.D. allows you to make a real impact by advancing knowledge in your field. Your research can have practical applications and contribute to societal progress.
- *Personal fulfilment.* For many, the pursuit of a Ph.D. is a deeply fulfilling and personally rewarding experience. It gives you a chance to explore your intellectual curiosity to the fullest.

- *Networking.* Graduate programs often provide opportunities to network with experts in your field, attend conferences, and collaborate on research projects. These connections can be invaluable in your future career.
- *Autonomy.* Ph.D. programs typically offer a high degree of independence. You have the freedom to choose your research topics and work at your own pace.
- *Global perspective.* Ph.D. programs typically are international, allowing you to collaborate with scholars from around the world, gain a global perspective, and potentially work in different countries.
- *Higher earning potential.* While financial gains should not be the primary motivator for pursuing a Ph.D., research suggests that, on average, Ph.D. holders tend to earn higher salaries over their careers compared to those with lower degrees.

However, it is essential to weigh these benefits against the challenges of a Ph.D. program, such as the time commitment, financial costs, and potential stress. It is also crucial to have a clear plan and career goals in mind when considering this path. One should discuss his or her intentions with mentors, advisors, and professionals in their desired field to make an informed decision. Ultimately, pursuing a Ph.D. can be a rewarding and transformative journey for those who are deeply passionate about their chosen area of study. As a doctoral student, you will be embarking on a challenging and rewarding journey that involves advanced research, critical thinking, and a deep dive into your chosen field of study. The expectations for doctoral students can vary depending on the program and institution, but here are some general expectations and responsibilities you can anticipate:

- *Coursework.* In the early stages of your doctoral program, you may be required to complete some coursework. These courses are designed to provide you with a strong foundation in your field and ensure you have the necessary knowledge and skills to conduct research.
- *Research.* The primary focus of your doctoral studies will be conducting original research. You will need to identify a research topic, develop research questions, and design and carry out experiments, surveys, or other research methods to answer these questions.
- *Knowledge of literature.* You will be expected to thoroughly review existing literature in your field to understand the current state of knowledge and identify gaps in the research that your work can fill.
- *Dissertation/thesis.* One of the key milestones of a doctoral program is the completion of a dissertation (Ph.D.) or thesis. This is a lengthy and original piece of research that contributes significantly to your field. Some doctoral programs offer other options, such as publishing a number of research articles.
- *Advisor/supervisor relationship.* You will work closely with a faculty advisor or supervisor who will guide and mentor you throughout your doctoral studies. Regular meetings with your advisor are crucial for getting feedback, discussing your research progress, and seeking advice.
- *Research assistantship.* As part of your research training, you may be required to serve as a research assistant. This involves assisting professors with their research, or participating in research projects.

- *Conferences and publications*. You will be encouraged to present your research at conferences and aim to publish your work in academic journals. This is important for sharing your findings with the academic community and building your reputation as a researcher.
- *Comprehensive examinations*. Some programs require comprehensive exams, also known as qualifying exams or prelims. These exams typically cover the coursework and literature relevant to your major chosen field and/or related (secondary) fields.
- *Time management*. Managing your time effectively is crucial. Doctoral programs are demanding, and you will need to balance coursework, research, and potentially teaching or assistantship responsibilities.
- *Ethical conduct*. You are expected to adhere to high ethical standards in your research, including avoiding plagiarism, conducting ethical experiments, and respecting the rights and privacy of research participants.
- *Persistence and resilience*. Doctoral programs can be mentally and emotionally challenging. You will need persistence and resilience to overcome obstacles and setbacks that may arise during your research or efforts to publish your work.
- *Self-motivation*. Doctoral studies often involve a high degree of self-directed work. You will need to be self-motivated and able to set and achieve your research goals.

Remember that every doctoral program is unique, so it is important to familiarize yourself with the specific requirements and expectations of the program of the institution and department you have chosen or are considering. Given the information on academic career and doctoral program requirements presented in this chapter, readers should be in a better position to decide whether to pursue an academic career, and, if so, they should choose an institution that is most likely to help them best prepare for such a career (guidelines for choosing doctoral programs are presented in Chap. 2).

Early career researchers who are pursuing a doctoral degree for nonacademic reasons (e.g., personal fulfilment, consulting) may wish to consider obtaining such a degree from other organizations that are in the business of granting doctoral degrees. Such organizations, which are known as "paper mills," are not accredited and have substantially lower requirements (e.g., online courses and exams, shorter time frames, lower costs), and they could serve the needs of those who do not wish to devote the resources to receive a Ph.D. degree that they do not plan to use for an academic career.

Because research is the core of an academic career, the requirements for a successful career focus greatly upon the factors that contribute to the parson's ability to conduct and publish impactful academic research. To conduct effectual academic research, several skills, attributes, and strategies are essential. In the interest of helping the reader better understand the landscape of expectations and activities of a person's academic career, I draw heavily from my own career experiences as examples. Many such experiences also form the bases for my views and comments on academic research, and they largely support my suggestions and advice to early career researchers offered throughout this book, as the reader can easily see some of their benefits.

In this chapter, I maintain that a person's ability to conduct and publish impactful or effectual academic research is based on three types of factors: skills, attitudes or mindsets, and strategies. Skills are the main type of factors researchers develop in formal settings such as doctoral programs. In contrast, attitudes and mindsets regarding research tend to define individual characteristics, which are not normally taught and not easy to develop. Finally, strategies refer to the way a researcher approaches major decisions concerning every stage of the research and publication process, from topic selection to writing and revising manuscripts. Such strategies typically are not formally taught. Some may be are acquired informally from the researcher's experiences in working with, or talking and observing other researchers in various settings (e.g., conferences) and receiving reviewer feedback on submitted manuscripts, and some other strategies may never be learned or employed during the researcher's entire academic career.

This book focuses on skills, attitudes, and strategies that are not formally taught in doctoral programs but are important in determining the likelihood a scientific study will be published in an academic journal. The present chapter discusses these skills as well as attitudes toward research. Because the major emphasis of this book is on research strategies and tactics related to each topic that is covered by a full chapter, strategies that promote impactful academic research are presented as they apply to materials covered in their respective chapters.

1.2.2 Required Skills

In this chapter, I maintain that there are three types of skills that can lead to successful academic research: conceptual, analytic, and communication.

Conceptual Skills Initially, researchers must cultivate and apply the necessary conceptual aptitudes. These encompass the capacity to contextualize a phenomenon or issue, position it within a suitable analytical framework, and evaluate its potential associations with similar phenomena. These skills hold particular significance in the development of theories and hypotheses. While subject matter knowledge is a prerequisite, it alone is insufficient for honing conceptual skills. Acquiring knowledge entails assimilating facts about a particular topic through self-study and interaction with peers, doctoral students, as well as participation in conferences, workshops, and seminars. However, the refinement of conceptual skills demands the ability to effectively apply this knowledge—a skill that is more challenging to acquire and cultivate.

The application of knowledge to research problems is particularly demanding because it necessitates creativity, abstract thinking, and, notably, imagination. As Albert Einstein once noted, "Imagination is more important than knowledge." I concur with the belief that a comprehensive understanding of one's field, the existing body of work, and the required tools for specific tasks significantly facilitate the generation of research ideas. Moreover, I firmly assert that ideas for research are not stumbled upon but crafted deliberately. With sustained contemplation of a problem or area, numerous research ideas can emerge. Often, this entails persistent reflection on the issue, with ideas occasionally surfacing unexpectedly, even during moments of relaxation or half-sleep. Additional skill applications are honed through trial-and-error experiences, collaborative efforts, constructive feedback from peers, and the study of established researchers' work and their research methodologies or approaches.

Analytic Skills Second, the researcher needs to have *analytic skills*. These skills refer to procedures involved in analyzing the problem or phenomenon, such as breaking it down into specific tasks that must be performed, interpreting and synthesizing data, and using analytic tools to come up with answers to research questions. Analytic skills can be developed or improved during one's doctoral studies. Development of analytic skills is largely the focus of most doctoral programs, which require students to take courses on research methodologies. They are normally acquired from one's own experiences, working with others, and taking courses in theory construction and methods (e.g., quantitative, qualitative). And they are typically the focus of courses and seminars in typical doctoral programs.

Communication Skills The third type of skills that promotes successful research is *presentation*. The researcher must have effective *communication skills* in order to effectively present his or her research findings to target audiences. These skills are important in crafting manuscripts for publication consideration, such as knowing how to position a study, structure a paper, and proactively address concerns of reviewers. Proficiency in writing is particularly crucial for two key reasons. First, the ability to write with greater ease and speed can significantly enhance one's productivity. Second, the style of writing can influence the clarity and perceived quality of one's manuscript, with the latter being a prominent criterion in the peer review process of many journals. Even in cases where a manuscript does not make a substantial contribution, well-written manuscripts are often regarded as "effective," as evidenced by an analysis of article readability in four marketing journals (Sawyer et al., 2008). From my own experience, I have found that challenges in writing often stem from a lack of understanding of the material that needs to be communicated or a clear strategy for presenting one's ideas. Effective writing commences with outlining the paper's key components, establishing the overall structure, and laying the groundwork for the paper before the actual writing process begins. Although communication skills, quality writing for academic journals in particular, are important, and writing and copyediting classes are widely available in universities, doctoral students are unlikely to be exposed to such learning experiences. Despite evidence pointing to the importance of quality writing for successful academic publishing (e.g., Sawyer et al., 2008; Summers, 2001), long-standing and frequent complaints of journal editors about poor quality of manuscripts received (e.g., Churchill &

Perrault, 1982; Varadarajan, 1996), this skill appears to remain largely undeveloped during the student's preparation for academic career. In view of this deficiency in doctoral student training and need for improving the writing of early career researchers, Chapters 2 and 10 provides some guidelines for quality writing.

1.2.3 Additional Factors that Contribute to Effectual Research

Although conceptual, analytic, and communication skills are essential for successful academic research, several other skills and aptitudes can also promote successful academic research and, therefore, are worth mentioning. Below is a list of them with a brief explanation:

- *Intellectual curiosity*. A natural inclination or desire to seek out information, explore new ideas, ask questions, and engage in learning for the sake of expanding one's mind and knowledge base, rather than out of external pressures or requirements.
- *Critical thinking*. The ability to analyze information critically, question assumptions, and evaluate evidence is fundamental to academic research.
- *Research methodology*. Proficiency in research methodologies, both quantitative and qualitative, is vital. This includes designing experiments, surveys, interviews, and data analysis techniques.
- *Familiarity with literature*. A strong understanding of the existing literature in one's field is essential. This involves the ability to identify gaps in knowledge and build on prior work.
- *Time management*. Effective time management is crucial to balance teaching, administrative duties, and research. It helps you stay productive and meet deadlines.
- *Collaboration*. Many impactful research projects involve collaboration with other researchers. Being able to work effectively in teams is essential.
- *Ethical awareness*. Understanding research ethics and maintaining the highest ethical standards is nonnegotiable in academia.
- *Adaptability*. Research can be unpredictable. Being adaptable and open to changing research directions when necessary is important.
- *Attention to detail*. Careful attention to detail is critical to avoid errors in data collection and analysis, which can undermine the credibility of your research.
- *Information management*. Organizing and managing the vast amount of information and data involved in research is a valuable skill.
- *Grant writing*. The ability to secure research funding through grant writing is often necessary to support your research endeavors.
- *Networking*. Building relationships with other researchers in your field and staying connected with developments in your area of study can lead to collaborative opportunities and access to resources.
- *Patience and perseverance*. Research can be a slow and challenging process. Patience and perseverance are essential to see a project through to completion.

- *Critical feedback reception*. Being able to accept and use feedback and criticisms from mentors, peers, and reviewers to improve your work is crucial for growth as a researcher.
- *Creativity*. Thinking creatively can help you approach problems from unique angles and develop innovative research ideas.
- *Mentoring*. If you are in a position to do so, mentoring junior researchers can enhance your own understanding and contribute to the growth of your field.
- *Self-motivation*. In academia, you often need to set your own research agenda and stay motivated despite setbacks or periods of slow progress.

Remember that these factors can vary in importance depending on your specific field of study. Additionally, academic research is a continuous learning process, and honing these skills over time is essential for long-term success. Going through a rigorous doctoral program should enable a person to develop many of these skills. However, receiving a doctoral degree alone is not a guarantee for a successful academic career. It is usually the work you do after receiving this degree that determines the academic trajectory of the professor.

Quite frequently, holders of a doctoral degree do not pursue an academic career. Rather, they seek employment in the industry as consultants, or in government agencies as specialists in various areas. And quite often, some of those who enter an academic career upon receiving a Ph.D. degree decide a few years later to do something different for a living, either because they do not like academics as a profession or because they do not think they can have a successful academic career. And the few who would pursue a doctoral degree only for prestige and status reasons likely will never consider an academic career.

1.2.4 Attitude Toward Research

The second type of factors that is important for conducting and publishing impactful academic research is the person's positive *attitude* and *mindset* toward academic research. These factors are more likely to be viewed as personality traits. Unlike other skills that can be developed in formal classes and research settings, a favorable attitude toward research is more difficult to acquire. While skills are integral elements that contribute to successful research, it is equally vital to approach research with the appropriate attitude. Personally, I firmly believe that an individual with the correct research-oriented mindset is more likely to acquire the skills and tactics essential for effective research, whereas a researcher possessing the skills and familiarity with strategies for productive research but lacking a favorable research attitude may not achieve comparable success. When I mention "attitude," I am encompassing all three dimensions of attitude—namely, cognitive, affective, and conative—which collectively shape a researcher's mindset, emotions, and behavioral inclinations.

1.2.5 The Mindsets and Habits of Successful Researchers

I have observed three key attributes in researchers who achieve success. First, they are deeply absorbed in their research, their minds consumed by research-related thoughts and tasks throughout the day. Even during interactions with others and leisure activities, these thoughts often intrude, driven partly by the need for anticipated outcomes. Successful researchers are inclined to initiate new investigations and plan fresh projects, either independently or collaboratively, even before concluding existing ones. Furthermore, they consistently have manuscripts in various stages of development.

Second, successful researchers are motivated to publish by their intellectual curiosity, a drive to learn and enhance their understanding, and to address questions that require imaginative and creative thinking. This motivation is akin to the curiosity displayed by individuals like George Washington Carver, a young African American with limited formal education, who was fascinated by peanuts and sought to unravel their composition. Carver eventually developed around 250 products from peanuts and became one of America's esteemed scientists. Successful researchers do not merely aim to meet the expectations of a specific journal; rather, they strive to create the best possible article for any journal. Their research and writing are not fueled by a desire for fame or recognition; instead, they are driven by the innate need to excel and extract the utmost from their abilities.

Finally, I am not aware of any accomplished researcher who approaches research as mere work or a burdensome task. Instead, these achievers derive immense enjoyment from their research endeavors. To them, research is a passion, a way of life, and, in many cases, even a hobby. The most successful researchers exhibit an unparalleled zeal and fervor for their work. They are successful because they love doing research. This perspective echoes the statement of Albert Schweitzer, a renowned and multifaceted figure in the twentieth century known for his achievements in the fields of philosophy, theology, music, medicine, and many more: "If you love what you are doing, you will be successful." Therefore, the habits of successful researchers are characterized by diligent mental engagement, a deep-seated passion for their work, and a consistent dedication to their research activities. These notions are parallel to the sentiment of Thomas A. Edison, one of America's eminent scientists, who stated that "Genius is 1% inspiration and 99% perspiration." The key to research success lies in the 99% perspiration—prolonged and committed engagement in the activity, whether pursued as a hobby or otherwise, ultimately leads to excellence in research in any field.

1.3 Ingredients of Success

I firmly believe that the prerequisites for achieving success in academic research mirror those needed for success in any sphere of life. This conviction stems from my fortunate experiences, which granted me the privilege of meeting some of the world's most accomplished individuals across various domains, including academia, sports, and business. I closely observed their habits and the strategies they employed to attain their objectives.

In academia, I had the opportunity to collaborate with and learn from some of the most prolific researchers. As a member of the Greek National track team, I interacted with some of the globe's most exceptional athletes. In my consulting role in the business realm, I co-directed extensive surveys and conducted focus groups involving self-made multimillionaires, leading to notable findings published in academic journals (e.g., Stanley & Moschis, 1984; Stanley et al., 1987) and in the widely acclaimed book, *The Millionaire Next Door*, authored by my late colleague Thomas J. Stanley. My observations have led me to the realization that the principles adhered to by successful individuals in one field hold true in others as well. And I am eager to share these insights with those aspiring to excel in academia, particularly those of you in the early stages of your academic career or contemplating such a path, believing that they might help you as you are trying to build a successful career.

1.3.1 Discipline

First and foremost, accomplished individuals excel at organizing their lives. They meticulously plan their daily routines and establish clear objectives for each day, week, and even longer timeframes, diligently adhering to their plans. They typically initiate their day early and rely on comprehensive "to-do" lists for guidance. For instance, I recall the disciplined daily routine of my esteemed mentor at the University of Wisconsin, where he dedicated the first two hours of each day to working on a book and the subsequent three hours on research projects, steadfastly avoiding interruptions such as phone calls. Similarly, I reflect on the work habits of a successful entrepreneur who credited his ability to achieve long-term goals to the attainment of shorter-term goals meticulously set for each year, month, week, day, and even hour.

1.3.2 Optimism

Furthermore, successful individuals tend to possess an innate optimism regarding both their future prospects and the ventures they embark upon. They maintain a positive attitude and outlook on life, undeterred by setbacks or disappointments. They recognize that learning and personal growth stem not only from favorable experiences but also from adverse ones. In my view, adversity has the potential to create new opportunities and expand horizons, enabling individuals to accomplish even greater feats.

For instance, when I failed to pass the eighth grade in high school, it compelled me to intensify my studies and transform into a more dedicated student. This transformation ultimately enabled me to secure admission to a Greek university with an acceptance rate of just 10% for applicants. Similarly, encountering the setback of failing my major Ph.D. exam twice, coupled with the polite suggestion to withdraw from the program due to the unprecedented requirement of publishing two sole-authored articles in top journals within my field, became a catalyst for enhancing my research skills. This experience spurred me to publish multiple articles during my doctoral studies and throughout my subsequent academic career.

1.3.3 Strive for Perfection

Moreover, accomplished individuals never settle for mediocrity and adhere to the belief that, in the words of a successful individual, "if better is attainable, then good is insufficient." They take immense pride not only in their areas of expertise but also in their capacity to consistently deliver work that is perceived as competent and flawless. This quality garners significant appreciation and admiration from their peers and colleagues. In contrast, producing subpar work becomes evident in the outcomes of their endeavors, leading to unfavorable perceptions of both the researcher and their work.

From my personal perspective, when I encounter a researcher who exhibits carelessness in paper writing, characterized by haphazard formatting and typos, I am inclined to infer that a similar level of carelessness might have permeated their data collection and analysis processes. This raises doubts about the validity of the findings they have reported. Ultimately, achieving success in research, or reaching the pinnacle in any field for that matter, necessitates the ability to identify and rectify flaws that could impede progress or hinder one's ascent to the top.

1.3.4 Make an Extra Effort

Having observed how successful individuals from diverse fields achieve their goals, I firmly believe that the disparity between success and failure is not as significant as commonly perceived. It hinges on the willingness to invest that extra effort that ultimately makes the distinction. This principle applies equally to academia, where it can signify the difference between a manuscript's acceptance and rejection. It manifests in the additional time spent meticulously proofreading a manuscript for errors or inaccuracies, the extra effort exerted to address reviewers' comments more effectively, or the added citation sought to substantiate a point.

It might come as a surprise to readers that the reason I chose an academic career can be traced back to a mere 20 extra minutes I devoted as an undergraduate student to review material for an exam. These extra minutes allowed me to craft a more thorough response to a question on the exam, resulting in a grade of B instead of a C for that exam and consequently in the course overall. This accomplishment was pivotal in securing a GPA of 2.5 at graduation, the minimum requirement for graduate school admission. It often boils down to that extra bit of effort that tips the scales between success and failure in various facets of one's life.

1.3.5 Self-Confidence

In general, successful individuals exhibit confidence in their abilities and possess a strong belief in what they can achieve—a principle that also holds true for successful researchers. This unwavering self-assurance motivates them to undertake research projects, even when faced with unfavorable odds, akin to my own experience when I, as a foreign doctoral student, aspired to publish two sole-authored articles in top marketing journals. I firmly believe that there is nothing more invaluable than possessing an attitude, mindset, or determination that empowers you to surmount obstacles and challenges encountered in life—an outlook that proclaims, "regardless of the circumstances, I will endeavor to transform them into opportunities for greatness."

I am convinced that in research, as in life, you can attain as much as you dare to envision and believe you can accomplish. When one genuinely believes in the possibility of an outcome, it has a remarkable tendency to materialize. As highlighted by my late colleague Dave Schwartz in his bestselling book, *The Magic of Thinking Big*, the core philosophy is encapsulated in the idea that "Thinking does make it so." This principle, embraced by legendary football coach Lou Holtz as a key to his monumental success, underscores the profound impact of one's beliefs on their aspirational goals and achievements.

1.3.6 Accept Criticism

Furthermore, accomplished individuals in many fields, including research, tend to possess an open-minded disposition and are amenable to considering multiple perspectives. They not only embrace criticism but often actively seek it. I firmly assert that the ability to accept criticism is a fundamental characteristic of successful researchers. Constructive feedback from colleagues and reviewers serves as a valuable means for researchers to reevaluate their viewpoints, identify weaknesses in their work, and enhance their skill sets. Given that criticism frequently originates from individuals qualified to assess one's research, it can be viewed as a form of instruction, offering researchers an opportunity to gain insights, evolve, and enhance their capabilities. To achieve success, researchers must continually refine their skills, and the acceptance of criticism, coupled with responsive action, serves as a robust method to remain current and foster professional growth.

1.3.7 Stay Focused

Lastly, based on my personal observations, successful individuals in general, and researchers in particular tend to channel their focus into a limited number of areas, as opposed to attempting to perform exceptionally across a broad spectrum. I consider this principle to be of great significance, whether applied to sports, business, or academia. When we disperse our resources, including time, effort, and financial investments, across numerous areas, specialties, or tasks, we often find ourselves performing suboptimal in each of these domains compared to the potential when we concentrate all our resources on a single, specific area. I firmly believe that individuals who publish across a wide array of areas run the risk of not establishing themselves as authorities or experts in any particular field.

1.4 About This Book

1.4.1 What Readers Will Learn

This book can help early career researchers make decisions in several areas of the research process that should increase their likelihood of conducting and publishing impactful research papers. It can help both those who are preparing and are in the process of developing research skills (e.g., doctoral students) as well as those who have already embarked on an academic career and wish to improve their skills at conducting and publishing impactful academic studies. The book provides guidance in the form of suggestions for strategies and tactics, from preparation for academic research to execution, writing, and publishing, often showing examples and illustrations, in the following areas:

- Selecting a university to pursue a Ph.D. degree
- Choosing and working with mentors, supervisors, and members of your dissertation committee
- Efficient navigation of the doctoral program
- Choosing a university to begin your academic career
- Developing and improving skills required for conducting effectual academic research
- Selecting viable areas for developing a long-lasting stream of programmatic research
- Preparing for programmatic academic research studies
- Choosing a specific topic or research question within a select research area or stream
- Choosing collaborators for conducting academic studies
- Developing a conceptual research framework, theory, and hypothesis
- Choosing viable research approach(es) for research questions
- Conducting literature reviews appropriate for different research questions
- Selecting proper methods for conducting academic research studies
- Conducting impactful cross-cultural academic research studies
- Preparing and "crafting" manuscripts for academic outlets
- Manuscript positioning and journal selection for submission
- Revising manuscripts: Responding to journal editors and reviewers
- Reviewing manuscripts and preparing comments for authors and journal editors
- Preparing a research proposal for dissertation, university support, agency funding, proprietary and syndicated study

- Developing networks of research collaborators
- Mentoring and working with doctoral students
- Increase research productivity, as measured by h-index
- Starting and successfully managing a research center
- Research ethics

Developing and implementing effectual strategies and tactics in these areas should enable the reader navigate successfully the academic research and publication process, especially during early stages of one's academic career, and could form the foundations for a long and successful career.

1.4.2 Book Chapters

I believe that there are seven areas where the employment of suitable strategies can significantly improve the early career researcher's likelihood of achieving research excellence in his or her academic career. More precisely, effective research strategies can be implemented when (a) choosing research topics, (b) adopting a research philosophy, (c) selecting a research approach, (d) employing a robust conceptual framework, (e) choosing research methods and designs, (f) navigating research procedures, and (g) developing manuscripts. The effectiveness of strong research skills, can be limited, if one's research strategies in these areas are inadequately conceived.

The majority of book chapters are organized largely according to these seven areas in sequence that describes the scientific process to knowledge creation, beginning with preparation and planning, followed by conceptualization and execution of research, and ending with the reporting of results, and some additional chapters are used as supportive materials to this process. Following the present chapter's overview of this book, Chap. 2 focuses on preparation for academic research, which begins with choosing a university to pursue a Ph.D. degree. It discusses the skills that one needs to develop while in the doctoral program and how to improve these skills. It also suggests ways to effectively navigate the program, such as getting organized for research and choosing research collaborators, and it suggests criteria for evaluating institutions to choose for beginning an academic career.

Chapter 3 discusses conceptual foundations of research, beginning with the definition of basic concepts used in academic research. It also discusses a procedure for conceptualizing a phenomenon of interest and presents research philosophies and approaches that can be employed for its investigation. Chapter 4 focuses on planning academic research projects. It suggests strategies for identifying viable research areas and choosing research topics, including the selection of a dissertation topic.

Chapter 5 focuses on strategies for selecting and developing conceptual frameworks. It presents a step-by-step process to developing conceptual frameworks, theories, and hypotheses, with examples, using both qualitative and quantitative data. Chapter 6 discusses specific research methods and designs. It familiarizes readers with the major types, their purpose, benefits, and suggests circumstances that favor their employment. Chapter 7 emphasizes research procedures for conducting academic studies. It highlights issues relevant to the use of specific methods and suggests strategies for effectively addressing them. Chapter 8 presents the main and emerging types of literature reviews. It informs the reader on their objectives and method and suggests their value in addressing research questions and problems. Chapter 9 covers cross-cultural research, especially challenges and issues facing early career researchers doing research in other countries. It discusses skills required, effective research strategies for cross-cultural research, and offers suggestions for effectual cross-cultural research with illustrations.

Chapter 10 discusses manuscript preparation, focusing on major components of published articles. It suggests information that should be included within each major component or section of the manuscript, including strategies for positioning a manuscript and steps that should be followed prior to its submission to a journal. Chapter 11 makes the early career researcher aware of criteria journal editors and reviewers use to evaluate a manuscript and make a decision to accept or reject it. And it provides guidelines for revising a manuscript that is conditionally accepted, suggesting effective strategies for responding to editor and reviewers' comments. Chapter 12 discusses ethics in research for every aspect of a professor's academic life. It includes ethical standards as they apply to the main stages of the research process, manuscript preparation, and working with colleagues.

Chapter 13 informs early career researchers of research strategies most effective at different stages of one's academic career. It includes strategies from the preparation stage (as a doctoral student) and beginning of academic career, to mid- and late-career and preparation for retirement, suggesting strategies for impactful research at each stage. Chapter 14 discusses research proposals that early career researchers may have to develop at various stages of their academic career. It offers details on specific types of proposals, including proposals for dissertation and external funding, with proposal samples. Finally, Chapter 15 highlights major ideas about academic research, a synopsis of the materials presented, and the author's personal observations and philosophy about the present state of academic research. And it includes some emerging trends that are likely to affect the way academic researchers around the globe conduct studies in the years to come.

1.4.3 Bases for Author's Views and Suggestions

My observations and recommendations throughout the entire book are based on my experiences, published research, and anecdotal experiences of other colleagues and professionals (e.g., mentors, collaborators, editors, reviewers) with whom I have interacted during my lengthy academic career. I draw upon both personal experiences and the experiences of others to construct narratives that underpin and reinforce my perspectives on devising effective strategies for academic research. And I draw heavily from my experiences while preparing for an academic career as a doctoral student, as well as from my experiences in various positions and roles that assumed at various stages of my academic career.

Professorial Experiences During my lengthy academic career, I performed a wide variety of activities in various capacities in the three broad areas of research, teaching, and service. In the area of research, I published hundreds of articles in scientific outlets and ten research books. I taught numerous courses and developed new ones, including a course on academic research and publishing, which I taught during my entire academic career in several universities around the globe. Most of the teaching notes and materials I used for this course are included in this book.

I also provided a wide variety of services to my university, universities in other countries, and other academic communities, industry groups, and government agencies. I founded and directed the Center for Mature Consumer Studies, which became globally known and one of the best sources of marketing information in the USA for several years, served as director of the doctoral program in my department for many years, and served on numerous universities, college, and department committees. I served on editorial board of top journals in my field, a reviewer for dozens of journals in several disciplines, and a consultant to major corporations, government agencies, and an expert witness on high-profile litigation case (georgepmoschis.com). Many of my research, teaching, and service-related activities and resulting experiences I gained from them form a large base of my views and suggestions included in this book.

Author's Experiences as Doctoral Student As a doctoral student and research assistant, I engaged in a wide variety of time-consuming activities, outside my normal responsibilities. Because I consider these activities very important in helping me prepare for conducting academic research, I am sharing these experiences with those who might be interested.

- Developed a filing system, which was used to catalogue article abstracts of every article in my field published in the previous 10 years.
- For written assignments (e.g., term papers), I worked with a copy editor to improve my writing skills and the quality of the assignments.
- Took more courses than required in the field of mass communications, related to my major field (marketing), taught by some of the country's best researchers.
- Collaborated with classmates in mass communications classes on pilot research projects, which served as bases for our dissertations and led to publications in top journals in our respective fields.
- Collaborated on small-scale projects with classmates that also resulted in several publications in respectable journals.
- Took the same class(es) or seminar(s) taught by prolific writers and researchers, sometimes more than once, because of new learning experiences rather than satisfying doctoral program requirements. I observed those scholars' work habits, writing styles, and approaches to research questions, and I tried to emulate them.
- Selectively read articles written by well-known authors and tried to study their writing and presentation styles.

- For my dissertation, I asked some of the most prolific researcher-writers in different disciplines to serve on my committee. They served as role models, mentors, and collaborators, helping shape my mindset and habits regarding academic research.
- Before my first regular employment at a university, I had ten articles from my doctoral student projects either published or accepted for publication in *all* major journals in my field (nine sole- or senior-authored), as well as one co-authored book.

Suggestions to early career researchers, especially doctoral students, are based not only on my experiences as a doctoral student. They are also based on my interactions with doctoral students in various roles and contexts, such as recruiting, advising, mentoring, supervising, teaching, and co-authoring with them.

References

Churchill, G. A., Jr., & Perrault, W. D., Jr. (1982). JMR editorial policies and philosophy. *Journal of Marketing Research, 19*, 283–287.

Sawyer, A. G., Laran, J., & Xu, J. (2008). The readability of marketing journals: Are award-winning articles better written? *Journal of Marketing, 72*(1), 108–117.

Stanley, T. J., & Moschis, G. P. (1984). America's affluent. *American Demographics, 6*(3), 28–33.

Stanley, T. J., Moschis, G. P., & Danko, W. D. (1987). Financial service segments: The seven faces of the affluent market. *Journal of Advertising Research, 27*(4), 52–67.

Summers, J. O. (2001). Guidelines for conducting research and publishing in marketing: From conceptualization through the review process. *Journal of the Academy of Marketing Science, 29*(4), 405–415.

Varadarajan, P. R. (1996). From the editor: Reflections on research and publishing. *Journal of Marketing, 60*, 3–6.

2 Preparing for Academic Career

The preparation for an academic career is a long process. It typically starts with formal training, and it can last as long as the person's academic career, because academics provide continuous opportunities for learning and growth. This chapter is confined to early preparation for such a career. It begins with guidelines for choosing an institution for formal training, followed by guidelines for navigating the doctoral program, which is required for successful academic career. Guidelines for improving one's skills in the doctoral program are provided next, including writing and research skills. And it offers suggestions for choosing collaborators, building research networks, and getting organized for research. The chapter ends with guidelines for choosing an institution for beginning one's academic career, as this decision is likely to have a significant impact on the person's professional trajectory.

2.1 Formal Training

Formal training typically takes place at an academic institution while the student is pursuing a Ph.D. degree. Opportunities for formal training are provided in the form of classes, working on projects with faculty and other students outside the classroom, and self-learning. It is very important for doctoral students to have learning opportunities outside the classroom, so that they can apply skills formally acquired in classes to project execution and writing for academic outlets. Therefore, choosing a university to pursue a Ph.D. degree that provides a landscape of learning opportunities is a crucial first step in preparation for an academic career.

G. P. Moschis, *Academic Research in Business and the Social Sciences*,
https://doi.org/10.1007/978-3-031-56548-9_2

2.1.1 Choosing an Institution

It is essential to carefully consider several factors when choosing a university to receive training for an academic career. Below are several key aspects to look for:

1. *Program reputation and accreditation*
   - Research the reputation of the university's doctoral programs in your field of interest.
   - Ensure the university is accredited by a recognized accrediting agency to ensure the quality of education and its doctoral degree.
2. *Faculty expertise*
   - Look for universities with faculty members who are experts in the research area you plan to pursue, if you have chosen one.
   - Consider their publications, research projects, and academic achievements.
3. *Facilities and resources*
   - Evaluate the availability of state-of-the-art laboratories, libraries, archives, and other research resources.
   - Consider availability of scholarships or assistantships, both level ($ annually) and length (years) of support by the department of your interest.
4. *Support services*
   - Investigate the availability of academic advisors and mentors who can guide you through your doctoral studies.
   - Check for career services and counseling.
5. *Program structure and requirements*
   - Understand the specific requirements of the doctoral program, including coursework, qualifying exams, and dissertation expectations.
   - Consider the flexibility of the program to accommodate your research interests, especially the option to choose an advisor, rather than be assigned to one, who will guide you through your program.
6. *Research opportunities*
   - Look for universities with research centers, institutes, or collaborations that align with your research interests.
   - Consider opportunities for interdisciplinary research.
   - Try to find out if there are opportunities to work with faculty on research projects by, for example, talking to doctoral students already in the same program.
7. *Graduation and job placement rates*
   - Research the university's track record in terms of doctoral graduation rates and postgraduation job placement at academic institutions, including the reputation of these institutions.
   - Check alumni outcomes and success stories by, for example, studying the trajectory of their professional achievements.
8. *Location and environment*
   - Consider the university's location and whether it aligns with your lifestyle, including cultural, social, and recreational opportunities in the area.
   - Assess the cost of living in the area where the university is located.

9. *Networking opportunities*
   - Assess the potential for networking with fellow students, faculty, and professionals in your field.
   - Explore opportunities to attend conferences, symposia, and workshops organized by the university, such as presentations by well-known researchers.
10. *Graduate student community*
    - Interact with current doctoral students to gain insights into their experiences and the sense of community within the program.
    - Consider the size of the doctoral student body in relation to the size of faculty who are active in research and its potential impact on your academic experience.
11. *Application process*
    - Understand the application requirements and deadlines for the doctoral program.
    - Prepare a strong application, including a compelling statement of purpose for seeking a doctoral degree (for academic career), with letters of recommendation.

In sum, choosing the right university for your doctoral studies is a critical decision that can significantly impact your academic and career trajectory. Take your time to research and visit potential institutions, and do not hesitate to seek guidance from professors, mentors, and current doctoral students to make an informed choice. And if you are presently at an early stage in a doctoral program of an institution that does not provide such opportunities, consider transferring to one that does. You will be better off in the long run.

2.1.2 Navigating the Doctoral Program

Earning a doctoral degree is a significant academic achievement that requires dedication, perseverance, and a substantial amount of time and effort. Many students apply for admission into a doctoral program without adequate knowledge of the expectations and demands, thinking that the doctoral program is a continuation of a Master's degree program. Many universities offer orientation seminars to help those who were recently admitted to the Ph.D. program decide if they have made the right decision. The specific requirements can vary depending on the country, institution, and field of study, but here are the general steps and requirements for earning a doctoral degree:

- *Meet admission requirements.* First, to be admitted into a doctoral program, you typically need to hold a bachelor's or master's degree. Admission requirements may also include standardized test scores (e.g., GRE), letters of recommendation, a statement of purpose, and possibly an interview.
- *Choose your field of study.* Next, you will need to decide on the field in which you want to earn your doctoral degree. This should align with your academic and career goals.

- *Find funding.* Doctoral programs can be expensive, so it is important to explore funding options. This can include scholarships, research assistantships, teaching assistantships, and fellowships. Most programs offer these types of financial support to doctoral students.
- *Coursework.* Once admitted, you will typically begin with required coursework in your field of study for up to two or three years. These courses will provide you with a strong foundation of knowledge and research skills in your area of interest.
- *Comprehensive examinations.* In many doctoral programs, you will need to pass comprehensive exams that test your knowledge in your field. These exams often come after coursework and before you begin your main research project(s).
- *Choose an advisor.* You will need to select a faculty advisor or mentor who will guide you through your doctoral research. This person will be instrumental in helping you shape your research project (dissertation). Some institutions assign an advisor to the student upon admission into the doctoral program.
- *Publish and present.* Throughout your doctoral program, you may be encouraged to publish your research projects in academic journals and present your findings at conferences. Some universities offer the option of publishing three articles in acceptable journals (e.g., Scopus) in leu of a completing the dissertation requirement. Other universities expect sole- or co-authored publications throughout the program, in addition to dissertation.
- *Proposal and research.* You will develop a formal research proposal outlining your main research project, which is usually your dissertation. Once approved, you will conduct your research, which typically takes anywhere from several months to one year (sometimes even longer), depending on the nature of the chosen research project.
- *Dissertation.* Your doctoral dissertation is the culmination of your research. It should make an original contribution to your field. In choosing a dissertation topic, do not be overly ambitious. The purpose of the dissertation should be to graduate by meeting the program's requirement, not to help change the world!
- *Defend your dissertation.* Writing and defending your dissertation is a significant part of the doctoral process. You will need to defend your dissertation before a committee of faculty members. This defense includes a presentation of your research and answering questions from the committee.
- *Final steps.* After successfully defending your dissertation, you will need to complete any additional program-specific requirements, such as publications or teaching requirements, before receiving your doctoral degree. Several universities now require doctoral students to publish at least one article out of their dissertations in acceptable journals. This can pose a challenge to students who normally do not receive formal training at writing manuscripts for journals and interacting with journal editors and reviewers (see Chaps. 10 and 11 for suggestions). Co-authoring such an article usually satisfies this requirement.
- *Suggested strategy for meeting publication requirements.* For doctoral programs that require candidates to publish an article out of their dissertation, I suggest the following:

(a) Revise your dissertation proposal, changing hypotheses to "propositions," and develop a manuscript based on a condensed version of your proposal for submission to a journal that is on your University's approved list (see examples—Prakitsuwan & Moschis, 2020; Yingwattanakul & Moschis, 2017), and submit this manuscript before or upon approval of your proposal by your dissertation committee.
(b) Incorporate any helpful reviewer suggestions into your research design and plan for data gathering.
(c) Complete your dissertation and develop one or more articles that include reviewer suggestions and findings (see examples—Prakitsuwan et al., 2022; Yingwattanakul & Moschis, 2019). In doing so, you will benefit from reviewer comments and increase the likelihood of having an article published out of your dissertation required for graduation.

Keep in mind that the specific requirements and timeline for earning a doctoral degree can vary widely across disciplines and institutions. It is important to consult with academic advisors and faculty members in your chosen field to ensure you are on the right path and meeting all the necessary requirements. Additionally, doctoral programs are a significant commitment, often taking several years to complete, so be prepared for a long but rewarding journey.

2.2 Improve Your Writing Skills

Evidence shows that well-written manuscripts have a higher likelihood of seeing publication light (Sawyer et al., 2008), suggesting that writing quality plays important role in reviewer and editor's decision. Yet, writing for publication in academic journals is not typically taught in doctoral programs. You are likely to learn writing skills and rules from different sources or individuals, including reviewers, copy editors, and guidelines seen in journal style sheets reporting on widely accepted rules about writing. For example, I learned from one of my colleagues who used to teach editing that single-sentence paragraphs should be avoided. And a copy editor told me that, and long paragraphs should be avoided, especially when they do not relate to a single idea, and sentences should not start with acronyms (e.g., AMA).

Before discussing ways to improve article writing skills, a distinction among the meanings of words "paper," "manuscript," and "article" is worth making, as properly used words can convey the impression of a competent writer. A paper is an unpublished document, a working draft that is shared informally for reasons such as to receive feedback from others or read at a conference. An unpublished document that is developed and submitted for publication to a journal or book publisher is normally referred to as "manuscript," and manuscripts that see publication light in journals become "articles."

2.2.1 General Guidelines for Improving Writing

Improving your writing quality is a valuable skill that can benefit you academically and professionally. The following tips will help you improve your writing:

- *Read extensively*. One of the best ways to improve your writing is to read regularly. Read a variety of articles, books, and publications in different genres and styles to expose yourself to diverse writing techniques and perspectives.
- *Practice regularly*. Writing is a skill that improves with practice. Set aside dedicated time to write regularly, even if it is just a few sentences or paragraphs a day.
- *Plan and outline*. Before you start writing, create an outline or plan for your piece. This helps you organize your thoughts and maintain a clear structure.
- *Clarity and conciseness*. Strive for clarity and conciseness. Use clear and straightforward language to convey your ideas. Avoid overly complex sentences or jargon.
- *Avoid plagiarism*. Always give credit to the original sources of information or ideas. Plagiarism is a serious academic and ethical offense. It is not only unethical but can also have serious academic and professional consequences.
- *Edit and revise*. Writing is a process, and your first draft is unlikely to be perfect. Edit and revise your work multiple times, focusing on clarity, conciseness, and coherence. Look for ways to improve sentence structure, eliminate redundancies, and enhance clarity.
- *Feedback*. Seek feedback from peers, mentors, or editors. Constructive criticism can help you identify areas for improvement. Do not hesitate to ask for feedback from peers, professors, or writing mentors. Constructive criticism can provide valuable insights into areas for improvement.
- *Read aloud*. Reading your work aloud can help you catch awkward phrasing, errors, and inconsistencies that may be harder to spot when reading silently.
- *Expand your vocabulary*. A rich vocabulary can make your writing more engaging. Regularly explore new words and their meanings. However, use them judiciously and ensure they fit the context.
- *Stay informed*. Keep up with current events, trends, and developments in your field or the subject you are writing about. This will help your articles stay relevant and timely.
- *Patience and persistence*. Becoming a skilled article writer takes time and effort. Be patient with yourself, and do not be discouraged by initial setbacks.
- *Practice different styles and genres*. Experiment with different writing styles and genres to expand your skills.

2.2.2 Guidelines for Improving Article Writing Skills

Improving your article writing skills is a valuable endeavor, whether you are a student, a professional, or someone who enjoys writing as a hobby. The following are some additional tips to help you enhance your article writing skills:

1. Learn to emulate top researcher-writers by reading their works carefully. Study the way these individuals structure their writing by, for example, how they start and end paragraphs, how their sentences flow and lead to the main point the intend to make, when and how they use references to support the statements they make, and how they amplify explanations of concepts by offering additional information or examples.
2. Take courses in writing, especially in academic writing (online, if such courses are not available at your institution) and copy editing.
3. Choose research collaborators who are known to be good writers, if you feel your experience or skill at writing is inadequate for the expectations of academic journals. Read carefully their writing and the editing they do on your own write-ups.
4. Use the services of professional copy editors; read and save the edits they make on drafts of your manuscripts before accepting their changes. There are always opportunities to learn something new about article writing by working with copy editors. Learning is a life-long process.

To summarize, enhancing writing abilities is typically achievable through self-directed learning, analyzing the presentation styles of good writers, collaborating with more skilled writers, and enrolling in writing and editing courses. Remember that writing is a continuous learning process. It is a skill that develops over time, and there is always room for improvement. Be open to learning, embrace feedback, and continue honing your article writing abilities through consistent practice and study. As you apply these tips and continue to write, you will see gradual improvement in your article writing skills.

2.3 Improve Your Research Skills

Improving your research skills is essential for academic success and for contributing to your field of study. Whether you are a student or a researcher, the following are steps you can take to enhance your research skills:

- *Understand research basics.* Start by gaining a solid understanding of research fundamentals (see Chap. 3). Learn about definitions of research terms, basic research methodologies, data collection techniques, and the research process.
- *Take courses in methods outside your main field.* Many important methodologies are developed outside your main discipline. Take at least one course taught by the most qualified faculty in the following areas: qualitative methods, structural equation modelling, and experimental designs.
- *Identify your research interests.* Choose topics that genuinely interest you. Passion for your subject matter will make the research process more engaging and motivate you to delve deeper.
- *Stay informed.* Regularly read academic journals, books, and articles related to your field. Staying informed about current research helps you identify gaps in knowledge.

- *Develop strong information literacy*. Learn how to effectively search for and evaluate sources of information. Familiarize yourself with databases, libraries, and online resources relevant to your field.
- *Use citations and references properly*. Understand the citation style (e.g., APA, MLA, Chicago) relevant to your discipline, and use it consistently. Properly cite sources to avoid plagiarism.
- *Set clear research goals*. Define specific research questions or objectives. Clearly articulate what you want to achieve with your research.
- *Create a research plan*. Develop a structured research plan with timelines, milestones, and tasks. This helps you stay organized and on track.
- *Learn how to analyze literature*. Learn to conduct literature reviews and analyses that help you draw conclusions about published studies. Learning methods such as meta-analysis, bibliometric analysis, and integrative literature review (see Chap. 8) can be valuable in understanding what has already been published on your topic and in identifying research trends and gaps in knowledge.
- *Select appropriate research methods*. Learn to choose research methods that are appropriate for your research questions. This could involve qualitative or quantitative approaches, such as surveys, experiments, interviews, or archival research (see Chaps. 6 and 7).
- *Ethical considerations*. Familiarize yourself with research ethics, including obtaining informed consent, protecting participants' privacy, and adhering to ethical guidelines in your field (see Chap. 12).
- *Seek guidance and collaboration*. Do not hesitate to seek advice and mentorship from professors, advisors, or experienced researchers. Collaborating with others can provide valuable insights and resources.
- *Attend conferences and workshops*. Participate in academic conferences, workshops, and seminars. These events offer opportunities to present your research, receive feedback, and network with experts in your field.
- *Write and publish*. Practice writing research papers, manuscripts, and reports. Submit your work to academic journals or conferences for publication. The process of writing and revising improves your writing and research skills.
- *Peer review*. Engage in peer review processes, whether as a reviewer or by seeking peer review for your own work. This helps you refine your critical analysis skills.
- *Stay organized*. Use tools like research management software, citation managers, and note-taking apps to keep your research materials organized.
- *Time management*. Manage your time effectively to balance research, coursework, and other responsibilities. Set aside dedicated time for research tasks during hours you feel alert and are likely to have limited disruptions.
- *Learn from failure*. Research can be challenging, and not all projects will yield the desired results. Learn from your failures and setbacks, and use them as opportunities for growth.
- *Stay curious and open-minded*. Cultivate curiosity and open-mindedness. Be willing to explore unexpected avenues in your research and consider alternative perspectives.

- *Reflect and iterate.* Regularly reflect on your research process and outcomes. Identify areas for improvement and refine your research skills accordingly.

Improving research skills is a continuous journey. By following these steps, you can enhance your research abilities and make meaningful contributions to your academic field.

2.4 Collaborative Research

Collaborative research is a process in which researchers from different backgrounds, disciplines, institutions, or geographic locations work together to conduct investigations, share resources, and combine their expertise to address complex research questions or solve problems. It is a common and valuable approach in contemporary research for several reasons:

1. *Diverse expertise.* Collaborative research allows researchers to tap into a broader range of expertise and perspectives than would be possible through individual efforts. Combining knowledge and skills from various disciplines can lead to more innovative and comprehensive solutions.
2. *Enhanced resources.* Collaboration often provides access to more resources, including funding, equipment, and research facilities. Partners can pool their resources to tackle larger and more ambitious projects.
3. *Increased productivity.* Collaborative research can lead to increased productivity. Multiple researchers can work simultaneously on different aspects of a project, accelerating the pace of research and the development of results.
4. *Interdisciplinary insights.* Collaborations between researchers from different fields promote interdisciplinary thinking. This can lead to the development of novel approaches and methodologies that might not have been considered in a single-discipline setting.
5. *Quality assurance.* Collaborative research often involves peer review and validation processes among the team members, which can enhance the quality and rigor of the research.
6. *Global reach.* Collaborations can transcend geographical boundaries, allowing researchers to access diverse populations, data sets, and environments. This global reach can be particularly valuable in fields like environmental science, public health, and international business.
7. *Problem-solving.* Complex challenges, such as those related to climate change, healthcare, and technology development, often require multidisciplinary approaches. Collaborative research can bring together the necessary expertise to address these challenges effectively.
8. *Networking opportunities.* Collaborative research provides opportunities for researchers to build networks and establish relationships with colleagues from different institutions and backgrounds. These connections can lead to future collaborations, career opportunities, and knowledge exchange.

9. *Mentorship and learning.* Collaborations can foster mentorship and learning opportunities, particularly for junior researchers. Working alongside experienced colleagues can help early-career researchers develop their skills and knowledge.
10. *Inter-institutional collaboration.* Collaborative research can strengthen ties between institutions and promote knowledge-sharing among universities, research centers, and organizations.
11. *Cross-cultural understanding.* Collaborations involving researchers from different countries and cultures can promote cross-cultural understanding and tolerance, fostering a more global perspective.

Collaborating on projects and developing research networks can help increase one's productivity and efficiency. Conducting studies and developing manuscripts often require the contribution of individuals who have different skills, ranging from conceptual to methodological and writing skills. Developing a manuscript shares similarities with constructing a house, involving various skilled individuals ranging from financiers to painters or carpet layers. Collaborating with experts who can bring diverse contributions to a research project can enhance productivity and provide opportunities for skill acquisition, especially in areas like data analysis and writing. Engaging with different sets of collaborators can exponentially increase both the quantity and impact of your publications, even if you are not the primary author. There are instances where individuals achieve a high citation count relative to their senior or sole-authored publications or expertise in a specific field.

Nonetheless, it is crucial to exercise caution and strategic thinking when selecting and working with collaborators. First, it is essential to establish clear roles and authorship order agreements before commencing a project. Many reputable institutions only recognize co-authored publications if the researcher's name appears at least second or third in the author sequence. Prominent universities often require a substantial number of senior or sole-authored publications for granting promotion and tenure, so researchers aspiring to build a robust publication record should avoid overcommitting to projects resulting in mere co-authorships. Second, careful selection of collaborators is paramount. Partners should have a track record of producing sole-authored or senior-authored publications, and their skills should complement rather than duplicate those of other group members.

In sum, successful collaborative research requires careful planning, clear communication, and effective management. Researchers must establish roles and responsibilities, define objectives, allocate resources, and establish mechanisms for decision-making and conflict resolution. It is also important to consider issues related to authorship, data sharing, intellectual property, and ethical considerations within the collaborative framework. Ultimately, collaborative research has the potential to generate impactful, drive innovation, and address some of the most pressing challenges. Researchers who engage in collaborative efforts are often better positioned to make meaningful contributions to their respective fields.

2.4.1 Choosing Collaborators

Choosing collaborators for your research is a crucial decision that can significantly impact the quality and success of your projects. The following are some steps and considerations to help you select the right collaborators:

- *Clarify your research goals.* Start by defining your research goals and objectives. What are you trying to achieve with your project(s)? Understanding your research direction will help you identify individuals with complementary expertise.
- *Identify the gaps in your expertise.* Assess your own strengths and weaknesses as a researcher. Identify areas where you lack expertise or experience, and consider finding collaborators who can fill these gaps.
- *Networking and professional relationships.* Leverage your professional network. Collaborating with individuals you know or have worked with before can be advantageous because you already have an understanding of their work ethic and capabilities.
- *Search for complementary skills.* Look for collaborators who possess skills, knowledge, or expertise that complement yours. For example, if you're an anthropologist, you might seek a collaborator with expertise in data analysis or statistics.
- *Consider interdisciplinary collaboration.* Interdisciplinary research can lead to innovative solutions. Seek collaborators from diverse academic backgrounds who can bring unique perspectives to your project.
- *Evaluate track records.* Review potential collaborators' past research projects, publications, and academic achievements. A strong track record in relevant areas can be a good indicator of their suitability.
- *Communication and teamwork.* Effective communication and teamwork are vital. Collaborators should be responsive, open to feedback, and willing to share credit and responsibilities. Assess their interpersonal skills during initial discussions.
- *Assess availability and commitment.* Ensure that potential collaborators have the time and commitment to actively participate in your research project. Discuss expectations and time commitments upfront.
- *Discuss authorship and responsibilities.* Clearly define roles and responsibilities within the research team, including authorship guidelines, and do this before starting a research project. This will help prevent disputes later on.
- *Funding and resources.* Consider the availability of funding and resources that potential collaborators can bring to the project. Ask them what they plan to "bring to the table" in terms of their intended contributions. This can be especially important for larger research endeavors that can produce multiple manuscripts where authorship order can be an issue.
- *Ethical considerations.* Ensure that potential collaborators share your ethical principles and are committed to conducting research with integrity and in compliance with ethical guidelines (see Chap. 12).

- *Compatibility.* Assess personal compatibility and work styles. Research collaborations can be long-term, so it is important to work with individuals who are compatible with your working style and values.
- *Start with small projects.* If you are unsure about a potential collaborator, consider starting with a smaller, less critical project to test the collaboration before committing to a larger endeavor.
- *Legal agreements.* In some cases, it may be necessary to formalize collaborations with legal agreements (e.g., memo/letter of understanding), especially if the project involves intellectual property, data sharing, or funding commitments.
- *Seek advice.* Do not hesitate to seek advice from mentors, colleagues, or experienced researchers who can provide insights and guidance on potential collaborators.

The following points summarize the benefits and risks of working with collaborators and suggest when an early-career researcher should work with collaborators:

2.4.2 Reasons for Working with Collaborators (Benefits)

- Improve the quality of a research project.
- Increase efficiency and productivity.
- Acquire certain skills.
- Synergy can better address a research problem.

2.4.3 Risks of Collaborative Research

- Overreliance on collaborative research can create the image one is not able to publish without others' help.
- Some institutions are looking for sole- and senior-authored publications, and they do not "count" publications of persons whose name appears beyond third place in authorship sequence or have contributed a small fraction to the total effort.
- The failure of a collaborator to perform as expected, either because of inability or because of other circumstances, can impede timely project completion.

2.4.4 When to Collaborate

- Collaborator's skills or resources are necessary, and you cannot complete a project without them.
- Collaborator's contribution is clear.
- Contribution is not going to have adverse or unfair effect on authorship sequence.

- Collaboration is on a project that falls within the researcher's chosen stream(s) of research.
- There is compatibility in working styles of collaborators and agreement about project execution and completion.

Remember that selecting the right collaborators is a dynamic process that may require time and careful consideration. It is essential to make informed decisions to ensure a successful and productive research partnership.

2.5 Getting Organized for Research[1]

Academic research has grown exponentially in the last three decades (Thelwall & Sud, 2022), consistent with the increasing trend toward interdisciplinary and collaborative research. This growth is accompanied by challenges, including difficulty in keeping up-to-date with the latest research developments. Also, researchers must cultivate skills for interdisciplinary teamwork and develop diverse knowledge and expertise to navigate these new contexts successfully. This evolving landscape requires a more structured approach to academic organization. An effective system of classifying and retrieving the available information is a must if one pursues any systematic research, as one cannot afford to do a new literature search whenever one writes a manuscript.

What researchers need, I think, is a method of classifying and retrieving the relevant literature and continuing to build or expand upon what one already knows. Establishing an efficient system for information organization and retrieval in academia is fundamental for rigorous and systematic research pursuits. To do this, the researcher must have an effective filing system to quickly determine what is known in specific areas, the gaps in knowledge, and how the new information one uncovers "fits" into what is already known. Researchers can leverage adaptable, free software tools to create more structured and organized knowledge libraries that enrich their knowledge, enhancing scholarly productivity.

The organizing style of such a filing system and software tools used could vary from person to person, but researchers should always have either a hard or, preferably, a soft copy of important articles and books within their field, along with a portable electronic data file. I find it helpful to organize my files using a conceptual model, grouping all examined dependent and independent variables in published studies, along with the nature of their discovered relationship (positive, negative, or nonsignificant), within that model. This way, when I want to explore, for instance, the impact of independent variable X on dependent variable Y, I can easily refer to my file and focus on the pertinent studies that have investigated that specific relationship.

With its array of features, Google Scholar is an effective tool for creating a structured search system. Its multifaceted functionalities, such as multiple keyword

[1] The author thanks Murtaza Haider for writing a major portion of this section.

searches, "related articles" showcasing linked content, and access to cited articles, aid in retrieving relevant articles, and they aid in understanding research impact and uncovering new sources. Additionally, receiving email alerts for authors' new publications ensures staying abreast of the latest research. Google Scholar's "Label" feature enables the creation of custom labels for topics, authors, or publication dates, enabling the users to create their personal knowledge library, thus streamlining information retrieval for swift access to specific content. These features empower researchers to organize scholarly articles efficiently, maintaining meticulous organization throughout their research journey.

Organizing and integrating researched material can be streamlined with a reference manager like Zotero. Zotero is a free and open-source reference manager that can extract bibliographic information from online sources like Google Scholar, attach PDFs, and organize libraries. Zotero groups, its online feature, enables collaboration with other users on its site; members can add content to a shared folder that all collaborators can see. Zotero seamlessly integrates with other applications, such as Microsoft Word and Google Docs, making it simple to create citations and insert them into documents. Researchers can use Zotero to highlight and annotate attached PDFs, extract highlighted text, and add their thoughts to synthesize the categorized and highlighted text into novel ideas.

Although annotations are critical to academic research writing, managing and synthesizing ideas from them can be difficult, necessitating the use of a knowledge management tool. Researchers can utilize Obsidian, a free knowledge management tool, to create "Notes" and organize their annotations and link various published resources. In Obsidian, any word in a note can be turned into a link to another note, allowing for easy navigation and exploration of thoughts and ideas. Notes' bidirectional linking and backlinking capacities enable researchers to combine new insights with existing knowledge, expanding the personalized knowledge base. Obsidian's interconnected web of notes helps researchers see how different pieces of information relate and fit together to identify patterns and develop insights.

Tools like Google Scholar, Zotero, and Obsidian streamline literature organization for an efficient system for organizing and retrieving academic information essential for research. Like my example of organizing files based on conceptual models, these tools can make accessing relevant literature easier, and they can systematically explore specific relationships within a researcher's field of study. These tools enable researchers to seamlessly navigate their field's knowledge, identify gaps, and leverage new insights for their academic work.

2.6 Looking for a Professorial Position

2.6.1 Interviewing

Before you decide to "go on the market," you should consider the timing of the defense of your dissertation and that of the event, such as the date of an annual conference of an association in your field, which allows you to interview with several universities. Members of an association normally receive messages that inform them of this event and of the member institutions that are looking for new faculty, as well as member doctoral students who are looking for professorial positions. Postings of institutions and students include brief descriptions of the position(s) available, and postings of students also describe their interests and specializations. These platforms allow interested parties to arrange job interviews during such conferences. Institutions are normally interested in interviewing *only* those doctoral students who have already defended their dissertations or have other evidence they will successfully do soon.

Look for announcements of openings, and evaluate the desirability of working at an institution that is hiring junior faculty. At this point, it is important to consider nonacademic factors, such as location (e.g., preference for institutions located in rural or urban institutions), working opportunities for your spouse (if married), cost of living, and schools (if you have children), and not to ignore the potential lifestyle you will likely have by working at a particular institution.

Next, look at the present faculty of the department that is hiring junior faculty (usually available on the University's website), and search the recent publications of each. Examine carefully the topics or areas of their research interest; assess the extent to which your interests (if any) overlap with theirs or your skills can complement theirs. Most likely, you would prefer working at an institution where there are opportunities for collaborative studies; compare with places where nobody is interested in the work you do or the skills that you have. And keep in mind that many departments often strive to develop the image of having an expertise in a particular research area or topic.

Finally, rank order the institutions that meet your criteria above in terms of desirability, being realistic about your chances of landing a job at these institutions based on the quality and reputation of the university from which you will be receiving your degree. For example, unless you are graduating from a reputable university, your chances of being hired by such a university are likely to be rather small. Normally, universities prefer to have faculty holding degrees from prestigious institutions. The largest number of institutions on your list, among those which are hiring, should be universities that have similar reputation to the university from which you will be receiving your doctoral degree, followed by several institutions that are less prestigious, and few that are more prestigious. Depending on economic conditions, the number of available positions varies and so is the number of those seeking employment.

After a candidate decides on the institutions that are looking for new faculty, the usual next step is to request his or her main advisor, mentor, or dissertation chair to write a "letter of introduction" to each university on the candidate's list. This letter is usually addressed to someone known by the candidate's advisor, and it is (and should be) highly confidential. Although the contents of this latter may vary depending on the institution, the expectation is that it will provide a candid assessment of the candidate's present and potential abilities to meet the hiring department's expectations for research and teaching, including the expected date of his or her graduation. The impact of this letter on the decision of members of the institution's recruitment committee usually varies based on the reputation and credibility of the candidate's advisor. Letters written by well-known and highly credible researchers have more impact, especially when the candidate's research focus is within his or her advisor's stream of research—hence the importance in choosing a credible advisor—and they are likely to help the candidate secure an interview with the members of the university's recruitment committee, although such interviews sometimes reflect a gesture of courtesy to the student's advisor.

Off-Campus Interviews It is not uncommon for institutions and prospective employees to arrange 20–30 interviews during the duration of a large conference. During these interviews, which normally last between 30 and 60 min, prospective employers determine the candidate's suitability for the available position(s), and prospective employees decide if they would be interested in working for an institution. Based on these interviews, employers decide on the candidates who do not meet their criteria or expectations as well as those who merit further evaluation and consideration. Similarly, candidates may obtain adequate information during this relatively short interview to decide the extent to which they would be interested in learning more about the available position(s). These interviews allow a university or department's recruitment committee to select approximately half a dozen of those they interviewed and find very attractive to invite for a campus interview. The goal of a university that is very interested in a particular candidate is to invite that person for a campus interview and, assuming interest remains strong, offer him or her a job with a short deadline for deciding, before other institutions do the same.

Campus Interviews A campus interview serves several purposes for the hiring institution and the candidate. During their visit, candidates are expected to make a presentation of their dissertations (proposal and/or completed study). The main purpose of this presentation is for the attending faculty members to evaluate the candidate's ability to communicate effectively and handle himself or herself when asked (often intentionally) difficult questions. Early-career researchers who are making a presentation to faculty members should be aware that they are likely to be "tested." They may be asked questions borderline line to being insulting, and they should try to keep their posture, rather than react in a way that they would be perceived enable to handle challenging questions, such as those often asked by students. It is not uncommon for an institution to ask a visiting candidate to make a presentation of their choice to a class of students, who are later asked to evaluate the teaching effectiveness of the candidate.

Campus visits also provide opportunities for candidates to meet with all members of a department's faculty and doctoral students. As these visits typically last more than 1 day, candidates should be asking questions they had not enough time to ask during the initial interview. Campus interviews also allow members of a department to assess the candidate's suitability for the position and, to the extent the candidate is very attractive, even do some "selling" of their university and other nonacademic factors (e.g., lifestyle, environment, entertainment options, weather).

2.6.2 Employers' Decision Criteria

In preparation for an academic career that emphasizes research, it is important for early-career researchers to learn about the opportunities an institution would provide to them for advancing their academic career. This requires both knowledge of the criteria a university uses to decide on the candidate's suitability for the available position, as well as learning about the factors that promote (or inhibit) professional development at a particular institution. Following are some *criteria and qualities employers are looking* for when they are hiring a junior faculty member.

- *Research and scholarly expectations.* A strong research record is important, particularly in research-oriented institutions. Employers are likely to assess candidates' publications or the impact of their dissertations on their field. And they also consider the candidates' potential for future research contributions.
- *Teaching excellence.* Effective teaching skills are essential. Employers are likely to look for candidates with a demonstrated ability to engage students, adapt teaching methods to diverse learning styles, and receive positive evaluations from students or colleagues. And in many cases, they look for faculty members who have an expertise and experience in teaching a particular subject.
- *Teaching philosophy and expectations.* Candidates should be able to articulate their teaching philosophy and demonstrate alignment with the institution's educational goals. Institutions are likely to seek individuals who show a commitment to innovative teaching methods and a willingness to continually improve their pedagogical approaches.
- *Collegiality and collaboration.* Collaboration is often key in academia. Many departments look for candidates who can work well with colleagues, mentor students, and contribute positively to the department's culture and community.
- *Service expectations.* Institutions also consider a candidate's willingness to engage in service to the institution, department, and profession. Candidates who have shown leadership in academic or community organizations may be particularly attractive to the hiring institution.
- *References and recommendations.* These factors weigh heavily on a department's decision to interview a candidate and hire him or her. The candidate's letters of recommendation from his or her major professor(s), especially those known to the faculty members of the hiring department, offer insights into the candidate's strengths, weaknesses, and potential fit within the department.
- *Diversity, equity, and inclusion.* Many universities prioritize diversity, equity, and inclusion initiatives. Show your commitment to these values in your application or during interviews by highlighting relevant experiences and ideas for promoting diversity and inclusion in your teaching and research.
- *Fit with departmental need.* Lastly, the candidate should align with the department's needs, whether it is filling specific expertise gaps, contributing to specific programs, or supporting the department's strategic goals.

- *Attractive resume.* Employers look closely at a candidate's resume. Seeing one's publications listed by title followed by a "co-authored with" notation, rather than listed by author name sequence, can be interpreted as a lack of senior-authored publications and inability to do research without help from others.

The exact weight of these criteria may vary depending on the specific department and institution. In practice, hiring committees often use a combination of information from interviews, candidate's teaching demonstrations, research presentations, and reference checks to assess candidates holistically and make informed decisions.

2.6.3 Decision Criteria of Candidates

Recent Ph.D. graduates or soon-to-graduate doctoral students seeking their first job at a research-oriented university should carefully consider several criteria to help them make an informed decision. The following are key factors one should consider when deciding on his or her first academic position:

- *Research fit.* Ensure that the university's research focus aligns with your own research interests and expertise. Look for departments or programs where your work can make a meaningful contribution and where there are potential collaborators or mentors in your field.
- *Location.* Consider the location of the university and its impact on your lifestyle and career goals. Think about factors like cost of living, proximity to family and support networks, and whether you prefer an urban, suburban, or rural setting.
- *University reputation.* Assess the reputation and ranking of the university and the department you are considering. A strong university with a good track record in your field can enhance your academic profile and research opportunities. Assess how the university is regarded within your specific field of study.
- *Resources and facilities.* Evaluate the research resources and facilities available at the university. Access to well-equipped laboratories, libraries, and funding opportunities can significantly influence your research productivity.
- *Teaching load*: Determine the expected teaching load and the balance between teaching and research at the university. Consider your teaching preferences and how they align with the institution's expectations.
- *Mentorship and support.* Investigate the availability of mentorship and support systems for early-career faculty members. Having experienced mentors and a supportive academic community can be invaluable for your professional development.
- *Tenure and promotion criteria.* Understand the tenure and promotion criteria at the institution you are considering. Clarify the expectations for achieving tenure and what it entails in terms of research, teaching, and service. Look for answers to specific questions about publication requirements for tenure and promotion, such as tiers of journals recognized by the department, number of publications expected in each tier, and whether they are expected to be co-authored, senior- or

junior-authored publications. Ask if the institution requires information on the co-authors' relative contribution to each co-authored article (e.g., percentage of contribution/effort, and if there is a minimum acceptable percentage for receiving credit) and if information about the nature of contribution to the article is required (e.g., data analysis, conceptual framework, writing and editing).

- *Faculty turnover.* Try to find out the approximate number of junior faculty members who were previously employed in a department. A large number of those previously employed who have left should raise concerns, and it would be worth investigating the reasons for their departure.
- *Research opportunities.* Look for universities with research centers, institutes, or collaborations that align with your research interests.
- *Collaborative opportunities.* Research-oriented universities often encourage interdisciplinary collaboration. Explore the potential for cross-departmental and interdisciplinary research projects and partnerships.
- *Student engagement.* Assess the level of student engagement and the quality of students in the department. A motivated and talented student body can enhance your teaching and research experiences.
- *Financial considerations.* Evaluate the compensation package, including salary, benefits, and startup funds for research. Determine whether the package aligns with your financial needs and expectations.
- *Professional development opportunities.* Research-oriented universities often offer opportunities for professional development, such as grants, sabbaticals, and travel funding. Investigate these opportunities and how they can support your career growth.
- *Course releases for research.* Availability of course releases for research, especially during summer months, and protocols for their awards should be a major consideration. If they are awarded on a competitive basis, information on the ratios of number of applicants to the number of releases is essential.
- *Long-term career goals.* Reflect on your long-term career goals and how the position you are considering aligns with them. Alternatively, consider whether this job will serve as a stepping stone to achieving your academic aspirations.
- *Location and lifestyle.* Consider the university's location and whether it aligns with your lifestyle. Evaluate the cultural, social, and recreational opportunities in the area.
- *Interview experience.* Finally, the interview process can provide valuable insights into the department's culture and your fit within it. Pay attention to your interactions with faculty, staff, and doctoral students during the campus visit.

It is essential to thoroughly research each potential institution, ask questions during interviews, and seek advice from mentors and colleagues in your field. Remember that academic job searches can be highly competitive, and it may take time to secure a position that aligns with your goals and qualifications. Ultimately, choose the position that aligns best with your research interests, career goals, and personal preferences, as this will set the foundation for a successful and fulfilling academic career. Continuously develop your skills, seek mentorship, and be persistent in your pursuit of an academic career at a research-oriented university.

2.7 Preparing for the Next Transition

Junior faculty members who are hired in their first professorial position are normally evaluated for promotion and tenure after 4–5 years (or longer, depending on the institution). Annual faculty member evaluations by administrators, such as department heads, often provide feedback and guidance to junior faculty, helping them understand their institution's expectations regarding their performance. During this relatively short time frame, junior faculty tend to follow three main trajectories, largely depending on the institution they chose. One group performs as expected or better than expected, with those in the latter group often receiving tenure and promotion earlier than normal. Because early-career researchers in this group tend to be mobile and are often courted by other universities, they must often assess their career goals and decide whether to stay at the same institution or move to one that is more attractive than the one they are presently serve. This group usually incudes individuals who started their first job at a university that had low research expectations relative to the faculty member's skills, in part because of market conditions—i.e., few job openings relative to the number of candidates. And those in this group who, for various reasons, are either unhappy at the present position or wish to work at a more prestigious university are likely to welcome an opportunity to move. Their publication record gives them the choice to do so when the opportunity arises.

A second group of early-career researchers performs adequately, but not well-enough to deserve consideration for promotion and tenure and are often given extra time before they are considered. Many individuals in this group perform below expectations either because they underestimated the institution's expectations or due inadequate skills and (possibly) interest in research. It has been my experience that individuals in this group who are promoted to the rank of Associate Professor and are awarded tenure are likely to remain at the same institution, and they are unlikely to build the publication record that would justify promotion to Full Professor. These individuals are often labelled as "associates for life" not only because their record is not strong enough for further promotion but also because they do not meet the criteria of Full Professor at other comparable institutions. And because they do not do much research, they are often required to teach a larger-than-normal number of classes.

The third group consists of junior faculty members who perform below expectations during the first years of their employment, either because they have underestimated the institution's expectations or because they make up their minds that they are in the wrong profession. Those in the first category are likely to be informed (often informally) that they are not a good fit with their institution's needs, and they are likely to start seeking employment opportunities at other institutions that have lower expectations for the ranks of Assistant or Associate Professors, before they are formally considered for promotion or tenure. And many of those in the latter category decide to leave academia and work in the industry or government agencies.

Thus, in preparation for an academic career, those looking for their first employment should evaluate their research and teaching skills relative to the expectations or demands of the institution they are considering. Working at universities that have higher performance expectations than junior faculty are willing or able to meet can have consequences on their academic career and well-being in general. The more prestigious universities also expect more from their junior faculties, and there is a "price" these individuals must pay for a position at these universities, usually in the form of chronic stress and time that must be devoted to teaching and research. Such positions are ideal for those who have the skills and aptitude for effectively enacting their expected roles and immensely enjoy what they do, and work tends to be their hobby and entertainment. In contrast, those who have the skills but also other interests and responsibilities, and not as a strong passion for their work, usually prefer working at a less prestigious or demanding institution.

A strategy that I often recommend to my doctoral students who seek my advice is rather than trying to secure your first job at one of your aspirational schools that have high expectations, start your career at a place where you are likely to "feel comfortable" but have adequate opportunities for growth and advancement. If you can exceed that institution's expectations, you will have the option to go to a more prestigious place where you can also feel comfortable and enjoy additional benefits (e.g., a higher salary, more research support). And if you decide to stay at the same institution, you can still enjoy additional benefits, such as salary supplements and prestigious titles (e.g., Chair, Professorship), as long as you continue to perform and remain marketable. Your institution is likely to try to keep you from "defecting" to another university. After all, it is more the contributions that you make to your discipline than the prestige of the university one works for that brings fame.

References

Prakitsuwan, P., & Moschis, G. P. (2020). Well-being in later life: A life course perspective. *Journal of Services Marketing, 14*(2), 152–167.

Prakitsuwan, P., Moschis, G. P., & Shannon, R. (2022). Using the life course paradigm to study financial well-being in late life. *Asia Pacific Journal of Marketing and Logistics, 34*(1), 60–74. https://doi.org/10.1108/APJML-06-2020-0415

Sawyer, A. G., Laran, J., & Xu, J. (2008). The readability of marketing journals: Are award-winning articles better written? *Journal of Marketing, 72*(1), 108–117.

Thelwall, M., & Sud, P. (2022). Scopus 1900–2020: Growth in articles, abstracts, countries, fields, and journals. *Quantitative Science Studies, 3*(1), 37–50.

Yingwattanakul, P., & Moschis, G. P. (2017). Life course perspectives on the onset and continuity of preventive healthcare behaviors. *The Journal of Primary Prevention, 38*(5), 537–550.

Yingwattanakul, P., & Moschis, G. P. (2019). A life course study of the effects of experienced life events on the onset and continuity of preventive healthcare behaviors. *Health Marketing Quarterly, 36*(1), 1–21.

Research Foundations

3

Academic research is built upon several key foundations that provide the framework for the systematic investigation of questions or problems. These foundational elements are essential for producing credible and valuable contributions to knowledge. In a scientific study, the main foundations of that guide academic research can include the following: (a) definition of the issue or topic under investigation and the specific goals and aims of the study; (b) a review prior research to understand what is already known about the topic and determine area(s) where further research is needed; (c) a theoretical basis for the study; (d) the overall approach to the study and the guiding the research design; and (e) results and their interpretation in the context of the study's goals and research questions.

A solid grasp of these foundations of academic research is essential for guiding the entire research process, from the formulation of questions to the communication of findings. It empowers early-career researchers to contribute meaningfully to their fields and establishes a strong foundation for their future academic endeavors. This chapter informs early-career researchers of the basic conceptual foundations they should be familiar with when conducting academic studies, including the definition and meaning of commonly used research terms, the process of conceptualizing a phenomenon under investigation, the types of literature reviews they can do, and the basic research approaches commonly employed in academic studies.

3.1 Conceptual Foundations

3.1.1 Commonly Used Terms

As a basic requirement for conducting academic research, one should be familiar with the meaning of terms often used to describe research-related concepts such as "variable," "hypothesis," and "theory." To begin with, the term *concept* is defined in

G. P. Moschis, *Academic Research in Business and the Social Sciences*,
https://doi.org/10.1007/978-3-031-56548-9_3

Merriam-Webster Dictionary as "something conceived in the mind…a thought or notion." It can be an abstract idea generalized from particular instances. A *variable* is an objective or subjective factor that varies in value, intensity, level, or strength and is subject to change. If it varies or changes as a result of other factors, it is called *dependent* variable, but if it causes other variables to vary or change, it is called *independent* variable. Thus, a variable can be both dependent and independent. A *construct* is a variable that consists of other variables.

In addition, variables can be given several other names, depending on the role they are expected to play in an empirical study. When studying the relationship between an independent variable (e.g., variable X) and dependent variable (e.g., variable Y)—i.e., the presumed effects of variable X on variable Y—a variable that is theorized to affect the strength and the direction of this relationship, such as variable Z, is known as *moderating* (or moderator) variable. When the investigator wishes to see the influence of the independent variable on the dependent variable in the absence of the moderating variable Z, this variable can serve as a *control* variable by holding its value constant. For example, if gender influences the relationship between two variables, the researcher can analyze the relationship between the two variables for men separately from women participants of the study. When variable X can only affect variable Y by changing the value of variable Z, which in turn affects variable Y, variable Z is known as *intervening* or *mediating* variable. Thus, a mediating variable (or mediator) explains the process through which two variables are related; it represents the "change" mechanism. When variable Z is presumed to affect both the dependent and independent variables, it is called *antecedent* variable.

In modelling relationships between variables, as in the cases of path analysis and structural equation modelling (SEM), model variables can take other names such as exogenous, endogenous, and latent variables (e.g., Olobatuyi, 2006). Exogenous variables are factors in the model whose values cannot be affected by other factors in the model, and they can only affect other variables in the model. Endogenous variables are variables in the model whose values or measures are determined by another variable in the same model. And latent variables, also known as indicators and manifest variables, are variables that cannot be directly observed or measured (also known as "unobservable variables"), but are assumed to be present based on observable and measurable variables.

A *hypothesis* is a conjectural statement about the relationship between two or more variables, or sets of variables—one dependent and the other independent. It is a tentative statement for which there is no empirical support for or against it. A hypothesis is subject to empirical testing for the purpose of *falsifying* rather than establishing causality between variables, as causality can only be inferred in social and behavioral sciences. In order to establish causality, three conditions must be satisfied: (a) significant covariation (correlation) between the dependent and independent variable; (b) time-order of occurrence—i.e., the independent variable must occur or change before the dependent variable; and (c) elimination of all possible factors that may affect the dependent variable, other than the independent variable tested. Survey data can only satisfy the first condition, and experiments can satisfy only the first two conditions, and it is impossible to know and account for all possible factors that can affect the dependent variable (for a more extensive discussion of these conditions, see, e.g., Churchill & Brown, 2004).

In the real world, where decisions concerning policy and practice are made with incomplete information, theory and data often help guide such decisions. And "causality" is often determined based on information from one or more of the following three sources: the decision makers' knowledge (e.g., legislators, marketers), those affected by the decision maker's actions (e.g., public, consumers), and information provided by third parties (e.g., researchers). For example, in one of the author's seminars for food store retailers, attendees whose company was offering senior discounts to older customers were asked if they thought these promotional offerings available during certain days of the week were effective. And the response was affirmative because, in the words of one executive, "there are a lot more white-hair customers shopping on senior days." These responses, however, were not consistent with findings of our studies at the Center for Mature Consumer Studies (CMCS), where older consumers were asked if they had switched brands or stores because of senior discounts. In a subsequent time series experiment (see Chap. 6), it was determined that the increase is store traffic (sales) during senior days was followed by a decrease in store traffic during other days of the week, with senior discounts having trivial effects on the store's weekly sales. Similarly, companies that position their offerings to appease a segment of customers could alienate customers in other segments (Moschis, 2022). These examples raise the issues of (a) the base(s) that should be used for inferring causality and (b) the context in which causality should be assessed for effective decision-making.

When testing relationships between variables, it is important to keep in mind that one tests the null hypothesis, i.e., that there is no relationship between the variables, and should take steps to make it difficult for the null hypothesis to be rejected. For example, if one has a reason to believe that the driver's gender plays a role in experiencing a car accident, a hypothesis stating that "there are significant sex differences in the number of car accidents" would be easier to accept (i.e., easier to reject the null hypothesis) than stating the gender that is more or less likely to have a car accident. Thus, hypotheses should be directional. And any emerged relationship between variables in hypothesis testing should be viewed as a mere rejection of the null hypothesis, rather than inferring causality (Popper, 1959). Even in the presence of strong evidence regarding the possible causal effects of a variable, as in experimental studies, researchers should exercise caution in interpreting results and suggesting course of action. One should keep in mind that the emerged *statistically significant* relationships may not necessarily be *managerially significant*. For example, a business manager who is told that his company's annual expenditures on advertising that consists of 5% of its annual sales was (statistically) significant in causing an increase of 2% in annual sales volume might not want to spend much on advertising.

Tentative or conjectural statements about the relationship between variables that are not empirically tested in a given study should not be stated as "hypotheses"; they should be stated as *propositions*. As in the case of hypotheses, propositions can be theory-driven and/or data-driven. They provide conceptual directions for future research and are the bases for hypotheses to be tested in empirical studies.

A *theory* is a set of systematically related statements, including some law-like generalizations, which is empirically testable (Hunt, 1983). Theories help explain, understand, and predict phenomena. A good theory should explain the "what," "why," and "how" (Salthouse, 1991). For example, when investigating the relationship between age and brand loyalty, a theory should state *what* type of relationship exists between the two variables, such as a negative relationship, and *why* the negative relationship (e.g., family size decreases with age, reducing the diversity of family preferences for brands of a product); and it should explain the *how* or the change mechanism(s) (e.g., reduction in coercive strategies used by children in the household that would affect parental yielding). Theories are held tentative, pending additional evidence that could modify, or provide a new theory, or specific conditions for explanation. A theory must be empirically testable, but its "survival" as an explanation of a phenomenon depends not only on empirical results but also on alternative explanations of the emerged relationships. It is for this reason that the strongest test of a theory is the absence of alternative theoretical explanations of empirical findings derived from hypothesis testing—i.e., the same findings but based on different theoretical formulations.

A *theoretical perspective* refers to a set of similar types of theories in behavioral and social sciences, each having different sets of assumptions or views about the real world. For example, the psychological perspective assumes that behavior is driven by subjective factors within the individual such as motives, needs, and attitudes. In contrast, the sociological perspective assumes that behavior is shaped by one's social environments (e.g., family, friends) in which he or she has been embedded. A *multi-theoretical framework* is a combination of multiple and diverse theoretical perspectives and theories. It offers a more comprehensive and realistic explanation of a phenomenon, in part because the various theories and perspectives tend to be viewed as complementary rather than competing (e.g., Elder et al., 2003). Multi-theoretical frameworks are often conceived in the form of conceptual frameworks, which are commonly presented graphically as diagrams (e.g., Moschis, 2019). A *conceptual framework* is a theoretical structure or a set of interconnected concepts and ideas that provide a systematic and organized way of understanding a particular phenomenon or topic within a specific field of study. It serves as a foundation for research, guiding researchers in their exploration, analysis, and interpretation of data. Multi-theoretical frameworks are becoming increasingly important in academic research, as researchers recognize that not only phenomena cannot be adequately explained by single theories or theoretical perspectives but also because the various diverse theories and perspectives tend to be interdependent (e.g., Shanahan et al., 2016).

A *paradigm* refers to "the operating rules about the appropriate relationship among theories, methods and evidence that constitutes the actual practice of the members of a particular scientific community, research program, or tradition" (Alford, 1998, p. 2). Alford distinguishes among three major paradigms: empirical/quantitative, interpretive, and historical (see "Philosophical Paradigms" in this chapter). An *argument* is an explanation of a phenomenon based on integration of theories, methods, and evidence derived from all three paradigms. It "deals with the ways in which theoretical claims and empirical generalizations are constructed within multivariate, interpretive, and historical paradigms of inquiry" (Alford, 1998, p. 8). It is believed to offer the most satisfactory explanation of a phenomenon (Alford, 1998).

Researchers, in their attempts to communicate to others their perceived reality and knowledge about a topic, often use an existing model or develop a new one. A *model* is a mere representation of reality. A model can take various forms such as iconic (e.g., diagram, graph), mathematical (e.g., $y = f(x)$), and verbal that describes the variables and their relationships. Models are not necessarily theories, but all theories are models by definition. Models are useful in scientific research for several reasons. First, a model serves as a skeleton or outline of much of the information presented, helping the reader "walk though" the materials presented in a systematic fashion by relating model elements to text. It is for this reason models should be placed before presenting the study's hypotheses in an article. Second, it helps summarize the discussion of the main concepts, their meanings, and relationships among them. Third, a model helps the researcher communicate his or her ideas to others by showing how the main concepts presented are related.

3.1.2 The Research Question

Theories are integral parts of the scientific process to creating knowledge, which entails a systematic approach to knowledge construction that involves (a) observing a phenomenon; (b) providing a tentative explanation of the phenomenon, either in the context of existing theories or in the form of hypotheses or propositions; (c) gathering data to test the hypotheses or propositions; and (d) interpreting the emerged results to provide an understanding. Development of assumptions about the phenomenon under investigation (research question or problem) heavily relies on theories and existing data. The researcher's task is to identify the relevant theories that might explain the phenomenon under investigation and/or the relevant data that will help us understand and provide tentative explanations of the phenomenon of interest.

A "phenomenon of interest" can take the form of an issues, concern, or problem, while the research question aims at generating knowledge relevant to addressing it. Alford (1998) asserts that a research problem must be broken down into two parts that are needed to define both empirical and theoretical questions:

> The theoretical question orients you toward the theoretical concepts within the relevant literature and frames the empirical question with theoretical justification. Why did something happen? What explains what exists?...The empirical question directs you toward certain kinds of evidence that is necessary to answer the theoretical question. What happened? What's going on?... (pp. 30–31)

Therefore, it is important to correctly state the issue or describe the phenomenon, as incorrectly stating it could lead to the wrong question or description, evidence that will answer it or help understand it, and relevant theoretical frameworks that would justify it.

It should be noted, however, that the scientific process to knowledge creation has greater value in addressing theoretical than empirical research questions. The latter type of question is data-driven, while theoretical questions are theory-driven and presume the presence of evidence that gives rise to theoretical questions. For example, a research question such as "are older people more prone to car accidents?" is an empirical one whose answer depends on evidence or data. The theoretical question suggests the presence of empirical evidence and seeks an answer, such as "why are older people more prone to car accidents?"

At this juncture, it is important to emphasize the importance of making accurate interpretation of the data in creating theoretical questions. For example, using the same data, the investigator may ask, "why are younger people disloyal to brands," rather than asking, "why are older people loyal to brands?" I had this experience in looking at the age distribution of residents of various states, such as Florida and Iowa, that show a high concentration of the older population. While one would be tempted to theorize that Florida's weather might attract older people, this theory is not likely to be helpful in explaining Iowa's high proportion of elderly residents. An alternative interpretation of these data creates the need for answering the question: "Are younger persons more likely than older persons in these states to move to other states, compared with those in the remaining states?" These theoretical interpretations and empirical questions are likely to lead researchers to different directions in terms of selecting theories to explain these phenomena. Explaining the relatively high number of a state's older population who prefer to stay put would make theories that explain stability in behavior relevant, but explaining the higher inclination of the state's younger population to leave their state would require the employment of theories that explain change in behavior.

3.1.3 Types of Literature Reviews

The first step in addressing a research question, issue or problem, is to obtain knowledge of (or draw upon) what is already known. This frequently requires a literature search, as new information becomes available daily. The manner in which a literature review should be conducted depends on the reason one undertakes the review, and there are several types of reviews suitable for different reasons.

Literature reviews are an essential part of academic research, providing a comprehensive overview of existing literature on a specific topic or research question. There are several types of literature reviews, each serving a distinct purpose in the research process. The most common types of literature reviews are briefly discussed in the paragraphs that follow. More elaborate discussion of the various types of literature reviews, including their objectives and the procedure(s) for conducting each, are discussed in Chap. 8.

Systematic Literature Review A systematic literature review is a rigorous and structured approach to reviewing and synthesizing existing research on a specific topic. It involves a systematic search for relevant sources using predefined criteria. The primary purpose of a systematic literature review is to provide an objective and evidence-based summary of existing research on a specific topic, with a focus on minimizing bias, identifying patterns, assessing the quality of studies, and informing evidence-based decision-making and future research directions.

Meta-analysis Meta-analysis is a statistical approach to literature review that focuses on quantitative data. It involves the synthesis of numerical data from multiple studies to draw statistical conclusions about the topic. Meta-analyses are often used to provide more precise estimates of effect sizes in empirical research, such as the impact of a particular intervention or treatment.

Narrative Literature Review This is the most traditional and common type of literature review. A narrative literature review is a comprehensive and systematic summary of existing research on a particular topic, concept, or area of study; it allows flexibility and subjectivity in the process. Its purpose is to provide a comprehensive understanding of the current state of knowledge, identify research gaps, and inform future research endeavors and decision-making in both academic and practical contexts.

Semi-systematic Literature Review A semi-systematic literature review represents a middle ground between a fully systematic review and a narrative review. It combines elements of both systematic and narrative reviews, offering a structured approach to reviewing existing literature while allowing for some flexibility and subjectivity in the process.

Integrative Literature Review Integrative reviews aim to provide a comprehensive analysis of the literature by synthesizing both qualitative and quantitative studies. They go beyond summarizing findings and seek to identify overarching themes, patterns, and relationships in the literature.

Critical Literature Review A critical literature review involves evaluating and analyzing existing research in a systematic and critical manner to gain a deep understanding of the current state of knowledge on a specific topic. Critical reviews involve a deep and critical evaluation of the existing literature. The emphasis is on assessing the quality of the sources, their methodology, and their contribution to the field. It may also involve identifying biases, contradictions, or limitations in the literature.

Theoretical Literature Review Theoretical review provides a comprehensive overview of existing theories, their evolution, and the contributions made by scholars, which is essential for developing a strong theoretical foundation for one's research. This type of review focuses on developing or extending a theoretical framework. It examines the existing theories and models in the literature, identifies gaps, and proposes new theoretical constructs or models.

Conceptual Literature Review A conceptual review explores and clarifies key concepts and definitions within a specific field or topic, typically leading to the development of a new or revised measure. It often provides a taxonomy to guide further research.

Bibliometric Review A bibliometric review, also known as bibliometric analysis or bibliometric study, is a systematic examination of published academic literature using quantitative methods. It analyzes citation patterns, trends, and relationships in the academic literature in order to quantify and evaluate the scholarly output and influence of the literature, including journals, articles, and authors.

Grounded Theory Literature Review A grounded theory literature review typically involves a systematic exploration of existing literature using grounded theory methodology. Grounded theory is a qualitative research approach that emphasizes the generation of theory from data rather than testing existing theories.

3.2 Variable Conceptualization

Conceptualization is the process of development and clarification of concepts. That is, clarifying a concept with words and/or examples to create a precise verbal definition. This clarification process needs to take place as a word in English (or any language for that matter) can hold a variety of meanings, depending on its usage, its context, and its user. Therefore, conceptualization is the process by which researchers attempt to define that which they attempt to study as precisely as possible. For example, the term "social status" could hold different meanings, such as wealth (millionaire), prestige (academic professor), and power (military general). The various meanings give rise to dimensions or domains of the term "social status." Thus, in this case, the concept "social status" can have the three dimensions that have been identified. As not all dimensions are directly observable, a researcher must use proxy variables, which are referred to as "indicators," to measure the latent dimension. For example, using the social status dimension of power, in military general context, the following indicators may be used: the number of people under supervision, annual budget, and amount of equipment under control. Thus, concepts, dimensions, and indicators are variables. However, their main key difference is in the level of abstraction.

The term "concept" is highly abstract and may contain many dimensions, while dimensions are somewhat less abstract and may contain several indicators that are concrete and observable. Although, in its strictest sense, concepts, dimensions, and indicators can all be variables, in an operational sense, a concept usually contains more than one dimension, and each dimension may contain several indicators.

Variable conceptualization, therefore, refers to the process by which the researcher defines the concept or idea he or she is looking to explore, using words and examples to describe its meaning, and attempts to assign objective properties to it so that it can be used for statistical analysis. This process is often referred to as *concept explication.*

3.2.1 Concept Explication

The key to successful research is the careful definition of the major concepts in the study. A fuzzily defined concept may enter into statistical relationships with other variables, but the meaning of those relationships can be no clearer than the meaning of the concept itself. The process by which concepts are defined for scientific purposes is called *explication.* This section presents a brief description of the concept explication process based on Carl Hempel's (1952) suggestions in his monograph *Fundamentals of Concept Formation in Empirical Science*, in a revised and condensed five-page format developed by the late Steven H. Chaffee, who made it available to students at the University of Wisconsin's School of Mass Communications.

Selecting the Concept One must start with at least a general notion of what he or she wants to study, or a commonly used label that would be interested in analyzing. At this preliminary stage, about all one can decide is what to focus on. The researcher's thinking about that "focal variable" should change quite a bit as he or she studies it and learns more about it. Early-career researchers should try to select a concept that is (a) amenable to empirical observation and (b) likely to fit into relationships that will be important for their field. Generally, one should avoid adopting "canned" operational definitions from other people's research, unless they have been widely used in previous studies that have appeared in leading scientific journals in the relatively recent past. In the event there are no widely used or agreed upon definition of a concept, one can make a contribution by a fresh start that might lead to innovative studies.

Literature Search After deciding on the focal variable or concept, the next step is to do a search to find the various types of definitions that have been used. At this stage it is not particularly relevant to catalogue the various relationships that have been found between the concept and other variables. Keep a list of all the ways in which the concept has been defined for research purposes. You can ignore purely abstract definitions, for example, where the concept is given some meaning that could not be tied to empirical observations in the real world, or cases where the term is used without definition. You may also find cases where the concept has been used by some other name. Keep those on your list too. It is the empirical usage of the concept that is important, not the label that is put on it.

Levels of Definition The definitions of concepts that can be found in the literature can be placed into three basic categories: nominal definitions, definition of the meaning, and empirical definitions of the concept. A *nominal definition* is when a set of operational procedures is given an arbitrary name by stipulation, without any "reduction statements," linking the name to the measure. This is usually the most common type of definition and often the least useful. It can usually be spotted by the obvious gap between the label and the measure. Some examples are as follows: "intelligence" is what an IQ test measures," "consensus" consists of a majority vote," and "brand loyalty is repeat purchase of the same brand."

A *definition* via *meaning* analysis is a more useful type of definition. This type of definition expresses the meaning of a higher-order term by listing in the lower-order concepts it subsumes. The lower-order terms are more "primitive," in that there are more clearly tied to operational definitions. This list of lower-order concepts is expendable and replaceable, in most cases. That is, new terms can be added to it, and others may disappear. And any such changes also change the meaning of the concept. For example, "mass media" are newspapers, books, magazines, radio, television, film, and electronic media, and "social media" refer to Facebook, Instagram, Tweeter, WhatsApp, etc. (note that these lists are clearly expandable).

An *empirical definition* consists of listing the necessary and sufficient conditions for observation of the concept. This form of definition is most valuable in scientific contexts, as alterations in the underlying concepts at a lower level do not fundamentally alter the essence of the overarching concept. However, it is important to note that empirical analysis typically serves as the outcome of research rather than its initial phase. Nonetheless, empirical definitions are essentially hypotheses, subject to adjustment as our understanding of the concept deepens. For instance, "information seeking" entails an individual taking action to augment their exposure to a particular kind of communication content, with some degree of uncertainty regarding the content they will receive, and a certain level of motivation stemming from that uncertainty.

Level of Analysis The next step is to distinguish between two kinds of attributes that are called property terms and relational terms. A property term is an attribute that is observable for one person or one object, in isolation from other persons or objects. A relational term is only observable in the interaction of two persons, or the comparison of two objects, or in some similar two-unit relationship. Many of the attributes that researchers are interested in are relational in nature. Strangely, they are often operationalized as if they were properties, in that only one person is observed at the time. This kind of anomaly is a serious error in research procedure. Early in the process of explication, one should decide whether the focus variable is a property or a relational term. Any further work with the concept should stick to whichever level of analysis one has decided on. For examples, income is a property term, but socioeconomic status (SES) is a relational term. So, if one is interested in SES but have data only on income, he or she should be treating the data as a relational (e.g., "relative income"). Similarly, information-seeking can be thought of as the property of an individual. But it may be relational to other forms of behavior. For instance, it preempts other forms of communication, in that person can only do one thing at a time. So, the explication might well lead one into defining a whole typology of forms of communication, which are mutually exclusive. It should be clear that concepts such as power, obedience, and knowledge are relational for most purposes.

Assessing Definitions After the researcher has narrowed his or her thinking to a few alternative definitions, these definitions should be assessed by applying several criteria. *Specificity* is important in a definition. The greater the specificity of the definition, in terms both of details of observation and of reduction sentences linking the various elements of the concept, the better. For example, it is more useful to report that someone "watched Channel 15 from 7 to 9 PM yesterday" than to say he "watched TV last night." Similarly, it is more helpful to ask study participants to report their "total household income from all source, after taxes last year" than to report their "annual income."

Another criterion for assessing a definition is ensuring that the concept under consideration is not a *reification*—i.e., naming attributes that one might imagine that exist but cannot be observed. In the case the researcher suspects that there is some key factor that has not been observed, that factor should be given empirical meaning by careful research. In that case, the researcher proposes a *hypothetical construct*, the hypothesis being that it exists, and the first test of the research should be a "validity check" on its existence. When you provide operational evidence of a hypothetical construct, it retains the more secure status of a variable. If a hypothetical construct remains unobserved, it is considered a reification, and other researchers are unlikely to be persuaded by your references to it. The important thing is to recognize the status of all elements of one's definition and to design research that will demonstrate their empirical content. Examples of common reifications in psychological and social studies include concepts such as "dissonance," "group cohesiveness," and "attitude." Although these concepts have never been observed, they hold important position in certain formulations. The danger is that they may not exist except in the minds of their theoreticians. Marketing researchers often experience this problem when they attempt to study consumer attitudes toward the so-called "low-involvement products," such as chewing gum and paper napkins. When consumers are asked to express their attitudes toward brands of such products, it is likely that their responses represent mere responses to measurement instruments rather than their thoughts and feelings.

Invariance of usage of a term is also important in assessing concepts and their definition. Although the term should be used by the same person consistently, this is not always the case. Rather, the same term is frequently used to refer to different things at different times. Even more common is the error of shifting levels of analysis without making any terminological distinction. For example, the term "attitude," which refers to a learned predisposition to respond to a stimulus in a favorable or unfavorable way, is not the same as "preference." A person, for example, may have a favorable attitude toward several brands but show preference only for one, while another person may show preference for the same brand without holding favorable attitude toward any of the same brands. Similarly, the term "generation," which is appropriate for analyzing families and other kinship systems, is misapplied to differences between age groups in society as a whole, as in the notion of a "generation gap."

Inter-observer invariance in the use of the concept, meaning that everyone uses the concept to mean the same thing, is the ultimate criterion and often the most difficult to achieve. But it is a useful goal to strive toward, and careful explication of the other vocabulary criteria in explication will help toward it.

Setting Boundaries Perhaps the most important step in explication is to decide on clear-cut boundaries for your concept. In the meaning analysis, this is simply a matter of considering whether or not to include the various lower-order concepts in the definition. If you can formulate a clear-cut rule for such a decision, you are on your way to a more versatile definition—i.e., an empirical analysis. In empirical analysis, boundaries are set by considering which conditions are necessary and/or sufficient, and which are neither necessary nor sufficient. In both cases, this stage of explication consists of stripping the concept of "surplus meaning." For example, various writers have described the adoption process as a series of stages including awareness, evaluation, trial, and adoption. An explicator looks at this list and decides that, whatever the heuristic the value of the total model, it includes too much. All that seems to be necessary are awareness and adoption. The evaluation and trial stages may occur in some case, but not in all, so they are surplus elements of the concept and can be dropped.

Tentatively Define Attempt to formulate a satisfactory definition through empirical analysis. You might discover that it can be surprisingly concise and straightforward. The goal is to ensure that this definition aligns with your intended meaning for the concept and excludes any unintended inclusions. In cases where an empirical definition proves elusive, it may be necessary to conduct further research. In such instances, return to meaning analysis and work on a list of lower-order concepts. Keep in mind that this represents an intermediate step in refining your concept.

Next, define the concept operationally. For every element within each concept that you retain in your ultimate definition, it is imperative to specify at least one operational definition. The greater the scientific rigor applied and the clearer the reduction statements linking each operation to your conceptual definition, the better. While it may not be necessary to enumerate all possible operational definitions, it is crucial to demonstrate that each element in your definition can be observed in real-world experiences.

Operational definitions can take various forms, such as interview questions, experimental manipulations, unobtrusive observations, content categories, and more. The key at this final stage of elucidation is to explicitly articulate all your reasoning. This ensures that anyone reading your work will understand (a) what actions you have taken, (b) how you perceive these actions conceptually, and (c) the rationale behind your choices. In the initial planning phases of a research project, it is vital to refine operational definitions into precise terms. This serves as evidence that you can accomplish this task effectively when designing an empirical study in the future.

3.2.2 An Example

The reader can see several elements and stages in the concept explication process already highlighted in this section in one of my earlier articles (Moschis, 1976). In this article, I follow the step-by-step process of concept explication suggested by Hempel's monograph (1952) described in the previous section. I explicate concepts such as social comparison, information seeking, and group influence, using the same terminology mentioned here. In explicating "social comparison," for example, I find two meanings and definitions of the concept: reflected appraisal and comparative appraisal. I briefly discuss the meaning of these two processes—i.e., the former entails cognitive and overt activity between two persons, while the latter may take place only at the cognitive level and at a distance. After the meaning analysis stage, I discuss the two concepts in the context of empirical analysis, by using research to specify the conditions that are necessary for inferring their presence or operation (as both are hypothetical constructs). For example, both processes require that there be similarities in interests, attitudes, and lifestyles between the evaluation seeker and the reference person(s), and the necessary and sufficient condition for comparative appraisal is only the evaluation seeker's perceived similarities between oneself and the reference person(s), while reflected appraisal requires both similarities and overt interaction.

Following the conceptual discussion of social comparison and the distinction between the two processes (i.e., conceptual definitions), I operationally define the two variables in the "methods" section. The operational definition for comparative appraisal is the respondent's perceived level of similarity in specific cosmetic product preferences (i.e., specificity), and the operational definition for reflected appraisal is the strength of the respondent's motivation to obtain information from those similar to herself for self-evaluation and gratification purposes in a face-to-face confrontation.

The final step entails the development of measures, which should derive from the necessary conditions that are required for "observing" the presence of the two processes. Measures are developed based on empirical analyses of the concepts of reflected appraisal and comparative appraisal, focusing on the necessary conditions that must be present to ensure non-reification. For example, items in the scale of reflected appraisal, such as "I like to talk about cosmetics with friends," derive from the necessary condition of overt interaction with peers about cosmetic products, and responses to this statement could measure the extent to which this social comparison process operates. And extreme responses to the statement "I am more interested in cosmetics than most of my friends" suggests low similarity, hence low-perceived similarity.

In the same article, the reader can see how other concepts in the reported study are explicated. Also, of additional benefit to novice researchers is the distinction among a conceptual definition, an operational definition, and a measure that is made in this article. Unfortunately, this distinction is not often made in empirical studies, where researchers interested in studying a variable are simply looking for its measure, ignoring the extent to which that measure taps any construct domains or reflects necessary conditions for its presence. The inherent shortcomings of this practice can be seen in the analysis of early measures of compulsive buying by Ridgway et al. (2008). Their review of literature in this article highlights the shortcoming of adopting "canned" definitions, and their analysis reveals two conceptual definitions (meanings) of compulsive buying—obsessive-compulsive and impulse-control disorder—rather than one. Careful explication and making a distinction between conceptual and operational definitions of variables and constructs help researchers develop better measures. Additional examples of conceptual and operational definition of variables and their derived measures can be seen elsewhere (Moschis & Churchill, 1978).

3.3 Research Philosophies

3.3.1 Programmatic Research

Many researchers possess a multitude of research ideas. However, research ideas that are scattered and lack systematic relationships within a single area are unlikely to be in the best interest of researchers. Researchers may be enticed to publish on multiple topics for various reasons, such as a multitude of opportunities, collaboration prospects, or data availability. Nonetheless, such a strategy often results in the perception of the researcher as an ad hoc scholar, lacking a distinct identity. Researchers who have a prolific publication record across several topics, with relatively little focus on any particular one, tend not to be recognized as experts in any specific field.

In contrast, a researcher who consistently conducts research in a single area or a select few related areas—referred to as "programmatic research"—is more likely to establish a reputation as an expert in that specific domain. Programmatic researchers often receive invitations to speak at universities on their specialized topics or are asked to serve as expert witnesses in litigation cases. It is important to note that this does not imply that ad hoc research lacks value for the researcher; in fact, ad hoc researchers often accumulate extensive publication records and high citation scores, as measured by h-index (see "Metrics" in Chap. 11). However, they may be easily identified and perceived as "opportunistic" due to their frequent co-authorships and the absence of single or senior-authored publications.

I hold a strong belief in the preference for programmatic research over ad hoc research. Engaging in research within a specific domain enables the researcher to cultivate expertise, conduct subsequent investigations more efficiently and effectively, and gain recognition for their contributions in that field. Granted, it can be more challenging to generate fresh ideas within a relatively narrow area, in contrast to ad hoc research where one can explore ideas across several areas. However, many ad hoc researchers often approach an area, perhaps for the first time, with limited prior knowledge of the subject they are studying, placing their work at a disadvantage as it is typically reviewed by individuals with greater expertise in the field. Therefore, I strongly advocate for programmatic research strategy, where researchers immerse themselves in a specific area, fostering personal growth and contributing to the body of knowledge.

My assertion finds support in the results of a bibliometric analysis of publications in one of the most respected marketing journals by Hoffman and Holbrook (1993). This analysis ranks my programmatic research favorably in relation to the number of my published articles in the same journal. Specifically, Hoffman and Morris performed a bibliometric analysis of the 42 most published authors in the *Journal of Consumer Research* during the journal's first 15-year time span (1974–1989), which overlaps with approximately the first 10 years of my academic career. They developed two scores that tap two major components: the symmetric component, which reflects reciprocal intellectual structure (i.e., how frequently these researchers cited the work of others in that group), and the asymmetric component, which "presumably reflects some aspect of intellectual influence referred to by such terms as 'prominence or visibility' (McCain, 1990, p. 203), 'importance' (Paisley, 1990, p. 296), or 'eminence' (White, 1990, p. 103)" (Hoffman & Holbrook, 1993, p. 509), all of which convey a sense of superiority, distinction, and recognition, often earned through exceptional achievements, expertise, or contributions in one's field. This analysis ranks me *fifth* on the symmetric component, although I had only four publications in that journal during the first 10 years of my academic career, compare with most of the remaining authors who had longer careers and more than six publications during the entire 15-year period, and it ranks me *first* on the asymmetric component, a great achievement during the first 10 years of my academic career. It is for this reason that I would often advise my doctoral students that it is more advantageous to have 5 publications in esteemed journals on a single topic than to accumulate 25 publications in those same journals on 25 different topics.

3.3.2 Philosophical Paradigms

In their efforts to create knowledge, researchers subscribe to different research philosophies that drive their research methods of data collection and analysis. Alford (1998) classifies the main views on seeking knowledge into three paradigms of inquiry that he labels as "multivariate," "interpretive," and "historical," each having advantages and disadvantages and seemingly most appropriate for specific situations.

Multivariate/Positivistic The multivariate paradigm provides multiple theoretical interpretations of a phenomenon and utilizes the conventional empirical methodology rooted in positivist science, encompassing the utilization of surveys and experiments. This method has faced scrutiny concerning its efficacy in deepening our comprehension of socially constructed phenomena, giving rise to concerns related to prediction and control. These challenges, in turn, have played a role in the emergence of the humanist perspective in recent years.

Humanistic As a research approach, the humanistic paradigm has philosophies and assumptions in direct contrast to those that underscore the positivistic approach to research (e.g., Hirschman, 1986). This paradigm seeks subjective explanations of culturally constructed and shared meanings of observed phenomena. Humanistic methods, when properly used, can provide insights into a phenomenon and enhance understanding that quantitative methods are not likely to offer (e.g., Belk et al., 2013; Hirschman, 1986). This may be one of the reasons why certain emerging multidisciplinary fields, as exemplified by Shanahan et al. (2016), are increasingly adopting a combination of humanistic and positivistic approaches, which includes employing various data collection methods. Each method has the potential to supplement the others and, in some cases, validate the results and conclusions derived from specific methods. This, in turn, contributes to a more comprehensive explanation and improved understanding of the phenomena being studied.

Historical The *historical* paradigm seeks explanations of the evolution of phenomena, placing emphasis on processes and sequence of events (Alford, 1998). For example, the "wheel of retailing" is offered as an explanation the transition of a relatively small discount store to a high-end establishment. It explains the reason why the majority of new retailers start with a low-cost, low-margin business model to entice potential customers, and, with increasing sales volume, they offer more services (events) and gradually shift to a high-cost, high-revenue model, creating opportunities for smaller firms to market low-cost, low-margin products. To compete with the new entrants, the larger firms are forced to go back to their original business model, visually depicting this upmarket journey on a circular diagram or chart.

In a similar vein, the relatively recent *bibliometrics* method of seeking knowledge can be viewed within the context of the historical paradigm. It enables researchers to examine the evolutionary streams of a specific field and shed light on the emerging areas in that field (Ninkov et al., 2022). For example, biometrics analysis identified the increasing in importance sustainable business practices and the evolving streams of sustainable consumer research in recent decades (Haider et al., 2022).

A research project that employs multiple methods based on all three paradigms is likely to be more favorably perceived and appreciated by reviewers and readers than a study that employs a single method. While the use of multiple paradigms is advocated (Alford, 1998), it is highly likely that researchers must choose among them because of several constraints such as time, costs, and journal word/page limits. Furthermore, the proper implementation of each approach becomes an issue partly because a researcher is not likely to have the high level of competency required in applying each method, unless he or she has been exposed to rigorous training in them. Most researchers today tend to be more familiar with methods derived from one paradigm and less competent or familiar with others. And each method is becoming increasingly specialized in itself and customized to better address different situations (e.g., multiple regression vs. Cox regression vs. regression mixture models). This is perhaps one of the reason studies that employ multiple methods tend to be co-authored, as each co-author likely contributes to the study in different ways. Thus, to enhance publication likelihood, the strategies suggested to early-career researchers are either become proficient in several methods or develop working relationships with researchers who have skills that complement yours.

3.3.3 Philosophical Approaches

Philosophical approaches to research problems or questions entail the embracing of either an inductive or deductive approach within scientific inquiry. The first approach requires the introduction of a theory, typically borrowed from a different discipline, proposing its applicability to explain a phenomenon within the researcher's own field, and subsequently evaluating the theory's effectiveness in elucidating that particular phenomenon. Conversely, the second involves gathering and analyzing both qualitative and quantitative data and the subsequent effort to derive meaning from these data. The approach lends itself to data interpretation, exploratory analysis, and creative thinking, often leading to the generation of novel theories. Subsequent sections provide a more comprehensive explanation of each of these two approaches.

Deductive Approach The deductive approach to research starts with a general theory or hypothesis and then tests it using specific observations or data. It moves from the general to the particular. It works as follows:

1. *Theory or hypothesis.* Researchers begin with a well-defined theory or hypothesis. This theory is often based on existing knowledge, previous research, or established principles.
2. *Prediction.* From this theory, researchers derive specific, testable predictions or hypotheses about what should happen in a particular situation.
3. *Data collection.* Researchers collect data through experiments, surveys, or observations to test the predictions derived from the theory.
4. *Analysis.* The collected data is then analyzed to determine whether it supports or contradicts the predictions made by the theory.
5. *Conclusion.* Based on the analysis, researchers draw conclusions about the validity of the theory or hypothesis. If the data supports the predictions, the theory is strengthened; if not, it may need revision or rejection.

The deductive approach is common in quantitative research, where the goal is to test existing theories or hypotheses rigorously. It is often associated with the scientific method, where researchers aim to confirm or disprove a hypothesis through empirical evidence. The deductive approach is used when the arguments or explanations for the phenomenon under investigation are based on laws, rules, or accepted principles. It begins with the general and ends with specifics; it goes from a theory to hypothesis to data in order to confirm or contradict the theory. This approach aims at testing or applying existing theories, while the inductive approach aims at new theory formulation from existing data. My article (Moschis, 1976), "Social Comparison and Informal Group Influence," uses the deductive approach to test a theory as it applies to a specific consumption context.

The research methodology for deductive approach that is commonly preferred is quantitative research in the form of pre-experimental, quasi-experimental, true-experimental or ex post-facto ("after the fact") research designs. Generalization can be made from quantitative research because the data are collected value-free (i.e., they are independent of measurement), and an objective reality exists, which means that there is no bias (Neuman, 2000). The data obtained through quantitative means, survey in particular, are not biased because the researchers have no direct relationship with the participants and can by no means influence them. For quantitative approach, the intent is usually to test theories deductively by gathering evidence to support or contradict the hypotheses derived from theories.

Inductive Approach The inductive approach is a research method that is the opposite of the deductive approach. It starts with specific observations or data and then seeks to develop broader generalizations and theories based on those observations. It moves from the particular to the general. Here is what it entails:

1. *Data collection.* Researchers begin with collecting data, often through observations and interviews.
2. *Pattern recognition.* They then look for patterns, trends, or commonalities within the collected data. These patterns may not have been expected or predicted in advance.
3. *Generalization.* Once patterns or themes emerge from the data, researchers formulate general theories or propositions to explain these patterns. These theories are often developed incrementally as more data are collected and analyzed.
4. *Refinement.* The inductive approach may involve further data collection and analysis to refine the emerging theories or propositions.
5. *Conclusion.* The final result is a theory or framework that is grounded in the observed data. It may serve as a foundation for future research or further testing.

The inductive approach is commonly used in qualitative research, where the goal is to explore and understand phenomena deeply, rather than to test predefined hypotheses. Contrary to the deductive approach, inductive approach works its way from data to theory, when the arguments are based on experiences or observations and interpretations. Building theory from case studies involves using empirical evidence from one or more cases to create theoretical constructs and propositions (Eisenhardt, 1989). However, for qualitative research, the intent is to gather information to inductively formulate theories by identifying common themes (Creswell & Plano Clark, 2011). The research objective is tested through open-ended questions in order to learn from participants and leave room for participants to come up with new ideas. Examples of the employment of the inductive approach to theory development can be seen in several studies (e.g., Belk et al., 2013; Fournier, 1998; Hirschman, 1992).

Research methodologies commonly employed in the inductive approach include mainly qualitative research in the form of case studies, field studies, ethnographic and anthropological studies, and document and phenomenological analyses. These methods assume that all data is value laden because subject and object are interdependent and there is no objective reality. Thus, the data obtained qualitatively cannot be considered neutral, so it cannot be generalized (Neuman, 2000). Since qualitative research is usually conducted in a natural setting, the researcher is the one who collects the data. Therefore, it is up to the researcher to collect the words of participants and analyze their body language. Furthermore, the presence of the researcher or what the researcher says can influence the participants, introducing bias in the data.

Differences and Use The key difference between these two approaches lies in their starting points and processes. Inductive research starts with data and seeks to derive theories, while deductive research begins with theories and tests them with data. Trochim (2006) refers to the two approaches as "broad methods of reasoning" (p. 1). He characterizes induction as the process of moving from specific instances to a general conclusion, while deduction commences with a general premise and proceeds to specific implications. Arguments rooted in experience or observation are most effectively conveyed in an inductive manner, whereas arguments grounded in established laws, rules, or widely accepted principles are better suited for deductive expression. Similarly, Creswell and Plano Clark (2011) delineate the deductive researcher as one who operates "top-down," starting from a theory, formulating hypotheses, and collecting data to either support or challenge the theory (p. 23). Conversely, they describe the inductive researcher as someone who operates "bottom-up," utilizing participants' perspectives to construct broader themes and generate a theory that interconnects these themes (p. 23).

In research, the two primary types of analysis commonly employed are quantitative (deductive) and qualitative (inductive). While there may be some divergence of opinion among researchers regarding the most suitable method for conducting research and gathering data, these two approaches are not mutually exclusive and often address the same question using distinct methodologies. Both approaches come with their respective strengths and weaknesses, and the choice between them hinges on factors such as the research question, objectives, and methodology.

Both approaches make use of published works. Literature reviews for qualitative approach are less extensive than the quantitative approach. This is because quantitative approach uses literature review to justify the research and identify theories and purpose of the study. In contrast, literature reviews in qualitative research are used to provide evidence for the purpose of the study, and no theories are identified because theory formulation will be drawn from interpreting the information from the collected data.

There seems to be disagreement among researches as to which approach is the best method (Soiferman, 2010). Different approaches are suitable for answering different questions. For example, if you want to test a theory or make an inference about a population, quantitative research would be more appropriate. If you want to uncover deeper meaning of phenomena, to explain or build a theory, qualitative research would be more appropriate.

In my experience, the first approach tends to yield more credible and safer results. It is particularly suggested to early-career researchers, as experts in the latter approach have emphasized the necessity of possessing extensive knowledge and experience in qualitative research, which is typically acquired over many years of work (Belk et al., 2013). The deductive approach that is based on theory either makes predictions that can be corroborated or falls short in explaining the phenomenon of interest. For instance, a well-established theory like cognitive dissonance, originally developed in psychology to elucidate post-decisional cognitive and behavioral tendencies, can be utilized to forecast consumer post-purchase behaviors, especially for significant acquisitions like appliances. An article assessing the theory's capability to predict post-decisional behaviors regarding major appliance purchases finds publication in prestigious journals such as the *Journal of Marketing*, even when the theory fails to accurately predict behavior in the specific context (Hunt, 1970). Similarly, during my doctoral studies at the University of Wisconsin, I employed Festinger's theory of social comparison to elucidate the influence of reference groups on consumer decisions. I condensed the theory's explanation, conducted a small-scale survey involving 200 consumers, and crafted a well-written manuscript (with the assistance of a copy editor, given my proficiency in English as a foreign student) that was accepted by the prestigious *Journal of Marketing Research* (Moschis, 1976).

Journal editors and reviewers are generally more inclined to accept the introduction and application of a new theory in a field, even from a lesser-known researcher or with less-than-optimal methods, compared with a new theory or novel interpretation of a phenomenon proposed by someone who lacks recognized authority on the subject. However, a well-established authority who has previously published widely cited articles in a particular area, such as on the topic of consumption and "the extended self" (Belk, 1988), and possesses extensive experience in employing the inductive method, would encounter minimal difficulty in publishing another paper in a reputable journal using the inductive method to explain consumers' extended selves in new contexts, such as within the digital realm (Belk, 2013).

References

Alford, R. R. (1998). *The craft of inquiry*. Oxford.

Belk, R. W. (1988). Possessions and the extended self. *Journal of Consumer Research, 15*(2), 139–168.

Belk, R. W. (2013). Extended self in a digital world. *Journal of Consumer Research, 40*(3), 477–500.

Belk, R., Fischer, E., & Kozinets, R. V. (2013). *Qualitative consumer & marketing research*. Sage Publications.

Churchill, G. A., & Brown, T. J. (2004). *Basic marketing research* (5th ed.). South-Western.

Creswell, J. W., & Plano Clark, V. L. (Eds.). (2011). *Designing and conducting mixed methods research* (2nd ed.). Sage.

Eisenhardt, K. M. (1989). Building theories from case study research. *Academy of Management Review, 14*(4), 532–550.

Elder, G. H., Johnson, M. K., & Crosnoe, R. (2003). The emergence and development of life course theory. In J. T. Mortimer & M. J. Shanahan (Eds.), *Handbook of the life course* (pp. 3–19). Plenum Publishers.

Fournier, S. (1998). Consumers and their brands: Developing relationship theory in consumer research. *Journal of Consumer Research, 24*(4), 343–373.

Haider, M., Shannon, R., & Moschis, G. P. (2022). Sustainable consumption research and the role of marketing: A review of the literature (1976–2021). *Sustainability, 14*(7). https://doi.org/10.3390/su14073999

Hempel, C. G. (1952). *Fundamentals of concept formation in empirical science*. University of Chicago Press.

Hirschman, E. C. (1986). Humanistic inquiry in marketing research: Philosophy, method, and criteria. *Journal of Marketing Research, 23*, 237–249.

Hirschman, E. C. (1992). The consciousness of addiction: Toward a general theory of compulsive consumption. *Journal of Consumer Research, 19*(2), 115–179.

Hoffman, D. L., & Holbrook, M. B. (1993). The intellectual structure of consumer research. *Journal of Consumer Research, 19*(4), 505–517.

Hunt, S. D. (1983). *Marketing theory: The philosophy of marketing science*. Irwin Publishing Company.

Hunt, S. D. (1970). Post-transaction communications and dissonance reduction. *Journal of Marketing, 34*(3), 46–51.

McCain, K. W. (1990). Mapping authors in intellectual space: Population genetics in the 1980s. In C. L. Borgman (Ed.), *Scholarly communication and bibliometrics* (pp. 194–216). Sage.

Moschis, G. P. (1976). Social comparison and informal group influences. *Journal of Marketing Research, 13*, 237–244.

Moschis, G. P. (2019). *Consumer behavior over the life course*. New York: Springer.

Moschis, G. P. (2022). *Marketing to the aging population*. New York: Springer.

Moschis, G. P., & Churchill, G. A. (1978). Consumer socialization: A theoretical and empirical analysis. *Journal of Marketing Research, 15*(4), 599–609.

Neuman, W. L. (2000). *Social research methods: Qualitative and quantitative approaches* (4th ed.). Allyn & Bacon.

Ninkov, A., Frank, J. R., & Maggio, L. A. (2022). Bibliometrics: Methods for studying academic publishing. *Perspectives on Medical Education, 11*(3), 173–176. https://doi.org/10.1007/s40037-021-00695-4

Olobatuyi, M. E. (2006). *Definition of basic terms and concepts. A user's guide to path analysis* (pp. 21–52). University Press of America.

Paisley, W. (1990). The future of bibliometrics. In C. L. Borgman (Ed.), *Scholarly communication and bibliometrics* (pp. 281–299). Sage.

Popper, K. (1959). *The logic of scientific discovery*. Basic Books.

Ridgway, N. M., Kukar-Kinney, M., & Monroe, K. B. (2008). An expanded conceptualization and a new measure of compulsive buying. *Journal of Consumer Research, 35*(4), 622–639.

Salthouse, T. A. (1991). *Theoretical perspectives on cognitive aging*. Lawrence Erlbaum Associates.

Shanahan, M. L., Mortimer, J. T., & Johnson, M. K. (Eds.). (2016). *Handbook of the life course: Volume II*. Springer.

Soiferman, K. (2010) ERIC - ED542066 - Compare and contrast inductive and deductive approaches. Retrieved from https://eric.ed.gov/?id=ED542066

Trochim, W. M. K. (2006). Research methods knowledge base. Retrieved from http://www.socialresearchmethods.net/kb/. (8/24/2023).

White, H. D. (1990). Author co-citation analysis: Overview and defense. In C. L. Borgman (Ed.), *Scholarly communication and bibliometrics* (pp. 84–106). Sage.

Planning Research Projects

4

This chapter focuses on planning the research project. It begins with strategies and tips that can help identify viable opportunities for research, followed by suggestions for prioritizing them. Next, the chapter provides guidelines for selecting viable research topics and framing theoretical and empirical questions to be addressed in a scientific study, and it offers examples of research areas and topic identification. In addition, the chapter suggests a step-by-step process of dissertation topic identification and project planning.

4.1 Identifying Research Opportunities

The development of publishable manuscripts requires careful research planning. During the literature review, researchers should pinpoint areas with potential contributions, whether they are in the realms of theory, concept, or methodology. Consequently, their studies should aim to address and enhance one or more of these areas. It is worth noting that a new or relatively unexplored topic offers a broader range of potential contributions and multiple publication opportunities with thorough planning. For instance, when planning my dissertation within the consumer socialization conceptual framework that I developed in the mid-1970s, I selected variables intended to contribute to theory development, methodology, marketing practice, and public policy.

In the planning phase, researchers should steer clear of tackling issues that necessitate the creation of new conceptual definitions and measures. Such endeavors are fraught with risk and entail developing instruments that consume journal space and require validation of their accuracy and reliability. It is preferable to utilize and cite previously established and widely recognized measures, as these have withstood tests of validity and reliability and are less likely to raise objections. Furthermore, researchers should avoid employing methods, samples, and measures that have

G. P. Moschis, *Academic Research in Business and the Social Sciences*,
https://doi.org/10.1007/978-3-031-56548-9_4

faced criticism in prior studies (e.g., Summers, 2001). Alternatively, if there is a need to use such methods, they should make an effort to elucidate the rationale or steps taken to minimize their potential adverse effects, as exemplified in the case of employing online panels (e.g., cf., Goodman & Paolacci, 2017; Wessling et al., 2017) (for additional procedural guidelines in project design and execution, refer to Summers, 2001).

4.1.1 Prioritizing Research Opportunities

One critical aspect of effective research lies in the strategic selection of research opportunities available to investigators. In most studies, researchers aim to explore novel problems, issues, or phenomena within a specific field, such as consumer behavior or marketing. They possess a toolbox comprising methods and approaches, including analytic techniques and theories, to analyze and elucidate these problems or phenomena. This array of choices results in a collection of research opportunities that can be categorized into four distinct groups, as outlined in Table 4.1.

The assessment of the four categories of research opportunities should take into account potential risks, rewards, and career goals at different stages of the person's academic life. Set A opportunities pose the least risk but also offer limited potential rewards. To exemplify, in the case of studying the connection between materialism and life satisfaction (as indicated in Table 4.1), researchers may need to establish a foundation by drawing upon existing theories. They can explore factors that explain contradictory findings, like the moderating or mediating effects of variables suggested by the conflicting values perspective (Burroughs & Rindfleisch, 2002), such as religion and chronic stress. Alternatively, researchers might want to tackle the long-standing question of causality between the two variables by applying a known method to disentangle their reciprocal effects, as shown by Laisawat et al. (2012). Such studies, grounded in a single method, are most suitable for publication in B- or C-level journals.

Set B opportunities encompass the utilization of an existing method or established theory to address a novel research problem or issue. These opportunities, by nature, carry the potential for a high risk-to-reward ratio since they often pertain to specific situations. For instance, when employing existing theories and methods to elucidate the adoption of a new technology or identify early adopters, one may not uncover fresh or unexpected findings distinct from prior studies on new product adoption. Furthermore, the suitability of an existing method or theory for addressing the new problem may come into question, especially when other available theories or methods could potentially be more fitting, as the new problem may be amenable to multiple approaches. Consequently, research papers stemming from Set B opportunities are best suited for publication in lower-tier journals, unless the projects capitalize on these opportunities to address crucial and timely issues with substantial implications, such as investigating the impact of cigarette advertising and anti-smoking messages on young individuals, as seen in the work of Pechmann and Knight (2002).

Table 4.1 Grid of research opportunities

		Methods & Tools	
		Existing	New
Problem/ Issue	Existing	A	C
	New	B	D

Four sets of opportunities available to researchers:

Set A—Opportunities that involve the application of a known method to address an existing problem or issue. An example would be the study of the relationship between materialism and life satisfaction in different contexts (e.g., countries, subcultures) to help answer previously-reported contradictory findings about the nature of the relationship.

Set B—Opportunities that involve the application of an existing method to address a new problem or issue. An example would be the use of diffusion theory and appropriate existing analytic methods (e.g., discriminant analysis) to explain or predict early adopters of smart-home gadgets or robotics (e.g.,"Alexa").

Set C—Opportunities to apply a new method or approach to address an existing/known issue or problem. An example would be the application of the life course paradigm to understand differences in adults' materialistic values.

Set D—Opportunities that involve the application of a new method or approach to a relatively new problem. An example would be the application of the life course approach to understand and explain the onset, development, continuity and change in consumption patterns over the person's entire life span.

Source: Moschis (2019a)

In contrast to research opportunities within Set B, those found in Set C offer the most favorable reward-to-risk ratio. As previously mentioned, these research endeavors involve the application of fresh theories or methods to address existing problems. Employing these new approaches demonstrates an innovative way of tackling the problem, and testing a novel theory in a different context provides evidence of its generalizability or its limitations, as exemplified by the application of cognitive dissonance to post-purchase behavior in appliance buyers (Hunt, 1970). As I mentioned earlier, my initial research projects as a doctoral student applied new theories or approaches to established marketing issues. For instance, a small-scale survey was designed that employed communication and psychological theories to elucidate how consumers utilize product information and are influenced by their peers, resulting in multiple publications in reputable journals (Moschis, 1976a, b, 1980).

Conversely, research opportunities in Set D carry the highest risk but also hold the greatest potential for reward. The heightened risk stems from the likelihood that many reviewers and readers may not be familiar with either the method or the novel issues being addressed. It becomes the researcher's responsibility to educate and persuade their audiences about the merits of the innovative approach in addressing new problems and issues. While a comprehensive explanation of the new method is often necessary and expected, most journals impose page limits on articles, making it challenging for authors to provide in-depth explanations of the new method and pertinent research issues, and even more difficult to demonstrate its application using quantitative or qualitative data. Nevertheless, researchers who can effectively conceive, execute, and communicate research ideas in this realm are likely to make a substantial contribution to their field.

Research opportunities in Set D often involve the exploration of fresh conceptual frameworks that can be constructed by drawing inspiration from diverse disciplines. I firmly believe that the quest for innovative research concepts should extend beyond the boundaries of one's own field. This practice has a rich history in applied or interdisciplinary fields like marketing, where researchers frequently leverage theories from various domains such as psychology, sociology, and neuroscience. The primary objective is to adopt these ideas and tailor them, if necessary, to address marketing-related challenges effectively. An even more formidable endeavor entails the integration of multiple theories into a comprehensive conceptual or theoretical framework. To illustrate this undertaking, we can consider the new product adoption process, a topic familiar to most readers.

In his groundbreaking article, "The Process of Innovation and the Diffusion of Innovation," published in 1967, Tom Robertson was the first to apply Everett Roger's sociological model to the marketing of new consumer products. By reframing innovation as a process rather than a singular outcome, he introduced marketers to a novel consumer challenge: the necessity of comprehending how innovations propagate from their point of origin to their eventual users or adopters. Additionally, Robertson expanded the definition of "innovation" to encompass three distinct types: continuous, dynamically continuous, and discontinuous. He integrated preexisting diffusion theories from various fields, including economics (Schumpeter's), anthropology (Barnett's), and polling expert Roper's (concentric-circle) theory, into his innovative conceptual framework. Furthermore, he demonstrated how additional concepts, hypotheses, and theories such as Raymond Bauer's (perceived risk) and Katz and Lazarsfeld's (two-step-flow) could be seamlessly incorporated into the original adoption model to elucidate the process of adopting new products. Robertson's article laid the groundwork for a significant portion of the research on the diffusion of innovations in consumer behavior over the past half-century, and his pioneering contributions continue to shape marketing textbooks today.

While opportunities within Set D may seem enticing, they tend to be rare and demand a profound understanding of the subject matter. To illustrate, crafting my conceptual consumer socialization model for my dissertation required four years of immersing myself in the realm of socialization. Similarly, it took approximately a decade to create my initial, rather straightforward conceptual life course model (Moschis, 2007), which I later refined into a more comprehensive version (Moschis, 2019b). It is advisable for researchers to accord higher importance to opportunities in Set C, assign lower priority to those in Set B, and the choice between Sets A and D should hinge primarily on the researcher's background and their stage within their academic career. Early-career researchers should prioritize opportunities in set C, followed by research opportunities in set A.

4.1.2 Topic Selection

The second strategy involves the choice of a research subject or domain. Journals attract a diverse readership, and typically "popular" topics garner more attention and readership than less popular ones. This necessitates an analysis of the "product life cycles" and the selection of a subject that is currently in its growth phase within this cycle. Naturally, the chosen topic should align with the researcher's personal interests and ideally harmonize with their pursuits in teaching and consulting. However, a word of caution is warranted: it is essential to be wary of trends or subjects that may take considerable time to gain traction. It is unwise to invest substantial effort in an area that appears to be in its growth phase based on appearances or claims but may not actually be or could take an extended period or never reach that stage. An illustrative example is the highly acclaimed (by practitioners) domains of videotex and teletext in the 1970s and 1980s, which laid the foundation for today's Internet system.

In 1980, I was engaged as a consultant for Payment Systems, Inc., a subsidiary of American Express based in Atlanta, with the task of monitoring and reporting on technological advancements in the banking and retail industry. During that period, there were over 100 field studies and experiments related to videotex and teletext, referred to as "home information systems" at the time, which had been documented in trade publications throughout the 1970s. Utilizing solely publicly available sources, I composed a manuscript to inform the academic community about these emerging technological developments, given that the findings of all these studies were proprietary. However, my submission to the *Journal of Consumer Research* was politely declined, citing reasons such as insufficient audience knowledge, interest, or demand, as well as a lack of available reviewers. In simple terms, the subject was still in its "development" phase, not even at the introductory stage in its product life cycle.

Over a span of more than five years, I continued to observe the outcomes of these proprietary studies, witnessing consumers' reluctance to embrace these technologies in their original forms, which cast doubt on their prospects for adoption (e.g., Moschis et al., 1985; Moschis & Stanley, 1984). The uncertainties within the technological landscape, combined with demographic shifts highlighting the aging of the consumer base, led me to shift my research focus away from the earlier topic and begin delving into studies of older consumers. It took an additional decade of technological changes that played a pivotal role in transforming the original home information systems into what we now know as the Internet. (Further guidance on selecting viable research topics is provided later in this chapter.)

4.2 Identifying Viable Areas of Research: Some Illustrations

A suitable domain for programmatic research, whether it pertains to a new phenomenon, theory, method, or general research approach, should exhibit several of the following characteristics:

1. Represents a relatively novel area within the researcher's discipline, with only a limited number of researchers actively publishing in the field
2. Offers clear advantages over previously employed methods or approaches
3. Addresses existing research gaps identified by scholars within one's discipline
4. Is at its growth stage within the "product life cycle" in one or more disciplines
5. Experiences increasing popularity as a research approach across various fields of study
6. Aligns with the researcher's prior expertise or familiarity with related subjects
7. Holds the potential to make substantial contributions to both knowledge and practice
8. Demonstrates a high demand for information on the topic that surpasses the currently available supply
9. Is supported by facts or trends indicating its enduring relevance as a research subject
10. Can be investigated using multiple research methodologies

In the following sections, I draw from my personal experiences to elucidate the rationale behind my decision to concentrate on three specific areas (consumer socialization, older consumer behavior, and life course research) for pursuing programmatic research, providing a connection between each of these areas and several of the features listed above to substantiate my choices.

Consumer Socialization The subject of consumer socialization gained prominence and relevance in the field of marketing during the 1970s due to concerns raised by consumer advocacy groups regarding the adverse effects of advertising on young individuals. Simultaneously, the Federal Trade Commission (FTC) expressed interest in understanding the impact of marketing activities on youths and their families, with the aim of enacting legislation to regulate advertising targeting children. The scarcity of data to support effective legislation prompted the FTC to sponsor numerous empirical studies in the 1970s to generate valuable information (FTC, 1978). This initiative provided motivation for several scholars to embark on research related to consumer socialization.

Even scholars like Tom Robertson, who had previously focused on the diffusion process in the 1960s, recognized that consumer socialization was in its nascent stages within the product life cycle. As a result, he entered this field and established the Center for Research on Media and Children (CRMC) at the Wharton School of Business. Consequently, the conditions at that time favored dedicating time and effort to this area, making the decision to prioritize consumer socialization for programmatic research a logical one. Moreover, opportunities for contributing to both theory and practice abounded not only because the field was relatively new but also because there was limited competition, with only a few researchers actively publishing in this domain.

Although the concept of consumer socialization had been prevalent in other disciplines for many years, it had long suffered from a notable absence of a comprehensive conceptual framework that could serve as a blueprint for amalgamating previous research, conducting empirical investigations, and interpreting qualitative data. In various fields, studies lacked socialization models that would elucidate the relationships between pertinent variables, the theoretical underpinnings for these relationships, and the empirical evidence supporting them. Therefore, I seized the opportunity to develop a general conceptual model as the subject of my dissertation at the University of Wisconsin (Moschis, 1978; Moschis & Churchill, 1978). This decision was motivated by the escalating interest in the subject, the scarcity of conceptual socialization models available in other disciplines, and the growing demand for information that exceeded the available supply (three of the ten characteristics shown early in this section).

Older Consumer Behavior The 1980 US Census data took both marketing professionals and academia by surprise, as it revealed the significant purchasing power of the older consumer segment. Until that point, neither the industry nor academia had given much attention to the elderly market, partly due to prevailing perceptions that the elderly were financially disadvantaged. Furthermore, little consideration had been given to the expanding size of the older market, attributed to the increasing life expectancy that had added nearly two decades to the average lifespan during the first half of the twentieth century, as well as the impending age wave of 78 million baby boomers. As this newfound information became widely disseminated in mainstream media and trade publications, companies began developing initiatives to tap into the older consumer market. This emerging development created research opportunities, given the limited body of published research and credible information available on the topic of older consumer behavior before 1980, which hindered marketers from making informed decisions.

While both academic researchers and practitioners recognized the growing significance of the expanding older demographic segment, they faced a substantial deficit in their knowledge and training when it came to addressing the needs of this consumer group. Marketers possessed limited insights into the aging process, whereas gerontologists were well-versed in the characteristics of older individuals but lacked expertise in marketing to them. This gap presented an opportunity that I identified, positioning myself as an authority in the realm of marketing to mature consumers. To establish this expertise, I pursued postdoctoral studies in gerontology and simultaneously engaged in activities that cultivated the perception of expertise. These activities included conducting research through my newly established Center for Mature Consumer Studies (CMCS), creating and instructing a graduate course focused on marketing to older adults, and authoring the initial books on marketing to the aging population.

Several factors from the aforementioned list, as discussed earlier in this section, favored my transition into this emerging field of consumer studies. The subject matter was fresh, underserved in terms of research, with only a limited number of academic researchers actively publishing. Additionally, the global significance of the older consumer market was poised to increase due to shifting demographics. What worked in my favor was that I did not need to start from scratch in educating myself about this subject because I already possessed some familiarity with the existing literature. I perceived the applicability of the socialization approach to the examination of consumers at any life stage (e.g., Bellenger & Moschis, 1981; Moschis, 1981), and I had previously employed my consumer socialization model in the study of older consumers (e.g., Smith & Moschis, 1984a, b, 1985; Smith et al., 1981, 1982).

By the mid-1980s, I had compiled a comprehensive consulting report on the mature market for BellSouth Corp., summarizing all previously published studies. Concurrently, I had completed my book titled *Consumer Socialization: A Life Cycle Perspective*, in which I documented a substantial body of prior research on older consumers. Around the same time, I observed that the area of consumer socialization for young individuals had reached the "maturity" stage in the product life cycle, evident through reduced government funding and the discontinuation of Wharton's CRMC, among other signs. Given the uncertainties surrounding the likelihood and timing of adoption of the older generation's version of today's Internet, I made a significant shift in my research focus and began exclusively studying older (or "mature") consumers.

Swiftly, I gained recognition as a prominent authority, perhaps even the foremost authority, on the subject of marketing to the mature market, both within academia and the industry. When there is a strong demand for information on a specific topic that exceeds the available supply, the value of one's research tends to skyrocket, and researchers in that field quickly earn the distinction of being the "experts" in their domain. Engaging in programmatic research on a topic characterized by high demand for information, and where few researchers are pursuing similar investigations, often leads to visibility and recognition.

Life course research While investigating consumer socialization among various age groups, I became increasingly convinced that understanding behavior at any life stage necessitates a comprehensive study that takes into account consumers' prior life experiences and future expectations as critical determinants of their current conduct. This viewpoint had been expressed previously by other consumer researchers who advocated for studying consumers across their entire lifespan (e.g., Moschis,

2019b). However, their efforts were hampered by a lack of robust theoretical and methodological foundations for examining consumer behavior throughout one's life. Past attempts to investigate consumer behavior across the life course were largely devoid of theoretical underpinnings, fragmented, and scattered, reflecting disconnected endeavors stemming from diverse research traditions. These endeavors often revolved around examining people's behavior at different life stages in isolation from their earlier life experiences, as exemplified by studies focused on stages in the family life cycle, aiming to explain observed changes in behavior based solely on age or stage-related differences (e.g., Moschis, 2019b).

During my postdoctoral training in gerontology in the late 1980s, as I attended seminars on aging, I was exposed to literature from various disciplines that highlighted a shift in the study of old age. The focus was transitioning from examining older individuals within age groups to investigating the processes of aging itself. During this period, the research agenda, which previously centered on understanding human behavior at specific life stages, began to merge with new avenues of scientific inquiry, giving rise to the emergence and increasing adoption of paradigms that integrated prior approaches into more comprehensive research frameworks. The life course approach stood out as one such research framework (Moschis, 2019b).

The life course approach was evolving into an interdisciplinary framework for examining diverse forms of behavior. While social scientists had long recognized the potential utility of the life course paradigm in comprehending time and context-dependent market and consumption phenomena, the consumer behavior literature had, and still has, been somewhat lacking in systematic efforts to embrace this approach for investigating various behavior types (Moschis, 2019b). This research approach had gained substantial traction across multiple fields but had not yet diffused widely within the realm of consumer research (Billari, 2009).

The life course approach seemed to fulfill numerous theoretical and methodological prerequisites necessary for advancing research aimed at comprehending not only consumer behavior at specific life stages but also the evolution and alterations in consumer behavior patterns over time. This framework offered the foundation I had been searching for a considerable duration to establish connections between an individual's consumer behaviors at a particular life stage and their life and consumption experiences during earlier life stages. Consequently, my research interests gradually shifted from attempting to comprehend consumers at various life stages to exploring consumer behavior throughout the entirety of their lives.

Exploratory analyses of both cross-sectional and longitudinal data collected at CMCS in the early to mid-1990s, along with my postdoctoral work in the field of gerontology, generated enough interest in life course research to motivate my doctoral students to undertake dissertations on this subject. Given the absence of comprehensive multi-theoretical conceptual models in other disciplines, initial conceptual life course frameworks were relatively straightforward and incorporated a limited number of variables based on restricted theories (e.g., Lee et al., 2001; Mathur et al., 1999). Recognizing opportunities to approach the study of various consumption phenomena from a life course perspective, I developed a relatively simple conceptual life course model and presented this research framework as a viable approach for investigating the initiation, development, or transformation of consumer behaviors (Moschis, 2007). This conceptual model has served as the foundation in more than three dozen studies examining various forms of consumer behavior, based on data collected in over ten countries, as detailed in one of my recent books (Moschis, 2019b). Furthermore, it has formed the basis for the development of the more comprehensive life course model (Moschis, 2019b) utilized by the authors of several studies, including those published in the two-part special issues of the *Journal of Global Scholars of Marketing Science* (Mathur, 2019, 2020).

4.3 Selecting a Dissertation Topic

4.3.1 Preliminary Considerations

In selecting a dissertation topic, students should consider several factors before deciding on the topic. First, students should assess their overall skills and interests. Ideally, a dissertation topic should be of interest to the student, and it should be compatible to one's skills. For example, if student does not have strong qualitative skills, he or she should not select a topic that requires the employment of qualitative methodologies. Similarly, students who do not have strong methodological or quantitative skills should not select a topic that requires the use of rigorous analytical techniques. And the student should have some interest in the topic that would prompt him or her to spend adequate time reading the relevant literature.

Second, a dissertation topic should be consistent with the potential advisor(s)' research interests and research streams. A student who selects a topic that is not consistent with the recent research interests of potential advisors available at his or her department runs the risk of not finding an advisor to supervise his or her dissertation. In contrast, an advisor interested in the student's topic will be more willing to spend time reading his or her work and making helpful comments on the material submitted. I often advise my doctoral students before they select a dissertation topic to visit their department faculty members, and try to learn about their current research interests and topics they are working on, and even ask them for a copy of their CVs. In doing so, the students will have a very good idea about the research areas that that faculty members are working on and are likely to show interest in serving on the student's dissertation committee. Furthermore, faculty who are interested in the topic and are working in that particular area would be more helpful to the student, and the student is likely to have a better dissertation because of the relatively more useful advice and assistance he or she may receive from one's dissertation committee members.

Third, the student should consider situational and environmental factors. These factors include things like the timely of the topic, whether the topic is doable from the standpoint of time that it would take to complete the dissertation, accessibility to data, and the resources that will be required to carry out the research project.

Ideally, the doctoral student should select a topic that will not require a great deal of time to complete, because things can change over a longer period of time that would put the student in a precarious position. For example, I can think of several cases where the student's supervisor took a job at another university, forcing the student look for another advisor. Usually, faculty members who are productive researchers and can be affective advisers for the student also have more opportunities for employment at other universities and they tend to be mobile. In contrast, those who do not do much research, especially junior faculty, might not be able to keep their positions at the present university and might be forced to seek employment at different institution or place. To reduce such a risk, I often suggest the student have not one but two co-advisors, especially faculty members who have been working together on projects and are familiar with the student's topic.

4.3.2 Strategies

Dissertation topic selection is a process that should begin from the very first year the student is in the program. During the first year, every doctoral student should assess his or her strengths and weaknesses with respect to areas where they potentially can develop a dissertation topic. Early in the program, they should attempt to gain wide knowledge about several areas and assess their interests in these areas; and they should build an inventory of various topics that interest them. Once such an inventory is developed, the student should examine the faculty's interests in these areas in attempt to find overlapping topics or areas of mutual interest with faculty members. This is likely to reduce the list of areas that student is interested in. The research ideas on this shorter list should be assessed in the context of the life cycle of each topic, that is, whether the idea is novel or has been overly researched or it is at this early stage of its life cycle.

This can be done by considering two factors. First, whether their idea has the potential for growth in particular field, and second whether the idea or topic is going to be viable for a long period of time. Research ideas on topics such as technology usually have short life cycles because they are quickly replaced by new forms of technology. And articles on such topics become quickly obsolete. For example, what we have learned and published in the 1980s and 1990s about the original form of the Internet became obsolete a few years later. Changes in technology make demands on researchers to constantly keep on updating their knowledge and skills which can be a daunting task.

A dissertation topic should have the potential for a long "life cycle," and research on this topic should be appealing to several groups for a relatively long period of time. For example, one can look at the demographic changes globally and determine that the aging of the Earth's population is going to be taking place for a long period of time. Therefore, research on aging consumers should be appealing to several groups for many decades to come. Thus, in attempting to gain broad knowledge about different topics during his or her first year in the doctoral program, the student should keep in mind the topic's potential for growth and a long life cycle. This can be done while the student is preparing for his or her qualifying exam, which is often in the form of a written qualifying paper or written examination.

Where does one find viable topics for dissertation? Recent review articles are good sources. In reading articles on a particular topic, one should make the following lists: (a) issues not adequately addressed, (b) inventory of contradictory findings on a particular topic or issue, and (c) recommendations for future research, which may also pertain to the first two areas. Based on these lists, the student should develop a set of research questions on each topic on which he or she should request faculty input in order to narrow down the list of viable research topics. The student is strongly advised not to seek ideas in areas where very little research has been published. Although intuitively appealing, such an area may not be familiar to faculty members who are likely to be advisers for the student's dissertation, nor to journal reviewers and readers. As I mentioned earlier in this book, the Internet technology at its initial stages was not familiar to the academic community, because research conducted by companies at that time was proprietary and not subject to publication.

During the second year in the doctoral program, the student should make an initial effort to write a dissertation proposal. This proposal should be relatively short and should focus on research questions that could be addressed. It should briefly outline the scope of the project, the research questions or issue addressed, the methods that should be used, expected findings and how these would advance knowledge, the audience(s) that would be interested in the results and their implications, including journals (additional suggestions for developing such a proposal are outlined in the next section). This short proposal should be given to potential faculty members who may serve on the student's dissertation committee. Based on faculty input and feedback, the student should be able to select an advisor and (with the main advisor's assistance) determine the committee members of his or her dissertation.

It is highly desirable for the student to use such a proposal to conduct a pilot study—i.e., a smaller-scale study than the one planned for the dissertation, and collect data relevant to addressing some of the research questions. And, ideally, the student should develop a manuscript based on this pilot study and submit it to a lower-level journal. In doing so, the student could benefit in many ways. First, the entire research process, from research questions to be addressed to the manuscript submission and journal feedback, is likely to expose the student to issues not familiar to him or her, contributing to one's learning and preparation of the main dissertation proposal. In this pilot study, one can examine things such as the properties of the planned measurement instruments, familiarize himself or herself with appropriate analytic methods, become aware of response rates of certain populations, accessibility to potential study participants, and the like. Reviewer feedback, comments and criticisms, could also be constructive in this regard. Such information could be helpful in developing the final proposal, and it should make the student aware of the issues and concerns of the reviewers regarding a similar manuscript. It is also advisable to include this pilot study and its results in the student's final dissertation proposal, as a base for certain areas of the main proposal. Finally, if the pilot study is published, the student would be able to graduate upon completion of his or her dissertation from an institution that requires a publication out of one's dissertation for awarding the doctoral degree.

4.3.3 Preparing the Dissertation Proposal

In developing their dissertation proposal, students should keep in mind that they are trying to sell or market their idea to their Department's faculty or their potential supervisor. Therefore, they should try to make their dissertation topic as marketable as possible. This means that the short version of the proposal they develop to present to faculty, who might have interest or ability to serve on the student's dissertation committee, should emphasize the following:

1. The topic should be relevant to a wide variety of groups (e.g., researchers, practitioners, legislators), and reasons for its relevance to these groups should be briefly stated.
2. A wide variety of journals should be interested in publishing the study results, because these journals have previously published similar or related studies (shown in the references that are used).
3. The proposed research is doable, within the proposer's means, such as skills, finances, and required time for completion, and that it is totally controllable by the proposer and not subject to uncontrollable conditions (e.g., permission to obtain required data, availability and ability to use required software, access to company employees).
4. The research topic should be of interest to as many faculty members as possible, based on their previous and present research projects. And the required methodologies (e.g., qualitative research, SEM) are within the expertise of present faculty.
5. Let faculty know that you prefer potential publications from the proposed study, as well as future studies on the main research topic (s), to be co-authored by one or more members of the student's dissertation committee.
6. If the research topic falls within the research stream of potential supervisors, emphasize how the proposed study and its principal investigator may be viewed as branded "products" of their main dissertation supervisor(s) by extending their research.

With these considerations in mind, the student should develop a short version of his or her proposal to present to potential dissertation committee members and advisor(s). This version should not be longer than 10–12 pages, including tables, figures, and references.

Short Version of Dissertation Proposal The purpose of the short version of the student's proposal is to make it possible for faculty members to determine if they would be interested in serving on the student's dissertation committee. The following outline of structure and contents is suggested for an empirical study:

Introduction (1–2 pages). This section should have a minimum of three paragraphs, each including, respectively, (a) the importance of the topic and its relevance to various groups, (b) existing gaps in knowledge or needed research on the topic, and (c) purpose and objectives of the proposed study.

Background (3–4 pages). This section should include (a) the proposed conceptual or theoretical framework appropriate for your study, including its relevance for the study objectives, (b) select variables derived from the theoretical or conceptual framework as potential explanatory factors of your concept of interest, and (c) your main hypotheses derived from theories and research findings. If possible, show your hypothesized relationships in the form of a model (diagram or figure).

Methods (1–2 pages). This section should include the proposed research design (e.g., survey, experiment), sample size, measures, methods of data analysis, and statistical tests for model and hypothesis testing.

Expected contribution (1–2 pages). The last section should clearly state the expected contribution of the proposed study in the context of gaps in knowledge or needed research stated in the introduction. It should spell out what readers are going to learn from this study that they do not already know, and why this additional knowledge is important to the various groups that are mentioned in the proposal's introduction. In this section, the student should be able to clearly communicate whether the study's intended contribution is going to be theoretical, methodological, empirical, or conceptual (for more information on a study's intended contribution, see Chap. 10).

References, *tables*, and *appendixes* should also be included, as needed (for more details on preparing a complete proposal and its contents for a quantitative, qualitative, or a mixed methods study, see "Thesis or Dissertation Proposal" in Chap. 14).

Choosing a Dissertation Supervisor and Committee Members I am aware of different formats of doctoral programs across countries in terms of requirements, procedures, expectations, and the like. And even within the same country, requirements and expectations for graduation differ. For example, some universities expect students to publish before receiving their doctoral degree, others require publication out of their dissertation for granting the degree, and others have no such expectations. Similarly, universities in some countries assign a faculty member to the student upon entering the doctoral program, with the student expected to work with and be mentored by that same faculty member throughout his or her program of studies, including dissertation. In such a program, the student is expected to be "shaped" by his or her advisor's expertise and research interests. In contrast, most universities in countries like the United States allow the student to assess his or her interests and skills when entering the program and choose the supervisor of the main research project (dissertation) after taking courses and completing other requirements for graduation. In this section, I am outlining suggestions for students who are given the freedom of choosing the supervisor of their dissertation.

After the student receives feedback from faculty on the short version of their proposal, he or she should attempt to form a dissertation committee by first deciding on the one person (or two, if necessary) who would work closely with the student at every stage of the dissertation. Before asking a faculty member to be the dissertation's supervisor, the student should try to learn more about the person's work habits and life in general. A potential advisor should show evidence of ability to work with other committee members and provide feedback to the student's work submitted. Other students who were supervised by a potential advisor could be useful sources of information in this regard. In addition, the student should try to determine the likelihood the person under consideration will work in his or her Department for the time it will take to prepare the final dissertation, defend it, and complete the proposed study. Nontenured faculty (e.g., assistant professors) without an established research track record who have not been working at their university for several years would be a risky choice. Although tenured professors with established track records are also likely to have employment opportunities at other universities, they would be less likely to move if they have established their "roots" at a particular place, such as own homes, have career-oriented working spouses and school-age children.

Another consideration in choosing a dissertation supervisor includes the extent to which the person is willing or able to invest time into the student's dissertation. Most faculty see high opportunity costs in supervising a dissertation, unless they see a potential benefit in doing so; and they often agree to serve on the student's dissertation in various capacities, if they have some control over the process and outcomes of the proposed dissertation, such as other persons who should serve on the student' dissertation committee and co-authorship of the resultant publications. Therefore, if there are no conditions specified by the potential supervisor, it is suggested the student let the potential supervisor know, formally or informally, that a number of publications out of the student's dissertations would be co-authored.

Doctoral students should prefer supervisors whose areas of research interests, expertise, and stream(s) of published research are close to the proposed dissertation topic. Such individuals are likely to have a vested interest in the student and his or her dissertation for two main reasons: First, the expected co-authored publications are likely to add to their image as experts on the research topic, and second, the student who studies under their supervision and published in the same area of their expertise likely will be viewed as their "branded product." In contrast, potential supervisors who offer to direct a dissertation on a topic they are not familiar with, or do not show any potential for contribution to areas of student's dissertation (e.g., methodology), especially when they expect co-authorship, should be avoided. These individuals, most likely, will play a "ceremonial" role of the chair of the student's dissertation committee, expecting or hoping other committee members to provide substantive feedback and guidance.

After a student selects a supervisor, he or she is ready to start preparing the complete dissertation proposal, if other requirements in their doctoral programs (e.g., qualifying papers, prelim exams) are not of higher priority. Concurrently, he or she should seek advice and suggestions from the supervisor in selecting the other members of the dissertation committee based on need for assistance in areas of the student's dissertation. While developing the various parts of the dissertation proposal, the student may have the need for advice on topics his or her supervisor might not be as familiar with (e.g., methodology) where a committee member may offer assistance. Therefore, committee members should be selected as early as possible after selecting the dissertation supervisor.

References

Bellenger, D. N., & Moschis, G. P. (1981). A socialization model of retail patronage. In K. Monroe (Ed.), *Advances in Consumer Research* (Vol. IX, pp. 373–378). Association for Consumer Research.

Billari, F. C. (2009). The life course is becoming of age. *Advances in Life Course Research, 14*(3), 83–86.

Burroughs, J. E., & Rindfleisch, A. (2002). Materialism and well-being: A conflicting values perspective. *Journal of Consumer Research, 29*(3), 348–370.

FTC. (1978). *Staff report on television advertising to children*. Federal Trade Commission. U.S. Government Printing Office.

Goodman, J. K., & Paolacci, G. (2017). Crowdsourcing consumer research. *Journal of Consumer Research, 44*(1), 196–210. https://doi.org/10.1093/jcr/ucx047

Hunt, S. D. (1970). Post-transaction communications and dissonance deduction. *Journal of Marketing, 34*(3), 46–51.

Laisawat, S., Atchwahn Jantara, A., Fon Sim Ong, F. S., & Moschis, G. P. (2012). Clarifying the relationship between materialism and well-being: Testing for reciprocal and third-variable effects. *Journal of Global Scholars of Marketing Science*, 1–25.

Lee, E., Moschis, G. P., & Mathur, A. (2001). Life events and changes in patronage preferences. *Journal of Business Research, 54*, 25–38.

Mathur, A. (2019). George P. Moschis tribute special issue: His philosophy and contributions (Part I). *Journal of Global Scholars of Marketing Science, 29*(4), 359–371.

Mathur, A. (2020). George P. Moschis tribute special issue: His philosophy and contributions (Part II). *Journal of Global Scholars of Marketing Science, 30*(1), 1–3.

Mathur, A., Moschis, G.P. & Lee, E. (1999). Stress and consumer behavior: Coping strategies of older adults. *Journal of Marketing Practice: Applied Marketing Science*, No. 6/7/8; 233-47 (MCB University Press).

Moschis, G. P. (1976a). Social comparison and informal group influences. *Journal of Marketing Research, 13*(August), 237–244.

Moschis, G. P. (1976b). Shopping orientations and consumer uses of information. *Journal of Retailing, 52*(Summer), 61–70, 93.

Moschis, G. P. (1978). *Acquisition of the consumer role by adolescents*. Research monograph 82, College of Business Administration, Georgia State University, (also available as unpublished doctoral dissertation, University of Wisconsin, 1976).

Moschis, G. P. (1980). Consumer information use: Individual vs. social predictors. *Communication Research, 7*(April), 139–160.

Moschis, G. P. (1981). Socialization perspectives and consumer behavior. In B. Enis & K. Roering (Eds.), *Review of marketing* (pp. 53–56). American Marketing Association.

Moschis, G. P. (2007). Life course perspectives on consumer behavior. *Journal of the Academy of Marketing Science, 35*(2), 295–397.

Moschis, G. P. (2019a). Pathways to successful academic research: A life course perspective. *Journal of Global Scholars of Marketing Science.*. Issue 4: George P. Moschis tribute special issue, part one, *29*(4), 372–408.

Moschis, G. P. (2019b). *Consumer behaviour over the life course: Research frontiers and new directions*. Springer Publishing, Inc.

Moschis, G. P., & Churchill, G. A. (1978). Consumer socialization: A theoretical and empirical analysis. *Journal of Marketing Research, 15*(4), 599–609.

Moschis, G. P., & Stanley, T. J. (1984). Home information systems: Recent developments and implications. In *Proceedings of the winter educators' conference*. American Marketing Association.

Moschis, G. P., Goldstucker, J. L., & Stanley, T. J. (1985). Will consumers let computers do the walking? *Business Horizons, 28*(2), 22–29.

Pechmann, C., & Knight, S. J. (2002). Intentions about cigarette consumption. *Journal of Consumer Research, 29*(1), 5–19.

Smith, R. B., & Moschis, G. P. (1984a). Consumer socialization of the elderly: An explanatory Study. In T. C. Kinnear (Ed.), *Advances in Consumer Research* (Vol. XI, pp. 548–552). Association for Consumer Research.

Smith, R. B., & Moschis, G. P. (1984b). Effects of advertising on the elderly consumer: An investigation of social breakdown theory. In R. Belk et al. (Eds.), *Proceedings of the annual educators' conference* (pp. 1–5). American Marketing Association.

Smith, R. B., & Moschis, G. P. (1985). A socialization perspective on selected consumer characteristics of the elderly. *Journal of Consumer Affairs, 19*(Summer), 74–95.

Smith, R. B., Moschis, G. P. & Moore, R. L. (1981). *Impact of mass communication on consumer decision making of the elderly*, presented at the Association for Education in Journalism Annual Convention, Michigan State University, August 8–11, 1981.

Smith, R. B., Moschis, G. P. & Moore, R. L. (1982). *Social effects of television advertising on the Elderly*, presented at the theory and methodology division, Association for Education in Journalism Annual Convention, Ohio University, July 25–28.

Summers, J. O. (2001). Guidelines for conducting research and publishing in marketing: From conceptualization through the review process. *Journal of the Academy of Marketing Science, 29*(4), 405–415.

Wessling, K. S., Huber, J., & Netzer, O. (2017). MTurk character misrepresentation: Assessment and solutions. *Journal of Consumer Research, 44*(1), 211–230. https://doi.org/10.1093/jcr/ucx053

Conceptual Framework and Theory Development

5

5.1 Conceptual Frameworks

A conceptual framework is a structure that researchers use to best explain the relationship they expect to see between variables, or the characteristics of the phenomenon they investigate. This term is used often interchangeably with "model" and "theory." And although all conceptual frameworks and models are not necessarily theories, theories and theoretical frameworks are normally viewed as conceptual frameworks. A conceptual framework forms the basic foundation for conducting a study, helping to summarize either the basic constructs and their expected relationships in a deductive investigation, or the outcomes of the inductive inquiry. They evolve and change as knowledge accumulates (Miles et al., 2014). As Miles et al. (2014: 20) put it: "Conceptual frameworks are simply the current version of the researcher's map of the territory being investigated. As the explorer's knowledge of the terrain improves, the map becomes correspondingly more differentiated and integrated." Thus, a conceptual framework becomes increasingly refined, elaborate, and comprehensive as knowledge accumulates and forms the basis for its expansion and revision, which may also suggest the use of different methodologies (Ravitch & Riggan, 2016).

A conceptual framework typically consists of key concepts or variables related to the topic of study; it specifies the relationships between these concepts, which are often linked together to form a coherent structure. And it may propose hypotheses or theories about how these concepts interact or influence each other. Researchers use these hypotheses to guide their research questions and design. For example, in a study about the factors influencing academic achievement, concepts like socioeconomic status, parental involvement, and student motivation might be included.

A conceptual framework helps to contextualize the research within existing knowledge. It identifies relevant theories and prior research that inform the study's theoretical basis. A well-defined conceptual framework provides clarity and structure to a research study, making it easier for both researchers and readers to

G. P. Moschis, *Academic Research in Business and the Social Sciences*,
https://doi.org/10.1007/978-3-031-56548-9_5

understand the study's objectives and its place within the broader academic discourse. The choice of a conceptual framework depends on the research question, the field of study, and the level of theoretical development within that field.

Researchers also use the conceptual framework as a guide for collecting and analyzing data. It helps them determine which variables to measure, what data to collect, and how to interpret the results. In some cases, a conceptual framework can contribute to theory development within a specific field. By testing and refining the framework through research, researchers may contribute to the development of new theories or the refinement of existing ones.

5.1.1 Types of Conceptual Frameworks

Conceptual frameworks can vary in complexity, ranging from simple diagrams illustrating relationships between a few key concepts to elaborate theoretical frameworks with multiple interconnected elements. There are three basic types of conceptual frameworks commonly used in academic studies. The most common consists of elements that are interconnected and graphically presented in figures. Their intent is to show the key concepts and relationships among them, often (but not always) suggesting causal links among them, and they are most frequently seen in deductive research. The model in Fig. 5.1 in this chapter is an example of such a conceptual framework.

Another type of conceptual framework is in a form of categorical or hierarchical structure, often graphically shown and accompanied by descriptive information of the classes or groups into which a phenomenon is categorized. The widely known

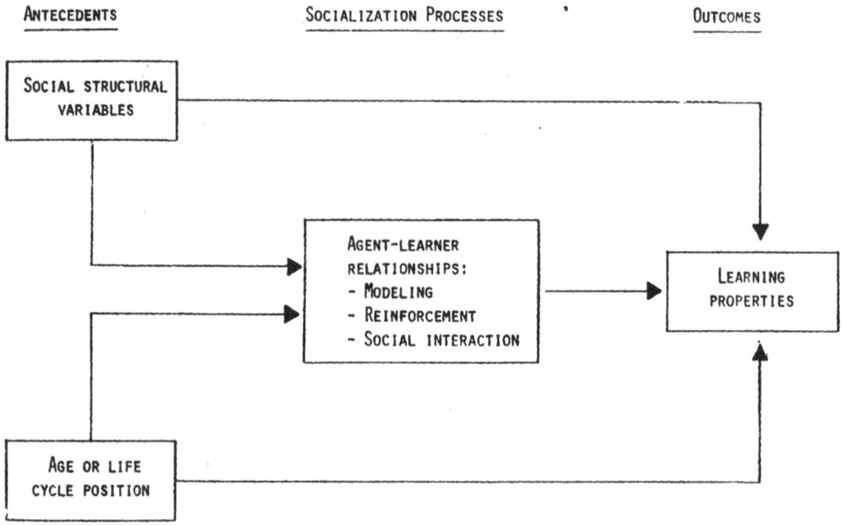

Fig. 5.1 Conceptual model of consumer socialization. (Source: Moschis & Churchill, 1978)

theory of Maslow's hierarchy of needs is an example of this conceptual framework that can be presented visually or verbally. Such frameworks, which are often based on theories, are often depicted as taxonomies that are developed based on quantitative and qualitative studies. There are no clear relationships, if any, between classes or categories that are easy to verify empirically, making them most useful for qualitative inquiry because they can be used to interpret qualitative data. For example, based on Maslow's model, bicycle ownership may satisfy social (status) needs of consumers in a third-world country but psychological needs of consumers in a developed country.

The third type of conceptual framework is expressed in mathematical terms, where the phenomenon under investigation is always expressed in a mathematical equation, and often supplemented by verbal description and pictorial representation to enhance understanding. They are useful in deductive research, more useful in predicting than explaining the phenomenon of interest. Examples of these conceptual frameworks can be seen in Cox's proportional hazard model and in Weibull's model (cf., Vuchinich et al., 1991).

5.1.2 Choosing and Using a Conceptual Framework

A well-constructed conceptual framework serves various purposes, including the organization and categorization of existing research, the identification of knowledge gaps, the formulation of hypotheses, and the validation of variable selection or inclusion in one's study. To guide the selection of a conceptual framework, specific criteria are proposed. First, the framework should be comprehensive, featuring classifications or variable categories that are both mutually exclusive and exhaustive. Second, it should align with the research question, as frameworks borrowed from unrelated disciplines are often unsuitable for addressing certain types of problems and research inquiries, leading to their improper applications. Last, the ideal conceptual framework should have garnered a degree of recognition or acceptance within one's field or related disciplinary domains. An illustrative example of a conceptual framework meeting these criteria is the "hierarchy of effects" model, which can assess the impact of advertising and various communication forms across cognitive, affective, and behavioral dimensions.

For early-career researchers who contemplate using a conceptual framework or theory developed in another discipline should ensure that this model is suitable for their research questions. And most importantly, they should not try to "adapt" it to meet their needs. Examples of frameworks that have been misused in the field of consumer behavior include various attitude models. These models were developed to explain the formation and change in people's attitudes, but researchers used them to explain various forms of behavior, prompting criticism after they were used in studies that appeared in credible journals (e.g., Wilkie & Pessemier, 1973). Labeling theory is another theoretical framework that was developed to explain development and change in older persons' perceptions of their aging "self." It is not to be employed to explain the older person's behaviors, as was it was applied (Tepper,

1994), because it has been argued that the theory does not lend itself to empirically testing to explain perceptions, making it even more doubtful it can be tested to explain behavior (Moschis, 2000).

In sum, in this author's opinion, a conceptual framework should do the following:

- Classify variables into mutually exclusive and exhaustive categories.
- Enable one to use multiple or mixed research methods.
- Provide opportunities for its improvement.
- Allow its testing, or parts of it, not only by means of acceptable methods but also (ideally) by illustrating new/emergent methodologies.

In deductive research, the study normally begins either with the use of an available conceptual framework or with one that the researcher develops based on available literature regarding (a) existing, known and often measurable concepts and relationships among them and (b) new concepts and relationships that are produced by means of the researcher's integration, synthesis, and interpretation, and it ends either with its validation and enrichment in helping understand variables and their relationships, or its modification and expansion. In contrast, researchers using the inductive approach work in a reverse sequence. They start with attempting to understand the phenomenon under investigation by first identifying relevant concepts it subsumes and their meanings, as well as the implied or subjective relationships among them, and they end with *their* theory and relevant propositions that beg validation for their support. There is usually more rigor in the process of discovery than in developing conceptual frameworks deductively.

5.2 Conceptual Framework Development

If researchers cannot find a conceptual framework that fits their needs, they may consider developing their own. This task is much more difficult and harder to "sell" because such a framework often must integrate existing model(s) into a modified version, which should then be supported with theory and data that one must marshal to justify it. Ravitch and Riggan (2016) discuss multiple strategies and practices for developing conceptual frameworks using quantitative and qualitative methods.

5.2.1 Quantitative Approach

The quantitative approach to conceptual framework development aims at the construction of a model consisting at variables that are presumed to be causally linked, with some in a sequential fashion. Almost in every conceptual framework that is built using the quantitative approach, the variables that comprise it take one or more of the following four forms: (a) antecedent variables, (b) outcome or criterion variables, (c) process or mediating variables that explain the mechanisms by which antecedent variables affect outcome variables, and (d) contextual variables, which can take the form of moderating variables (or moderators), or control variables, which can affect the remaining three variables and the relationships between them.

The specific variables that are to be included in the conceptual model should be based on theory and/or research. For example, if the researcher is interested in understanding individual differences in brand loyalty and results of previous research show a positive link between age and brand loyalty, then age should be included as antecedent variable along with brand loyalty, the criterion variable. Similarly, if theory suggests that age has a positive effect on brand loyalty, then age should be included in the conceptual framework as an antecedent variable, even in the absence of previous studies that show such a link. And it goes without saying that the strongest justification for including variables in a conceptual model is both theory and research that suggest a link between variables—i.e., the presence of theory and supportive research justifying their inclusion. However, it should be noted that not every variable, or relationship between variables, included in a conceptual framework needs to be justified on the basis of theory or research. Variables and relationships between variables in a conceptual framework or model can be included on the basis of deduction. For example, if theory and/or research shows that variable A has a positive effect on variable B, and variable B has a positive effect on C, then it can be deduced that variable A should have a positive effect on variable C. In a similar vein, if variable X and Y share similar properties as, for example, in the case of education and income, and variable X is theorized to lead to brand loyalty, then variable Y should also be related to brand loyalty in a similar fashion.

The first step in developing a conceptual framework or model is to do a literature review, first using key words that should include the name of the variable of interest or phenomenon, and later additional words that might provide explanations for the variable of interest or phenomenon under investigation, such as "predictors of (phenomenon)," "(phenomenon) explanations," or "determinants of (phenomenon)." Review articles in particular tend to be helpful in presenting knowledge about the phenomenon of interest, often summarizing the types of variables that are relevant to the study of the concept of interest (for choosing the proper literature review, see Chap. 8). Once the key types of variables are identified, it is relatively easy to use them in developing a conceptual framework. In the next two sections that follow, I use two examples from my own work to illustrate the process of developing a conceptual framework. The first is based on a summary statement about state of knowledge, and the second is based on more elaborate review and analyses of materials.

Using Text to Build a Figure: An Example Although socialization research had been widespread across disciples for several decades prior to the seventh decade of the twentieth century, with researchers addressing topics such as political, occupational, and marital socialization, I could not find a conceptual framework of socialization to use as a blueprint for my proposed dissertation topic, "Consumer Socialization." Therefore, I decided to develop my own conceptual framework. The quotation below comes from a literature review (Moschis, 1978):

> McLeod and O'Keefe maintain that a complete socialization theory must deal with five types of variables: (1) content or criterion behavior; (2) agent or source of influence; (3) learning process involved in socialization; (4) social structural constraints effecting learning; and (5) age or lifecycle position of the influencee. (p. 8)

This paragraph suggested the types of variables that should be included in a consumer socialization conceptual framework, which serve as the basis for the conceptual model shown in Fig. 5.1. Specifically, content or criterion behavior is the outcome of socialization (defined broadly to include consumption-related behaviors), age or life cycle is an antecedent variable, agent or source of influence and learning process suggest that learning takes place during the person's interaction with socialization agent, and social structural constraints suggest variables serving as antecedents or moderators.

A Step-by-Step Process In most cases, a literature review is not likely to be so clear as to reveal the types of factors that should be included in a conceptual framework, forcing the researcher to develop a model by analyzing, cataloging, and interpreting relevant findings and theories. For the early-career researcher who has had limited experience in developing conceptual frameworks, I suggest a step-by-step simple process *when using the deductive approach* to research:

1. Review literature relevant to your topic or the phenomenon you want to understand and investigate (e.g., "brand loyalty"). Make a list of research findings that shows every factor that has been found in previous studies to be associated or related (e.g., correlated) with brand loyalty, noting the nature of the reported statistically significant relationship (positive or negative). For example, (a) "age is positively related to brand loyalty," (b) "frequency of discussion of consumption matters among family members has a negative relationship with brand loyalty," and (c) "the negative relationship between age and brand loyalty is stronger among larger than smaller families."
2. Put those variables that affect others shown in the above statements into three categories: antecedents (age in statement a), processes (frequency of discussions in statement b), and moderators (family size in statement c). You now have an incomplete conceptual model because the only condition that is satisfied for a good theory, which should be incorporated into a conceptual model, is the negative link between age and brand loyalty, as there is absence of explanation(s) for this association and the process(s) that link(s) age to brand loyalty.
3. Develop another list of findings for every variable that is associated with those variables found to be related to your main concept (brand loyalty)—i.e., every antecedent, process, and moderator variable. For example, (a) "age is negatively associated with family size," (b) "age is negatively associated with the frequency of discussion of consumption matters among family members," and "frequency of discussion of consumption matters among family members is negatively associated with family size."

The result of these steps is the development of a conceptual model that consists of two antecedent variables (age and family size) that lead to the process or mediating variable (frequency of discussion of consumption matters among family members), which leads to brand loyalty, with the two antecedents having also a direct impact on brand loyalty, and family size moderating the direct effects of age. You now have a conceptual framework built on empirical findings.

4. The last step in the process is to "dress up" as many of the relationships of this model with theories and research findings, which would explain the reason(s) for the relationships between its variables. Providing one or more theoretical explanations for the emerged finding in previous studies offer stronger support for each relationship. And the larger the number of relationships that can be explained by theories, the more credible the conceptual framework. After the last step is completed, the model should be explained briefly, with regard to its main variables and expected relationships, followed by discussion of each relationship by first stating the reason or theory in support of the relationship, and lastly citing empirical findings in support of the relationship. This discussion can be offered as a justification for proposing each relationship as a hypothesis.

For future research on the same topic, researchers can expand their conceptual framework by identifying other variables (e.g., antecedents, mediators, moderators) that might influence the relationships between the independent and dependent variables. This revision and expansion should be based on relevant theories and results from other studies.

5.2.2 Qualitative Approach

When using the inductive approach to research, development of a conceptual framework, novice researchers with relatively limited experience in qualitative research should follow the steps and suggestions of Anfara and Mertz (2015) and Ravitch and Riggan (2016). Their suggested procedure for developing a conceptual framework can be summarized as follows:

1. Define and describe the phenomenon (e.g., repeat choice of brand, stability of choice over time), state the reason(s) for its investigation, and decide on the qualitative research methodology you plan to use (e.g., grounded theory, phenomenology, case study, ethnography, content analysis; discussed in Chap. 6).
2. Contextualize the phenomenon (e.g., product category), actors (family members), and settings where the phenomenon can be observed (e.g., supermarkets).
3. Conduct in-depth interviews with a small number individuals who live with other family members, asking them questions about their feelings and experiences with a product in the specified category, including how purchasing decisions are made within the family and how the product is consumed, and audio-tape the interviews and transcribe them.

4. Examine the literature on the topic (e.g., brand loyalty; e.g., Fournier, 1998; Chaudhuri & Holbrook, 2001) as well as topics related to the phenomenon (e.g., theories and research on stability and change in other forms of behavior) to inform yourself on previous studies and relevant theories in other disciplines that might be helpful in data coding and understanding this pattern of behavior.
5. Use keywords and phrases to code the data from interviews (see suggestions by experts, e.g., Belk et al., 2013), and use these codes to understand and make interpretations about processes and connections between theory and data. For example, comments by a middle-aged mother of two, such as "My 4-year-old always talks about this brand when he sees it advertised on TV" and "My child wouldn't let me pick the brand that I and my husband like," suggest that this informant has low brand loyalty. The interpretation of this phenomenon is that TV ads influence young children, who make product requests that parents yield to them, and it helps understand the reason age is negatively related to brand loyalty, as older people are more likely to live in smaller families without children. Thus, family systems theory (e.g., Watson, 2012) can explain these interactions.

   Another set of comments (codes) by an elderly informant about a brand, such as "reliable," "worth the money," and "no reason to take a chance on an unfamiliar brand," provide a complementary understanding of the phenomenon based on Heckhausen and Schulz's (1995) lifespan theory of control. The theory explains how behavior changes over the life course, focusing on control strategies that shift due to opportunities and constraints encountered. With age in later life, people experience cognitive and physical losses that make the control of their external environment increasingly difficult and increase the likelihood of failure of their efforts that can have negative effects on their self-esteem. To cope with perceived potential failures in attempting new projects, older adults become increasingly hesitant to engage in new activities, and they develop increasingly stronger preferences for activities that they feel comfortable performing.
6. You can now develop your verbal or iconic conceptual framework and suggest propositions. The framework should integrate the two theories that are embedded within sociological and psychological theoretical orientations, family systems, and control theory, respectively. And propositions could derive from each theory. Alternatively, a researcher can use an overarching multi-theoretical conceptual framework suitable for studying the onset, stability, and change in behavior in general, such as the life course paradigm (LCP), within which to locate the two theories (Moschis, 2019).

The article by Fournier (1998) provides an excellent illustration of the process involved in building a conceptual framework for studying consumer brand relationships. Her work helps develop a typology of consumer brand relationships useful in understanding the notion of brand quality.

While the two different approaches, deductive and inductive, to developing a conceptual framework have merit and are commonly used in various disciplines, it can be easily seen in this example that a mixed methods approach would be better than either one alone (the discussion of the "Mixed Methods" approach is in Chap. 6). The researcher could integrate data and conclusions from each method to better understand the phenomenon, support his or her conceptual framework, reach a final conclusion, and even suggest avenues for further research.

It is important to recognize that any initial conceptual framework is susceptible to adjustments over time, driven by changing environmental factors and the accumulation of new knowledge. A case in point is the original consumer socialization framework in the consumer behavior field presented by Moschis and Churchill (1978), which has more recently been incorporated into the broader life course conceptual model (e.g., Moschis and Mathur, in press; Moschis et al., in press; Prakitsuwan et al., in press). This shift reflects a contemporary trend observed in various disciplines, where the concept of socialization has become an integral component of the life course paradigm, as exemplified by the work of Elder (1994).

5.3 Theory Construction and Hypothesis Development

Theories are very important in the scientific world. They allow scientists to predict, understand, describe, and explain phenomena of interest. Theories prevent scientists from being dazzled by the complexity of the empirical world by providing a linguistic tool for organizing it (Bacharach, 1989). Research is normally done to address a problem or research question, and theory and hypothesis development should start with the statement of the problem or research question. Development of assumptions about the phenomenon under investigation (research question or problem) heavily relies on theories and existing data. The researcher's task is to identify the relevant theories that might explain the phenomenon under investigation (i.e., deductive approach) and/or the relevant data that will help us understand and provide tentative explanations of the phenomenon of interest (i.e., inductive approach).

The next section discusses two approaches to theory construction and hypothesis development for addressing a research question or problem: using existing theory or theories (deductive) and building new theories (inductive).

5.3.1 Theory and Hypothesis Development from an Integrative Literature Review

Because the integrative literature review appears to be most appropriate for theory construction (see Chap. 8), this section outlines guidelines and recommendations based on this type of review, and it offers an example to illustrate the process of theory and hypothesis development based on existing knowledge. The example used is "supermarket patronage," as such a behavior demonstrates empirical regularities (Hunt, 1983)—i.e., the phenomenon "loyalty" to the same store. It is also assumed that concept explication has identified two domains of the phenomenon: behavioral consistency (repeat patronage) and loyalty in the form of psychological commitment (affect) or strong positive attitude toward supermarkets. And it was decided that the latter domain or meaning of the concept was not relevant to supermarkets—i.e., excess meaning or reification—prompting our focus on the single domain of behavioral consistency, and that the term "loyalty" refers to behavioral consistency over time. Note that larger numbers of domains of a concept could make additional theories and research findings relevant, requiring more elaborate literature review and analyses.

Preliminary Steps

1. Describe the phenomenon as broadly as possible (e.g., it concerns a person's stability and change in behavior, making theories that explain stability and change in every discipline relevant).
2. Make two lists of study findings from your literature review: one that contains information (empirical findings, theories, etc.) from studies directly relevant to the phenomenon (e.g., variables that correlate with your focal variable) and those indirectly relevant because of the phenomenon's similarities (e.g., brand loyalty, loyalty to other types of retail outlets) and another list consisting of information from sources outside one's discipline (theories and empirical findings) regarding broader forms of stability and change in other forms of behavior (e.g., employment, residence, marriage), including the correlates of such behaviors.
3. Assess every item on each list, and mark it to show whether the information contained is empirical (E), theoretical (T), or descriptive of a process (P) in nature, and whether the information applies to the specific phenomenon under investigation (S) or to general phenomena under which the specific phenomenon can be subsumed (G).
4. After you complete these tasks, go back to the list that contains general information not directly relevant to the phenomenon of interest, and look at the theories and supportive empirical evidence that explain stability and change in other forms of behavior—i.e., independent variables. You might see more than one theory that explains such behaviors, and you might see other theories and empirical findings that relate to these theories.
5. Begin to draft a tentative explanation of the phenomenon under investigation by (a) discussing relevant theories and supportive findings that explain people's inclination to maintain stable patterns of behavior, followed by findings related to the focal variable that support the notion that the general theory, which explains general patterns of behavioral stability, might also explain the specific pattern of supermarket patronage (loyalty).

To help the reader understand how to organize and integrate findings from the literature search (items #1 through #3 above), and the specific tasks involved in steps #4 and #5, the following list of finding is assumed to have emerged from the literature search:

Samples of findings from literature search and their classification are as follows:

1. Store loyal customers tend to be more satisfied with their retail establishments they patronize (S, E).

2. Life changes have been negatively associated with brand loyalty (S, E).
3. There is a positive relationship between perceived control and life satisfaction (G, E).
4. People who work in a routine type of jobs are more satisfied with their work than those who face constant change and uncertainty (G, E).
5. Trying to re-establish homeostasis is an effortful process because it taxes the persons adaptive resources (G, P).
6. People are constantly striving to achieve a homeostatic state (G, P).
7. Disruptions of balanced psychological states create mental disequilibrium (G, E).
8. An unexpected event disrupts a person's homeostatic state (G, E).
9. Solving a problem that has been a source of psychological dislocation helps one re-establish psychological equilibrium (G, P).
10. Feelings of anxiety and tensions are reduced by taking action that reduce such feelings (G, P).
11. Those with high levels of self-esteem are less likely than the lower self-esteem counterparts to experience aversive psychological feelings (G, E).
12. People with higher levels of self-esteem are more satisfied with their life than those with lower levels of self-esteem (G, E).
13. People who experience aversive psychological feelings (e.g., anxiety, stress, tensions) tend to be very unhappy (G, E).
14. Cognitive consistency theory suggests the people are most satisfied with life to the extent they experience a harmonious state of mind (G, T).
15. When faced with potentially threatening situations, people react in a way that helps them diminish the potential threat (G, P).
16. A person sense of control over his or her environment increases one's self-esteem (G, T).
17. Control theory states that because people need to be certain about their future, their actions are aimed at achieving certain desired outcomes, and if they are not certain about their future, they are not likely to be happy (G,T).
18. Successful resolution of a problem may enhance one's sense of personal control over his or her environment

(Legend: G=general, S=specific, T=theoretical, E=empirical, P=process)

Based on these findings from the review of the literature, the following guidelines are suggested for writing up your argument or thesis and developing hypotheses deductively:

1. Select those theoretical statements that would suggest possible explanation(s) of the phenomenon, keeping in mind that there might be more than one theory (explanation) or explanations that might be complementary rather than competing.
2. Select the theory that appears to be most relevant based on findings of literature search, and write a sentence that offers a tentative explanation of the phenomenon. For example, "People are loyal to supermarkets in order to avoid aversive psychological feelings related to change."

3. Now you are ready to start elaborating on your thesis or argument. First, always begin with established theories that explain the general or broad pattern of behavior, offering empirical support for them, and, next, suggest that the specific theory that explains the general pattern of behavior can help explain the specific type of behavior (loyalty to supermarkets). And for every statement, use the results of your literature review to support your statement. Begin with theories which argue that people do not like change, and discuss how and why change makes people unhappy, offering empirical support—(i.e., explanation, with supportive evidence from the results of your literature search). An example of a write-up is as follows:

   People don't appear to like change. Change disrupts balanced psychological states and creates a psychological disequilibrium (#7) and aversive feelings, such as anxiety, stress, and tension that make people unhappy (#13). These feelings prompt one to re-establish homeostasis (#11), which is effortful process because it taxes the person's adaptive resources (#5). An unexpected event, such as being unable to locate a product in an unfamiliar supermarket, is likely to disrupt a person's homeostatic state and create aversive feelings (#8). Cognitive consistency theory suggests the people are most satisfied with life to the extent they experience a harmonious state of mind (#14). When faced with potentially threatening situations, such as considering shopping at an unfamiliar supermarket (i.e., change), people react in a way that helps them diminish the potential threat (#15); and they may repeat past behavior (e.g., patronize the same store) rather than facing unknown or uncertain outcomes of their new actions (e.g., shop in a different supermarket) (#17), with such repeat behaviors viewed as coping responses to present or potential stress (#10) within the context of control theory.

   Control theory states that because people need to be certain about their future, their actions are aimed at achieving certain desired outcomes; and if they are not certain about their future, they are not likely to be happy (#17). Successful resolution of a problem may enhance one's sense of personal control over his or her environment (#18), helping one re-establish psychological equilibrium (#9), and such a sense of control may increase the person's self-esteem (#16), which can enhance satisfaction with life (#12). The positive relationship between perceived control and life satisfaction reported in the literature (#3) offers support for control theory, while the uncovered positive link between store loyalty and satisfaction with retail establishments (#1) suggests that control theory may explain the reason people are loyal to supermarkets. Therefore, change in the form of patronizing a different supermarket may create psychological dislocation and aversive feelings that erode well-being, prompting people to avoid such a change because they want to maintain control over the outcomes of their patronage decisions (#18). In contrast, continuous patronage of the same retail establishment or vendor may occur when the person is experiencing more life changes than usual, as suggested by the negative relationship life changes and brand loyalty (#2), avoiding additional changes that would add to his aversive feeling he or she is experiencing due to the increase number of life changes. The preceding discussion suggests the following hypotheses:

H1: Personal control is positively associated with store loyalty.

H2: The greater the number of life changes a person experiences within a specified period of time, (a) the lower his or her level of satisfaction with life, and (b) the higher his or her store loyalty.

The reader can notice that these hypotheses concern relationships between variables based on the reasons for these expectations. What appears to be missing from the proposed theory of store loyalty that should be included in the list of hypotheses is the third condition or characteristic of a good theory—i.e., the mechanism(s) or process by which changes affect store patronage behavior (see Chap. 3). This entails the testing of one or more constructs that tap a person's "aversive feelings" as a mediating variable. Using the concept of "stress" as a mediating variable (distinction can also be made between acute and chronic stress), the following hypothesis can be stated:

H3: Stress experienced within a certain period of time mediates the effects of life changes experienced within the same time on store loyalty, with greater levels of stress resulting from life changes leading to higher levels of store loyalty.

Offer a Strong Test of Your Theory The theory builder should take one last step to convince the reader that the proposed theory has merit. Earlier in this book (Chap. 3), I mentioned that a strong test of a theory is the absence of alternative explanation(s) of the phenomenon under investigation. The theory builder may want to demonstrate this point by testing an alternative theoretical formulation. In looking for alternative explanations, he or she could ask a question such as: "Why a person would *not* be loyal to a store?" Thus, instead of seeking explanations of loyalty, one can look for explanations of disloyalty.

The theory builder may reason that the boredom of shopping at the same store, seeing the same products or store layout, etc. might prompt one to switch stores. In line with this thinking, he or she may consider personality characteristics, such as need for novelty, as possible factors, and may consider the personality trait of sensation-seeking (Zuckerman et al., 1964) to be closest to the concept (trait) of novelty-seeking, with the two traits closely related (De Fruyt et al., 2000). Therefore, the sensation-seeking construct of four domains that can be obtained from the 40-item sensation-seeking scale (SSS) can be used to test an alternative explanation of store loyalty.

H4: Sensation-seeking is inversely related to store loyalty.

Finally, the reader should notice that the proposed theory, like any other theory, is subject to modification, expansion, and even replacement, and it could be integrated with complementary theories to provide a more complete explanation of the phenomenon. For example, additional variables could be tested as mediators, besides stress (e.g., anxiety, tensions), and also moderating variables should be considered based on theory and research (e.g., self-esteem, and characteristics such as family size).

5.3.2 Theory and Proposition Development from Depth Interviews

When some qualitative researchers use the phrase "theory development" or "theory building," they use the term theory to refer to "a system of ideas or statements explaining some phenomenon" (Belk et al., 2013: 139). And these researchers use the phrase "building new theory" to "encompass identifying new concepts or construct or processes to help us understand something about the phenomenon, identifying new variants in a phenomenon and the factors that help us understand and explain them, and identifying exceptions that delineate when an existing theory is relevant and/or challenging the adequacy of existing theory" (p. 139).

For theory building, generally, qualitative researchers look at variation in relationships between codes that apply to elements that describe a phenomenon, and sequence of events leading to outcomes, which are "complex and underdetermined" (Belk et al., 2013: 153). Codes are names the researcher assigns to words, sentences, paragraphs, and even to chunks of text consisting of sentences or paragraphs. And although "outcomes are never fully determined by the individual, social, cultural, and community factors that are identified through qualitative data analysis," they may distil the relationship they identify into propositional statements (p. 153). Nevertheless, Belk and associates assert that: "Interpreting groups of codes as elements of a phenomenon, as processes, or as explanations for outcomes of a phenomenon can constitute a new theoretical contribution if your insights are novel" (p. 150). And they give examples of relating codes to one another as elements, processes, and outcomes. Relating codes to one another as elements is viewed as a theoretical contribution known as "mapping" a construct, while process theories are developed to provide explanation of the sequence of events leading to an outcome. Theories that explain the conditions that give rise to a phenomenon of interest (outcome), or the consequences of that phenomenon, are never fully determined and form the bases for propositions. Causality between elements or codes is not often explicitly stated, but is usually implied in the words and statements used to describe theory, such as "is a function of" (Kozinets et al., 2010: 86), "brand relationship quality effects" (Fournier, 1998: 366), and "etiology of addiction" (Hirschman, 1992: 155).

Building theory from qualitative or quantitative data is a process that is commonly referred to as "grounded theory." It involves making two types of interpretations of text: idiographic and cross-person analysis (Strauss & Corbin, 1990). The first interpretation focuses on the individual, while the latter attempts to uncover relationships across individuals. Fournier's (1998) research on brand relationships illustrates these methods in detail. Her idiographic analysis shows " how the projects, concerns, and themes that people use to define themselves can be played out in the cultivation of brand relationships and how those relationships, in turn, can affect the cultivation of one's concept of self" (p. 359), and her cross-person analysis reveals 15 meaningful forms of consumer-brand relationships as a typology, which serves as a conceptual framework for future research.

Another approach to theory building that is increasingly becoming popular among qualitative researchers is the use of preexisting theory in order to build a new theory. In the consumer field, for example, Fournier (1998) uses theories of human relationship quality to build her theory of consumer-brand relationship quality, a construct of six-faceted brand relationship quality that she offers as an alternative to brand loyalty. Furthermore, she asserts that this research contributes to theory development on brand personality by understanding the processes through which brand personality is created, developed, and changed over time. Belk and associates (2013) offer several other examples of studies that have used this approach.

Developing a theory from qualitative data is a complex and iterative process that involves careful analysis and interpretation of data. The following steps can help guide you through this process:

1. *Familiarize yourself with qualitative research methods.* Before you start, ensure you have a strong understanding of qualitative research methods. Familiarize yourself with different approaches such as grounded theory, thematic analysis, content analysis, and narrative analysis (see Chaps. 7 and 8).
2. *Define your research question.* Begin with a clear research question or objective. Your theory will be centered around this question, so it needs to be well-defined and specific.
3. *Data collection.* Collect your qualitative data using appropriate methods like interviews, focus groups, observations, or content analysis. Ensure that your data are relevant to your research question.
4. *Data organization.* Organize your data systematically. This may involve transcribing interviews, creating data matrices, or using qualitative data analysis software like NVivo or ATLAS.ti to manage your data efficiently.
5. *Data coding.* Start coding your data. Coding involves systematically categorizing and labeling segments of your data (e.g., themes, concepts, or patterns). You can use open coding (developing categories from scratch) or axial coding (relating categories to each other) depending on your research approach.
6. *Memo writing.* Write memos or reflective notes during the coding process. Memos can help you record your thoughts, ideas, and interpretations as you work through the data. They also provide a record of your analytical journey.
7. *Constant comparative analysis.* Engage in constant comparative analysis, a key component of grounded theory. Compare new data with existing codes and categories to refine and develop your theory. Look for similarities and differences within your data.
8. *Theory development.* As you code and analyze your data, you will begin to notice patterns and themes emerging. These patterns can serve as the basis for your theory. Pay attention to both commonalities and anomalies.

9. *Theoretical sampling (grounded theory).* In grounded theory, consider conducting additional data collection (theoretical sampling) to validate and refine emerging concepts and categories. This helps ensure your theory is grounded in the data.
10. *Triangulation.* Use triangulation by comparing your qualitative data with other data sources or by involving multiple researchers in the analysis process. This can enhance the validity and reliability of your theory.
11. *Constantly refine and revise.* The development of a theory is an iterative process. Continuously revisit your data, codes, and emerging theory. Refine and revise as needed to develop a coherent and well-substantiated theory.
12. *Theoretical saturation.* In grounded theory, you aim for theoretical saturation, which means you stop collecting data when no new insights or categories emerge, and your theory is well-developed and supported.
13. *Write your theory.* Once you have developed a robust theory supported by your qualitative data, write it up in a clear and concise manner.
14. *Member checking (suggested).* If possible, consider sharing your emerging theory with participants for their feedback. This can provide valuable insights and enhance the credibility of your theory.
15. *Continued theorizing.* Remember that theory development is an ongoing process. Your theory may evolve over time as new data and insights emerge or as it is tested by other researchers in the field.

Remember that qualitative theory development is both art and science. It requires a deep understanding of your research area, creativity in interpreting data, and rigor in the analysis process. Collaboration and peer review are also crucial to ensure the validity and reliability of your theory.

References

Anfara, V. A., & Mertz, N. T. (2015). *Theoretical frameworks in qualitative research* (2nd ed.). Sage.

Bacharach, S. B. (1989). Organizational theories: Some criteria for evaluation. *The Academy of Management Review, 14*(4), 496–515. https://doi.org/10.2307/258555

Belk, R., Fischer, E., & Kozinets, R. V. (2013). *Qualitative consumer & marketing research*. Sage.

Chaudhuri, A., & Holbrook, M. B. (2001). The chain of effects from brand trust and brand affect to brand performance: The role of brand loyalty. *Journal of Marketing, 65*(2), 81–93.

De Fruyt, F., Van De Wiele, L., & Van Heeringen, C. (2000). Cloninger's psychobiological model of temperament and character and the five-factor model of personality. *Personality and Individual Differences, 29*(3), 441–452. https://doi.org/10.1016/S0191-8869(99)00204-4

Elder, G. H. (1994). Time, human agency, and social change: Perspectives on the life course. *Social Psychology Quarterly, 57*(1), 4–15.

Fournier, S. (1998). Consumers and their brands: Developing relationship theory in consumer research. *Journal of Consumer Research, 24*(4), 343–373.

Heckhausen, J., & Schulz, R. (1995). A life-span theory of control. *Psychological Review, 102*(2), 284–304.

Hirschman, E. C. (1992). The Consciousness of addiction: Toward a general theory of compulsive consumption. *Journal of Consumer Research, 19*(2), 115–179.

Hunt, S. D. (1983). *Marketing theory: The philosophy of marketing science*. Irwin Publishing Company.
Kozinets, R., De Valk, K., Wojnicki, A., & Wilner, S. (2010). Networked Narratives: Understanding word-of-mouth marketing in online communities. *Journal of Marketing, 71*(March), 71–89.
Miles, M. B., Huberman, A. M., & Saldaña, J. (2014). *Qualitative data analysis: A methods sourcebook*. Sage.
Moschis, G. P. (1978). *Acquisition of the consumer role by adolescents*. College of Business administration, Publishing services division. Georgia State University.
Moschis, G. P. (2000). Consumer behavior in later life: Multidisciplinary approaches and methodological issues. *Research in Consumer Behavior, 9*, 103–128.
Moschis, G. P. (2019). *Consumer behavior over the life course: Research frontiers and new directions*. Springer Publishing, Inc.
Moschis, G. P., & Churchill, G. A. (1978). Consumer socialization: A theoretical and empirical analysis. *Journal of Marketing Research, 15*(4), 599–609.
Moschis, G. P., & Mathur, A. (in press). Children and adolescent consumer behavior: Insights from the life course paradigm. *Journal of Consumer Behavior*.
Moschis, G. P., Prakitsuwan, P., & Mathur, A. (in press). Financial socialization: Insights from the life course paradigm. *Journal of Financial Counseling and Planning*.
Prakitsuwan, P., Moschis, G. P., & Mathur, A. (in press). A study of financial socialization in life course context. *Journal of Financial Counseling and Planning*.
Ravitch, S. M., & Riggan, M. (2016). *Reason and rigor: How conceptual frameworks guide research* (2nd ed.). Sage.
Strauss, A., & Corbin, J. M. (1990). *Basics of qualitative research: Grounded theory procedures and techniques*. Sage Publications, Inc.
Tepper, K. (1994). The role of labeling processes in elderly's consumer responses to age segmentation cues. *Journal of Consumer Research, 20*, 503–519.
Vuchinich, S., Teachman, J., & Crosby, L. (1991). Families and hazard rates that change over time: Some methodological issues in analyzing transitions. *Journal of Marriage and Family, 53*(4), 898–912.
Watson, W. H. (2012). Family systems. In *Encyclopedia of human behavior* (2nd ed., pp. 184–193).
Wilkie, W. l., & Pessemier, E. A. (1973). Issues in marketing's use of multi-attribute attitude models. *Journal of Marketing Research, 10*(Nov.), 428–441.
Zuckerman, M., Kolin, E. A., Price, L., & Zoob, I. (1964). Development of a sensation-seeking scale. *Journal of Consulting Psychology, 28*(6), 477–482.

6 Research Approaches and Designs

Research approaches and methods that are employed for knowledge creation derive from the philosophical paradigms (multivariate/positivistic, interpretive/humanistic, and historical) that are briefly described in Chap. 3. The present chapter focuses on the positivistic and humanistic paradigms because academic research in business and social sciences has been largely based on these two paradigms and in part because the historical paradigm is often integrated within the two paradigms and is viewed as a distinctive paradigm only in the field of "history" (Alford, 1998). It discusses the key features of, and differences between, the positivistic and humanistic paradigms and their main research approaches or traditions, and it comments on the desirability of their employment in academic studies. This chapter also discusses the mixed methods approach, which integrates the positivistic and humanistic paradigms and has been increasing in popularity as an approach that capitalizes on the strengths of the two traditional approaches and overcomes many of their limitations. Finally, the chapter evaluates these approaches and offers recommendations for their use in academic studies.

6.1 Differences Between Positivistic and Humanistic Research

The two research approaches that are based on the positivistic and humanistic paradigms have distinctive features. They make different assumptions, use different processes for knowledge creation, and have different goals. These differences are discussed in greater detail by Hirschman (1986). They include main *differences in the assumptions* made by the positivists, compared to those made by humanists, respectively: knowledge is discovered rather than created; there is a single objective reality rather than multiple subjective realities; causality is present among phenomena or elements rather than absent; and inquiry is and should be value-free and objective rather than inherently value-laden (Hirschman, 1986).

G. P. Moschis, *Academic Research in Business and the Social Sciences*,
https://doi.org/10.1007/978-3-031-56548-9_6

Next, there are *differences in the methods* positivists and humanists use to accomplish their goals, ranging from the way they conceptualize a phenomenon and the research process to preliminary exploratory steps and main analyses they perform to reach conclusions. For example, the positivist researcher sees the phenomenon or main concept embedded in causal relationships, with variables and relationships clearly delineated. In contrast, the humanist researcher sees the phenomenon as an amorphous "mass" whose contents and textures the researcher wants to understand. The positivist researcher would perform an exploratory investigation in order to better refine the variables—i.e., increase their reliability and validity and the presumed causal relationships among them. In contrast, the humanist investigator would attempt to learn as much as possible about the phenomenon, discard any preconceptions, and understand the phenomenon in various contexts. In a way, the researcher attempts to "break down" the amorphous mass into more coherent ideas or concepts.

Researchers who employ the two approaches also use *different analyses*. The positivist researcher would try to test his or her model and/or hypothesized relationships between variables and make causal inferences between variables based on statistical tests of significance. In contrast, the humanist investigator would personally immerse in the phenomenon and systematically use his or her prior knowledge, intuition, and empathy to make interpretations of the data collected via personal observations and other forms (e.g., Belk et al., 2013). In doing so, the researcher becomes the "instrument" of data collection.

Also, the two methods *differ in drawing conclusions* based on their findings. At the final stage of the investigation, the positivist researcher would draw conclusions about relationships between variables in his or her attempt to explain the phenomenon, using these relationships to either describe the nature and characteristics of the phenomenon under investigation or infer its explanation from the emerged relationships, and, ultimately, these conclusions would serve in confirming, revising, or building a theory to explain a phenomenon and would suggest action in different times and contexts (Hunt, 1983).

In contrast, at the final stage of the investigation, the humanist researcher attempts to use information obtained about the phenomenon in the forms of observations and personal experiences and translate it into a verbal interpretation. At this stage, the humanist researcher would assemble the concepts, ideas, and their meanings he or she has "extracted" from the original amorphous mass and use them as clues, to help in translating them into a comprehensive whole. This process involves analysis solely from the perspective of the researcher who has participated in the culture or group being studied. Thus, the end product of inquiry is one or more interpretations of a phenomenon, which may take the forms of narratives or themes constructed by the investigator. As Hirschman (1986) puts it, "humanistic inquiry involves no right ending, only the right process" (p. 243).

Finally, the two methods *differ in the criteria used to evaluate findings*. Criteria used to assess the quality of the findings from positivistic studies, such as internal and external validity, reliability, and objectivity, are inappropriate for evaluating humanistic studies. Rather, the analogous criteria to those of positivistic research are credibility, transferability, dependability, and confirmability, respectively (cf. Hirschman, 1986). One method for evaluating the *credibility* of humanistic research is to submit the researcher's interpretation of the phenomenon to the study participants (referred to as "informants") and seek their responses as to its truthfulness or accuracy. *Transferability*, which is analogous to external validity, is concerned with "the transferability of one manifestation of a phenomenon to the second manifestation of the phenomenon, recognizing implicitly that no two social contexts are ever identical" (Hirschman, 1986: 245); it is *not* concerned with the generalizability of findings across time, populations, or contexts. It can be assessed on a post hoc basis by constructing an alternative interpretation of the same phenomenon in a different social context and comparing the two.

Dependability, which is analogous to reliability in positivistic research, is assessed by using multiple investigators to study the same phenomenon and make interpretations. As investigators are the "instruments" used for data collection and analyses, greater consistency in interpretations across researchers, but not perfect correspondence (as one does not see perfect reliability coefficients in the instruments of positivistic research), would suggest a more dependable construction of the phenomenon investigated. Finally, *confirmability* in humanistic research, which is analogous to objectivity or neutrality in positivist inquiry, can be achieved by using one or more outside auditors who are to assess the extent to which the interpretation drawn from the data gathered by the researcher is logical and unbiased. The auditors' task is, based on their own experience with the subject matter and informant characteristics (e.g., age, subculture), to determine if the researcher's interpretation is logically consistent with their own experience with, and knowledge of, the informant's subculture (e.g., race, organization). Stronger evidence of the accuracy or credibility of the interpretation can be produced by auditors with diverse backgrounds and fields of reference.

Researchers who attempt to understand these differences, or contemplate using one or both research approaches, should not assume that one is superior or inferior to the other. Rather, they should keep in mind that each method of inquiry provides equally valuable information and a parallel path to the other in creating knowledge (Hirschman, 1986). Although they may be used for different purposes, they could also be used as complementary to help explain phenomena, enhance understanding, and create knowledge.

6.2 Positivistic/Quantitative Research Designs

6.2.1 Cross-Sectional (Descriptive) Designs

Surveys The most common method of obtaining information is through surveys that can be in various forms such as mail, telephone, personal interviews, mall intercepts, and online surveys, where a sample of elements (e.g., individuals) taken from the parent population is measured only one time. They all are forms of cross-sectional studies aimed at estimating parameters in a population of interest (e.g., percentage of people who support a candidate), describing the characteristics of certain groups or objects (e.g., product users, dealers), and making predictions. In academic research, cross-sectional studies are primarily used to test hypotheses (e.g., Churchill & Brown, 2004). When information is obtained from the same elements more than one time, either by asking the same individuals different questions or the same questions as in earlier surveys, the research becomes a *longitudinal study*. Basic marketing research books provide details on the specific methods of cross-sectional studies, including their purpose, advantages, and disadvantages.

Panels A panel is a sample of elements drawn from the parent population from which measures of variables are obtained over time. When the same measures are obtained from the same sample over time, the panel is referred to as a *continuous panel*, and when different measures are obtained, it is known as a *discontinuous panel*. (e.g., Churchill & Brown, 2004). Panels are useful in designing longitudinal studies but are expensive to maintain, and the information they provide is often of questionable value, especially when it is obtained from online panels (Goodman & Paolacci, 2007; Wessling et al., 2017). In fact, some journals have announced that they do not accept studies based on online panels. However, the panel is the only research design that allows the researcher to assess the effects of variables over time, especially when their effects are delayed, and they are a much better substitute for cross-sectional studies which use retrospective measures to determine variable effects over time.

Although commercial panels have received criticism, there are commercial firms that have panels that are likely to provide valid information for academic purposes. Qualtrics is one such firm, which tries to keep panel members for a long time by using them as "panel workers," who are compensated for the time they spend completing surveys. In addition, this firm uses questions that screen out participants who show certain characteristics such as low knowledge about a subject matter. This author's experience with panels has been generally favorable. For example, in our earlier consumer socialization studies, I used middle-school and high-school students to obtain information over time in order to assess the long-term and short-term effects of socialization agents (e.g., school, mass media) on the development of consumer cognitions and behaviors (Moschis & Moore, 1982). Several years later at the Center for Mature Consumer Studies (CMCS), we used panels of older adults to assess age-related changes in their consumption-related cognitions and habits (e.g., Lee et al., 2012; Mathur et al., 2008). Examining the individual's actual change that occurs over time is more valid than implying change from the observed age-group difference that can be obtained from cross-sectional studies. Thus, carefully designed panel studies can produce invaluable information.

6.2.2 Experimental (Causal) Designs

Experiments are research designs where variables are observed and recorded under different conditions. In an experiment, the investigator (experimenter) deliberately intervenes in the research process and has some degree of control over the variables and the conditions under which they are observed. The experiment consists of exposing an experimental unit (e.g., a group of customers, a group of salesmen) to an experimental variable (e.g., advertising, training program) and measuring the effect on the dependent variable (e.g., units sold, sales calls). In a typical experiment, for example, the researcher uses two groups (group O1 and group O2) and an experimental stimulus (treatment X). One group (known as "experimental group") is exposed to X, and the other group serves as a control group. The experimenter then compares the values of the measure of "effects" (variable Y) in the two groups, testing for statistical significance of the mean scores of Y in the groups (O1 vs. O2). The chief significance of experimentation is the ability it gives the researcher to regard the experimental treatment as the cause of the effect he or she measures.

The main problems encountered in experiments are of two general types, one internal to the experiment and the other external to the experiment. Internal problems are encountered in seeking to obtain valid data that show the effects on the dependent variable from exposure to the experimental variable—i.e., problems of internal validity. External problems are those encountered in collecting data in such a way that one can conclude that the effect of the experimental variable on the dependent variable in the experimental situation is the same as the change that will take place in the entire universe of experimental subjects, if they were all exposed to the experimental variable—i.e., problem of external validity. Experimental situations that offer the tightest control over internal validity may also be the most reactive and raise the most concern over external validity. Although internal validity has been held up as the researcher's goal, in business we are concerned with the task of predicting the effect on the universe in general.

A key feature of experimental studies is the *experimental design*, which is the specific plan for research having certain logical and statistical qualities. Different experimental designs are suitable for certain objectives, and several are most suitable for *laboratory experiments* that can account for sources of internal invalidity (see sources of invalidity in Chap. 7). For example, the *posttest only with one treatment and control group design* involves the randomized selection of two groups, exposing one group to the experimental treatment (e.g., training program) and comparing scores on measures (e.g., knowledge) between the two groups. Variations of this basic randomized design can include a design that involves three groups, with two experimental treatments—when a comparison of two treatments is desired (e.g., two different training programs), where scores can be compared between the groups that are exposed to the two experimental treatments as well between groups receiving the program and the group that was not exposed.

When the experimenter wishes to determine the incremental change in the effect variable, a baseline is needed. For example, the level of knowledge on a subject matter would need to be assessed for both experimental and control groups, prior to exposing one group to the experimental treatment, and the *pretest-posttest control group design* would be appropriate for this purpose. And if there is reason to believe that exposure to the pretest interacts with the effects of the experimental treatment, the *Solomon four-group design* is appropriate. For this design, two of the four groups are pretested, and only one group in each category receives the experimental treatment. In doing so, the experimenter can assess separately the incremental effects of a treatment (for more information on these and additional designs, see Shadish et al., 2002).

While these designs are most appropriate for laboratory experiments, another set of experimental designs is most appropriate for *field experiments*, which are conducted in natural settings. If properly conducted, field experiments produce results that are externally valid at the expense of internal validity. Thus, the experimenter is not very sure about the true effects of the experimental treatments. Some field experiments take the form of quasi-experimental designs, such as *time-series experiments*, where several measures of the effect variable are taken over time before and after the experimental treatment; and some take the form of test market. They are particularly useful if the effects of cause variables manifest over a long period of time. Field experiments tend to be more difficult to conduct in part because of the difficulty of controlling variables other than experimental treatments, as well as longer required time and higher costs (Churchill & Brown, 2004). They are most relevant and useful for commercial purposes rather than academic research.

6.3 Humanist/Qualitative Research Designs

Qualitative research involves the collection and analysis of nonnumerical data, such as text, video, and audio. It is used for the purpose of understanding a wide variety types of phenomena in the form of concepts, experiences, opinions, and behaviors. The terms "postmodernism" and "interpretivism" are often used to refer to all work that uses qualitative data. Belk and associates (2013) see the relevance of qualitative research to a broad range of problems and issues, and they view all forms of qualitative research as interpretive. Thus, unlike quantitative research, which involves the collection and analysis of numerical data for statistical analysis, qualitative research involves the collection of data for interpretation in order to gain in-depth insights into a problem, generate new ideas for research, and develop theory inductively.

This section distinguishes two forms of qualitative research: exploratory and interpretive. Although it can be argued that every form of exploratory research is interpretive, the distinction is made because on some occasions data from exploratory studies can be put into numeric formats for interpretation and conclusion drawing. For example, when organizations experience time and budget constraints, they often collect data from focus groups, which are normally viewed as exploratory research designs (e.g., Churchill & Brown, 2004), as a substitute for expensive large-scale and time-consuming cross-sectional studies. Also, based on my own consulting experience with large companies, conclusions based on large-scale cross-sectional studies are fairly similar to those reached from data on the same topic(s) collected from a large number of focus groups in different contexts. And software packages are available that allow researchers to quantify responses to open-ended questions using keywords from transcribed audio and video recordings of personal and focus-group interviews.

6.3.1 Exploratory

The term "exploratory research" is often used to describe a wide variety of research designs, such as the in-depth interview, literature search, analysis of select cases, focus groups, and experience survey (for a detailed discussion of these designs, see, e.g., Churchill & Brown, 2004). Exploratory research is used for different reasons by those subscribing to a different research philosophy. Positivists use exploratory research as a stepping stone to conducting descriptive and causal studies. They rely on results from the various exploratory designs they may use to (a) develop hypotheses and theories by, for example, analyzing the results of published empirical research and (b) generate ideas in order to do better descriptive studies by, for example, using information from these research designs to develop better instruments.

On the other hand, qualitative researchers use exploratory research, such as case studies and focus groups, for understanding the meaning of phenomena and observations (Belk et al., 2013). They consider the method as "a complete and internally consistent approach to theory construction, testing, and revision process when used competently by a researcher" (Hirschman, 1986: 239). Thus, the same exploratory research design is used differently according to the needs of the investigator. And one could argue that all qualitative research designs may be viewed as forms of exploratory research, although they may not be used exclusively for qualitative inquiry.

6.3.2 Interpretive

The term "interpretive" is used to refer to all forms of qualitative research as well as only to specific types of qualitative work. For the purpose of the present discussion, it is assumed that the term is used to refer to all forms of qualitative research, including forms of exploratory research. Interpretive research is widely used in several fields of business, behavioral, and social sciences to study a wide variety of phenomena; it is used to understand how people experience the world and life in general. Examples of research questions interpretive research can try to answer:

- How do older people experience aging?
- What does socialism mean to college students?
- How do people around the world experience climate change?
- How are health clubs perceived by their members in the United States?
- How do social media shape political ideologies in teenagers?

Research Traditions Research designs in qualitative research are known as "research traditions." Researchers often use different terms to refer to the same research tradition. Belk et al. (2013) acknowledge the differences in language used not only for specific research methods but also for broad terms such as "interpretive." They classify all qualitative research traditions into six categories: existential phenomenology, hermeneutics, postmodernism, critical, semiotics, and neopositivism, and they outline the kinds of research questions each is appropriate for addressing (for a detailed explanation of each and the types of questions it addresses, see Belk et al., 2013: 21–25):

- *Existential phenomenology* addresses questions about the "nature of people's lived experiences."
- *Hermeneutics* addresses questions about "how cultural notions are shaping specific kinds of experiences and actions."
- *Postmodernism* addresses questions about "how taken-for-granted understandings of phenomena can be challenged."
- *Critical* addresses questions about "what factors contribute to the oppression or marginalization of some group of actors and/or how these conditions could be alleviated."
- *Semiotics* address questions about "how specific words, phrases, gestures, myths, images, products or practices within a symbol system acquire meaning."
- *Neopositivism* addresses questions "regarding the factors that help to explain a particular phenomenon, or the consequences that may arise when a particular phenomenon occurs."

Others classify qualitative research traditions into rather different types of categories, which share some similarities with those presented by Belk and colleagues. For example, according to Creswell and Poth (2017), qualitative research traditions include grounded theory, ethnography, case study, phenomenological research, and narrative research.

Grounded Theory Grounded theory is a dynamic and iterative process, where the researcher is actively involved in shaping the theory as it emerges from the data This involves breaking down the data into discrete parts and assigning codes to represent concepts or ideas. The primary goal of grounded theory is to generate a theory that is "grounded" in the data, meaning it emerges from the study itself rather than being imposed beforehand. Starting with systematic data collection, it is important to approach the research with an open mind, allowing the theory to develop organically from the data rather than being constrained by preconceived notions. Grounded theory is particularly useful when researchers want to understand and explain complex social processes and interactions.

Ethnography Ethnography is a qualitative research method that involves the study of people and cultures in their natural environment. Researchers using the ethnographic method immerse themselves in groups or organizations to understand their cultures. They engage in detailed observation of people during their ordinary daily lives, using direct observations, interviews, and audio and video recordings. When using the ethnographic method to develop theory, the process is often characterized by a deep engagement with the culture or community under study; it involves the detailed study and description of the culture, behavior, and practices of a particular group or community. The goal of ethnography is to gain a deep understanding of the social world of the group being studied from the perspective of the participants themselves. It has been used to study a wide range of topics, including cultural practices, social interactions, rituals, healthcare systems, and educational settings.

Case Study A case study is an in-depth, context-rich investigation of a specific case or cases, aiming to provide a nuanced understanding of complex phenomena within their natural settings. It is an in-depth exploration of a particular instance or phenomenon within its real-life context. The case study method involves a detailed and holistic examination of a specific case or cases to gain a rich understanding of the complexities and nuances inherent in that situation. It is a flexible approach that allows researchers to delve deeply into specific instances and generate theories that are contextually rich and nuanced. When using this method to develop theory, the process is characterized by a detailed examination of the case, often leading to the emergence of theoretical insights. Case studies are often used when the researcher aims to explore a phenomenon in its natural setting, understand the context, and generate insights rather than test hypotheses.

Phenomenology Phenomenology is a philosophical approach that focuses on the study of human consciousness and the subjective experiences of individuals. Phenomenological research offers a systematic and rigorous approach to understanding the lived experiences of individuals, providing a foundation for the development of theories that capture the essence of human phenomena. It is a method where researchers investigate a phenomenon or event by describing and interpreting participants' lived experiences, such as how older persons experience aging and the meaning of work and money. It seeks to understand and describe the essence of these experiences as they are lived and perceived by individuals themselves, rather than through preconceived theories or interpretations.

Narrative The narrative tradition subsumes a group of designs that rely on the spoken or written words or visual representation of individuals. These designs typically focus on the lives of individuals as told through their own stories; they examine how stories are told to understand how participants perceive and make sense of their experiences. The narrative method involves the collection and analysis of stories or narratives shared by individuals to understand their experiences, perspectives, and meanings attributed to certain events or phenomena. It seeks to understand and interpret these by allowing participants to share their stories and perspectives in their own words, providing a rich and nuanced understanding of various phenomena, such as trauma, illness, and migration. When using the narrative method to develop theory, the process is focused on identifying patterns and themes within the collected narratives to construct a theoretical framework.

6.4 Mixed Methods Research Designs

Mixed methods research is an approach that combines both quantitative and qualitative research methods within a single study to gain a more comprehensive and nuanced understanding of a research problem or question. In mixed methods studies, investigators intentionally integrate quantitative and qualitative data rather than keeping them separate.

6.4.1 Purpose and Use

The basic idea underscoring this approach is that the integration of quantitative and qualitative data maximizes the strengths and minimizes the weaknesses of each type of data, thus allowing researchers to capitalize on the unique strengths of the two approaches while compensating for their respective limitations. Mixed methods research is becoming increasingly popular as a research approach, allowing for a deeper exploration of a research question by utilizing a blend of qualitative and quantitative data. It can answer complex research queries that cannot be solved with either qualitative or quantitative research. But using mixed methods does not simply mean doing two studies using different methods, one qualitative and another quantitative study separately. Mixed methods research goes beyond a mere collection of qualitative data through interviews or assembling diverse forms of qualitative evidence, such as observations and interviews, or multiple types of quantitative evidence, like surveys and diagnostic tests. It encompasses purposeful gathering of both quantitative and qualitative data, harnessing the unique strengths of each to address research inquiries. And it suggests the integration of the two methods in order to better answer a research question.

The research questions suitable for mixed methods require both quantitative and qualitative research, such as "How does a blue color worker's perception of life after retirement (qualitative) help explain levels of their monthly investments in retirement accounts (quantitative)?" Following are additional examples of research questions that mixed methods research can address:

- To what extent does change in sales of 7–11 stores (*quantitative*) reflect customer perceptions of these stores (*qualitative*) in Bangkok?
- How do sales persons' perceptions of their job description (*qualitative*) relate to differences in their performance (*quantitative*)?
- How do people's experiences of their health club membership during a trial period (*qualitative*) explain their intentions to become regular members of facility X (*quantitative*)?
- How do young people's beliefs about global warming (qualitative) help explain their levels of green product consumption (quantitative)?

However, the mixed method research design can also be used on a post hoc basis to help explain emerged and unexpected findings. Empirically established linkages in a theoretical model can be used to help interpret qualitative data. For example, Minowa and Belk (2020) used qualitative data to illustrate the relationships among variables in Moschis' (2019) conceptual life course model. They helped better understand the model's empirically supported linkages between early-life experiences of traumatic events and consumer behaviors in the context of romantic gift-giving of mature Japanese consumers.

Furthermore, findings from quantitative studies can be used to help understand findings from qualitative studies. For example, in one of my seminars for supermarket executives, several Florida CEOs could not understand the reason(s) their weekly sales were unchanged after introducing special "senior days" with deep discounts, observing increase in the number of older customers during these days, and hearing older shoppers in focus groups saying that they were shopping on senior days. One of our surveys at the Center for Mature Consumer Studies (CMCS) had revealed that the various types of sales promotion offerings would not motivate older shoppers to switch stores, but they would make them switch only the days of their weekly shopping.

6.4.2 Types of Mixed Methods Research Designs

There are several types of mixed methods research designs, each with its own unique characteristics and purposes. The design of a mixed methods study usually can take one of the following forms: convergent parallel, embedded, explanatory sequential, and exploratory sequential, fully integrated, and multiphase.

Convergent Parallel In a convergent parallel design, quantitative and qualitative data are collected concurrently and analyzed separately. After both analyses are completed and conclusions are drawn, they are compared to draw a general conclusion. The goal is to compare and contrast the findings to look for convergence, divergence, or complementarity between the two data types. The results can provide a more robust understanding of the research question. For example, in assessing the effectiveness of reduced prices offered to store X's older shoppers on "senior days," an investigator could conduct depth interviews with older shoppers during the week of these promotions are offered and also examine store records that show sales volume on different days of the same week. He or she can then relate the conclusions of one method to those reached by the other to determine the extent to which the "senior days" promotion is effective.

Explanatory Sequential In this type of mixed research, the investigator first collects and analyzes quantitative data. This is followed by gathering and analyzing qualitative data. This approach best applies to a research problem where researchers believe the qualitative data will explain the results from the analyses of quantitative data. The emphasis is on using qualitative data to explain or elaborate upon the quantitative findings. This design should be used when qualitative data are likely to be needed in order to contextualize and explain the findings of the quantitative study. This design is sometimes referred to as "QUAN → QUAL."

This design is particularly useful when quantitative data alone cannot fully address the research question or when unexpected results need further exploration. For example, if a researcher wants to determine the extent to which discounts to older shoppers on "senior days" a store has recently begun to offer increase a store's sales (an empirical question), he or she could first use a time-series experiment (Shandish et al., 2002) to examine store sales figures for every day of the week for a few weeks and compare sales figures for the days that these promotions are offered to figures for the remaining days of the week, and he or she could also examine and compare weekly sales figures across weeks. In order to determine the reason(s) for the observed increase in sales during "senior days," whether they reflect sales from new patrons or additional spending by existing customers or simply change in their shopping habits during the week (a theoretical question), the researcher could do in-depth interviews with older shoppers during "senior days" to help understand differences in sales volume and answer the main (empirical) research question.

Exploratory Sequential This mixed methods design is inverse to the explanatory sequential. In this design, researchers first collect and analyze qualitative data that lead to one or more quantitative studies. This type of mixed methods research is used when there is a reason to believe that a topic needs to be adequately explored before collecting any quantitative data. This design is sometimes referred to as "QUAL → QUAN." It is often used when little is known about a research area, and qualitative data can help generate hypotheses and formulate research problems. There are several reasons the exploratory sequential design is used. For example, exploratory research in the form of review of literature and theories relevant to the topic can help formulate research questions and lead to hypothesis development that could be tested using a quantitative study. Exploratory research in the form of depth interviews and focus groups also can provide useful information for developing instruments (e.g., questionnaires and their contents) and for identifying the relevant domains of psychological constructs (e.g., Churchill & Brown, 2004) that are to be used in a subsequent quantitative study.

Embedded/Nested Design The embedded design, also known as "nested design," is when the quantitative and qualitative data are collected concurrently, but one type of data takes precedence over the other. Secondary data are collected and analyzed to provide additional insights or context; they are typically used to validate or triangulate the primary data. Integration occurs by using the secondary data to enhance or support the primary data findings. The conclusions reached by analyzing the data set of the main (primary) research design are better explained, understood or supported by results from the secondary data set. For example, when Moore and Lutz (2000) attempted to determine advertising's impact in conjunction with children's product usage experiences and found these influences to differ between younger and older children, they used data from in-depth interviews to gain insights into these age differences in order to understand of how older and younger children relate to advertisements and product consumption. These researchers employed an embedded design, using qualitative data to understand, strengthen, or supplement conclusions from their primary (experimental) design.

Fully Integrated Design In this design, qualitative and quantitative data are collected concurrently and are fully integrated during data analysis and interpretation. The goal is to create a comprehensive and holistic understanding of the research problem by merging both types of data from the outset.

Multiphase Design This type of design involves multiple phases of data collection, where each phase builds upon the previous one. Researchers may start with a qualitative phase, followed by a quantitative phase, and then further qualitative or quantitative phases as needed. It allows for iterative exploration of the research question.

The choice of a specific mixed methods design depends on the research question, the objectives of the study, and the resources available. As researchers formulate their research questions, they should try to directly address whether qualitative and quantitative methods should be combined in their study. If the research question can be sufficiently answered by either quantitative or qualitative research alone, a mixed methods approach may not be needed. Researchers must carefully consider how to blend qualitative and quantitative approaches to enhance the overall rigor and validity of their research

6.5 Evaluation of Approaches

As both types of approaches to research (qualitative and quantitative) have much to offer, it is in the best interest of early academic researchers to develop the skills required for conducting effectual research in both areas. Besides learning to do both types of research, it is equally important to learn when to use each type and when one should use a specific "mixed methods" research design.

6.5.1 Positivistic

Quantitative research is a mode of inquiry that is employed often to develop knowledge deductively, when the research question calls for hypothesis testing, measuring or describing a known concept or phenomenon, and estimating parameters of factors. It calls for estimating measurable variables and relationships among them that can be generalized to larger populations and facilitate the comparison of groups. Quantitative research has the potential to provide measurable evidence that can be used in theory building by testing hypotheses for the purpose of falsifying relationships between variables or for establishing probable causal relationships between them. Because the positivistic approach relies on the scientific process (Hunt, 1983), where quantitative methods are used, it produces results that can be replicated and generalizable, creating the perception that they are more reliable than results of the humanistic approach.

Positivistic inquiry involves assumptions that often fail to live up to reality, such as the belief that the researcher and phenomenon are independent and the experiment can be done regardless of human emotion and that there is a single (objective) reality. Perhaps the main drawback of the positivist approach is the potential of error in every quantitative study. Errors can occur at every stage in the scientific process, from statement of the research question to the interpretation of the emerged results. First, the possibility of error can be in the statement of the research question or problem because of the wrong assumption that can lead to the wrong hypothesis and affect the entire research study. For example, if the researcher wishes to explain the demographic "phenomenon" of high concentration of older population in Florida, he or she could make an error in incorrectly stating the research question: "Why do older people move to Florida?" The researcher could then decide to do a focus group or in-depth interviews with older persons who recently moved to Florida to determine the relevant theory, variables, and hypotheses that should be investigated in a quantitative survey of a large sample of people with the same characteristics drawn from every State of the Union. He or she may, for example, hypothesize a positive relationship between the older person's preference for a warm climate and his or her likelihood to move to Florida or another sun-belt state. Errors in stating research questions usually occur because the researcher is not very familiar with the phenomenon, hence the reason for exploratory research in the form of published documents (e.g., Census data, articles), because such information would have revealed that only 5% of the older population moves to a different place after retirement and other states like Pennsylvania and Iowa have almost equally high percentages of older residents. Based on this information, the researcher could have conducted focus groups or depth interviews with younger adults who had moved out of these three states and used results to reframe the research question as: "Why do younger people move out of certain states?" This would have produced a completely different study and set of findings. Thus, inadequate knowledge about a topic and incorrect interpretation of the available information can lead to errors in the statement of the research question.

Another major source of error in quantitative studies derives from selecting participants for the study and obtaining information from them. As only a relatively small number of elements (participants) are selected from the universe for cross-sectional and experimental studies, four types of error can occur in the selection process: frame, selection, nonresponses, and sampling error. *Frame or noncoverage error* arises because of failure to include some elements of the defined population in the sampling frame—i.e., the list from which the participants are selected. *Selection error* can occur when some elements of the population have a greater likelihood of being included in the study. *Nonresponse error* arises because of failure to obtain information from elements of the population that were selected for the study. *Sampling error* is the difference between the value of a variable that was estimated from the responses of participants and the actual value of the variable that can be estimated based on the total population that is represented by the study participants.

Additional errors can occur in the process of obtaining information from the participants of a cross-sectional study or experiment. These errors are mainly due to the instrument used and are known as "*measurement errors.*" They can be the result of improperly designed instrument (e.g., questions, scale) that contains ambiguous questions, as well as invalid and unreliable scales. Measurement errors can also arise from the respondent's inability or unwillingness to provide accurate responses, and they can also arise because of the researcher's inability to obtain accurate responses. Podsakoff et al. (2003) offer a comprehensive discussion of measurement errors due to these and other factors.

Processing errors are errors that occur after data collection, such as editing, coding, data entry, programming, and data analysis. Finally, errors can arise in the process of explaining the findings. These are known as "errors of explanation" because the researcher makes statements about his or her findings that are largely invalid or are not supported by the study findings. For example, stating that a course was effective in creating knowledge would be invalid in the absence of a control group or proper basis for comparing the course's effectiveness (e.g., compare to other similar courses, students who did not take the course). Similarly, stating or implying that laboratory findings apply to the real world would not be valid. The most common mistake a novice researcher makes is to make definitive statements about causality based on hypothesis confirmation even in cross-sectional studies, such as "variable X affects variable Y," when the conditions for establishing causality were not met in the study (see Chap. 3).

Thus, despite merit in quantitative studies, one is never certain about the validity of the emerged findings in part because of the magnitude of errors that may have occurred during the research process. Of all possible sources of error, only sampling error can be estimated, and in most cases, the estimate of this error is of little value to the researcher interested in hypothesis testing (other than showing variable variance). The magnitude and incidence of these errors can only be reduced rather than totally eliminated. Churchill and Brown (2004) suggest methods of identifying and reducing many of these errors in surveys. With respect to specific types of measurement errors, Podsakoff and associates (2003) provide guidelines helpful in reducing the likelihood of occurrence of these errors and their effects in cross-sectional studies. Similarly, Sawyer (1975) suggest procedures for reducing demand artifacts in laboratory studies (strategies for reducing measurement errors and demand artifacts are presented in Chap. 7). While efforts to reduce various forms of error can be costly and time consuming, at a very minimum, early career researchers should do pretesting of their questionnaires and experiments (see ***Pretesting questionnaires and experiments*** in Chap. 7).

6.5.2 Humanistic

A significant advantage of qualitative research lies in its concentration on the contexts and significance of human lives and experiences, primarily for the purpose of conducting inductive research or research leading to theory development. Qualitative data play a crucial role in aiding researchers in comprehending processes, particularly those that evolve gradually, and offer intricate insights into the surrounding settings or contexts. Qualitative research generally focuses primarily on processes rather than outcomes, which are "complex and underdetermined" (Belk et al., 2013:

153). This suggests caution in making interpretations that lead to the identification of concepts that may be reifications, not only because qualitative data are subject to the interpreter's subjective evaluations but also because the implied links among elements, processes, and outcomes cannot be objectively verified. Yet, an inherent advantage of qualitative methods is the identification of concepts for which measures do not exist.

If one accepts the argument that scientific knowledge should (a) be independent of time and context, (b) not allow for different meanings of its concepts or their relationships, and (c) be testable (replicable) (Hunt, 1983), one wonders about the value of knowledge produced by qualitative studies. The mere fact that qualitative researchers often consider themselves "instruments" in research because their observations, interpretations, and analyses are filtered through their own personal lens raises issues of the reliability and validity of their findings. And while dependability (i.e., data interpretation by more than one researcher) is offered as a criterion for assessing the reliability of their interpretations, there is no objective test analogous to Cronbach's coefficient alpha or acceptable level of inter-interpreters' agreement, such as Cohen's kappa (inter-rater reliability) coefficient, unless the interpretations are coded into categories. The "benefit" of gaining different insights into a phenomenon because of investigators' personal differences in experiences undermines theory development. As qualitative research deviates from rigidity, it creates its own problems when it comes to theory development. Specifically, the interpretive perspective does not provide guidelines for understanding relationships between qualitative and quantitative methodology, or among data instruments or theories. Nor does the approach enable us to adjudicate between rival interpretations of the world. Moody (1988) points out a danger inherent to the interpretive perspective: "The danger here is that qualitative methods inspired by the humanities could simply result in further fragmentation and could deepen the spreading relativism in our view of social reality" (p. 24).

It is worth noting, however, that this approach to theory build implies time-dependencies and causality because it describes the process(es) from events that lead to certain outcomes. And researchers rely on informants' ability to reconstruct the events and process(es), which can be problematic, in part because the study of processes require the study of changes over unspecified lengths of time. In fact, much of the qualitative work relies on informants' ability to provide information about their past in the form of events, emotions, and attitudes. While there are few objective criteria for confirming the validity of such information in qualitative studies, research indicates that individuals can reliably recall significant life events, such as marriage, graduation, and retirement, regardless of their age or life stage (Rodgers & Herzog, 1987).

However, the recollection of less important events seems to decline at monthly rates ranging from 2 to 5 percent (Tausig, 1982), with telescoping error (i.e., the fact that most people recall events that occurred more recently than they actually did), and recall loss (forgetting that an event happened at all) compounding this problem (Churchill & Brown, 2004). Therefore, the precision of recall assessments concerning experiences from earlier in life, particularly when gauging psychological constructs, becomes a concern. Longitudinal studies investigating the dependability of psychological measures on an annual basis reveal that these measures lose reliability when evaluated for periods exceeding 2 years in the distant past (Henry et al., 1994). Comparatively, measures taken over time intervals are generally more dependable, albeit more challenging and costly to acquire, when compared to retrospective measures. Nevertheless, recent advancements in methodological approaches, including the utilization of sophisticated data-gathering tools like the life grid method (Blane, 1996), the structure of autobiographical memory, and the event history calendar (e.g., Axim et al., 1999; Belli, 1998), have enhanced the precision of retrospective measures. Although the use of longitudinal qualitative designs help overcome such weakness, these methods are hardly seen in qualitative studies due to the required time, cost, and analytic skills (Hermanowicz, 2016).

6.5.3 Mixed Methods Research

Mixed methods research designs capitalize upon the strengths of quantitative and qualitative approaches, enriching and deepening understanding of quantitative results with qualitative data and validating qualitative findings with quantitative data. This approach offers more flexibility in designing research because it is not tied to established research paradigms, allowing the combination of theory development and hypothesis testing in a single project. And to the extent quantitative and qualitative results converge, a process known as "triangulation," they add credibility to the study's conclusions.

Mixed methods research is particularly useful when there are conflicting or differing results in different studies on a particular topic. For example, a review of studies that investigated older consumers' responses to money-saving incentives (e.g., senior discounts, "sales" promotions) revealed conflicting findings. Some studies have revealed that, compared to younger consumers, older consumers are deal-prone and would switch brands to take advantage of the "deals," while other studies had shown that older consumers were more brand loyal and less likely to switch brands because of money-saving offers. Thus, even when the results from different studies using the same or different approach differ, differences in the findings provide opportunities for more discoveries. A mixed methods research approach was employed by our team at CMCS to help resolve these differences. Depth interviews with a small number of shoppers revealed that these shoppers had well-established "relationships" with more than one brand in various product categories, and they would switch from one of these brands to another to take advantage of special offers, making them appear both brand loyal and deal-prone. A follow-up cross-sectional survey with a large national sample confirmed this explanation, finding that the largest majority of study participants would buy one of their preferred brands, but not an unknown brand, in response to these promotional offers. Thus, the mixed methods research design helped us understand and contextualize conflicting findings of previous studies, and it helped us integrate qualitative and quantitative results by merging the two types of data to conclude and generalize the relationship between age and consumer response to money-saving incentives in different contexts.

Although mixed methods research appears superior to either quantitative or qualitative research, it has inherent drawbacks that often limit its use. It is more expensive to conduct and takes more time. And the adequate discussion of the methods and results, which is expected by journals and their reviewers in order to favorably evaluate one's manuscript, results in lengthy manuscripts that take more journal space; they adversely affect length-to-contribution ratio, which is often a criterion for manuscript evaluation, and affect publication likelihood. And a single investigator, in most cases, is not likely to have the skills required to effectively execute both quantitative and qualitative studies, in part, because the vast majority of researchers nowadays are likely to have received training in, and subscribe to, one of the two main research philosophies. As quantitative and qualitative methods become increasingly sophisticated and demanding, early career researchers must spend a considerable amount of time learning state-of-the-art research skills. Lastly, when findings do not converge, additional resources might be needed to help resolve the differences that could be the result of error or inadequate training and skills.

Most academic researchers tend to subscribe to either positivistic or humanistic paradigm in seeking knowledge, not only because of their philosophical orientations but also because their skills and abilities to publish are better aligned with one of these two paradigms. Researchers who contemplate using mixed methods research designs should either attempt to develop or brush up on their qualitative and quantitative skills. Alternatively, they should collaborate with researchers who have the knowledge and required skills to effectively execute the different designs. Because journal reviewers tend to be experts in increasingly specialized areas and methods used, manuscripts should accordingly meet higher standards, especially with regard to methods used.

Traditional methods of data analysis become increasingly obsolete, as new methods and software become available and more appropriate for answering research questions, forcing authors to demonstrate state-of-the-art skills and knowledge throughout the research process. For example, reviewers may challenge the assumption that all participants of a study are equally affected by factors included in a model and request an SEM analysis among subpopulations and latent subgroup mixture models to account for differences (Jedidi et al., 1997). Similarly, Cox regression may be more appropriate for multivariate analysis in some situations, as this analytic method outperforms traditional techniques, including OLS regression, logit, probit, and discriminant analysis (Fraser et al., 1994). And the traditional approach to testing for mediation (Baron & Kenny, 1986) is not as effective when compared to other methods (Mackinnon et al., 2002; Pieters, 2007) and available software packages. For example, Hayes' PROCESS macro for SPSS (Hayes, 2018) allows the test of a moderated mediation model (Clement & Bradley-Garcia, 2022) and the estimation of direct and indirect effects in single and multiple mediator models (parallel and serial), two- and three-way interactions in moderation models, and conditional indirect effects in moderated mediation models with single or multiple mediators or moderators.

References

Alford, R. R. (1998). *The craft of inquiry*. Oxford.

Axim, W. G., Pierce, L., & Ghimire, D. (1999). Innovations in life history calendar applications. *Social Science Research, 28*(3), 243–264.

Baron, R., & Kenny, D. (1986). The moderator-mediator variable distinction in social psychological research. *Journal of Personality and Social Psychology, 51*, 1173–1182.

Belk, R., Fischer, E., & Kozinets, R. V. (2013). *Qualitative consumer & marketing research*. Sage.

Belli, R. F. (1998). The structure of autobiographical memory and the event history calendar: Potential improvements in the quality of retrospective reports in surveys. *Memory, 6*(4), 383–406.

Blane, D. B. (1996). Collecting retrospective data: Development of a reliable method and a pilot study of its use. *Social Science & Medicine, 42*(5), 751–757.

Churchill, G. A., & Brown, T. J. (2004). *Basic marketing research* (5th ed.). South-Western.

Clement, L. M., & Bradley-Garcia, M. (2022). A step-by-step tutorial for performing a moderated mediation analysis using process. *The Quantitative Methods for Psychology, 18*(3), 258–271. https://doi.org/10.20982/tqmp.18.3.p258

Creswell, J. W., & Poth, C. N. (2017). *Qualitative inquiry and Research design: Choosing among five approaches* (4th ed.). Sage.

Fraser, M. W., Jenson, J. M., Kiefer, D., & Popuang, C. (1994). Statistical methods for the analysis of critical life events. *Social Work Research, 18*(3), 163–177.

Goodman, J. K., & Paolacci, G. (2007). Crowdsourcing consumer research. *Journal of Consumer Research, 44*(1), 196–210.

Hayes, A. F. (2018). *Introduction to mediation, moderation, and conditional process analysis: A regression-based approach* (2nd ed.). Guilford Press.

Henry, B., Moffitt, T. E., Caspi, A., Langley, J., & Silva, P. A. (1994). On the 'remembrance of things past': A Longitudinal evaluation of the retrospective method. *Personality Assessment, 6*(2), 92–101.

Hermanowicz, J. C. (2016). Longitudinal qualitative research. In M. L. Shanahan, J. T. Mortimer, & M. K. Johnson (Eds.), *Handbook of the life course* (Vol. II, pp. 491–514). Springer.

Hirschman, E. C. (1986). Humanistic inquiry in marketing research: Philosophy, method, and criteria. *Journal of Marketing Research, 23*(August), 237–249.

Hunt, S. D. (1983). *Marketing theory: The philosophy of marketing science*. Irwin Publishing Company.

Jedidi, K., Jagpal, H. S., & DeSarbo, W. S. (1997). Finite mixture structural equation models for response-based segmentation and unobserved heterogeneity. *Marketing Science, 16*(1), 39–59.

Lee, E., Mathur, A., Fatt, C. K., & Moschis, G. P. (2012). The timing and context of consumer decisions: Insights from the life course paradigm. *Marketing Letters, 23*(3), 793–805.

Mackinnon, D. P., Lockwood, C. M., Hoffman, J. M., West, S. G., & Sheets, V. A. (2002). A comparison of methods to test mediation and other intervening variables. *Psychological Methods, 7*(1), 83–104.

Mathur, A., Moschis, G. P., & Lee, E. (2008). A Longitudinal study of the effects of life status changes on changes in consumer preferences. *Journal of the Academy of Marketing Science, 36*(2), 234–246.

Minowa, Y. & Belk, R.W. (2020). Qualitative approaches to life course research: Linking life story to gift giving, *Journal of Global Scholars of Marketing Science, 30*(1), 60–75, https://doi.org/10.1080/21639159.2019.1613905

Moody, H. R. (1988). Toward a critical gerontology: The contribution of humanities to theories of aging. In J. E. Birren & V. I. Bengston (Eds.), *Emergent theories of aging* (pp. 19–40). Springer.

Moore, E. S., & Lutz, R. J. (2000). Children, advertising, and product experiences: A multimethod inquiry. *Journal of Consumer Research, 27*(1), 31–48. https://doi.org/10.1086/314307

Moschis, G. P. (2019). *Consumer behavior over the life course: Research frontiers and new directions*. Springer Publishing, Inc.

Moschis, G. P., & Moore, R. L. (1982). A longitudinal study of television advertising effects. *JouLee, Ernal of Consumer Research, 9*, 279–287.

Pieters, R. (2007). Meaningful mediation analysis: Plausible causal inference and informative communication. *Journal of Consumer Research, 44*(3, October 2017), 692–716. https://doi.org/10.1093/jcr/ucx081

Podsakoff, P. M., MacKenzie, S. B., Lee, J. Y., & Podsakoff, N. P. (2003). Common method biases in behavioral research: A critical review of the literature and recommended remedies. *Journal of Applied Psychology, 88*(5), 879–903.

Rodgers, W., & Herzog, A. R. (1987). Interviewing older adults: The accuracy of factual information. *Journal of Gerontology, 42*(4), 387–394.

Sawyer, A. G. (1975). Demand artifacts in laboratory experiments in consumer research. *Journal of Consumer Research, 1*(4), 20–30.

Shadish, W. R., Cook, T. D., & Campbell, D. T. (2002). *Experimental and quasi-experimental designs for generalized causal inference*. Houghton, Mifflin and Company.

Tausig, M. (1982). Measuring life events. *Journal Health and Social Behavior, 23*(1), 52–64.

Wessling, S. K., Huber, L., & Netzer, O. (2017). MTurk character misrepresentation: Assessment and solutions. *Journal of Consumer Research, 44*(1), 211–230. https://doi.org/10.1093/jcr/ucx053

7 Research Settings and Procedures

7.1 Quantitative Studies

7.1.1 Surveys

Sampling A common question or concern is about the proper *sample size* that should be drawn. The required sample size is based on several factors, including the type(s) of analysis, variable measurement, and general study objectives. For example, for multivariate analyses (e.g., multiple regression, factor analysis), the common rule of thumb is that a sample size should be ten times larger than the total number of variables analyzed. If the investigator is interested in subgroup analyses (e.g., investigating relationships among age groups), larger numbers of subgroups would require larger samples, especially in studies that do not contain sampling quotas for subgroups. In structural equation modeling (SEM), the sample size depends on the number of variables or indicators and model fit; it could be as low as two to three times the number of variables if there is a good fit. The important factor in hypothesis or model testing is to use samples that can produce sufficient variance in the distribution of variable values. If the distribution of the values on variables is highly skewed, larger samples might be needed to obtain adequate distribution of values (e.g., via transformation of variable values). As a rule of thumb, for hypothesis testing involving two variables and estimation of reliability Alpha, a few hundred elements are needed (about 300, according to Nunnally 1967). Three to five hundred would be adequate for all practical purposes. And using larger samples would be counterproductive and dangerous, unless subgroup analyses are required. Very large sample sizes tend to produce significant relationships between variables, when such relationships actually do not exist.

Types of Samples Another question related to sampling concerns the *type of sample* that should be drawn. Generally, there are two types of samples: probability samples, where every element in the parent population has an equal and known

G. P. Moschis, *Academic Research in Business and the Social Sciences*,
https://doi.org/10.1007/978-3-031-56548-9_7

chance to be included in the sample, and nonprobability, which can be drawn based on factors such as availability and convenience and where elements have an unknown and unequal chance to be included in the sample. Although investigators normally attempt to obtain a probability sample and even identify elements of the population that would make up this sample, it is rather rare this will happen (unless all elements identified can be included in the sample). But it is very likely that some elements of the population (e.g., individuals, dealers, stores) will not be included in the sample for various reasons, such as unwillingness to participate in the study. And this raises the issue of sample representativeness, as the sample obtained may not accurately represent the characteristics of the sample population. Generally, the larger the number of elements the investigator wants to be included in the sample but are excluded, the higher the concern with sample representativeness. For example, response rates in cross-sectional studies based on surveys are in single digits, raising questions about sample representativeness.

Even when one wishes to work with probability samples and does everything possible to obtain such samples (e.g., increase in response rate via multiple mailings or calls), the investigator most likely will be working with *nonprobability samples*. As a precaution against criticism, the researcher should show that he or she has made every effort possible to obtain a sample representative of the population of interest or ascertain that the sample represents the parent population. One acceptable method to do this is by comparing early respondents to late respondents where the data collection method used allows for such a comparison. For example, in mail surveys where all questionnaires are sent out to respondents on approximately the same date, returned questionnaires can be marked on the dates they are received; and based on the total number of questionnaires returned, they can be classified as "early" (usually consisting of one-third of all questionnaire returned early) and "late" (usually consisting of one-third of all questionnaires received late). Because it has been shown in studies that late respondents are similar to nonrespondents, statistical tests of group comparison should be performed to determine the extent to which the two subsamples differ, not so much in terms of values on variables but mainly on relationships between the hypothesized variables. Thus, hypothesis testing is required for each of the subgroup; hence, the reason sample sizes of 300–500 are suggested. But the important thing to keep in mind is not the representativeness of the sample but the needed variance on variables in the hypotheses. Normally, low participation rates in cross-sectional studies that may produce nonprobability samples may not be as serious, as long as sufficient variance in variables can be obtained, unless the sample is highly idiosyncratic (Churchill & Iacobucci, 2005), as in the case of panels.

Panels Several recommendations are in order for designing panel studies for academic purposes. First, the initial sample size should be rather large. For example, jn planning a longitudinal study at CMCS, we used two samples of 10,000 adults that produced an average of 17% response rates, with half of them agreeing to participate in follow-up studies (or about 850 respondents per survey). Five years later, only about 40% of those who agreed actually completed surveys, resulting in an average sample size of 340. Second, anonymity is extremely important. As all of our CMCS surveys were anonymous, in the same studies we asked those who completed surveys the first time to let us know of their interest in participating in a follow-up survey by providing us with their names, date of birth and addresses on a pre-paid postcard that was mailed with the first survey, and asking them to mail it separately from their completed survey. This ensured respondent anonymity. And because we were using date of birth to determine the person's exact chronological age, we were able to match the two questionnaires for the same respondent from his or her date of birth and gender (only a couple of respondents had the same birthday), keeping study participants anonymous.

7.1.2 Experiments

Normally, experiments are conducted in two different types of settings. Laboratory and natural or real-life settings. In laboratory settings, because the experimenter has greater control over the variables whose effects wishes to determine, the emerged results (effects) are most likely the cause of variable manipulation; and they are said to be "internally valid." However, there are factors that by themselves could produce changes in the test scores that might be mistaken for the result of variable manipulation (experimental treatment) within the experimental setting. These factors are known as *sources of invalidity* or *threats to internal validity* and are the following:

- *History*. History refers to the flow of events taking place outside the experiment which might change the participants' awareness of, or reaction to, the subject under investigation; they can affect most, if not all, of the persons involved in the research study. The longer the time lapse between O1 and O2, the greater the possible effects of history on the measured change.
- *Maturation*. Maturation refers to all those biological or psychological processes that systematically affect people with the passage of time independent of specific outside events, such as growing older, hungrier, more bored, and tired.
- *Testing*. Testing refers to learning or mental conditioning of the test units, which arises as a result of a pretest or first measurement; it is the reaction to the pretest or first measurement. Therefore, it is important to avoid situations where pretesting procedures have a reactive effect that sensitizes the respondents or changes their responses.
- *Instrumentation* (or measurement variation). This refers to the change in the measurement instrument used in the two measurements, which might account for the differences found.
- *Statistical Regression*. Statistical regression is the phenomenon of measurement scores "shifting" toward the mean in a retesting as a result of choosing (or including) people who expressed attitudes and/or behavior that were at "extremes" during the first test.

- *Selection*. Selection is when one group might well have differed even without the occurrence of the experimental treatment as a result, for example, of the characteristics of that group (e.g., self-selection during the recruitment).
- *Mortality*. Mortality refers to the loss of some subjects between the before and after measurements. It is usually ignored but it must be considered when the mortality rate is different between experimental and control groups.

External Validity Questions about external validity deal with interactions. Interaction is the situation where the effect of one factor depends upon the particular level of another factor. *Threats to external validity* arise from the possibility that one cannot legitimately extrapolate from a set of experimental conditions. How much should one be concerned with external validity? The answer depends on what is at stake—i.e., the significance of the decision to be made based on the findings of the experimental study. When the decision involves large sums of money or major considerations, the projectability of the experimental findings to mass untested population is of greater significance.

Researchers conducting experimental studies, reviewers of academic papers, as well potential users of information based on experimental studies should be familiar not only with factors that may produce invalid results in an experiment but also with methods that help reduce them and, generally, with the main ingredients of the experiment method. In the sections that follow, I briefly discuss the reasons these experiments are conducted. I outline how experiments are conducted and, finally, I briefly discuss methods that are often used to help reduce the potential of obtaining invalid results from experimental studies. More details on these topics are available in other sources (e.g., Sawyer, 1975; Shadish et al., 2002).

Objectives of Experiments Experiments are mainly conducted for the purpose of establishing a causal relationship between two variables. As briefly mentioned in Chap. 3, three conditions must be met in order to establish a "cause-and-effect" relationship: (a) concomitant variation, that is, variation in the intensity of one variable (hypothesized to be the "causal" factor) results in parallel variation in another variable whose value is determined by the first variable. To the extent that this association is statistically significant, it serves as a basis for inferring, not proving, a causal relationship. Hypotheses tested based on data from surveys simply reveal whether there is an association between the variables in the hypothesized relationship to conclude the presence of potential causality. But experiments go a step further to test for the presence of the second condition that is required for inferring causality—i.e., (b) time order of occurrence. This condition puts restrictions on the timing of the changes in the two variables. If one variable is the cause of another, change in the cause variable must occur prior to the change in the effect variable. (c) Elimination of all other possible causes or factors that can affect outcome variable is the third condition that must be met. Proving the causal effect of a variable requires knowledge of and the ability to eliminate all possible explanations other than the cause variable under consideration. This condition is essentially impossible to meet, as proving that the cause of the outcome variable is the sole result of one specific factor defies logic.

When conducting an experiment, the investigator normally has two main goals: first, to accomplish the study's objectives, and, second, to control for factors that can contaminate the emerged findings. Not every experimental design is suitable for addressing every research objective and allows the investigator to control for factors that are threats to validity.

At this stage, it is worth mentioning how threats to validity can be significantly reduced, if not totally eliminated. To begin with, randomization—i.e., selecting or assigning units to groups randomly—can control for possible effects of regression, self-selection, and instrumentation. If we assume that certain extraneous variables might operate in an experimental situation but we cannot specify them, then we may assume that these extraneous variables will be "randomized out"—i.e., will equally affect both the experimental and control groups. The effects of history can be controlled by making observations for both experimental and control groups at the same time. And one can assume that maturation and testing effects are present in both groups equally the same. Finally, interaction, which refers to the combined effects of two or more independent variables, is mainly a threat to external validity.

Design of the experiment is the stage that includes a number of decisions that must be made in order to test the hypothesized relationship(s). It includes decisions on variable *measurement*, whether to use mechanical measures (e.g., eye movement), verbal measures (e.g., spoken or written responses), or direct measures (e.g., sales volume), and the selection of appropriate control techniques. Two other important decisions at this stage are as follows: selecting an *experimental design*, the specific plan for research, such as those mentioned in the previous chapter, and *variable manipulation*, the intentional variation in the independent variable (usually in the form of physical change), which is known as "experimental treatment."

Procedures and Ingredients of Experiments Unlike surveys that are designed to describe relationships between variables, experiments go a step further by attempting to establish a cause-and-effect relationship. In designing an experimental study, the first step is a *statement of the problem or research question*, which is usually a statement that concerns the relationship between two or more variables, such as "what is the effect or influence of variable X on variable Y?" The next step is *hypothesis formulation*, which is a tentative statement about the nature of the relationship between two or more variables, such as variable X has a positive effect on variable Y. Hypotheses in experiments, as in other research designs, are formulated after examination of existing theories and/or evidence in the form of empirical regularities (e.g., uncovered relationships between variables in previous surveys, interpretation of qualitative data) that provide reasonable justification for the hypothesized relationships. Prior to designing the experiment, the investigator must *define the variables* involved in the hypothesized relationship.

A key area of decisions in an experiment concerns the *experimental procedures*—i.e., the approach the experimenter must take at each stage of the data collection process They include decisions concerning the experimental design, setting and physical arrangements, needed apparatus and their operations, greeting the subjects, instructions, data collection forms, and debriefing the subjects. After these decisions are made, the experimenter can conduct the experiment, analyze the results, and write up the report or develop a manuscript aimed at a specific journal. To summarize, key decisions in experiments include the following.

1. *Experimental Design:*
   - *Type of Experimental Design.* Specify the type of experimental design you plan to use (e.g., pretest-posttest control group, Solomon four-group design—see Chap. 6).
   - *Experimental Variables.* Clearly define the independent variable(s)—i.e., the factor(s) you will manipulate or treatments and dependent variable(s) (the outcome(s) you will measure).
   - *Experimental Conditions.* Describe the different experimental conditions or groups, if applicable.
   - *Control Variables.* Identify any control variables or factors that you will hold constant or control for in your experiment.
2. *Participants:*
   - Detail the characteristics of your participants, including demographics (e.g., age, gender) and any specific criteria for inclusion or exclusion.
   - Describe the sampling method and the anticipated sample size.
3. *Procedure:*
   - Provide a step-by-step description of how the experiment will be conducted, including any materials or equipment to be used.
   - Explain how participants will be assigned to different experimental conditions (randomization or matching).
   - Variable manipulation (ensuring significant change or difference in the independent variable, usually via a "manipulation check").
   - Describe any informed consent procedures and ethical considerations.
   - Debriefing.

Reducing Demand Artifacts Demand artifacts are unintended cues or signals that participants may pick up on, leading them to adjust their behavior in response to what they believe is expected of them. Reducing demand artifacts in laboratory experiments is crucial for obtaining accurate and reliable results. The following are several strategies to minimize demand artifacts in your laboratory experiments (for greater elaboration of several of them, see Sawyer, 1975):

- Implement double-blind procedures whenever possible. This involves keeping both the participants and the experimenters unaware of critical aspects of the study, such as the experimental conditions or hypotheses. This helps eliminate unintentional cues from experimenters that could influence participants' behavior.
- Develop clear and standardized instructions for participants. Ensure that instructions are delivered consistently across all conditions to minimize variations that could inadvertently communicate expectations.
- Use random assignment to place participants in different experimental conditions. This helps ensure that any extraneous variables are equally distributed across groups, reducing the likelihood that participants will infer the purpose of the study based on their assignment.

- Include a control group in your experimental design. This group can help you establish a baseline for comparison and control for demand artifacts by exposing participants to a neutral or placebo condition.
- Limit interactions between experimenters and participants, especially interactions that could reveal information about the study's hypotheses or expectations. If possible, use procedures that would reduce experimenter-participant interactions.
- While ethical considerations must be carefully weighed, in some cases, using deception can help minimize demand artifacts. However, it is crucial to debrief participants thoroughly at the end of the study to explain the true nature of the experiment and obtain their informed consent.
- Develop cover stories to mask the true purpose of the experiment. This can help distract participants from the actual focus of the study, reducing the likelihood of demand artifacts.
- Employ counterbalancing techniques to present experimental conditions in a different order across participants. This can help control for order effects and prevent participants from inferring the study's purpose based on the sequence of conditions.
- When feasible, collect responses anonymously. This can reduce the perceived scrutiny that participants might feel and minimize their inclination to conform to perceived expectations.
- Use pilot tests to identify and address any potential demand artifacts before the main experiment. Piloting allows you to refine your procedures and instructions based on participant feedback.

By incorporating these strategies into your experimental design and execution, you can enhance the internal validity of your research by minimizing demand artifacts and obtaining more accurate data. Remember to consider the ethical implications of your chosen methods and ensure that your research adheres to relevant ethical guidelines.

7.1.3 Measurement of Variables

In order to analyze data from cross-sectional and experimental studies, variables must be clearly defined and measured. Conceptual and operational definitions are prerequisites for valid measurement of a variable (see Chap. 3, "Concept explication"). Measurement of variables involves the assignment of numbers to units according to rules to represent variable categories. While many types of variables are relatively easy to measure either through observation (e.g., location of one's residence) or other information provided by the participant (e.g., date of birth for measuring chronological age), many of the common concepts are not directly measurable, as in the case of religiosity and political ideology. A researcher cannot look into a person's mind and observe whether, for example, a person holds liberal or conservative political views. However, a number of proxies can be used to gauge the strength of the person's political ideology or how religious someone is. For example, answers to questions such as: "How often do you think about God/Allah/Buddha?" "how often do you attend religious ceremonies?" or "How often do you pray?" can be used to help define how religious a person is. However, instruments that are used to measure variables can introduce errors that can affect results. Therefore, there should be a concern about the quality of measurement, as differences in quality will affect the statistical outcome of an investigation.

7.1.4 Reliability and Validity

There are two quality factors that need to be considered in measurement: reliability and validity. *Reliability* refers to the measurement instrument's ability to produce the same results in the form of scores for the same object or attribute across times and researchers. *Validity* addresses the question of the extent to which the instrument measures what it is supposed to measure (known as *construct validity*) or the extent to which the measure predicts something theoretically relevant (known as *predictive validity*) or how adequately the measure captures the most important aspects of the concept (known as *content or face validity*) (e.g., Churchill & Brown, 2004; Heeler & Ray, 1972).

Early career researchers who use or plan to use quantitative approaches to research are advised to familiarize themselves with methods of developing reliable and valid measures. Procedures for developing reliable and valid measures are discussed in detail elsewhere (e.g., Churchill, 1979; Churchill & Brown, 2004; Gerbing & Anderson, 1988; Heeler & Ray, 1972; Nunnally & Bernstein, 1994). As errors are unavoidable in measurement, researchers should not only be familiar with commonly accepted methods of developing measures but also with methods that can help reduce errors. Padsakoff and colleagues (2003) identify a wide variety of sources of error in measurement and offer methods for controlling them. And early career researchers who are interested in conducting empirical studies should familiarize themselves with these methods before they embark on a new study.

Reducing Common Method Bias Common method bias (CMB) is a potential issue in research studies that occurs when the measurement method used in a study is related to the measured constructs, leading to inflated relationships between variables. It can be a significant threat to the validity of research findings. Following are several strategies to reduce or control for common method bias in research studies (For greater elaboration of several of them, see Podsakoff et al., 2003):

- Collect data from multiple sources or methods. For instance, if you're using self-report questionnaires, supplement them with objective measures or data from other sources such as peer evaluations, supervisor ratings, or archival records.
- If possible, gather data at different points in time to minimize the influence of the same method on all variables. This temporal separation can reduce the likelihood of common method bias.
- Assure respondents of the confidentiality and anonymity of their responses. When participants feel their responses are confidential, they may be more honest,

reducing the potential for socially desirable responses that can contribute to common method bias.

- In self-report questionnaires, reverse code some items to create a more balanced response scale. This can help minimize response biases by making it less obvious how respondents should answer.
- If you have multiple constructs or variables measured within the same questionnaire, counterbalance the order of items to avoid systematic response biases. This involves presenting items in a different order for different participants.
- Mix different response formats within the questionnaire. For instance, use Likert scales for some questions and nominal scales for others. This can help reduce response biases associated with a single format.
- Employ statistical techniques to control for or assess common method bias. Some techniques include Harman's single-factor test, CFA (confirmatory factor analysis), and structural equation modeling (SEM). These techniques can help identify and account for the influence of common method bias on your results.
- Include a measure of social desirability in the instrument, and incorporate this measure into your analysis to control for socially desirable responses.
- Have experts in your field review your research design and measurement instruments to identify potential sources of common method bias and suggest ways to mitigate them.
- Ensure that data collectors are well-trained and aware of the potential for common method bias. They should follow standardized procedures to minimize the influence of their interactions with participants.
- Analyze your data under different assumptions about the presence and magnitude of common method bias to see how it might affect your results. Sensitivity analysis can help you understand the potential impact of common method bias on your findings.
- If possible, replicate the study using different methods or in different settings to see if the same results hold. If the findings are consistent across different studies, they can provide more confidence in the results.

Addressing common method bias is essential for ensuring the quality and credibility of research findings. Implementing a combination of these strategies can help reduce the potential for common method bias in your research studies.

7.1.5 Pretesting Questionnaires and Experiments

Pretesting questionnaires and experiments is essential for improving the quality of data obtained from a study's participants. Summers (2001) discusses common errors in pretesting and suggests sound methods for improving pretesting of questionnaire and experimental designs. Questionnaire pretesting is critical in developing new measures or revising existing scales, especially items used to measure constructs (e.g., statements to which participants are asked to respond). Researchers should use a small sample of participants (ideally at least 100) with characteristics similar to those to be included in the final study and obtain responses to the questions and statements. They should use histograms that show the distribution of responses to categories (e.g., % "strongly agree," "strongly disagree") to ensure an adequate number of responses to each response category. If the distribution of responses to a question is highly skewed, such as only "disagree" responses to the statement "I seldom text messages," the wording of the statement should change (e.g., "I sometimes text messages"). Inadequate variance on variables that are stated in hypotheses can lead to statistically insignificant or biased results, such as weak correlation coefficients. For new multiple-item reflective scale construction (used to measure constructs), initial assessment of the scale's Cronbach's alpha reliability can provide information on the items that need to be eliminated or replaced (by examining item-to-total correlations) because of their relatively low association with the average score of the remaining items of the scale.

For pretesting experiments, Summers (2001) indicates that experiments are more demanding than surveys, and newly developed research designs are likely to have serious defects that require rigorous pretesting. He suggests:

> In addition to pretesting the measures, researchers need to be concerned with whether (1) the experiment has a sufficient amount of experimental realism, (2) the experiment contains demand artifacts, (3) the manipulations provide the intended variance in the independent variables, and (4) the manipulation might be causing unintended variance in other variables that might have an impact on the dependent variables of interest. (p. 409)

7.2 Qualitative Studies

7.2.1 Data Collection Methods and Aids

Regardless of the research tradition employed (discussed in Chap. 6), each one usually involves using more than one method of data collection that can be in various forms. Data collection methods can be in the form of interviews, observations, focus groups, and surveys using questionnaires with open-ended questions, and they can also be in the form of secondary research, such as text from online search (e.g., articles), archival data from websites and blogs, or annual reports. The in-depth interview and observation are considered the main methods of data collection (Belk et al., 2013).

Belk and associates (2013) offer suggestions for conducting in-depth interviews, including how to prepare for the interview, recruit informants, and set the stage for the interview, and they provide guidelines for interviewing informants. For example, they suggest that the interview should be in the form of a conversation that follows the interviewer's protocol—i.e., list of topics to discuss—and they offer a list of specific guidelines. Similarly, the same authors discuss observational methods for ethnographic research as well as other forms of observation (e.g., during personal or online interviews), including their strengths and limitations. And they also discuss the use of a wide variety of data collection aids, such as audio-video recording, still photography, and other tech forms.

Technological developments in recent decades have been making possible the use of methods for collecting a wealth of information online that enable the researcher to perform a wide variety of analyses. For example, a process known as *data mining* allows the researcher to analyze large amounts of data and develop knowledge from sources such as websites and databases (inductively) that take the form of patterns of activities or "observations" (e.g., types and frequency of articles published, purchase of a product and related products). Another related process known as *opinion mining* involves the analysis of large amounts of unstructured text. Belk and associates (2013) offer details on the use of these and other technologies that enable researchers to collect data that can be used for various types of analysis, including *social network analysis* and *netnography*. These tools provide new and alternative platforms for data collection and analyses. *Social network analysis* (SNA) considers online social relationships as networks, focusing on both the structure and the patterns of their linkages. It helps understand patterns of influence within and between social networks of interest to marketers, such as word-of-mouth (also known as "word of mouse") and diffusion of new products. And *netnography*, which is "ethnography in the social space of online environments…seeks to maintain and analyze the cultural qualities of online interactions" (p. 108), enabling the researcher to learn more about a community or culture and its members.

7.2.2 Data Analysis and Interpretation

Data analysis requires coding, which can be defined as "reducing data into meaningful segments and assigning names for the segments" (Cresswell, 2007: 148). In case of coding text, the task involves assigning names to words, sentences, paragraphs, and even to chunks of text consisting of sentences or paragraphs, and more than one code can be used for the same text. The same task is involved in coding other forms of data from different sources. Coding is an important, daunting, and ongoing process where initially assigned codes may be revised later, as the coder gains insights from attempting to code additional data. It requires skills in interpreting data, skills that are acquired with experience in interpreting large sets of data collected from different groups and in different contexts (Belk et al., 2013). Experienced qualitative researchers (e.g., Belk and associates, 2013) offer several tips for effective coding based on the investigator's research question, his or her familiarity with the literature relevant to this question, and the research tradition one uses as a blueprint, and they offer examples in the context of these bases.

Coding qualitative data is a crucial step in qualitative research, especially when you're working with textual or non-numeric data. Qualitative data coding involves systematically categorizing and labeling data to identify patterns, themes, and insights. The following are general process guidelines on how to code qualitative data:

- Begin by thoroughly familiarizing yourself with the qualitative data. Read and reread the text, audio, or visual material to gain a deep understanding of its content.
- Decide on a coding system or framework that suits your research objectives. This could be a preexisting coding scheme or one you develop based on your research questions and the data.
- Start with open coding, which involves generating initial codes without trying to fit them into any preconceived categories. This process is often exploratory and helps you identify potential themes and patterns in the data.
- As you open code, create a codebook. This is a document that lists all the codes you've created, along with definitions and examples. This will help maintain consistency in your coding process.
- Go through the data systematically, applying the codes to relevant sections. You might use specialized software like NVivo, ATLAS.ti, or simply a spreadsheet or word processor to do this.
- As you code, continually compare new data with previously coded data to refine your coding categories and ensure consistency.
- Break down the data into manageable segments, such as paragraphs, sentences, or even individual words or phrases. This makes it easier to code and compare across the data.
- Write memos or notes as you code. These notes capture your thoughts, interpretations, and questions about the data and the emerging patterns.
- If multiple researchers are involved, ensure inter-coder agreement by having discussions, comparing codes, and resolving disagreements. This helps improve the validity and reliability of your coding.
- After open coding, you can move on to thematic coding. This involves organizing codes into broader themes or categories that capture the essence of the data. Themes should emerge naturally from the data, but you may also draw upon existing theoretical frameworks.
- Qualitative coding is often an iterative process. You may need to revisit your codes, codebook, and themes as your understanding of the data evolves.
- Consider using data visualization tools like word clouds, concept maps, or matrices to help identify patterns and relationships between codes and themes.
- Once coding is complete, write narrative summaries that describe the major themes and patterns you've identified. Use quotes from the data to support your findings.
- If possible, share your coded data and findings with participants to validate your interpretations. This is called member checking and can enhance the credibility of your research.
- Finally, integrate your coded data into your research report, using the themes and patterns you've identified to support your conclusions.

Remember that coding qualitative data is a nuanced and interpretive process. It requires careful attention to detail, an open mind, and an awareness of your own biases. Additionally, the specific methods and tools you use may vary depending on your research approach and the type of qualitative data you are working with.

7.2.3 Theory Development

Theory development in qualitative research is driven by the research tradition researchers follow, as the process of applying each tradition to developing theory differs in one or more of the tasks that must be performed. The following paragraphs summarize the processes involved in developing theory by applying each of the main research traditions.

Grounded Theory The researcher starts with systematic data collection, which often involves interviews, observations, or document analysis, depending on the research question. Data collection is ongoing and iterative, allowing for constant comparison and refinement of emerging concepts. Next, the analysis process begins with open coding, which involves breaking down the data into discrete parts and assigning codes to represent concepts or ideas. Codes are applied without preconceived categories and evolve as the researcher becomes more familiar with the data. Throughout the data analysis process, the researcher engages in constant comparison of new data with previously-coded data, attempting to identify similarities and differences, refining codes, and identifying patterns and relationships.

Once a significant amount of open coding has been done, axial coding resumes. Axial coding involves making connections between codes, grouping them into categories, and exploring relationships. This step helps in developing a more structured and organized set of concepts. Next, the process moves to selective coding, where a central category or core variable is identified. This is the main theme or concept that ties the other categories together. The goal is to develop a coherent and integrated understanding of the data around this central phenomenon.

As the theory begins to emerge, the researcher uses theoretical sampling to deliberately select new participants or data sources that will help refine and further develop the emerging theory. Theoretical sampling is based on the evolving concepts and categories identified in the ongoing analysis. Throughout the process, the researcher engages in *memoing*, which involves writing reflective notes on the researcher's thoughts, ideas, and insights. This helps in documenting the analytical process, making connections between codes, and refining emerging theories. The process continues until theoretical saturation is reached or when new data cease to provide additional insights or contribute to the development of the theory. At this point, the researcher can be confident that the theory is well-developed and grounded in the data. Finally, writing up the developed theory involves presenting the key concepts, relationships, and the central phenomenon, and it often includes a detailed description of the research process, the theoretical framework, and implications for future research.

Ethnography When using the ethnographic method to develop theory, the researcher begins by defining the scope and focus of his or her study, which often involves long-term immersion in the field. Next, the researcher engages in participant observation, which is a key element of ethnography. He or she spends an extended period of time observing and participating in the daily activities of the community or social group under study. This involves being present in the field, building relationships with participants, and gaining firsthand experience of their lives. The researcher records detailed field notes during and after each observation. These notes capture the researcher's observations, interactions, and reflections. Field notes are crucial for building a rich and detailed understanding of the cultural context and for identifying patterns and themes.

In addition, the researcher conducts in-depth interviews with members of the community. These interviews can provide deeper insights into individuals' perspectives, experiences, and cultural meanings. He or she uses open-ended questions to encourage participants to share their narratives and perspectives. The researcher also analyzes relevant documents, artifacts, and other cultural products within the community. This can include studying historical records, cultural texts, and any materials that contribute to the understanding of the community's practices and values. Researchers have to immerse themselves in the cultural context to gain a deeper understanding of the community's values, norms, and social dynamics. This may involve participating in rituals, ceremonies, or everyday activities to experience the culture firsthand.

Ethnographic research involves systematic data coding and the identification of recurring themes, patterns, and categories in the field notes, interview transcripts, and other data sources. This process often involves both open coding (initial exploration of data) and axial coding (identifying relationships and connections). Researchers allow the theory to emerge organically from the data. Rather than starting with preconceived hypotheses, they let patterns and themes shape the development of the theory. The goal is to generate a theory that is grounded in the cultural context and experiences of the participants.

Ethnographic researchers often use triangulation by combining multiple data sources. This involves cross-verifying information obtained through different methods, such as observation, interviews, and document analysis. Triangulation enhances the validity and reliability of the findings. The write-up should provide a detailed and nuanced account of the cultural context and the emergent theory.

The Case Method The case study as a method should be designed to address specific aspects of the phenomenon, and the research questions guide the exploration of the case. Therefore, the researcher must first define the research questions or objectives for the study. Once the research question is defined, the researcher begins by selecting a case that is relevant to the research question and has the potential to provide rich insights into the phenomenon under investigation. Cases can be individuals, groups, organizations, events, or any unit of analysis that aligns with the research focus.

The next step is to gather data from multiple sources, including interviews, observations, documents, archival records, and other relevant materials. In-depth interviews with key stakeholders or individuals associated with the case provide insights into perspectives, experiences, and contextual details that may not be apparent through other data sources. Engaging in participant observation or nonparticipant observation, depending on the research goals, provides a first-hand understanding of behaviors, interactions, and contextual factors. Triangulation, or using multiple data sources, helps in obtaining a comprehensive and well-rounded understanding of the case.

Analysis of relevant documents and artifacts associated with the case, including reports, emails, official records, or any other materials, can contribute to a comprehensive understanding of the case. Document analysis helps in triangulating findings and verifying information. This process often involves coding and categorizing data to uncover meaningful insights. The researcher's systematic analysis of the gathered information helps identify recurring elements and connections that form patterns, themes, and trends in the data. This allows theories to emerge from the patterns identified in the data. Theories can be conceptual frameworks or models that help explain the observed phenomena. These theories may be grounded in the specifics of the case but may also have broader applicability.

The last step involves refinement of the emerging theories based on ongoing analysis and validation through discussions with colleagues, peer debriefing, or presenting findings to experts in the field. This helps ensure the robustness and credibility of the theoretical framework. Finally, the researcher writes up the case study, including a detailed account of the case, the emergent theory, and its implications. The write-up should provide a narrative that allows readers to understand the context, the development of the theory, and its potential contributions to the field.

The case study research as a method to theory building has received limited attention among researchers in applied fields of business like marketing, compared with other disciplines in behavioral and social sciences. Summers (2001) attributes this to a number of reasons, including insufficient training of students in doctoral programs and positivists' negative reactions to results of qualitative studies because they are difficult to objectively verify. Yet, the case study as a method of theory building is likely to see increasing use across disciplines, as qualitative studies in general are increasingly becoming popular and integral parts of mixed-methods research. An excellent discussion of building theories from case study research is offered by Eisenhardt (1989).

Phenomenology The development of theory using phenomenology begins with the clear definition of the research question or phenomenon of interest, and it often begins with an open-ended question that seeks to explore the lived experiences of individuals within a specific context. Next, researchers purposefully select participants who have experienced the phenomenon under investigation, and they consciously set aside preconceived notions, biases, and assumptions about the phenomenon (a practice known as "bracketing").

Researchers conduct in-depth, open-ended interviews or use other methods (such as diaries, focus groups, or written reflections) to collect rich descriptions of participants' experiences. They encourage participants to narrate their experiences in detail, emphasizing sensory perceptions, emotions, and meanings. And they immerse themselves in the participants' narratives to gain a deep understanding of their experience, paying attention to the nuances, emotions, and contextual details conveyed in their descriptions.

After they transcribe the interviews or prepare the data for analysis, researchers engage in a process of thematic analysis to identify significant themes within the participants' descriptions. Themes are the essential aspects that capture the core features of the phenomenon. This involves organizing the data into clusters of meaning. The next step involves performing a descriptive phenomenological reduction, which involves systematically reducing the raw data to essential constituents, and it may include coding, categorizing, and organizing the identified themes to uncover the underlying structures and patterns inherent in the experiences. By distilling the commonalities and core elements that characterize participants' experiences, researchers identify the essence of the phenomenon, which represents the fundamental qualities that define the phenomenon across individual experiences. They construct individual and composite descriptions of the experiences. Individual descriptions capture the unique aspects of each participant's experience, while composite descriptions amalgamate commonalities to present a broader understanding of the phenomenon.

Finally, researchers construct a theoretical framework based on the identified essence and patterns. This is expected to capture the fundamental structures and meanings that emerge from the analysis. Phenomenological research often results in a detailed and rich narrative that communicates the essence of the phenomenon as experienced by participants; and phenomenological theories often focus on the universal aspects of the phenomenon. Thus, phenomenological research offers a systematic and rigorous approach to understanding the lived experiences of individuals, providing a foundation for the development of theories that capture the essence of human phenomena.

Narrative In narrative research, the primary data source is the narratives themselves. These narratives can take various forms, including written or spoken stories, personal accounts, interviews, diaries, autobiographies, or even visual representations. Narratives are seen as a way in which individuals make meaning of their experiences and construct their identities. Researchers are interested in understanding how people frame and communicate their experiences through storytelling. Narrative research pays attention to the context in which the stories are situated. This includes the cultural, social, historical, and personal context that influences the construction of the narrative.

Researchers engage in the interpretation and analysis of narratives to uncover themes, patterns, and meanings. This often involves coding and categorizing narrative elements, such as characters, events, emotions, and themes. Narrative researchers consider both emic (the insider's perspective) and etic (the outsider's perspective) viewpoints. They aim to understand how participants themselves interpret their stories while also providing an external analysis.

Researchers examine the structural elements of narratives, such as the plot, characters, setting, conflict, resolution, and use of literary devices. These elements can reveal important aspects of the story-telling process.

Depending on the research goals, narrative researchers may use various typologies or frameworks to classify and analyze narratives. For example, personal narratives, life stories, illness narratives, and fictional narratives are common categories. Interviews are often conducted to elicit narratives from participants. Researchers use open-ended questions to encourage participants to share their stories, allowing for deeper exploration and clarification.

Like other qualitative methods, narrative research may involve triangulation, which means using multiple sources of data or methods to enhance the validity and reliability of findings.

Narrative research results in the representation of findings through narratives or stories. Researchers may craft narratives that convey the essence of the participants' experiences, making the research accessible to a broader audience. Narrative researchers often engage in reflexivity, reflecting on their own role and subjectivity in the research process. This self-awareness helps in acknowledging potential biases and influences on the analysis.

Use of Preexisting Theory Another approach to theory building that is increasingly becoming popular among qualitative researchers is the use of preexisting theory in order to build a new theory. Belk and associates (2013) offer several examples of studies that have used this approach. It is worth noting, however, that this approach to theory building implies time-dependencies and causality because they describe the process(es) from events that lead to certain outcomes. And they rely on informants' ability to reconstruct the events and process(es), which can be problematic, in part because the study of processes requires the study of changes over unspecified lengths of time. And information collected retrospectively becomes decreasingly valid and reliable with time (Henry et al., 1994; Tausig, 1982), with telescoping error (i.e., the fact that most people recall events that occurred more recently than they actually did) and recall loss (forgetting that an event happened at all) contributing to this problem (Churchill & Brown, 2004).

7.3 Mixed Methods Research

7.3.1 Data Integration

In mixed methods research, the integration of data involves the merging, harmonization, and analysis of information obtained from both quantitative and qualitative research components. The integration of data is a crucial step in the majority of mixed methods research designs, serving to enhance researchers' understanding and lend credibility to the integration process. By combining data from quantitative and qualitative sources, researchers can gain valuable insights into their research questions. For example, a study examining the impact of technology on learning may use surveys to quantify data on students' use of classroom technology. At the same time, interviews or focus groups can provide qualitative data on students' experiences and perspectives. The goal of data integration in mixed methods research is to create a coherent and unified dataset that allows researchers to derive meaningful conclusions and insights from the amalgamated data sources.

Data integration in mixed methods research is a powerful approach that enables researchers to explore research questions from multiple angles, ultimately leading to richer and more robust findings. It underscores the importance of an interdisciplinary and collaborative approach to research, as it often requires expertise in both quantitative and qualitative research traditions. The concept of integration distinguishes contemporary perspectives on mixed methods from earlier views where researchers gathered both types of data but maintained their separation or blended them informally, rather than employing systematic integrative approaches. Nevertheless, one of the most formidable hurdles in mixed methods research pertains to the integration of disparate data types.

7.3.2 Methods of Data Integration

The literature has explored three approaches to data integration (Creswell & Plano Clark, 2011): data merging, data connecting, and data embedding.

Data Merging This integration entails the fusion of qualitative data, in the form of texts or images, with quantitative data represented numerically. This amalgamation can be accomplished by presenting results together within a study's discussion section, for instance, by initially reporting quantitative statistical findings followed by qualitative quotes or themes that either corroborate or challenge the quantitative results. It also can be achieved by making interpretations of qualitative data and supporting them by using results of the quantitative study. This procedure is common in several types of mixed methods research designs, as in exploratory and explanatory sequential designs (discussed in Chap. 6).

Connecting Data This type of integration involves analyzing one dataset (e.g., a quantitative survey) and then using information from the anonymous quantitative survey to invite a smaller number of those who completed the survey to a focus group or depth interview. In doing so, the integration occurs by connecting data on each respondent from the quantitative and qualitative studies and even making it possible for the participants in the follow-up study to remain anonymous, if they choose so (a method of connecting the results from both studies is explained earlier in "Panels" section).

Embedding Data In this form of integration, a dataset of a quantitative or qualitative study of secondary priority is embedded within the primary study (see "Types of mixed methods research designs" in Chap. 6).

The choice of data integration method should align with the research objectives and the specific research questions being addressed. Effective data integration in mixed methods research requires careful planning, transparency in reporting findings, and a commitment to ensuring that the integration process enhances the overall quality and depth of the research.

Benefits of Data Integration Although integration can be challenging due to the complexity of managing and analyzing both types of data, including special research skills at combining the different data set, it offers several advantages: First, combining both types of data provides a more holistic and comprehensive understanding of the research problem, enabling researchers to triangulate their findings. Second, integration helps validate the research findings by corroborating or explaining quantitative results with qualitative insights. Third, qualitative data helps contextualize quantitative findings, adding depth and meaning to statistical results, and qualitative data can lead to the exploration of unexpected relationships or phenomena, which may not have been captured in the quantitative phase.

References

Belk, R., Fischer, E., & Kozinets, R. V. (2013). *Qualitative consumer & marketing research*. Sage.

Churchill, G. A. (1979). A paradigm for developing better measures of marketing constructs. *Journal of Marketing Research, 16*, 64–73.

Churchill, G. A., & Brown, T. J. (2004). *Basic marketing research* (5th ed.). South-Western.

Churchill, G. A., & Iacobucci, D. (2005). *Marketing research: Methodological foundations* (9th ed.). South-Western.

Cresswell, J. (2007). *Qualitative inquiry and research design: Choosing among five approaches* (2nd ed.). Sage.

Creswell, J. W., & Plano Clark, V. L. (2011). *Designing and conducting mixed methods research* (2nd ed.). Sage.

Eisenhardt, K. M. (1989). Building theories from case study research. *Academy of Management Review, 14*(4), 532–550.

Gerbing, D. W., & Anderson, J. (1988). An updated paradigm for scale development incorporating unidimensionality and its assessment. *Journal of Marketing Research, 25*(2), 186–192.

Heeler, R., & Ray, M. (1972). Measuring validation in marketing. *Journal of Marketing Research, 9*(4), 361–370.

Henry, B., Moffitt, T. E., Caspi, A., Langley, J., & Silva, P. A. (1994). On the 'remembrance of things past': A longitudinal evaluation of the retrospective method. *Personality Assessment, 6*(2), 92–101.

Nunnally J. C. (1967). *Psychometric theory*. New York: McGraw Hill.

Nunnally, J. C., & Bernstein, I. H. (1994). *Psychometric theory* (3rd ed.). McGraw-Hill.

Podsakoff, P. M., MacKenzie, S. B., Lee, J. Y., & Podsakoff, N. P. (2003). Common method biases in behavioral research: A critical review of the literature and recommended remedies. *Journal of Applied Psychology, 88*(5), 879–903.

Sawyer, A. G. (1975). Demand artifacts in laboratory experiments in consumer research. *Journal of Consumer Research, 1*(4), 20–30.

Shadish, W. R., Cook, T. D., & Campbell, D. T. (2002). *Experimental and quasi-experimental designs for generalized causal inference*. Wadsworth, Cengage Learning.

Summers, J. O. (2001). Guidelines for conducting research and publishing in marketing: From conceptualization through the review process. *Journal of the Academy of Marketing Science, 29*(4), 405–415.

Tausig, M. (1982). Measuring life events. *Journal Health and Social Behavior, 23*(1), 52–64.

Literature Reviews 8

A literature review is a critical component of a scientific study and holds significant importance, as literature reviews serve several important functions within the research process:

- Literature reviews provide a comprehensive overview of existing knowledge on a particular topic. By reviewing prior research, scholars can establish the context within which their own research will contribute. This helps situate the study within the broader academic landscape.
- Through a thorough examination of existing literature, researchers can identify gaps, contradictions, or unanswered questions in the current body of knowledge. This identification of gaps helps justify the need for new research and informs the development of research questions or hypotheses.
- Literature reviews contribute to the development of a theoretical framework for a study. Researchers draw on existing theories and conceptual models to guide their own research design and analysis. This theoretical foundation helps structure the study and provides a basis for interpreting results.
- Literature reviews expose researchers to various research methodologies and methods employed in previous studies. This understanding is crucial for making informed decisions about the most appropriate research design, data collection methods, and analytical approaches for their own investigation.
- By reviewing existing literature, researchers can ensure they are not duplicating efforts or repeating studies that have already been conducted. This helps in avoiding redundancy and ensures that new research contributes meaningfully to the field.
- A literature review involves a critical evaluation of the strengths and weaknesses of prior studies. This critical analysis helps researchers assess the quality of existing research, consider potential biases, and weigh the credibility of different findings.

G. P. Moschis, *Academic Research in Business and the Social Sciences*,
https://doi.org/10.1007/978-3-031-56548-9_8

- Literature reviews guide decisions related to the research design, including the choice of variables, sampling methods, and data collection instruments. Researchers can learn from the successes and challenges of previous studies to inform their own methodological choices.
- Researchers use literature reviews to provide a rationale for their study. By demonstrating a clear understanding of the existing literature, scholars can justify the significance and originality of their research questions, hypotheses, or objectives.
- The findings from prior studies, as presented in a literature review, can be used to support or challenge hypotheses and research questions. This empirical support enhances the credibility and validity of the new research.
- Engaging in a literature review hones researchers' writing and communication skills. It requires synthesizing complex information, summarizing key findings, and presenting a coherent narrative that communicates the state of knowledge in the field.

In summary, literature reviews play a foundational and multifaceted role in academic research, providing a basis for the development of new studies, guiding research design and methodology, and fostering a deeper understanding of the scholarly conversation within a particular field of study.

Literature reviews can vary in terms of their focus, purpose, and methodology, and they are often classified based on several criteria. With regard to their objective or purpose, reviews can have a different focus or purpose. First, they can be descriptive, aimed to provide an overview of existing research on a particular topic or field without necessarily offering critical analysis or synthesis. They summarize what is known about a topic. Second, certain types of literature reviews attempt to answer a specific research question and follow a predefined methodology. Broad reviews cover a wide range of literature within a field or topic, aiming to provide a comprehensive overview, and focused reviews concentrate on a specific aspect, subtopic, or aspect of a broader field, delving deep into a narrow area of research. Third, literature reviews can also be analytical, going beyond description and including a critical analysis of the literature, highlighting trends, gaps, contradictions, and inconsistencies in the research. Theoretical reviews are a fourth type, focusing on the development and exploration of theories related to a specific topic. They analyze the evolution of theoretical frameworks and concepts. And finally, there are reviews that aim to map the existing literature on a broad topic, identify research gaps, and provide an overview of the available evidence without necessarily conducting a detailed quality assessment. Literature reviews also differ on the basis of the methodology and approach they use.

For example, qualitative reviews primarily involve the analysis and synthesis of qualitative research studies and textual data, while narrative literature reviews typically present the literature in a narrative or thematic format without following a specific systematic methodology. In contrast, quantitative reviews focus on the analysis and synthesis of quantitative research studies and numerical data, as in the case of systematic reviews that can include statistical analyses (e.g., meta-analyses) and synthesis of quantitative data from multiple studies. And, lastly, integrative literature reviews integrate both qualitative and quantitative research studies to provide a comprehensive understanding of a topic.

Additional bases on which literature reviews differ include time frame and research context. Historical reviews provide a historical perspective on the evolution of research within a field or topic, often tracing the development of key theories and concepts, while contemporary reviews focus on the most recent research and developments within a field, emphasizing current issues and debates. Theoretical literature reviews focus on theoretical frameworks and concepts, whereas applied literature reviews emphasize practical applications of research findings and their relevance to real-world problems.

Understanding these bases or criteria is crucial for selecting the appropriate type of literature review that aligns with the researcher's goals and objectives. Different types of literature reviews serve different purposes, and choosing the right one will enhance the quality and relevance of one's research. Because of these differences, once early career researchers decide on the type of review that best aligns with their study's purpose or research question, they should be familiar with the appropriate methods and procedures for conducting that particular review, including data sources, software, analyses, and methods of extracting, analyzing, and synthesizing data. They should be cognizant of the differences in methodologies suitable not only to different types of reviews but also within a specific type. For example, meta-analysis can be placed within the broad category of "systematic literature reviews." Similarly, Xiao and Watson (2019) discuss a typology of systematic reviews consisting of four categories based on their purpose: describe, test, expand, and critique.

Literature reviews are largely driven by the method(s) of synthesis of data; they often take the name of the specific approach(es) to the synthesis used. As earlier authors who presented literature reviews included methods of synthesis (e.g., Barnett-Page & Thomas, 2009; Xiao & Watson, 2019), this chapter also includes reviews that are based on the type(s) of synthesis employed.

8.1 Process of Literature Review

An effectual review comprises three primary phases: initiation, execution, and documentation (Kitchenham & Charters, 2007; Breretona et al., 2007). During the initiation phase, researchers formulate the problem or research question, outline research inquiries, and formulate a review protocol. In the execution phase, researchers pinpoint and choose primary studies and extract, scrutinize, and amalgamate data. In the documentation phase, researchers report their discoveries derived from the literature review.

Although various types of literature reviews have different purposes and can be classified in different ways according to their review purpose and the related literature review types, it is the "review methodology that differentiates the literature review types from each other" (Xiao & Watson, 2019: 95). Furthermore, Xiao and Watson (2019: 102) note that:

> Despite differences in procedures across various types of literature reviews, all the reviews can be conducted following eight common steps: (1) formulating the research problem; (2) developing and validating the review protocol; (3) searching the literature; (4) screening for inclusion; (5) assessing quality; (6) extracting data; (7) analyzing and synthesizing data; and (8) reporting the findings.

Xiao and Watson (2019) use the term "systematic review" to include almost every type of literature review. They describe in detail the eight-step procedure for conducting a systematic review and the tasks involved in each of these steps, which can be briefly described as follows (cf. Xiao & Watson, 2019):

1. *Formulating the Research Problem.* Defining the research problem or question is the pivotal initial stage in the review process. This step holds utmost significance as it shapes the entire literature review, influencing the selection of studies, methodology for data extraction and synthesis, and the presentation of findings. A clear articulation of the research question is essential for aligning all aspects of the review with the objective of addressing the research problem (Kitchenham & Charters, 2007).
2. *Developing and Validating the Review Protocol.* The review protocol should outline the methods employed in conducting the review, encompassing the research question, search strategies, criteria for quality assessment and inclusion, screening procedures, and strategies for data extraction, synthesis, and reporting. This step is crucial in establishing a systematic and comprehensive framework for the review process. It contributes to the reliability of the review because the same protocol can be used by others to repeat the study for verification.
3. *Searching the Literature.* This task involves identifying sources from the published literature, including electronic databases, backward searching (utilizing references in selected articles), and forward searching (exploring articles that cite the selected ones). It is a critical step in gathering relevant information to address the research question effectively.
4. *Screening for Inclusion.* The inclusion screening process requires evaluating each identified article to determine its eligibility for data extraction and analysis. Consistent across various literature reviews, this step involves establishing inclusion and exclusion criteria, guided by the research question and relevant methodology.
5. *Assessing Quality.* Quality assessment is a crucial step in refining the pool of selected studies before data extraction and synthesis. Standards for quality assessment vary among different review types, with no consensus on the methodology. The primary criterion is the degree of methodological unbiasedness in the reported studies.
6. *Extracting Data.* The data extraction process typically involves coding themes and concepts. Well-designed forms are employed to enhance efficiency and minimize individual reviewer judgments, reducing the likelihood of errors.
7. *Analyzing and Synthesizing data.* This task entails organizing the collected data according to the chosen review structure, potentially using charts, tables, and textual descriptions. The goal is to present a coherent synthesis of the information gathered.

8. *Reporting the Findings*. Researchers communicate the outcomes of the literature search, providing details such as inclusion and exclusion criteria along with justifications. Transparent reporting of literature search details enhances the reliability and reproducibility of the review, contributing to the overall integrity of the findings.

8.2 Types, Objectives, and Methods

This section briefly discusses the main types of reviews mentioned in Chap. 3. It briefly describes each one, stating their main purpose and objectives, as well as the methods and procedures for conducting each of the literature reviews.

8.2.1 Systematic

A systematic literature review, often referred to as a systematic review, is a research methodology designed to comprehensively and rigorously examine and synthesize existing research on a specific topic or research question.

Purpose and Objectives The primary purpose of a systematic literature review is to provide an objective and evidence-based summary of existing research on a specific topic, with a focus on minimizing bias, identifying patterns, assessing the quality of studies, and informing evidence-based decision-making and future research directions. One of its goals is to minimize subjectivity in source selection and data extraction. Systematic literature reviews aim to provide a comprehensive summary of the existing literature, including research articles, books, and other scholarly works. This minimizes the risk of omitting important studies and ensures that the review is comprehensive.

Methodology A systematic review follows a well-defined and systematic methodology. This includes clearly articulated criteria for selecting and evaluating studies, a comprehensive search strategy to identify relevant literature, and a systematic approach to data extraction and synthesis. The review sets explicit inclusion and exclusion criteria to determine which studies are eligible for inclusion. These criteria are established in advance and are typically based on specific research questions or objectives. This helps ensure that the review is focused on the most relevant studies.

A systematic review involves a comprehensive and systematic search of multiple databases and sources to identify all relevant studies on the topic. This minimizes the risk of selection bias and ensures that the review is based on a wide range of evidence. For this type of review, researchers systematically extract relevant data from the included studies, often using standardized forms. These data may include study design, sample size, outcomes, and key findings. Systematic reviews typically assess the quality of the included studies. This may involve evaluating the risk of bias, methodological quality, and the strength of evidence in concluded individual studies, critically appraising each study's research design, methodology, and reporting, which helps in determining the reliability of the evidence.

Systematic reviews use rigorous methods to synthesize and analyze the data from the selected studies, and they often include statistical meta-analysis, which combines data from multiple studies to provide a more precise estimate of the effects or associations under investigation. By synthesizing the data, systematic reviews identify systematic patterns, trends, and consistencies across studies. This type of literature review concludes by summarizing the findings from the included studies and may offer insights, implications, or recommendations based on the synthesized evidence. This is typically followed by a discussion of the review's limitations and a call for further research. Systematic reviews are often subject to peer review, ensuring that the methodology and reporting meet established standards.

Systematic literature reviews are highly regarded because of their rigorous and objective approach to evidence synthesis. They are useful for informing evidence-based decision-making, identifying gaps in the existing research, and guiding future research. However, conducting a systematic review is a time-consuming and resource-intensive process, and it often requires a team of researchers with expertise in the subject matter and research methodology. Snyder (2019) discusses additional features of systematic literature review.

8.2.2 Meta-Analysis

Meta-analysis, developed by Glass (1976), is a statistical approach to literature review that focuses on quantitative data. It involves the synthesis of numerical data from multiple studies to draw statistical conclusions about the topic. It is a powerful tool in research that enables the quantitative synthesis of findings from multiple studies to obtain a more robust and comprehensive understanding of a particular research question or topic. Meta-analyses are often used to provide more precise estimates of effect sizes in empirical research. They help researchers make more informed decisions and draw generalizable conclusions by considering a broader set of data than any single study can provide.

Purpose and Objectives The main objective of a meta-analysis is to combine the findings from different studies to produce a more comprehensive and reliable estimate of the effect of a particular intervention, treatment, or relationship. Instead of relying on the results of a single study, researchers collect and analyze data from multiple studies that have investigated the same or similar research questions.

Methodology The following steps outline the key tasks involved in conducting a meta-analysis:

1. *Define the Research Question*. The first step is to clearly define the research question or hypothesis that you want to investigate. This question should be specific and well-defined.

2. *Literature Search.* Researchers perform a systematic and exhaustive literature search to identify all relevant studies on the topic. This often involves searching through academic databases, journals, conference proceedings, and other sources.
3. *Inclusion and Exclusion Criteria.* Studies are then selected or excluded based on predetermined criteria. These criteria may include factors such as the study design, sample size, publication status, and other relevant characteristics.
4. *Data Extraction.* Data from the selected studies are extracted, often in a standardized format. This includes information on the study design, sample characteristics, measurement methods, and the outcomes of interest.
5. *Effect Size Calculation.* Researchers obtain effect sizes for each study. Effect sizes quantify the strength and direction of the relationship between variables or the impact of an intervention. Common effect size measures include Cohen's d, odds ratios, correlation coefficients, and risk ratios.
6. *Weighting Studies.* Studies are typically weighted in the meta-analysis, giving more importance to larger studies or studies with better methodologies. This helps ensure that the results are representative of the overall body of evidence.
7. *Statistical Analysis.* The collected data and effect sizes from the individual studies are then statistically combined using specialized meta-analysis software or statistical techniques. The most common method is a weighted average of the effect sizes, with the weights reflecting the relative size and quality of each study.
8. *Assessment of Heterogeneity.* Researchers also assess the heterogeneity, or variability, among the results of the included studies. High heterogeneity may indicate differences in study populations, methodologies, or other factors that need to be explored further.
9. *Interpretation of Results.* The results of the meta-analysis are interpreted to provide an overall estimate of the effect size, along with a confidence interval. This information helps researchers conclude the strength and significance of the relationship or intervention being studied.

A more detailed explanation of this method is available in other sources (e.g., Cheung & Vijayakumar, 2016; Hansen et al., 2022). And Xiao and Watson (2019) offer Ewing and Cervero's (2010) review as an example of this method.

Meta-analyses are highly regarded in research because they provide a quantitative synthesis of existing evidence, offering a more accurate estimate of the true effect size and increasing statistical power. Meta-analysis is particularly useful when individual studies have produced inconsistent or inconclusive results and when researchers aim to synthesize the evidence from these studies to provide a more comprehensive and precise estimate of the effect under investigation. It has several advantages, including the ability to provide more precise and generalizable results, detect patterns that may not be apparent in single studies, and address the issue of publication bias. However, it is important to note that the quality of a meta-analysis depends on the quality of the studies included, so rigorous study selection and data extraction are essential for a reliable meta-analysis.

8.2.3 Narrative Literature Review

A narrative review, also known as a traditional or qualitative literature review, is a type of academic research review that summarizes and synthesizes existing knowledge and research findings on a specific topic or research question. It is an organized, written account of published research articles, books, and other sources that are relevant to a particular research topic or question. This is the most traditional and common type of literature review. It aims to provide a comprehensive overview of the existing knowledge in a particular field, offering a narrative or descriptive summary of the research findings, methodologies, and theoretical frameworks used in the reviewed studies.

Purpose and Objectives The primary purpose of a narrative literature review is to bring together and synthesize information from various sources. By summarizing and organizing the existing literature, it allows researchers to gain a comprehensive understanding of the current state of knowledge in their chosen area of study. A narrative review helps in identifying trends, patterns, and inconsistencies in the existing literature. This is valuable for researchers seeking to understand the evolution of ideas and research findings over time. By analyzing the existing literature, a narrative review can identify gaps or areas where more research is needed. This can help guide future research endeavors and contribute to the development of research questions.

In some cases, narrative literature reviews contribute to the development or refinement of theoretical frameworks. These reviews can establish a theoretical framework or conceptual model that synthesizes and organizes the existing knowledge on a topic. By examining and comparing various theoretical perspectives within the literature, reviewers can identify emerging themes and concepts. This can be a valuable resource for researchers looking to develop their research hypotheses or frameworks.

Researchers often conduct narrative literature reviews as a preliminary step before embarking on new research projects. These reviews help researchers refine their research questions, select appropriate methodologies, and design more informed studies based on the existing literature. A narrative review can provide historical context and the evolution of ideas in a particular field. It can also help readers understand the current debates and controversies within the subject matter. A narrative review is valuable for providing an overview of a research field, and it helps identify trends, patterns, and inconsistencies in the existing literature. This is valuable for researchers seeking to understand the evolution of ideas and research findings over time. Narrative reviews can also help readers understand the current debates and controversies within the subject matter, and they help identify gaps and inconsistencies, highlighting areas where further research is needed. This can be particularly useful for researchers who want to contribute to a field by identifying areas where their research can make a valuable contribution.

Methodology Unlike systematic reviews or meta-analyses, which follow a more structured and rigorous methodology, narrative reviews provide a broader, more flexible, and qualitative or interpretive overview of the literature. This review method focuses more on gathering information that provides both substance and context to the author's argument than on assessing evidence quality. The data extraction process is informal, and the synthesis of the data involves merely descriptive comparisons, which can be subject to the researcher's bias, experience, and subjectivity (Xiao & Watson, 2019).

Because narrative reviews aim to provide a comprehensive and in-depth understanding of a particular topic or research area, they often cover a wide range of studies, including theoretical and empirical research, and may include historical context and background information. In a narrative review, the author synthesizes the findings and key insights from the selected studies. Instead of using strict inclusion and exclusion criteria as in systematic reviews, narrative reviews use a more flexible and qualitative approach to select and analyze studies. Researchers typically use their judgment to decide which studies are most relevant to the topic. They often provide their interpretation and analysis of the literature, discussing trends, controversies, and gaps in the existing research, and they may also offer insights, hypotheses, or recommendations for future research. This involves summarizing the main ideas, arguments, and conclusions from each source, with the goal of presenting a coherent and cohesive narrative. Therefore, narrative reviews can be more subjective because the selection of studies and the interpretation of findings are often influenced by the author's expertise and perspective. This subjectivity can be both a strength and a limitation, as it allows for a nuanced analysis but also introduces potential bias.

Narrative reviews usually have a structured organization, with sections like introduction, methods (to describe the review process), results (summary of the reviewed literature), and discussion/conclusion (interpretation and implications). They may also include a reference list citing the sources reviewed. Narrative reviews are commonly used in various academic disciplines, including social sciences, humanities, and healthcare. They are valuable for providing an overview of a research field, offering historical context, and highlighting areas where further research is needed. However, it is essential to recognize that narrative reviews may not be as rigorous as systematic reviews, and their findings may be more open to interpretation and bias. Following are the recommended steps for conducting a narrative literature review:

- Clearly define the scope of your review, specifying the research question or objectives you aim to address. This will guide your literature search and help maintain focus.
- Use academic databases, libraries, and other relevant sources to identify studies, articles, and books related to your topic. Perform keyword searches and consider using Boolean operators ("and," "or," and "not") to refine your search terms.
- Develop criteria for including or excluding studies. This may include criteria related to the publication date, study design, geographic location, or other relevant factors. Clearly articulate these criteria to ensure transparency and rigor.

- Use reference management tools (e.g., EndNote, Zotero, Mendeley) to organize and manage the references you gather during the literature search. This will help you keep track of sources and streamline the citation process.
- Screen the identified studies based on your inclusion and exclusion criteria. Review abstracts and full texts as needed to determine their relevance to your review. Keep detailed records of the selection process.
- Systematically extract key information from each selected study. This may include details about the study design, sample size, methodology, main findings, and conclusions. Create a structured template or spreadsheet for this purpose.
- Organize the information in a coherent and logical manner. Summarize the main findings of each study, identifying common themes, patterns, or trends. Discuss any conflicting results and note gaps in the literature.
- Structure your narrative review in a way that makes sense for your research question. Consider organizing the review chronologically, thematically, or by key concepts. Develop clear headings and subheadings to guide the reader through the review.
- Offer a critical analysis of the literature. Discuss the strengths and limitations of individual studies and evaluate the overall quality of the evidence. Consider the methodological rigor, sample representativeness, and potential biases.
- Highlight gaps in the existing literature and propose areas for future research. Discuss how your review contributes to the understanding of the topic and suggest potential avenues for further investigation.
- Write a clear, coherent, and well-structured narrative. Ensure that your review flows logically, and use transitions between sections to guide the reader. Cite relevant studies to support your points.
- Review and revise your narrative literature review. Seek feedback from colleagues or mentors to improve the clarity, coherence, and overall quality of your review.
- Conclude your review by summarizing the main findings, discussing their implications, and reiterating the contributions of your review to the existing body of knowledge.
- Ensure accurate and consistent citation of sources throughout your review.

Researchers and readers should critically evaluate the quality of the review and consider the qualifications and expertise of the author when assessing its reliability.

8.2.4 Semi-Systematic

A semi-systematic review is a research methodology that falls somewhere between a fully systematic review and a more traditional narrative literature review. It combines elements of both systematic and narrative approaches to reviewing the literature. Semi-systematic reviews provide a more organized and systematic approach to reviewing literature than purely narrative reviews while allowing for some degree of flexibility in the review process. This helps readers gain a clear understanding of the current state of knowledge on a specific topic.

Semi-systematic reviews are often conducted when a full systematic review is not feasible due to time constraints or resource limitations or when the research question does not require the level of rigor associated with a systematic review. While semi-systematic reviews may have more flexibility in the review process compared to purely narrative reviews, they still aim to minimize bias and subjectivity by following predefined criteria for study selection and data extraction. Semi-systematic reviews can serve as a foundation for further research by identifying gaps in the existing literature and suggesting areas where additional investigation is needed. They can also inform the development of research questions and hypotheses.

Purpose and Objectives The primary purpose of a semi-systematic review is to organize and synthesize existing research in a structured manner by embracing some flexibility to synthesize and summarize existing literature on a specific research question or topic. This helps readers gain a clear understanding of the current state of knowledge on a specific topic. This type of review aims to balance the need for a systematic and organized process with the recognition that not all research questions require the same level of strict adherence to systematic review methodologies. Thus, semi-systematic literature reviews aim to strike a balance between the rigor and structure of a systematic review and the flexibility of a narrative review. By following a structured approach to review and synthesize the literature, semi-systematic reviews aim to identify key themes, trends, and findings within the existing research.

Methodology By combining elements of both systematic and narrative reviews, a semi-systematic review offers a structured approach to reviewing existing literature while allowing for some flexibility and subjectivity in the process. This flexibility can be particularly useful when dealing with research questions or topics where a fully systematic approach may not be feasible or necessary.

Like systematic reviews, semi-systematic reviews start with clear research objectives and well-defined research questions. These questions guide the review process and help establish the focus and scope of the review. Similar to systematic reviews, a semi-systematic review sets explicit inclusion and exclusion criteria to determine which studies are eligible for inclusion. These criteria are established in advance and are based on the research questions. While the search strategy in a semi-systematic review is more structured than in a narrative review, it may not be as exhaustive as in a systematic review. Researchers typically conduct a systematic search of relevant databases, but they might also include additional sources at their discretion.

Data extraction in a semi-systematic review follows a systematic process, and researchers may use standardized forms to collect relevant information from the included studies. The analysis focuses on summarizing key findings and identifying common themes. Unlike systematic reviews, which often rely on quantitative analysis and meta-analysis, a semi-systematic review may include more qualitative and subjective elements. This allows for a more nuanced interpretation of the findings and may involve some narrative synthesis.

Researchers conducting a semi-systematic review should still provide transparent documentation of their methods, including criteria for study selection, data extraction procedures, and any deviations from the systematic approach. Similar to other types of reviews, a semi-systematic review concludes by summarizing the findings and discussing their implications. Researchers should also acknowledge the limitations of the review.

A semi-systematic review is often chosen when the research question is not as complex. However, it is essential for researchers to clearly justify their approach, be transparent about the methods they use, and ensure that their methodology aligns with their research objectives and the nature of the topic being reviewed. Snyder (2019) also discusses this approach and offers examples of semi-systematic reviews.

8.2.5 Integrative

The integrative literature review is a comprehensive and systematic approach to synthesizing existing research on a particular topic or research question. This type of literature review, like a narrative literature review, serves a specific purpose. It goes beyond summarizing findings and seeks to identify overarching themes, patterns, and relationships in the literature by synthesizing, analyzing, and critically evaluating the findings from multiple sources to gain a deeper and more holistic understanding of a particular topic or research question. It combines both qualitative and quantitative research to provide a more holistic view of the subject.

Purpose and Objectives The primary purpose of an integrative review is to provide a comprehensive understanding of a particular research topic by incorporating evidence from a diverse range of studies. It aims to synthesize and integrate findings from various sources to develop a more holistic perspective on the research question or topic. This involves combining data from quantitative and qualitative studies, as well as different research methodologies. By synthesizing information from multiple studies, the integrative review allows for the identification of common patterns, trends, and consistencies across the existing literature. Another goal is to identify gaps or inconsistencies in the current body of knowledge. This can help researchers and practitioners understand areas where further research is needed. Finally, the integrative review can contribute to theory development or refinement by organizing existing knowledge and proposing new conceptual frameworks or models.

Integrated literature reviews are typically conducted for the purpose of accomplishing one or more of the following objectives: (a) develop a new theory, (b) extend an existing theory, or (c) modify an existing theory. They can contribute to the advancement of knowledge within a field. And they can inform the direction of future research by highlighting gaps in the existing literature and suggesting areas where more investigation is needed. In cases where there are conflicting findings in the existing literature, an integrative review seeks to provide insights into why these discrepancies exist and whether they can be reconciled or explained by contextual factors. It can guide researchers in refining research questions and hypotheses.

Methodology The methodology for conducting an integrated literature review is largely driven by the purpose and objectives of the researcher's review. Consequently, the method (sources of data, search, and analyses) is going to be affected by the specific purpose of one's literature review. For example, if the purpose of the review is to develop a new theory, the inductive approach would be most suitable. A wide variety of databases and studies could be more helpful, and data from multiple sources could be interpreted and synthesized to develop hypotheses. In contrast, if the purpose of the review is to modify or extend a theory pertaining to a particular phenomenon (e.g., Internet addiction), theories and studies related to that particular phenomenon or related phenomena (e.g., obsessive-compulsive disorders, compulsive behaviors) are likely to be more relevant and helpful. And the search focus would be on factors that extend or modify a theory, such as moderating and mediating variables. The end goal in the first case could include the construction of a model or conceptual framework, and in the latter case, researchers would begin their literature search with keywords and concepts related to an existing theory, with a goal of its extension or modification.

An integrative literature review provides a foundation for evidence-based decision-making by offering a synthesized view of the current state of knowledge in a particular field. However, early career researchers should keep in mind that conducting an integrative literature review requires a thorough understanding of the research area, strong analytical skills, and the ability to critically evaluate and synthesize diverse sources of information. Additionally, it is essential to remain transparent in your methodology and document each step of the process for reproducibility and credibility. Dhollande et al. (2021) offer detailed guidelines for conducting integrative reviews.

8.2.6 Critical

A critical literature review, also known as a critiquing review, or a critical analysis of the literature (Paré et al., 2015), is a type of research review that goes beyond summarizing and synthesizing existing research. It attempts to provide an in-depth analysis of the existing literature on a specific topic, concept, or research question.

A critical review assesses the significance of each study in contributing to the understanding of the research question or topic and determines whether the study adds valuable insights or merely replicates existing knowledge. It identifies consistencies and contradictions in the existing literature, and it provides an analysis of how various studies agree or disagree on key findings or interpretations. Critical reviews may lead to the development of new theoretical models, hypotheses, or perspectives based on the analysis of existing literature. This type of review can be valuable for practitioners, policymakers, and researchers, as they provide an assessment of the quality and credibility of the research on a particular subject. This can inform evidence-based decision-making.

Purpose and Objectives A critical review seeks to determine whether the research methods and data analysis procedures were appropriate and credible by evaluating the validity and reliability of the findings reported in the selected sources. It highlights any methodological limitations or weaknesses in the studies under review. A critical review aims to identify any biases, assumptions, or potential conflicts of interest in the research. This helps in understanding the context and potential limitations of the findings.

Methodology Critical literature reviews critically assess the quality and rigor of the studies and sources included in the review by comparing them to an established set of criteria (Grant & Booth, 2009; Xiao & Watson, 2019). It involves a rigorous assessment of the quality, methodology, and significance of the studies reviewed by examining the research design, methodology, data collection, and analysis methods used in each study. This can include issues related to sample size, data collection, measurement instruments, and data analysis techniques.

A critical literature review is an in-depth examination of existing research and requires a keen analytical mind to assess the quality and validity of the sources. It helps you build a solid foundation for your own research by understanding what has been done, what is missing, and how your work can contribute to the field. Xiao and Watson (2019) offer Dieckmann et al.'s (2009) study as an example of critical review.

8.2.7 Theoretical

A theoretical literature review, often simply referred to as a "theoretical review," is a critical examination of existing literature focused on the development and exploration of theories related to a specific topic or research area. It focuses specifically on examining and evaluating existing theoretical frameworks, models, and concepts within a particular field of study. This type of review does not typically emphasize empirical findings or practical applications but rather centers on the examination of theoretical constructs and frameworks.

Purpose and Objectives The primary purpose of a theoretical literature review is to provide a comprehensive analysis of the theoretical foundations that underpin research in a specific area. A theoretical literature review aims to delve deeply into the theoretical foundations and constructs that form the basis of research in a specific field. It focuses on exploring the fundamental ideas, concepts, models, and theories, and it synthesizes and integrates various theoretical perspectives, models, and frameworks from different sources. This helps in building a comprehensive understanding of the subject matter from a theoretical standpoint.

Methodology This type of review does not typically emphasize empirical findings or practical applications but rather centers on the examination of theoretical constructs and frameworks. The review often clarifies key theoretical concepts, definitions, and terminology used in the literature. This is essential for establishing a shared theoretical understanding within the field. By examining existing theories and theoretical frameworks, a theoretical review can identify gaps and debates within the literature. It highlights areas where theories may conflict, require further development, or present opportunities for synthesis.

A theoretical literature review can contribute to the development of new theoretical models, concepts, or hypotheses. It offers insights for researchers seeking to create or extend theoretical frameworks. Theoretical reviews inform and guide research by providing a comprehensive theoretical foundation. They are valuable for researchers, educators, and practitioners in understanding the theoretical landscape of a field and can inform research, policy, and educational practices. In interdisciplinary research, theoretical reviews serve as bridges between different fields, helping researchers connect and apply theories from multiple disciplines to address complex issues. My early reviews of aging theories and conceptual frameworks in the multidisciplinary "discipline" of gerontology, as they may apply to the field of marketing, can be seen as examples of theoretical literature reviews (Moschis, 1990, 1994).

8.2.8 Conceptual

A conceptual literature review explores and clarifies key concepts and definitions within a specific field or topic. It provides a conceptual framework or taxonomy to guide further research. A conceptual review is a type of academic literature review that focuses on synthesizing and analyzing existing knowledge and ideas related to a specific concept or topic. It is a critical and systematic examination of the literature to understand how a particular concept is defined, discussed, and applied within a particular field or discipline.

Purpose and Objectives The goal of a conceptual review is to provide a comprehensive and clear overview of the current state of knowledge on a specific concept, which can serve as a foundation for further research, theory development, or practical applications. Conceptual reviews often clarify key concepts, definitions, and terminology used in the literature. This is important for establishing a shared understanding of the topic among researchers in different disciplines, where conceptual reviews can serve as bridges between different fields, helping researchers connect and apply theories from multiple disciplines to address complex issues. Conceptual reviews help identify inconsistencies in the ways the concept has been defined, the theoretical bases for these inconsistencies, and the need for further research for understanding and using the concept in empirical studies. A conceptual review can provide a framework or taxonomy to guide further research.

Methodology While theoretical reviews examine different theories, conceptual literature reviews aim to delve deeply into the theoretical foundations that underpin a particular topic or concept. They focus on exploring the fundamental ideas, concepts, and theoretical frameworks that define the meanings and definitions of a particular concept (see "Concept Explication" in Chap. 3). The review by Ridgway et al. (2008) for the purpose of developing a better definition and measure of the concept of compulsive buying exemplifies this type of literature review.

8.2.9 Bibliometric

A bibliometric review, also known as bibliometric analysis or bibliometric study, is a systematic examination of published academic literature using statistical and mathematical methods. It focuses on evaluating patterns, trends, and relationships within the literature. Bibliometric review assesses publication trends over time, identifying periods of increased or decreased research activity and recognizing shifts in research focus. It can trace how knowledge and ideas spread within a field by analyzing citation patterns and the dissemination of research across different journals and even countries.

Purpose and Objectives The purpose of a bibliometric review is to conduct an analysis of the academic literature in order to quantify and evaluate the scholarly output and influence of the literature. Bibliometric reviews aim to identify the most prolific and influential authors, research groups, and institutions within a particular field. They examine citation networks to identify influential or highly cited papers. Additionally, these reviews are often used to provide a comprehensive understanding of the state of knowledge in a specific area of study. By analyzing the literature, bibliometric reviews can identify gaps in research, areas with limited attention, and potential opportunities for future investigation.

Bibliometric reviews are commonly conducted in various academic disciplines to analyze the structure, trends, and impact of research within a specific field. These techniques are used to assess the impact factors of articles, authors, and journals. This helps identify the seminal works and key contributors to a field; it provides insights into the influence and visibility of research outputs. Bibliometric reviews can track research trends and guide decision-making related to collaborations and research funding. Collaboration patterns among authors and institutions are assessed to determine the extent of collaboration and its impact on research output. This information is valuable for understanding the academic landscape.

Methodology The first step in a bibliometric review is to identify and gather relevant academic publications. This can be done by searching academic databases, such as PubMed, Web of Science, Scopus, or Google Scholar, using specific keywords, authors, or publication sources. The selection of databases and search terms should be tailored to the research topic or question of interest.

Once the relevant publications are identified, researchers extract specific information from these publications. Commonly extracted data includes publication titles, authors, publication dates, abstracts, keywords, citations, and the affiliations of the authors. Some studies may also include additional data, such as the journal impact factor, funding sources, and the geographic origin of the publications.

The extracted data is then subjected to various quantitative and statistical analyses. These analyses may include the following: coauthorship analysis—i.e., identifying collaborations between authors and research groups; citation analysis, which involves examining how often publications are cited by other works and indicates their influence and impact; keyword analysis, which entails the identification of common keywords or terms used in the publications to understand emerging trends and topics within the field; journal analysis, which involves assessing the source journals or publication outlets to evaluate the quality and impact of research; and even exploring the geographical distribution of authors and institutions involved in the research.

Researchers often use graphical representations such as network graphs and bar charts to visually convey the results of their analyses. Visualization can help identify patterns and trends more easily. After conducting the analyses and generating visual representations, researchers interpret the findings in the context of their research question. They discuss the significance of the observed trends, highlight any knowledge gaps, and offer insights into the development and direction of the field. The bibliometric review concludes with a summary of the key findings and their implications for the field. Researchers may also suggest areas for future research based on the insights gained from the analysis.

Bibliometric reviews are valuable tools for researchers and policy makers, as they provide a data-driven overview of the academic landscape within a particular field. They can help identify influential authors and publications, track research trends, and guide decision-making related to research funding, collaborations, and academic publishing. Additionally, these reviews are often used to provide a comprehensive understanding of the state of knowledge in a specific area of study. However, it is essential to recognize that bibliometric reviews produce results that are merely descriptive based on the work others have done, inferring the quality and impact of articles, authors, and journals from citations. They are atheoretical, and the researcher's subjective interpretations of their findings may be open to bias. As such, these reviews make trivial theoretical, conceptual, and methodological contributions, if any (Summers 2001), and their empirical findings based on articles that are assessed to be of high quality based on impact scores have questionable relevance to business practitioners. (Stremersch et al., 2007). Donthu and associates (2001) offer guidelines for conducting a bibliometric analysis.

8.2.10 Grounded Theory

Grounded theory is a qualitative research methodology that aims to develop theories or explanations grounded in the data itself, rather than being driven by preexisting theories or hypotheses (Glaser & Strauss, 1967). A grounded theory approach to literature review is iterative and dynamic, emphasizing ongoing data collection and analysis to refine your understanding of the research topic. When using grounded theory to conduct a literature review, the purpose and objectives are aligned with its inductive and exploratory nature.

Purpose and Objectives The primary purpose of using grounded theory in a literature review is to generate new, contextually relevant theories. Grounded theory allows researchers to develop theories that emerge from the data rather than imposing preconceived notions onto the research. The primary objective is to approach the literature with an open mind and a lack of predetermined theories or hypotheses. Researchers aim to explore the data without imposing preconceived notions, allowing new theories to emerge from the information gathered. The objective is to build a conceptual framework that represents the relationships and connections between key concepts identified in the literature. This framework serves as a foundation for the grounded theory that will be developed based on primary data collected during the research. The ultimate objective is to contribute to theory development in the field by synthesizing and integrating findings from the literature into a coherent and contextually relevant grounded theory. This theory should offer new insights and perspectives that advance the understanding of the researched phenomenon.

Methodology Conducting a literature review based on grounded theory involves a systematic approach to gathering and analyzing existing research to develop a comprehensive understanding of a particular phenomenon. Following is a step-by-step guide on how to conduct a literature review based on grounded theory (see also Strauss & Corbin, 1998):

- Clearly articulate your research question or area of interest. Grounded theory is often used to explore social phenomena, so your question should be broad enough to allow for an inductive, exploratory approach.
- In grounded theory, data collection and analysis occur simultaneously. For a literature review, the "data" are the various studies and texts relevant to the research question or topic.
- Use academic databases, such as PubMed, JSTOR, or Google Scholar, to search for relevant literature. Identify key terms related to your research question and use them in your search.
- Review the abstracts and titles of the articles to determine their relevance to your research question. Select articles that provide insights or data related to your topic.
- In grounded theory, coding involves categorizing and organizing data. Open coding involves breaking down the data (in this case, literature) into discrete parts. Identify concepts and ideas emerging from the literature without imposing preconceived categories.
- Axial coding involves organizing the identified concepts and categories. This step seeks to establish relationships between codes, connecting them into a more coherent framework. It helps researchers to understand the relationships between different themes or concepts in the literature.
- Selective coding focuses on refining and integrating the identified codes into a more comprehensive theory or framework. It involves selecting the core category or central theme that unifies the various concepts derived from the literature.
- Use the constant comparison method, a foundational principle of grounded theory, by continually comparing new literature with existing codes and categories.

This process helps refine and expand your coding scheme as you discover new insights.

- A grounded theory literature review aims to integrate the emergent theory with existing knowledge. This involves situating the newly generated theory within the context of the broader literature, identifying gaps, and contributing novel insights.
- Grounded theory often involves theoretical sampling, which means selecting literature sources strategically to refine and validate emerging concepts. As you code and analyze the literature, identify gaps or areas where more information is needed to develop a comprehensive understanding. This may involve returning to the literature to seek additional information that helps build or refine the theoretical framework.
- Document your thoughts, ideas, and reflections throughout the process. Memos are written notes that capture your evolving understanding of the literature and the emerging theoretical concepts. These can serve as a valuable resource during the analysis phase.
- Once you have coded a sufficient number of articles, synthesize the findings to identify recurring themes, patterns, and concepts. This synthesis forms the basis for your grounded theory.
- Using the themes and concepts identified in your literature review, start developing a conceptual framework. This framework should articulate the relationships between key concepts and provide a foundation for your grounded theory.
- Organize your literature review to highlight the key themes, patterns, and concepts that have emerged from the literature. Discuss how these findings contribute to the development of your grounded theory.

Overall, a grounded theory literature review is characterized by its flexibility, inductive nature, and emphasis on developing theory from the ground up based on the data (literature) at hand. It is particularly useful for exploring complex phenomena and generating new insights from existing knowledge.

8.3 Emerging Methods

Xia and Watson (2019) analyzed the different methods used by researchers in various disciplines to conduct a systematic review, and they identified additional types of literature review methods that appear to be emerging within the systematic review category, albeit not as widely used: *Bayesian meta-analysis, scoping, meta-narrative, meta-ethnography, critical interpretive synthesis, textual narrative synthesis, thematic synthesis, and framework synthesis*. For each, they describe the methodology used for the review and the researchers who developed it and give examples of reviews based on each method. The various types of reviews do differ in the review protocol, selection of literature, and techniques for extracting, analyzing, and summarizing. They are briefly described in the sections that follow.

8.3.1 Bayesian Meta-Analysis

Bayesian meta-analysis is a statistical approach used to combine information from multiple studies in a systematic and coherent manner. It combines studies that incorporates Bayesian statistical methods. Bayesian methods provide a flexible framework for estimating parameters, making predictions, and updating beliefs based on both prior information and observed data. It extends traditional meta-analysis methods by incorporating Bayesian statistics, allowing for the integration of prior knowledge and beliefs into the analysis. In traditional meta-analysis, researchers typically use methods like inverse variance weighting to combine study-specific effect sizes and their standard errors. Bayesian meta-analysis, on the other hand, employs Bayesian principles to account for uncertainty in effect sizes, prior beliefs, and the hierarchical structure of the data.

In Bayesian statistics, probability is interpreted as a measure of belief or certainty. Bayesian methods incorporate prior knowledge, represented as a prior distribution, and update this knowledge based on observed data to obtain a posterior distribution.

Prior information reflects existing knowledge or beliefs about the parameters of interest before observing the new data. This information is combined with the likelihood of the observed data to derive the posterior distribution. The posterior distribution represents the updated beliefs about the parameters after incorporating both prior information and observed data. It is the result of multiplying the prior distribution by the likelihood function of the data (e.g., Spiegelhalter et al., 1999; Sutton & Abrams, 2001).

Bayesian meta-analysis allows for the estimation of parameters of interest, such as effect sizes, treatment effects, or other relevant measures, based on the combined evidence from multiple studies. This analysis can account for heterogeneity, which refers to variability in effect sizes across studies. Hierarchical models are often used to model this heterogeneity, allowing for the estimation of both within-study and between-study variability. Bayesian meta-analysis requires making specific modeling assumptions, such as the choice of prior distributions and the form of the likelihood function. Sensitivity analyses can be conducted to assess the impact of different modeling choices on the results. Bayesian meta-analysis allows for model comparison, where different models with varying assumptions can be compared based on their fit to the data and their ability to represent the underlying phenomena. Various software tools, such as WinBUGS, JAGS, and Stan, are commonly used for implementing Bayesian meta-analysis. These tools facilitate the specification and estimation of complex Bayesian models.

Bayesian meta-analysis provides a powerful and flexible framework for synthesizing evidence from multiple studies while explicitly incorporating prior knowledge and addressing sources of uncertainty. It allows the combination of both quantitative and qualitative data, as suggested by recent studies and Roberts et al.'s (2002) study that is provided by Xiao and Watson (2019) as an application example. Bayesian meta-analysis is particularly useful when dealing with small sample sizes, complex study designs, or when there is substantial heterogeneity between studies.

It offers several advantages over traditional meta-analysis approaches, including improved accuracy when using a small number of studies and enhanced estimation of heterogeneity (e.g., Hackenberger, 2020; Reis et al., 2023). However, academic research has yet to see widespread adoption of these statistical methods. This is in part due to researchers' unfamiliarity with the processes involved, according to Reis and associates (2023), who provide a practical tutorial for conducting random-effects Bayesian meta-analyses.

8.3.2 Scoping

A scoping literature review is a research methodology used to systematically map the existing literature on a particular topic, concept, or research question. It attempts to map the breadth and depth of the existing literature on a given topic. Scoping reviews provide a comprehensive overview of the key themes, concepts, and ideas within a specific field or research area and are often used to identify gaps in the literature, define key concepts, and determine the need for further research. While not as in-depth as systematic reviews or meta-analyses, scoping reviews may include a wider range of source types and do not typically assess the quality of sources. And they provide a summary and synthesis of the main findings and trends within the literature.The primary purpose of a scoping literature review is to provide an overview of the available research in a broad or emerging field, allowing researchers to identify key themes, gaps in the literature, and potential areas for further investigation. They provide a comprehensive overview of the key themes, concepts, and ideas within a specific field or research area. The aim of the review is to "provide a snapshot of the field and a complete overview of what has been done" (Xiao & Watson, 2019: 99). One of the main objectives of a scoping review is to identify gaps or areas where there is limited research. By identifying research gaps and areas where additional investigation is needed, scoping reviews can inform research priorities and help researchers focus their efforts on relevant and significant topics. This helps researchers understand what questions have been addressed and what areas need further exploration.

The initial framework for conducting a scoping review was proposed by Arksey and O'Malley (2005) and has since gained popularity across various fields. However, Levac et al. (2010) later provided extensions to address confusion and criticisms of the Arksey and O'Malley approach. Despite these attempts, there is still a lack of clarity, particularly when it comes to data analysis. To address these concerns, Joanna Briggs Institute (JBI) developed guidance for scoping reviews, led by a working group of methodological experts known as the Scoping Review Methodological working group.

Scoping reviews can clarify key concepts, definitions, and terminology used in the literature. This is particularly important in emerging fields where definitions may vary across studies. Researchers can use the findings of a scoping review to design new studies or refine research questions. This is especially valuable in interdisciplinary or complex research areas.

Scoping reviews have become increasingly popular in recent years, particularly in the health and social science disciplines, and they are broadly accepted as a helpful adjunct for informing new research projects (Pollock et al., 2021*).* A scoping review is particularly useful when you want to map the literature on a broad topic, explore the diversity of research approaches, and identify areas where more focused systematic reviews or primary research studies are needed *(Mak & Thomas,* 2022*). It may be a step before undertaking research or conducting another type of review, such as a systematic review, according to Mak and Thomas (*2022*). These and other researchers (Arksey & O'Malley,* 2005*; Pollack et al.,* 2021*) explain how to conduct a scoping review, while Xiao and Watson (*2019*) offer Malekpour, Brown, and de Haan's (*2015*) study as an example.*

8.3.3 Meta-Narrative Review

A meta-narrative review, subsequent to Kuhn's (1970) work on research paradigms, is a type of literature review that goes beyond summarizing individual studies and aims to synthesize and analyze the overarching stories or narratives present in a body of literature. In other words, it involves examining the broader themes, patterns, and perspectives that emerge across multiple studies or sources on a particular topic. In essence, a meta-narrative review goes beyond the traditional narrative review approach by focusing on the larger stories and narratives that shape a field of study. Unlike traditional literature reviews that focus on specific research questions or methodologies, it seeks to provide a holistic understanding of a subject by exploring the larger narratives that shape the discourse. A meta-narrative review recognizes and integrates diverse perspectives and paradigms within the literature. This might involve considering studies with different methodologies, theoretical frameworks, or even conflicting findings to capture the complexity of the topic.

A meta-narrative review involves a critical analysis of the underlying assumptions, ideologies, and theoretical frameworks that guide the studies included. It seeks to uncover implicit or explicit meta-narratives that influence how researchers conceptualize and study the topic. And it often considers the historical development of ideas within the literature. This includes tracing the evolution of theories, methodologies, and key concepts over time. Meta-narrative reviews may draw on literature from multiple disciplines, recognizing that complex topics often require interdisciplinary perspectives for a comprehensive understanding.

The synthesis of findings in a meta-narrative review involves constructing an overarching narrative that ties together the diverse elements of the literature. It is a valuable method for gaining a deeper understanding of the complexities and nuances present in the existing literature on a particular topic. By examining the overarching narratives, this review can identify gaps, contradictions, or inconsistencies in the existing literature, providing valuable insights for future research, and it might involve developing a conceptual framework that captures the major themes and relationships within the field.

Conducting a meta-narrative literature review involves a nuanced and comprehensive approach to understanding and synthesizing diverse perspectives within a specific field. Xiao and Watson (2019: 99) share Greenhalagh et al.'s (2004) view that: "Synthesis includes identifying all dimensions of the research question, providing a description of the contributions made by each research tradition, and explaining all contradictions in the context of the different paradigms." And they offer Greenhalagh et al.'s article as an example of a meta-narrative review because it considers overarching research traditions that affect the conceptualization of the diffusion of innovations. Green, Johnson, and Adams (2001) describe the narrative review methodology in greater detail.

8.3.4 Meta-Ethnography

Meta-ethnography is a qualitative research method used in the social sciences, particularly in fields like sociology, anthropology, and healthcare research (Noblit and Hare (1988). It is a method for synthesizing and interpreting qualitative data from multiple ethnographic studies to develop a new, higher-level understanding of a particular phenomenon or topic. Meta-ethnography is a valuable approach for generating novel insights and theoretical contributions in qualitative research. It is a form of qualitative synthesis that aims to go beyond summarizing individual ethnographic studies. Instead, it seeks to understand the relationships between the findings and concepts across multiple studies.

The term "meta-ethnography" reflects the central process of translating the concepts and interpretations from one study to another. Researchers aim to identify common themes, metaphors, or concepts that appear across different ethnographies. The ultimate goal of a meta-ethnography is to develop a "line of argument" synthesis. This involves constructing a new, integrative interpretation or theory that goes beyond individual studies. It is about creating a higher-level understanding or explanation of the phenomenon under investigation.

Meta-ethnography employs three distinct synthesis approaches (Noblit & Hare, 1988). The first method, termed *reciprocal translational analysis* (RTA), entails translating concepts from individual studies into one another, leading to the development of overarching concepts or metaphors. This process involves interweaving ideas from different studies. The second method, *refutational synthesis*, focuses on exploring and elucidating contradictions present in individual studies. The third method, *lines-of-argument* (LOA) synthesis, involves constructing a comprehensive understanding of the whole (such as culture or organization) through the examination of its constituent parts. The authors conceptualized this latter approach as a form of grounded theorizing.

When employing meta-ethnography, researchers engage in reciprocal translation, moving back and forth between the original studies and the emerging synthesis. This iterative process helps refine the interpretation and ensures that the overarching themes are grounded in the data. Researchers typically assess the quality of included studies, considering factors such as methodological rigor, data saturation, and the depth of ethnographic engagement. This quality assessment contributes to the overall credibility of the meta-ethnography. Similar to the notion of data saturation in individual ethnographic studies, meta-ethnography seeks conceptual saturation. This means that the synthesis continues until no new concepts or insights emerge from the analysis.

Meta-ethnography aims to be inclusive, considering a range of studies regardless of their size or publication status. This helps minimize publication bias and provides a more comprehensive view of the available ethnographic literature. Meta-ethnography is often conducted using Schutz's (1962) method, as explained by Xiao and Watson (2019) and illustrated using Britten et al.'s (2002) study as an example.

8.3.5 Critical Interpretive Synthesis

Critical interpretive synthesis (CIS) is a qualitative research method used to systematically review and synthesize diverse forms of evidence, with a focus on generating new insights and interpretations (Dixon-Woods et al., 2006). It combines elements of interpretive synthesis and critical analysis, emphasizing a reflexive, exploratory, and iterative process. This method represents an alteration of the meta-ethnography method. Critical interpretive synthesis was developed to accommodate diverse methodologies used in the literature by being less formal and standardized (Xiao & Watson, 2019).

Dixon-Woods et al. (2006) introduced CIS as an encompassing methodology applicable to the entire review process, extending beyond the synthesis phase. This approach involves an iterative refinement of the research question, literature search, and selection process (utilizing theoretical sampling), as well as the definition and application of codes and categories. Notably, CIS adopts a distinctive method for assessing quality, emphasizing relevance—specifically, the anticipated contribution to theory development—rather than relying on methodological characteristics to determine the "quality" of individual papers (cf. Barnett-Page & Thomas, 2009). The authors also underscore a defining characteristic of critical interpretive synthesis, highlighting its critical stance toward the literature by deconstructing research traditions or theoretical assumptions to contextualize findings.

There are no formal standards or guidelines for judging the quality of CIS. Rather, each review is evaluated separately and judged by different criteria by comparing it to other similar type of literature (Xiao & Watson, 2019). Although there are no standards or guidelines for assessing review quality, CIS uses a team of researchers for making interpretations of the literature, rather than relying on individual interpretations. Critical interpretive synthesis is a rigorous and reflexive approach that encourages a team of researchers to engage deeply with the evidence, question assumptions, and generate novel interpretations. It is particularly valuable when dealing with complex and multifaceted research questions that benefit from a critical and interpretive lens. Several writers explain the CIS method in great detail, compare it to meta-ethnography, and use examples to illustrate its application (e.g., Dixon-Woods et al., 2006; Flemming, 2010; Xiao & Watson, 2019).

8.3.6 Textual Narrative Synthesis

Textual narrative synthesis involves the systematic examination and interpretation of written or spoken language. Textual narrative synthesis, described and exemplified by Popay et al. (2006) and Lucas et al. (2007), is characterized by having a standard data extraction format by which various study characteristics (quality, findings, context, etc.) can be taken from each piece of literature. It is somewhat similar to a narrative review but more rigorous, as explained by Xiao and Watson (2019), whose description draws heavily from the works of Popay et al. (2006) and Lucas et al. (2007). In the context of a narrative synthesis, this may include analyzing texts such as academic articles, reports, interviews, or any other written documents relevant to a particular research question.

Textual narrative synthesis is a method that organizes studies into more homogeneous groups. Lucas et al. (2007) note its effectiveness in synthesizing evidence of various types, such as qualitative, quantitative, and economic data. Generally, studies are reported in a standardized format, covering characteristics, context, quality, and findings. Similarities and differences across studies are then compared. Additionally, structured summaries may be created to provide further elaboration on and contextualization of the extracted data (Harden et al., 2004). Textual narrative synthesis' standardized format of data extraction allows researchers to look for and extract similar information from the studies, such as context findings. This process can be facilitated by organizing the studies into homogeneous subcategories, and it could potentially involve the integration of textual data from various sources to construct a cohesive and comprehensive narrative that relates to the research question. In a textual narrative synthesis, researchers may engage in thematic coding of the textual data. This involves identifying recurring themes, patterns, or concepts within the texts. Thematic coding is a common qualitative research technique that helps organize and categorize textual data.

Because of the standardized coding format used, the review may include a number of studies that have similar characteristics (Xiao & Watson, 2019). The synthesis process involves constructing a narrative that integrates the identified themes and findings from the analyzed texts. This narrative aims to provide a richer understanding of the topic by exploring the relationships and connections between different pieces of textual evidence as they may relate to the research question. Researchers may interpret the meaning of the identified themes and contextualize them within the broader literature or theoretical framework. This step involves going beyond the surface-level description of findings and delving into the implications and significance of the synthesized narrative. Like many qualitative research methods, textual narrative synthesis often involves an iterative process. Researchers may revisit and refine their analysis as they move back and forth between the original texts and the emerging narrative. Xiao and Watson (2019) cite Rigolon's (2016) literature review of equitable access to urban parks as an example of a narrative synthesis review.

8.3.7 Thematic Synthesis

Thomas and Harden's (2008) approach to synthesis, which they term "thematic synthesis," combines and adapts approaches from both meta-ethnography and grounded theory. It is a qualitative research method used to analyze and integrate findings from multiple studies or sources on a particular topic. Thematic synthesis involves data extraction and synthesis based on thematic analysis, where themes are extracted from studies, grouped into categories, and synthesized into analytical themes that are used to answer the research question (e.g., Thomas & Harden, 2008; Xiao & Watson, 2019). This approach is commonly employed in reviews where the goal is to distill and synthesize qualitative data from various studies to identify overarching themes and generate new insights (Barnett-Page & Thomas, 2009; Xiao & Watson, 2019).

Development of analytical themes entails a process that begins with reading and rereading the primary studies or sources to gain a deep understanding of the content. It is followed by conducting line-by-line coding of the text from the primary studies. This involves breaking down the data into smaller units and assigning codes to capture the key concepts or ideas. Next, codes are organized into potential themes by looking for patterns, connections, and relationships within the coded data. This is the stage where initial themes emerge from the coded data, and it is followed by reviewing and refining the identified themes. This often involves revisiting the coded data and ensuring that the themes accurately capture the essence of the data. Themes may be combined, split, or modified during this process. The goal at this stage is to create a descriptive account or narrative that summarizes the themes and their relationships. This narrative helps in providing context and a coherent story that reflects the synthesized findings. While thematic synthesis is primarily concerned with the synthesis of findings, the credibility and rigor of the primary studies can impact the overall trustworthiness of the synthesis.

Thomas and Harden (2008: 101) describe this methodology; they suggest that "analytical themes are more appropriate when a specific review question is being addressed," and researchers should use these analytical themes as bases for constructing higher-order or overarching themes that cut across the initial themes. These higher-order themes provide a more abstract and comprehensive understanding of the phenomenon under investigation. Second- and third-order constructs can be developed from analytical themes, often by creating clusters of themes, and synthesis of the themes can be used to generate overarching insights or conclusions suitable for addressing broader or more general review questions. Xiao and Watson (2019) illustrate this type of review by referring to Neely et al.'s (2014) study that attempts to answer a research question through a thematic synthesis of the literature.

8.3.8 Framework Synthesis

Framework synthesis is a method of data analysis commonly used in qualitative research, particularly in thematic analysis. It provides a systematic and transparent approach to organizing and interpreting qualitative data. This method involves establishing a conceptual framework on a priori basis that will be used to structure the coding of the literature and modify the framework based on the evidence of the studies reviewed. The rationale behind framework synthesis is the substantial amount of textual data generated by qualitative research, such as transcripts and observational field notes. The sheer volume of information poses a challenge for rigorous analysis, and framework synthesis provides a highly structured method for organizing and analyzing this data (e.g., indexing using numerical codes, rearranging data into charts, etc.).

Framework synthesis stands out from other outlined methods by employing an a priori framework—informed by background material and team discussions—to extract and synthesize findings. While predominantly deductive, this approach allows for the incorporation of new topics emerging from the data, in addition to those identified by the framework. The resulting synthesis can be presented in the form of charts for each key dimension identified, facilitating the mapping of the nature and range of the concept under study and revealing associations between themes and exceptions (Brunton et al., 2006). Xiao and Watson (2019) present Lindell and Perry's (2000) work as example, where coded items are initially interpreted within a priori framework but are adjusted based on new evidence.

Framework synthesis is often applied when there is a need to address specific research questions, inform policy decisions, or provide evidence for practice. It is particularly useful when there is a need for a structured and transparent approach to synthesizing qualitative evidence. This method allows researchers to develop a comprehensive framework that captures key themes and patterns across multiple studies, providing valuable insights for decision-making and further research.

8.4 Other Review Types and Methods

Another group of review methods does not appear to be as widely known either because they have been used in limited fields or because they have enjoyed limited use across disciplines. They include the following: *meta-interpretation, meta-summary, meta-study, realistic, ecological triangulation, qualitative meta-summary,* and *content analysis.* Each of these review methods is briefly discussed by Xiao and Watson (2019) and/or Barnett-Page and Thomas (2009). These authors include in their discussion method description, previous scholars who have contributed to their development, and examples of studies that have used them and illustrate their application.

8.4.1 Meta-Interpretation

Meta-interpretation, introduced by Weed (2005), seeks to enhance the systematic review by aligning it with an interpretive approach, ensuring fidelity to the epistemology of the synthesized research (Weed, 2005). To achieve this, the focus is on selecting a research area rather than a specific research question. Employing "maximum variation sampling," the initial step involves identifying a few contrasting studies. Emphasizing "meaning in context" as a focal point, the analysis of these studies brings forth conceptual issues, prompting further iterations of literature selection until theoretical saturation is achieved (Weed, 2005).

Weed (2005) emphasizes the need for a "statement of applicability" to precisely delineate the boundaries and scope of the synthesis. Arnold and Fletcher (2012) meticulously adhere to the meta-interpretation method in their article, allowing for iteration in the systematic review process. They applied this method to discern subcategories and subsequently develop a taxonomy of stressors faced by sports performers.

8.4.2 Meta-Study

Paterson et al. (2001) have devised a comprehensive synthesis approach termed "meta-study." Their approach is based on earlier-established views (e.g., Zhao, 1991; Ritzer, 1991) that synthesis should be preceded by three analytical components: meta-data-analysis (analyzing findings), meta-method-analysis (analyzing methods), and meta-theory-analysis (analyzing theory). Together, these three analytical elements, leading to synthesis, constitute the methodology known as "meta-study" (Barnett-Page and Thomas (2009). Paterson et al. note that these different components of analysis can be conducted concurrently.

Paterson et al. (2001) conceptualized meta-data analysis in a manner akin to Noblit and Hare's meta-ethnography (as discussed above), wherein it is fundamentally interpretive and seeks to unveil similarities and discrepancies among accounts of a particular phenomenon. A meta-study allows the systematic analysis of a substantive body of qualitative work, allowing the authors to generate or expand theoretical frameworks based on a consolidation of knowledge. It involves a systematic approach to the collection and evaluation of research and consists of a number of steps, including a systematic literature search, data extraction, meta-method, meta-theory, meta-data-analysis, and meta-synthesis (Drew et al., 2019). Paterson et al. (2001) developed the meta-study method to investigate the experiences of adults living with a chronic illness (Barnett-Page and Thomas (2009), but researchers have subsequently used different processes of meta-analysis. For example, Xiao and Watson (2019) cite Anthony and associates' (2016) more recent work to illustrate how these researchers used their own process of meta-study.

8.4.3 Realistic

A realist review is a methodological strategy for conducting a literature review that focuses on comprehending the underlying mechanisms and contextual elements influencing the outcomes of interventions, with interventions viewed as independent variables in the forms of, for example, a treatment, program, or training course.

This method finds particular relevance in disciplines such as social sciences, public health, and education, where the effectiveness of interventions is often contingent on the context of implementation (Rycroft-Malone et al., 2012). This systematic approach involves synthesizing evidence from diverse studies, with a specific emphasis on understanding the mechanisms that clarify the reasons behind the success or failure (viewed as outcomes) of interventions in specific contexts.

Realist reviews, *also known as "syntheses,"* aim to surpass the mere identification of intervention effectiveness and strive to unveil the causal processes (i.e., mechanisms) and contextual factors contributing to their outcomes. Pawson et al. (2005: 21) assert that "traditional methods of review focus on measuring and reporting on program effectiveness, often find that the evidence is mixed or conflicting, and provide little or no clue as to why the intervention worked or did not work when applied in different contexts or circumstances, deployed by different stakeholders, or used for different purposes." Realist reviews are commonly employed to address questions such as: "what works, for whom, in what contexts, how, why, and to what extent" regarding intervention or program. This method involves scrutinizing individual programs to identify the contexts, mechanisms, and outcomes—known by the fundamental "formula": context + mechanism = outcome (often abbreviated as C + M = O), aiming to elucidate variations, whether intended or unintended, between them. Thus, to relate these notions to positivistic models, the emphasis of this method is on antecedents and moderating factors that determine the effectiveness of mechanisms.

Realist synthesis is a progressively favored method for reviewing and synthesizing evidence, emphasizing the comprehension of the mechanisms through which an intervention operates or fails to do so (Wong et al., 2020). Rycroft-Malone et al. (2012) as well as Pawson and associates (2005) describe in detail the process used for a realist review and synthesis to answer the question regarding the effectiveness of interventions and strategies in enabling evidence-informed outcomes. These authors also discuss strengths and challenges of conducting realist review, while Xiao and Watson (2019) offer Harden et al.'s (2015) as example of a realistic review.

8.4.4 Ecological Triangulation

Banning (2005) has introduced the concept of "ecological triangulation" or "ecological sentence synthesis," to analyze evidence regarding effective interventions for youth with disabilities. He adopts the idea of triangulation, where phenomena are examined from various perspectives, to suggest that constructing an "evidence base" for effectiveness requires, according to Xiao and Watson (2019), the cumulative synthesis and diverse evidence to determine "what intervention works for what kind of outcomes for what kind of persons under what kind of conditions" (Banning, 2005:1). It involves the disentanglement of the interdependent relationships among environments, individuals, and behavior.

The goals of ecological triangulation are very similar to those of a realistic review (Xiao & Watson, 2019). They involve unraveling the interdependent relationships among behavior, individuals, and environments (Barnett-Page and Thomas (2009). Xiao and Watson (2019: 100) also see similarities between ecological triangulation and meta-study "in that meta-method, meta-data, and meta-theory should be considered." They cite Banning's assertion that data extraction and synthesis should be aimed primarily at ascertaining the evidence from various cases (articles) that back interventions yield positive outcomes, considering aspects such as theory, method, and the examination of individuals and conditions. And they offer the studies by Fisher and associates (2014) and Sandelowski and Leeman (2012) as examples of ecological triangulation and how information should be presented in an ecological sentence synthesis.

8.4.5 Qualitative Meta-Summary

Sandelowski and Barroso (2007) introduced a technique they termed "qualitative meta-summary." This approach is a systematic and thorough method for amalgamating findings from various qualitative studies. It provides a structured way to analyze, interpret, and summarize qualitative data in order to identify common themes, patterns, and overarching concepts that emerge across a body of literature. Sandelowski and Barroso (2007: 99) explain this approach:

> Qualitative metasummary is a quantitatively oriented aggregation of qualitative findings originally developed to accommodate the distinctive features of qualitative surveys. Yet these findings are similar in form and mode of production to the descriptive findings researchers often present in addition to the results of bivariate and multivariable analyses. Qualitative metasummary, which includes the extraction, grouping, and formatting of findings, and the calculation of frequency and intensity effect sizes, can be used to produce mixed research syntheses and to conduct a posteriori analysis of the relationship between reports and findings.

Unlike other methods discussed here, qualitative meta-summary is a novel and distinctive approach to managing a compilation of qualitative studies. The process of qualitative meta-summary typically includes a thorough examination of qualitative research findings, extracting key insights, and distilling them into a condensed and meaningful representation. Unlike some other qualitative research synthesis methods, qualitative meta-summary is characterized by its aggregative nature. Notably, it is aggregative in nature; that is, findings are accumulated and summarized rather than "transformed." It involves the accumulation and summarization of findings rather than transforming them. Meta-summary functions as a means of creating a "map" of the content in qualitative studies and, as highlighted by Sandelowski and Barroso (2007: 151), it "reflects a quantitative logic."

One of the main advantages of a qualitative meta-summary is its ability to create a comprehensive "map" of the content found in various qualitative studies. This method allows researchers to distill the essence of qualitative research findings, providing a clearer and more accessible understanding of the commonalities and trends present in the analyzed studies. It is important to note that while the term "meta-summary" suggests a quantitative element, this approach is applied to qualitative data and aligns with the logic of qualitative inquiry. Herber et al. (2017) illustrate the application of this approach to synthesizing research studies on self-care.

Meta-summary reviews often involve a more standardized and structured approach to data extraction and synthesis, making them suitable for quantitative and qualitative studies alike. To exemplify this, Xiao and Watson (2019) refer to the study by Limkakeng et al. (2014) who employed meta-summary techniques to distill themes related to patients' decision-making regarding participation or refusal in medical research within emergency settings.

8.4.6 Content Analysis

Although the method of content analysis has been used by researchers for several decades (e.g., Stemler, 2001), it only recently has been viewed as an approach to synthesizing the results of studies reviewed (Barnett-Page and Thomas 2007). Researchers using this approach (e.g., Evans & Fitzerald, 2002; Suikkala & Leino-Kilpi, 2000) condense text into fewer content-related categories. Synthesizing the results of a content analysis involves bringing together the findings from individual content units to draw meaningful conclusions and insights. By systematically synthesizing the results of content analysis researchers can contribute valuable insights to their research field.

Conducting a literature review based on content analysis involves two steps. First, the researcher conducts the standard content analysis. This involves the employment of customary procedures and research skills, such as those discussed by Stemler (2001), and it usually requires a team of researchers. Second, results from the standard content analysis are synthesized to obtain meaningful insights and conclusions. The following is a synopsis of the main steps involved in synthesizing the results of a content analysis:

First, researchers begin by identifying the key themes, topics, or categories that emerged during the content analysis process. These are the central elements that your analysis focuses on. The next step may involve the creation of a detailed coded book that outlines the definitions and criteria for each theme or category. This ensures consistency in coding across the content. If the content analysis involves quantitative data (e.g., frequency counts or percentages), a compilation of these statistics for each theme or category can provide a quantitative overview of the prevalence of different content elements. The next step may involve examining individual content units, considering their context, and identifying patterns or variations. And, if there are multiple cases or sources in one's content analysis, a comparison of the findings across cases is needed, looking for commonalities, differences, and trends. This step helps to identify broader patterns that may be present in the overall dataset.

An important step in the process is the integration of the quantitative and qualitative findings to provide a comprehensive understanding of the content. This involves weaving together the statistical summaries with qualitative insights to present a nuanced and thorough interpretation. Of equal importance is the exploration of any relationships or associations between different themes or categories. This step helps in understanding how various elements interact and contribute to the overall content. And researchers consider the broader context within which the content exists, which may involve examining historical, cultural, or environmental factors that could influence the meaning and significance of the content. Finally, based on this analysis, conclusions are drawn about the overall patterns, trends, or messages present in the content, followed by a discussion of the implications of these findings and their significance in the context of the review's objectives. The article by Mikkonen and Kääriäinen (2020) is offered by Barnett-Page and Thomas (2009) as an example of this review method.

8.5 Hybrid and Recent Review Methods

Finally, Xiao and Watson (2019) point out that it is possible for researchers to mix or combine methods and create hybrid reviews; they report that seven percent of all literature reviews are hybrid and offer as an example the study by Malekpour, Brown, and de Haan (2015). There appears to be a trend toward the development and use of hybrid methods of literature reviews in recent years. For example, Herber and associates (2019) use meta-synthesis techniques to integrate statements of findings that were derived previously through meta-summary techniques leading to a new situation-specific theory. And researchers in the areas of business integrate literature review methods to develop new ones (e.g., Paul et al., 2023).

In its annual call for papers on systematic reviews, the editor and associate editors of the *International Journal of Consumer Studies* state (Paul et al., 2024);

> We highly recommend the use of a well-grounded methodological approach to conducting systematic reviews, which may include, but are not limited to, the following types of systematic reviews: *theory-based reviews* (e.g., Gilal et al., 2019; Hassan et al., 2016; Tanrikulu, 2021), *theme-based reviews* (e.g., Hao et al., 2019; Kahiya, 2018; Paul et al., 2017; Rana & Paul, 2017; Rosado-Serrano et al., 2018), *framework-based reviews* (e.g.; Paul & Benito, 2018; Lim et al., 2020; Pradhan et al., 2023), *theory-context-characteristics-methodology (TCCM)-based reviews* (e.g., Hassan et al., 2022; Chen et al., 2021; Paul & Rosado-Serrano, 2019; Çelik et al., 2023), *theory development reviews* (e.g., Paul, 2019; Paul & Mas, 2019; Pansari & Kumar, 2017), *hybrid-narrative reviews* (e.g., Dabić et al., 2020; Sharma et al., 2023, Buphapant & Brandão, 2023), *bibliometric analysis* (e.g., Randhawa et al., 2016; Xiao et al., 2023) and *meta-analysis*. (e.g., Rana & Paul, 2020; Barrari et al., 2020)

And in another recent article, Paul et al. (2023) present "a more impactful type of systematic review, the framework-based review," and they "list and summarise some of the popularly used frameworks, TCCM (theories-contexts-characteristics-methods; Paul & Rosado-Serrano, 2019), ADO (antecedents-decisions-outcomes;

Paul & Benito, 2018), 5W+ H (who, when, where, what, why, how; Callahan, 2014) and IMO (input-mediators-outcomes; Ilgen et al., 2005)" (emphasis theirs).

While readers are likely to be familiar with some of these types of reviews and methods, I assume some readers want to know the reasons all these methods are viewed as systematic reviews and the reason many of the methods discussed earlier in this chapter, such as integrative, narrative and most of the qualitative review methods (e.g., ground theory, case method) are not included on these lists. I must apologize to them for not having good answers. I was not aware that these methods are the most widely used, impactful, or popular, as claimed by the Journal Editors, and failed to learn about them in time to include in this book. And I would have tried to learn the evidence or criteria used to determine their popularity, wide use, and effectiveness over a large number of other well-known review methods. I can also see that the Editors either used or developed some of these methods.

As the field of literature reviews is expanding and continuously evolving, new methods continue to appear in the literature, and earlier versions of the original literature reviews are presented and are claimed to be more impactful than the previous ones, as in the case of framework-based review (Paul et al., 2023), or even new as in the case of bibliometrics that was first used in the field of consumer behavior more than 30 years ago (e.g., Hoffman & Holbrook, 1993; Stremersch et al., 2007). As new software programs are becoming available and researchers in some disciplines (e.g., business), who are relatively unfamiliar with them, want to know more about their applications, more elaborate descriptions of these methods are seen in the literature (e.g., Donthu et al., 2001). Some methods are "introduced" with a slightly different name, and some others are even claimed by their authors to be new, as in the case of bibliometrics where the authors maintain that they "introduced bibliometric analysis as a technique that effectively synthesizes large quantities of bibliometric data to present an overview of a field's performance and intellectual structure" (Lim & Kumar, 2024: 18). Apparently, the guidelines given to readers to enhance their comprehension of the method, albeit beneficial, were viewed by the authors substantial and "seminal" to the point they considered the bibliometrics method as new, deserving publication in the journal their co-author was serving as editor (Donthu et al., 2001). Such developments make it difficult for the reader to see the differences among these methods and choose those most appropriate for their needs.

To keep earlier career researchers from becoming more confused with "new and improved" versions of established review methods, as well as newly introduced ones that are often touted by their developers as widely accepted (e.g., Paul et al., 2023), this chapter does not discuss these methods, either due to a lack of credible evidence regarding their value, because of their relatively limited use, or because of questionable incremental improvement of their value over established versions. However, these methods are mentioned (with citations), for those interested in learning more about them and assessing their efficacy.

8.6 Choosing the Most Appropriate Review

Each type of literature review serves a unique purpose, and the choice of the most appropriate type depends on your research objectives, the nature of your topic, and the methodology you want to employ. Snyder (2019) asserts that as a research method, the literature review can provide the basis for building a new conceptual model or theory; it can provide an overview of a certain issue, existing knowledge, or gaps in knowledge, helping to create research agendas; it is useful in examining the accuracy or validity of a certain theory or competing theories, and it can help map the development of a particular field over time. And depending on the goal of the literature review, the method that should be used will vary as well.

Snyder (2019) further discusses the purpose of three types of literature reviews: systematic, semi-systematic, and integrative, offering examples of studies that have used these reviews to accomplish certain research goals. For example, if the researcher is interested in addressing a research question, a systematic review of the literature should reveal the result of studies that directly or indirectly have addressed the question, helping draw conclusions for action. If one is interested in understanding and explaining a phenomenon, an integrative review of qualitative and quantitative studies would be appropriate, as such a review could provide new insights that can lead to the development of new theories or the modification of existing ones. This can be accomplished by organizing, interpreting, and integrating existing findings and theories to provide new insights into an issue or a phenomenon under investigation. Finally, if the researcher is interested in understanding how a topic has been conceptualized and studied in different disciplines, including theoretical perspectives employed, a semi-systematic review could be most helpful. Such a review is suitable when explicating concepts and developing new conceptualizations and measures of variables (e.g., Ridgway et al., 2008).

Thus, it is essential to clearly define the type of literature review that best aligns with your research goals before embarking on the review process. Although the task of choosing the appropriate type of literature review appears to be straightforward, the proliferation of the methods used for conducting a review creates additional challenges to early career researchers who may not be as familiar with the various types of reviews within broader categories. Furthermore, some types of reviews are very broad in scope and include one or more other types of reviews that are narrower in scope. For example, systematic reviews can include reviews based on meta-analysis. Similarly, researchers often use the term "systematic review" to refer to specific types of reviews, such as "meta-narrative" (e.g., Greenhalgh et al., 2004) as well as other types of qualitative and quantitative reviews presented here (Xiao & Watson, 2019), and other researchers use the term "systematic review" to include quantitative reviews, including bibliometrics (Paul et al., 2024). The decision to choose the type most suitable and effectual for one's research objective becomes even more challenging because some of the reviews can accomplish similar objectives, which puts an extra burden on the researcher to know how to conduct a literature review using each of these methods. For those early career researchers not familiar with most of these types of review, I recommend the following steps:

1. Clearly define the purpose of the review. This will eliminate those review types or methods whose objectives do not align with your study's objectives.
2. Examine the remaining and eliminate those you think you don't know enough about to perform the review effectively. This step likely will eliminate qualitative reviews that you need to have experience in conducting.
3. Eliminate those types that have not been widely used across disciplines.
4. Evaluate the remaining using criteria that align with your personal circumstances such as time and resources required (e.g., software); eliminate those that do not meet these requirements.
5. If more than one type of review or method is suitable for your research objectives, choose the one that you feel that you have the required skills for conducting.

Xiao and Watson (2019) also offer early career researchers a conceptual approach that can be used to find the most appropriate review type or methodology. They make suggestions based on the purpose of the literature review, which can be used to identify the most suitable review type, citing articles that established the specific type of review and providing an example of each literature review type.

References

Anthony, D. R., Gucciardi, D. F., & Gordon, S. (2016). A meta-study of qualitative research on mental toughness development. *International Review of Sport and Exercise Psychology, 9*(1), 160–190.

Arksey, H., & O'Malley, L. (2005). Scoping studies: Towards a methodological framework. *International Journal of Social Research Methodology, 8*(1), 19–32.

Arnold, R., & Fletcher, D. (2012). A research synthesis and taxonomic classification of the organizational stressors encountered by sport performers. *Journal of Sport and Exercise Psychology, 34*(3), 397–429.

Banning, J. H. (2005). Ecological triangulation: An approach for qualitative meta-synthesis. *What works for youth with disabilities* project. US Department of Education, School of Education, Colorado: Colorado State University.

Barnett-Page, E., & Thomas, J. (2009). Methods for the synthesis of qualitative research: A critical review. *BMC Medical Research Methodology, 9*, 59. https://doi.org/10.1186/1471-2288-9-59

Breretona, P., Kitchenhama, B. A., Budgenb, D., Turnera, M., & Khalilc, M. (2007). Lessons from applying the systematic literature review process within the software engineering domain. *Journal of Systems and Software, 80*(4), 571–583.

Britten, N., Campbell, R., Pope, C., Donovan, J., Morgan, M., & Pill, R. (2002). Using meta ethnography to synthesise qualitative research: A worked example. *Journal of Health Services Research & Policy, 7*(4), 209–215.

Brunton, G., Oliver, S., Oliver, K., & Lorenc, T. (2006). *A synthesis of research addressing children's, young people's and parents' views of walking and cycling for transport*. EPPI-Centre, Social Science. Research Unit, Institute of Education, University of London.

Cheung, M. W. L., & Vijayakumar, R. (2016). A guide to conducting a meta-analysis. *Neuropsychology Review, 26*, 121–128. https://doi.org/10.1007/s11065-016-9319-z

Dhollande, S., Taylor, A., Meyer, S., & Scott, M. (2021). Conducting integrative reviews: A guide for novice nursing researchers. *Journal of Research in Nursing, 26*(5), 427–438. https://doi.org/10.1177/1744987121997907

Dieckmann, N. F., Malle, B. F., & Bodner, T. E. (2009). An Empirical Assessment of Meta-Analytic Practice. *Review of General Psychology 13*(2), 101–15.

Dixon-Woods, M., Cavers, D., Agarwal, S., Annandale, E., Arthur, A., Harvey, J., Hsu, R., Katbamna, S., Olsen, R., & Smith, L. (2006). Conducting a critical interpretive synthesis of the literature on access to healthcare by vulnerable groups. *BMC Medical Research Methodology, 6*(1), 1.

Donthu, N., Kumar, S., Mukherjee, D., Pandey, N., & Lim, W. M. (2001). How to conduct a bibliometric analysis: An overview and guidelines. *Journal of Business Research, 133*, 285–296.

Drew, K., Morris, R., Tod, D., & Eubank, M. (2019). A meta-study of qualitative research on the junior-to-senior transition in sport. *Psychology of Sport and Exercise, 45*, 101556.

Evans, D., & Fitzgerald, M. (2002). Reasons for physically restraining patients and residents: A systematic review and content analysis. *International Journal of Nursing Studies, 39*, 739–743. https://doi.org/10.1016/S0020-7489(02)00015-9

Ewing, R., & Cervero, R. (2010). Travel and the built environment: A meta-analysis. *Journal of the American Planning Association, 76*(3), 265–294.

Fisher, C. L., Maloney, E., Glogowski, E., Hurley, K., Edgerson, S., Lichtenthal, W. G., Kissane, D., & Bylund, C. (2014). Talking about familial breast cancer risk topics and strategies to enhance mother–daughter interactions. *Qualitative Health Research, 24*(4), 517–535.

Flemming, K. (2010). Synthesis of quantitative and qualitative research: An example using critical interpretive synthesis. *Journal of Advanced Nursing, 66*(1), 201–217.

Glaser, B., & Strauss, A. (1967). *The discovery of grounded theory*. Aldine.

Glass, G. V. (1976). Primary, secondary, and meta-analysis of research. *Educational Researcher, 5*(10), 3–8.

Grant, M. J., & Booth, A. (2009). A typology of reviews: An analysis of 14 review types and associated methodologies. *Health Information and Libraries Journal, 26*(2), 91–108.

Green, B. N., Johnson, C. D., & Adams, A. (2001). Writing narrative literature reviews for peer-reviewed journals: Secrets of the trade. *Journal of Sports Chiropractic & Rehabilitation, 15*(1), 5–19.

Greenhalgh, T., Robert, G., Macfarlane, F., Bate, P., & Kyriakidou, O. (2004). Diffusion of innovations in service organizations: Systematic review and recommendations. *The Milbank Quarterly, 82*(4), 581–629.

Hackenberger, B. K. (2020). Bayesian meta-analysis now—Let's do it. *Croatian Medical Journal, 61*(6), 564–568. https://doi.org/10.3325/cmj.2020.61.564

Hansen, C., Steinmetz, H., & Block, J. (2022). How to conduct a meta-analysis in eight steps: A practical guide. *Management Review Quarterly, 72*, 1–19. https://doi.org/10.1007/s11301-021-00247-4

Harden, A., Garcia, J., Oliver, S., Rees, R., Shepherd, J., Brunton, G., & Oakley, A. (2004). Applying systematic review methods to studies of people's views: An example from public health research. *Journal of Epidemiology and Community Health, 58*, 794–800. https://doi.org/10.1136/jech.2003.014829

Harden, S. M., McEwan, D., Sylvester, B. D., Kaulius, M., Ruissen, G., Burke, S. M., Estabrooks, P. A., & Beauchamp, M. R. (2015). Understanding for whom, under what conditions, and how group-based physical activity interventions are successful: A realist review. *BMC Public Health, 15*(1), 1.

Herber, O. R., Bücker, B., Metzendorf, M.-I., & Barroso, J. (2017). A qualitative meta-summary using Sandelowski and Barroso's method for synthesizing qualitative research to explore barriers and facilitators to self-care in heart failure patients. *European Journal of Cardiovascular Nursing, 16*, 662–677. https://doi.org/10.1177/1474515117711007

Herber, O. R., Kastaun, S., Wilm, S., & Barroso, J. (2019). From qualitative meta-summary to qualitative meta-synthesis: Introducing a new situation-specific theory of barriers and facilitators for self-Care in Patients with Heart Failure. *Qualitative Health Research, 29*(1), 96–106.

Hoffman, D. L., & Holbrook, M. B. (1993). The intellectual structure of consumer research. *Journal of Consumer Research, 19*(4), 505–517.

Kitchenham, B., & Charters, S. (2007). *Guidelines for performing systematic literature reviews in software engineering*. In EBSE technical report. Software Engineering Group, School of

Computer Science and Mathematics, Keele University, Department of Computer Science, University of Durham.
Kuhn, T. S. (1970). *The structure of scientific revolutions* (International encyclopedia of unified science) (Vol. 2(2)). University of Chicago Press.
Levac, D., Colquhoun, H., & O'Brien, K. K. (2010). Scoping studies: Advancing the methodology. *Implementation Science, 5*(1), 69. https://doi.org/10.1186/1748-5908-5-69
Lim, W. M., & Kumar, S. (2024). Guidelines for interpreting the results of bibliometric analysis: A sensemaking approach. *Global Business and Organizational Excellence, 43*(2), 17–26. https://doi.org/10.1002/joe.22229
Limkakeng, A. T., Jr., Herling de Oliveira, L. L., Moreira, T., Phadtare, A., Garcia Rodrigues, C., Hocker, M. B., McKinney, R., Voils, C. I., & Pietrobon, R. (2014). Systematic review and meta-summary of attitudes toward research in emergency medical conditions. *Journal of Medical Ethics, 40*(6), 401–408.
Lindell, M. K., & Perry, R. W. (2000). Household adjustment to earthquake hazard: A review of research. *Environment and Behavior, 32*(4), 461–501.
Lucas, P. J., Baird, J., Arai, L., Law, C., & Roberts, H. M. (2007). Worked examples of alternative methods for the synthesis of qualitative and quantitative research in systematic reviews. *BMC Medical Research Methodology, 7*(1), 4.
Mak, S., & Thomas, A. (2022). Steps for conducting a scoping review. *Journal of Graduate Medical Education, 14*(5), 565–567.
Malekpour, S., Brown, R. R., & de Haan, F. J. (2015). Strategic planning of urban infrastructure for environmental sustainability: Understanding the past to intervene for the future. *Cities, 46*, 67–75.
Mikkonen, K., & Kääriäinen, M. (2020). Content analysis in systematic reviews. In H. Kyngäs, K. Mikkonen, & M. Kääriäinen (Eds.), *The application of content analysis in nursing science research*. Springer. https://doi.org/10.1007/978-3-030-30199-6_10
Moschis, G. P. (1990). Approaches to the study of consumer behavior in late life. *Advances in Consumer Research, XVIII*, 517–520.
Moschis, G. P. (1994). Consumer behavior in later life: Multidisciplinary contributions and implication for research. *Journal of the Academy of Marketing Science, 22*(3), 195–204.
Neely, E., Walton, M., & Stephens, C. (2014). Young people's food practices and social relationships. A thematic synthesis. *Appetite, 82*, 50–60.
Noblit, G. W., & Hare, R. D. (1988). *Meta-ethnography: Synthesizing qualitative studies*. Sage.
Paré, G., Trudel, M.-C., Jaana, M., & Kitsiou, S. (2015). Synthesizing information systems knowledge: A typology of literature reviews. *Information & Management, 52*, 183–199.
Paterson, B. L., Thorne, S. E., Canam, C., & Jillings, C. (2001). *Meta-study of qualitative health research. A practical guide to meta-analysis and meta-synthesis*. Sage Publications.
Paul, J., Khatri, P., & Duggal, H. K. (2023). Frameworks for developing impactful systematic literature reviews and theory building: What, why and how? *Journal of Decision Systems*. https://doi.org/10.1080/12460125.2023.2197700
Paul, J., Martinez, L. F., Singh, R. K., & Koklic, M. K. (2024). Systematic literature reviews in consumer studies. *International Journal of Consumer Studies*, Call for Papers—Annual Special Issue: Submission period: February 15–May 31, 2024 https://onlinelibrary.wiley.com/page/journal/14706431/homepage/callforpapers. Downloaded on January 5, 2024.
Pawson, R., Greenhalgh, T., Harvey, G., & Walshe, K. (2005). Realist review: A new method of systematic review designed for complex policy interventions. *Journal of Health Services Research and Policy, 70*(1), 21–34.
Pollock, D., Davies, E. L., Peters, M. D., et al. (2021). Undertaking a scoping review: A practical guide for nursing and midwifery students, clinicians, researchers, and academics. *Journal of Advanced Nursing, 77*, 2102–2113.
Popay, J., Roberts, H., Sowden, A., Petticrew, M., Arai, L., Rodgers, M., Britten, N., Roen, K., & Duffy, S. (2006). *Guidance on the conduct of narrative synthesis in systematic reviews*. A product from the ESRC methods programme Version 1:b92.

Reis, D. J., Kaizer, A. M., Kinney, A. R., Bahraini, N. H., Holliday, R., Forster, J. E., & Brenner, L. A. (2023). A practical guide to random-effects Bayesian meta-analyses with application to the psychological trauma and suicide literature. *Psychological Trauma: Theory, Research, Practice, and Policy, 15*(1), 121–130. https://doi.org/10.1037/tra0001316

Ridgway, N. M., Kukar-Kinney, M., & Monroe, K. B. (2008). An expanded conceptualization and a new measure of compulsive buying. *Journal of Consumer Research, 35*(4), 622–639.

Rigolon, A. (2016). A complex landscape of inequity in access to urban parks: A literature review. *Landscape and Urban Planning, 153*, 160–169.

Ritzer, G. (1991). *Metatheorizing in Sociology*. Lexington Books.

Roberts, K. A., Dixon-Woods, M., Fitzpatrick, R., Abrams, K. R., & Jones, D. R. (2002). Factors affecting uptake of childhood immunization: A Bayesian synthesis of qualitative and quantitative evidence. *The Lancet, 360*(9345), 1596–1599.

Rycroft-Malone, J., McCormack, B., Hutchinson, A. M., et al. (2012). Realist synthesis: Illustrating the method for implementation research. *Implementation Science, 7*, 33. https://doi.org/10.1186/1748-5908-7-33

Sandelowski, M., & Barroso, J. (2007). *Handbook for synthesizing qualitative research*. Springer Publishing Company.

Sandelowski, M., & Leeman, J. (2012). Writing usable qualitative health research findings. *Qualitative Health Research, 22*(10), 1404–1413.

Schutz, A. (1962). Collected papers. Vol. 1. Martinus Nijhoff. 1964. *Collected papers* 2.

Snyder, H. (2019). Literature review as a research methodology: An overview and guidelines. *Journal of Business Research, 104*, 333–339.

Spiegelhalter, D., Myles, J. P., Jones, D. R., & Abrams, K. R. (1999). An introduction to Bayesian methods in health technology assessment. *British Medical Journal, 319*(7208), 508.

Stemler, S. (2001). An overview of content analysis. *Practical Assessment, Research, and Evaluation, 7*, Article 17.

Strauss, A., & Corbin, J. (1998). *Basics of qualitative research: Techniques and procedures for developing grounded theory*. Sage.

Stremersch, S., Verniers, I., & Verhoef, P. C. (2007). The quest for citations: Drivers of article impact. *Journal of Marketing, 71*(3), 171–193. https://doi.org/10.1509/jmkg.71.3.171

Suikkala, A., & Leino-Kilpi, H. (2000). Nursing student-patient relationships: A review of the literature from 1984–1998. *Journal of Advanced Nursing., 2000*(33), 42–50. https://doi.org/10.1046/j.1365-2648.2001.01636.x

Sutton, A. J., & Abrams, K. R. (2001). Bayesian methods in meta-analysis and evidence synthesis. *Statistical Methods in Medical Research, 10*(4), 277–303.

Thomas, J., & Harden, A. (2008). Methods for the thematic synthesis of qualitative research in systematic reviews. *BMC Medical Research Methodology, 8*(1), 1.

Weed, M. (2005). Meta interpretation: A method for the interpretive synthesis of qualitative research. *Forum Qualitative Sozialforschung/Forum: Qualitative Social Research, 6*(1).

Wong, G., MacPhee, M., Merrett, K., Miller, K., Taylor, S., & Pawliuk, C. (2020). The realist review process workshop [presentation]. https://doi.org/10.14288/1.0390457.

Xiao, Y., & Watson, M. (2019). Guidance on conducting a systematic literature review. *Journal of Planning Education and Research, 39*(1), 93–112. https://doi.org/10.1177/0739456X17723971

Zhao, S. (1991). Metatheory, metamethod, meta-data-analysis: What, why and how? *Sociological Perspectives, 34*, 377–390.

9 Cross-Cultural Research

Cross-cultural research is a systematic and comparative study of different cultures, societies, or cultural groups to understand and analyze the similarities, differences, and interactions between them. This type of research aims to explore various aspects of human behavior, beliefs, values, customs, and practices across diverse cultural contexts. Cross-cultural research often involves the collection and analysis of data from multiple cultures or cultural groups to uncover patterns, relationships, and insights that can contribute to our understanding of how culture influences various aspects of human life.

Cross-cultural research involves comparing cultural groups or societies to identify variations and commonalities in behavior, attitudes, and other cultural phenomena. It often draws from various academic disciplines, such as anthropology, psychology, sociology, and communication studies, to provide a holistic understanding of cultural differences and similarities. Researchers collect quantitative data using standardized methods to ensure consistency and reliability in cross-cultural comparisons, and they use qualitative methods to understand various types of cultural phenomena (e.g., rituals, customs) and people in these cultures.

Cross-cultural studies are an integral part of various academic disciplines and international business. Cross-cultural research holds significant importance in the academic, social, and practical realms for several compelling reasons:

1. Cross-cultural research fosters a deeper understanding of different cultures, societies, and their unique attributes. It helps individuals and societies appreciate the richness and diversity of human experiences, values, and worldviews.
2. In an increasingly interconnected world, understanding and bridging cultural gaps is crucial. Cross-cultural research provides insights into how to navigate and bridge these gaps, both in interpersonal interactions and on a larger scale in international relations.

G. P. Moschis, *Academic Research in Business and the Social Sciences*,
https://doi.org/10.1007/978-3-031-56548-9_9

3. Research findings from cross-cultural studies help promote cultural sensitivity and respect, reducing the potential for misunderstandings, stereotypes, and cultural biases. This sensitivity is particularly vital in diverse workplaces, educational settings, and global business environments.
4. Cross-cultural research can inform the development of effective public policies and programs. It provides policymakers with evidence-based insights into how cultural factors impact issues like healthcare, education, social welfare, and immigration.
5. Within academia, cross-cultural research enriches various disciplines, including anthropology, psychology, sociology, linguistics, and communication studies. It contributes to the advancement of theoretical frameworks and the development of new research questions.
6. Businesses operating on a global scale benefit from cross-cultural research by understanding consumer behavior, marketing strategies, negotiation techniques, and workforce management in diverse cultural contexts. This knowledge can lead to improved competitiveness and profitability.
7. Effective communication across cultures is critical in our interconnected world. Cross-cultural research provides insights into communication styles, nonverbal cues, and language use, facilitating better intercultural interactions.
8. Cross-cultural research is invaluable in education, informing curriculum development, teaching strategies, and approaches to fostering cultural competence among students. It helps educators create inclusive and culturally sensitive learning environments.
9. Many global challenges, such as climate change, pandemics, and economic inequalities, require international cooperation. Cross-cultural research can shed light on how cultural factors influence perceptions of these issues and contribute to collaborative solutions.
10. By fostering empathy, understanding, and tolerance among individuals from different cultural backgrounds, cross-cultural research plays a role in promoting peace and reducing conflicts based on cultural differences.

To summarize, cross-cultural research is a vital tool for promoting cultural understanding, facilitating effective cross-cultural interactions, informing policy and business decisions, and advancing academic knowledge. It has far-reaching implications for addressing contemporary global challenges and promoting a more inclusive and interconnected world. The findings from cross-cultural research can have practical applications in fields such as international business, intercultural communication, education, and public policy, helping individuals and organizations navigate cultural diversity more effectively. Overall, cross-cultural research contributes to our knowledge of how culture shapes human behavior and provides insights that can enhance cultural understanding, cooperation, and communication in an increasingly globalized world.

9.1 Conceptual Frameworks

In cross-cultural research, theoretical and conceptual models serve as frameworks to guide the study of cultural differences and similarities. These models help researchers organize their investigations, develop hypotheses, and understand the complex interplay of cultural factors. This section discusses several theoretical and conceptual models commonly used in cross-cultural research.

9.1.1 Theories and Models

Hofstede's Cultural Dimensions Theory Geert Hofstede's (1980) model identifies several dimensions of culture, including individualism-collectivism, power distance, uncertainty avoidance, masculinity-femininity, and long-term orientation. Researchers use these dimensions to analyze and compare cultures, helping to explain variations in behavior, values, and attitudes.

Trompenaars' Cultural Dimensions Fons Trompenaars proposed a model that includes his seven dimensions of culture, which is a framework for understanding cultural differences in various contexts, particularly in the business world (e.g., Trompenaars and HampdenTurner, 1997). Dimensions are as follows: universalism-particularism, individualism-communitarianism, specific-diffuse, neutral-emotional, sequential-synchronic, internal-outer direction, and achievement-ascription. These dimensions assist researchers in understanding cultural differences in decision-making, communication, and conflict resolution.

Hall's High-Low Context Communication Edward T. Hall (1976) introduced the concept of high-context and low-context communication styles. High-context cultures rely heavily on nonverbal cues and contextual information, while low-context cultures prioritize explicit verbal communication. This model helps explain com munication variations across cultures. Hall's work has been influential in understanding how cultures differ in their communication styles, particularly in terms of the reliance on explicit verbal communication versus nonverbal cues.

The Cultural Intelligence (CQ) Framework Developed by David Livermore (2015), the CQ framework is designed to assess and enhance an individual's or an organization's ability to work effectively in culturally diverse settings. It consists of four components: metacognitive, cognitive, motivational, and behavioral CQ. This model helps researchers and practitioners understand how individuals can adapt to different cultural contexts.

Social Identity Theory Tajfel and Turner's Social Identity Theory (1979) explains how individuals categorize themselves and others into social groups and derive their identity from these group memberships. The theory focuses on the development of social identity and intergroup behavior, helping understand how intergroup dynamics, such as stereotypes and prejudices, influence behavior and perceptions across cultures.

Acculturation Models Berry (1992) introduced a model of acculturation that classifies individual adaptation strategies along two dimensions. The first dimension pertains to whether an individual retains or rejects their native culture, while the second dimension relates to the adoption or rejection of the host culture. From these two dimensions, four acculturation strategies emerge: (a) assimilation, where individuals adopt the cultural norms of the dominant or host culture over their original culture; (b) separation, where individuals reject the dominant or host culture in favor of preserving their culture of origin, often facilitated by immigration to ethnic enclaves; (c) integration, where individuals can adopt the cultural norms of the dominant or host culture while maintaining their culture of origin, often leading to biculturalism; and (d) marginalization, where individuals reject both their culture of origin and the dominant host culture.

Acculturation models, like Berry's bidimensional model (integration, assimilation, separation, and marginalization), help researchers study how individuals or groups from different cultures adapt to a new cultural environment. These models provide insights into the acculturation strategies employed by individuals in diverse cultural contexts (Berry, 2017; Schwarz and Unger, 2017).

Cultural Syndromes Theory This theory, particularly focusing on dimensions like individualism and collectivism, as presented by Triantis (1993), posits that cultures can be characterized by distinct cultural syndromes, which are patterns of behavior, cognition, and emotion prevalent in a particular culture. Researchers use this framework to analyze the prevalence and impact of cultural syndromes across cultures.

Cross-Cultural Psychology Theories The field of cross-cultural psychology has produced various theories and models, such as Markus and Kitayama's (1991) theory of independent and interdependent selves, that examine how cultural factors shape human psychology and behavior. The theory contrasts two fundamental ways in which individuals in different cultures may perceive themselves in relation to others and their social context.

Cultural Ecological Models Cultural ecology theories emphasize the relationship between culture and the physical environment. These models explore how cultural practices, beliefs, and adaptations are influenced by geographical and environmental factors. Berry and associates (1992) are known for their work on the ecological theory of cultural development. The ecological theory emphasizes the interaction between culture and the environment in shaping cognitive and behavioral patterns across different societies.

Critical and Postcolonial Theories Critical theories refer to a diverse set of perspectives that share a common commitment to critiquing and challenging social structures, power dynamics, and dominant ideologies. These theories often seek to uncover hidden assumptions, question established norms, and promote social justice. Postcolonial theories are a diverse set of intellectual frameworks that critically examine the legacies, impacts, and ongoing effects of colonialism. Postcolonialism and critical theories focus on power dynamics, colonial legacies, and issues of inequality in cross-cultural interactions. They are particularly relevant for research addressing social justice and decolonization.

Life Course Model This model is based on the life course paradigm (LCP), which is considered "one of the most important achievements of social science in the second half of the 20th century" (Colby, 1998, p. *x*) and is widely used internationally and across disciplines (Elder et al., 2003). It was developed by the author, who operationalized the tenets and paradigmatic principles of LCP and used them to develop a conceptual framework that has been employed for studying a wide variety of consumption-related phenomena of varying durations in numerous cultural contexts (e.g., Mathur, 2019, 2020; Moschis, 2019, 2021).

These theoretical and conceptual models provide researchers with frameworks to study cultural phenomena systematically, make cross-cultural comparisons, and gain a deeper understanding of the intricate interplay between culture and human behavior. Researchers often select the most appropriate model(s) based on their research objectives and the cultural dimensions they intend to explore.

9.1.2 Cultural Dimensions

Cultural dimensions are a framework used in the field of cross-cultural psychology and communication to understand and analyze the variations in cultural norms, values, and behaviors among different societies. These dimensions were initially developed by Geert Hofstede, a Dutch social psychologist, and have since been expanded upon by other scholars. They provide a structured way to compare and contrast cultures, helping individuals and organizations navigate the complexities of intercultural interactions. Several of these dimensions are integral parts of the conceptual models discussed in the previous section. Following are some of the most well-known cultural dimensions and their relevance:

1. *Individualism vs. Collectivism.* This dimension indicates the degree to which a culture prioritizes individual goals and autonomy (individualism) as opposed to group goals and interdependence (collectivism). Understanding this dimension helps in managing teamwork, leadership, and decision-making styles in diverse cultural contexts.
2. *Power Distance.* Power distance assesses the willingness to embrace hierarchical authority and the allocation of power within a society. Cultures with high power distance exhibit a greater acceptance of unequal power distribution, whereas those with low power distance typically value more egalitarian relationships. Knowledge of power distance can assist in adapting management and communication styles.

3. *Uncertainty Avoidance.* This dimension evaluates a culture's capacity to tolerate ambiguity and risk. Cultures characterized by high uncertainty avoidance often adhere to strict rules and rituals, while those with low uncertainty avoidance are generally more flexible and receptive to change. Recognizing this dimension helps in negotiations and managing expectations in unfamiliar environments.
4. *Masculinity vs. Femininity.* This dimension assesses the extent to which a culture values traditional masculine traits (e.g., competitiveness, assertiveness) versus feminine traits (e.g., cooperation, nurturance). Understanding this dimension is crucial for developing marketing strategies and managing workplace dynamics.
5. *Long-Term Orientation vs. Short-Term Orientation.* This dimension reflects a culture's time perspective. Cultures with a long-term orientation emphasize persistence, thrift, and perseverance, while those with a short-term orientation focus more on immediate rewards and results. Recognizing this dimension can be helpful in strategic planning and relationship-building.
6. *Indulgence vs. Restraint.* This dimension, also introduced by Hofstede, measures a society's approach to gratification and impulse control. Cultures with high indulgence allow for the gratification of desires, while cultures with high restraint emphasize the regulation of one's desires. Awareness of this dimension can aid in marketing and lifestyle-related decision-making.
7. *Communication Styles.* Understanding cultural dimensions can also help in grasping communication styles. For example, high-context cultures (e.g., Asian cultures) rely heavily on nonverbal cues and shared context, while low-context cultures (e.g., Western cultures) place greater emphasis on clear verbal communication.

Several of these dimensions are also seen in the results of the Global Leadership and Organizational Behavior Effectiveness (GLOBE) project, one of the leading cultural frameworks in the fields of management and psychology research that has been introduced by an international team of hundreds of collaborating researchers. This project has developed and assessed nine distinct cultural dimensions across 62 countries, which form ten clusters composed of groups of countries found to share similarities in numerous cultural aspects.

The nine dimensions include institutional collectivism, power distance, in-group collectivism, uncertainty avoidance, humane orientation, performance orientation, future orientation, gender egalitarianism, and assertiveness.

The relevance of cultural dimensions lies in their ability to enhance intercultural understanding and effective communication, which is crucial in the increasingly globalized world. By recognizing and respecting these dimensions, individuals and organizations can avoid misunderstandings, foster better relationships, and make more informed decisions in diverse cultural settings. However, it is important to note that these dimensions provide a broad framework and should not be used to stereotype individuals or oversimplify complex cultural realities. Additionally, cultures are not static, and they can evolve over time, so it is essential to use these dimensions as a starting point for cultural analysis rather than as rigid categories.

9.1.3 The Role of Context in Cross-Cultural Research

Context plays a crucial role in cross-cultural research. Cross-cultural research aims to understand and compare behaviors, beliefs, attitudes, and other aspects of human life across different cultural groups. The role of context in this type of research cannot be overstated, as it profoundly influences the interpretation and generalizability of findings. The following are some key points to consider:

1. *Cultural Specificity*. Context helps researchers appreciate the cultural specificity of phenomena. Many behaviors and beliefs are deeply rooted in cultural norms, values, and traditions. Without understanding the cultural context, researchers may misinterpret or oversimplify findings, leading to inaccurate conclusions.
2. *Cultural Relativity*. Context helps researchers acknowledge that what may be considered "normal" or "appropriate" in one culture may differ significantly in another. Cultural relativity emphasizes the importance of understanding behaviors and beliefs within their cultural context rather than imposing one's own cultural standards.
3. *Research Design*. Context influences research design. Researchers must tailor their methods, measurements, and data collection techniques to suit the cultural context they are studying. This may involve adapting surveys, questionnaires, or interview protocols to be culturally sensitive.
4. *Language and Communication*. Language is a crucial aspect of context. Researchers must consider linguistic nuances, idioms, and cultural-specific terms that can affect communication. The choice of language for surveys or interviews also matters, as it can impact response quality.
5. *Sampling and Participant Selection*. Context informs the selection of participants. Researchers must consider who represents the target cultural group and how best to access them. This may involve working with local collaborators who understand the cultural context.
6. *Interpretation of Findings*. The interpretation of research findings should always be contextualized. Researchers should avoid making sweeping generalizations about cultures based on limited data. Findings should be framed in the context of the specific cultural group studied.
7. *Ethical Considerations*. Ethical considerations in cross-cultural research are heavily influenced by context. What is considered ethical in one culture may not be in another. Researchers must be aware of and respect local ethical standards and ensure informed consent.
8. *Historical and Socioeconomic Context*. Historical and socioeconomic factors also play a significant role. Understanding the history of a culture and its current socioeconomic conditions can provide important insights into the behavior and beliefs of its members.
9. *Cross-Cultural Competence*. Researchers need cross-cultural competence, which involves cultural sensitivity, awareness, and the ability to adapt to different contexts. Training in cross-cultural research methods and ethics is essential.

10. *Applicability and Generalizability.* The role of context affects the extent to which research findings can be applied or generalized to other cultural groups. Researchers must carefully consider the limits of generalizability based on the context of their study.

In summary, context is integral to the entire cross-cultural research process, from conceptualization and data collection to analysis and interpretation. Researchers must be acutely aware of the cultural context in which they work, and their findings should always be presented with sensitivity to that context. This approach ensures that cross-cultural research is respectful and meaningful and contributes to a deeper understanding of human diversity.

9.2 Use of Quantitative Methods

9.2.1 Sampling

Sampling challenges arise when trying to create a representative sample of a foreign population. Differences in population size, demographics, and geographical distribution can make it difficult to select a sample that accurately reflects the entire population. Researchers must also grapple with the challenge of selecting culturally appropriate sampling methods, as what works in one country may not be suitable in another.

9.2.2 Measurement

Ensuring the use of reliable and valid measurement instruments in cross-cultural research is essential for obtaining meaningful and accurate results. In order to achieve this, the researcher should consider doing the following:

- Conduct a comprehensive literature review to identify existing measurement instruments that have been used in similar cross-cultural research. Look for instruments that have already been tested and validated in the countries you are interested in.
- Reach out to experts in the field of your research who have experience with cross-cultural studies. They can provide valuable insights and guidance on selecting appropriate instruments.
- If the measurement instrument is in a language different from the target countries, you may need to translate it and back translate it. This translation should be conducted by bilingual experts and undergo a rigorous process to ensure linguistic and cultural equivalence.
- Before using the instrument in your main study, conduct pilot tests in the target countries. This helps identify potential issues with the translation and cultural adaptation and allows for adjustments.
- Evaluate the reliability of the measurement instrument in each country. Common reliability measures include Cronbach's alpha for internal consistency and test-

retest reliability. Ensure that the instrument produces consistent results over time and across different samples.
- Assess the validity of the instrument. This involves examining whether the instrument measures what it is intended to measure. Types of validity to consider include content validity, construct validity, and criterion validity.
- Conduct cross-cultural validation studies to ensure that the instrument works effectively in different cultural contexts. This may involve comparing results from different countries to assess measurement invariance (Steenkamp and Baumgartner, 1998).
- Ensure that your sample size is sufficient and diverse enough to provide robust findings. A larger and more diverse sample can help identify potential issues with the instrument's performance in different subgroups.
- Seek feedback from experts in the target countries regarding the cultural relevance and appropriateness of the instrument. They can provide insights that may not be apparent to non-native researchers.
- Keep in mind that cultures evolve over time, so even if an instrument initially works well, it is essential to continuously monitor its performance in different countries and be prepared to make adjustments if needed.
- Respect ethical guidelines and obtain informed consent when administering instruments in other countries. Ensure that your research follows ethical standards in each cultural context.
- When analyzing data collected using a measurement instrument, use appropriate statistical techniques to account for potential cross-cultural differences. For example, you may need to employ multigroup confirmatory factor analysis to assess measurement invariance (Steenkamp and Baumgartner, 1998).

9.2.3 Reliability and Validity

Numerous commonly employed measurement instruments that include a combination of wording styles, encompassing both positively phrased items and negatively phrased items, as seen in measures related to materialism and well-being, have demonstrated effectiveness when used with individuals in the United States. However, they raise concerns about their reliability and validity when applied in cross-cultural contexts. These concerns have been highlighted in studies conducted by Wong et al. (2003), Eastman et al. (1997), Ger and Belk (1996), Iwata et al. (1995), and Nakano (2001). To illustrate, research has shown that measures incorporating mixed-worded items, which are designed to assess psychological well-being (e.g., optimism and anxiety) and which appear to be unidimensional for participants in the United States, actually split into distinct positive and negative factors for Asian Americans. This phenomenon has been observed in studies conducted by Wong et al. (2003), Nakano (2001), Cheng and Hamid (1997), and Suzuki et al. (2000).

Wong et al.'s (2003) research delves into the complexities of utilizing mixed-worded scales in cross-cultural investigations. Other scholars, such as Schwarz (2003), also suggest that issues associated with mixed-worded item (MWI) scales often arise within subcultural groups, including those defined by ethnicity, age, and race. While existing research indicates that challenges linked to MWI scales tend to be more prominent in specific cross-cultural and subcultural contexts, the underlying causes remain unclear, as noted by Wong et al. (2003). Several hypotheses have been advanced to shed light on why MWI formats may present difficulties for particular groups, encompassing disparities in their comprehension, interpretation, and response to reverse-worded items. These disparities might be influenced by factors such as age, cultural differences, religious beliefs, or contextual elements, as proposed by Schwarz (2003) and Wong et al. (2003). Nevertheless, it is important to highlight that these suppositions, while intuitively plausible, have not been subjected to rigorous empirical testing.

Diamantopoulos et al. (2006) suggest that responses to questions may differ based on content and presentation, with the latter differing due to response styles. They find that response styles differ across different stimulus formats and that response style effects impact cross-national comparisons in an inconsistent way. As cultures and subcultures are typically defined by factors such as religion, ethnic identity or background, and citizenship, it is difficult to isolate the factor(s) responsible for participant or informant responses to questions in surveys or in-depth interviews, especially in cross-national studies. Thus, researchers must account for the level of measurement invariance due to cultural factors but also the effects of these factors on the influence of variables in their models (Baker et al., 2013a).

In one of our studies, we investigate potential reasons for variations in reliability coefficients by analyzing cross-sectional data from three countries: the United States, Japan, and Malaysia (Moschis et al., 2011). Our analysis aims to test and potentially disprove these variations. The hypotheses we examine pertain to the impact of question and item context, format, sequence, and aging in these three countries. While our findings do align with some of the hypotheses, they also raise additional concerns about the potential sources of measurement differences. Moreover, they call into question the suitability of measures originally developed in the United States for application in other countries and among subcultures within countries. This highlights the importance of testing these instruments in specific contextual settings before their widespread use.

My general experience in testing instruments developed in the United States in more than a dozen countries in every continent is the following: First, negatively worded items (NWI) do not perform well as positively worded items (PWI) on scales administered to adults in Latin American and Asian countries. This may be due to cultural norms in these countries, such as acquiescence (Wong et al., 2003) or difficulty in responding to the NWI format (Diamantopoulos et al., 2006). For example, our studies in Asian countries where we use measures of subjective well-being that consist of mixed-worded items (MWI) (e.g., Rosengberg, 1965) and only PWI (Diener et al., 1985) find the items on MWI split into PWI and NWI factors for the former scale. This poses an additional problem when we attempt to use social desirability scales that contain MWI (e.g., Strahan and Gerbasi, 1972), as MWI scales tend to consistently produce relatively low reliabilities.

Second, regardless of cultural context or country, including the United States, people appear to have greater difficulty in responding to wordings of NWI than PWI formats. This is shown in the work of Richins (2004), where she attempts to develop a shorter version of the material values scale (MVS). Nearly every "poorly performing" item that was eliminated from the original 18-item scale, as well as shorter versions of it (15- and 9-item scales), was NWI. Therefore, my advice to early career researchers is as follows: Don't use MWI scales, or use scales with only PWI.

Finally, when using scales with "agree-disagree" response formats for items that measure constructs, I suggest you avoid including a midpoint category (e.g., "neither agree nor disagree"), especially in Asian countries. Instead, transform "agree/disagree" wording into "somewhat agree/disagree" or "tend to agree/disagree." A midpoint response category is an invitation for participants not to think much before they respond, or they are not sure; it can generate highly skewed distributions, with up to 90% of responses to 5-point scales shown as midpoint responses in some cases, potentially affecting scale reliability and study results.

9.3 Use of Qualitative Methods

The choice of qualitative research methods for academic studies in other countries should be guided by the research questions, objectives, and the specific cultural and contextual factors of the study. Qualitative research is versatile and adaptable.

9.3.1 Data Collection Methods

Data collection qualitative methods that are commonly used and particularly appropriate for international research include the following: ethnography, in-depth interviews, focus groups, and case studies.

Ethnography Ethnographic research involves immersive fieldwork and participant observation. (see Chap. 8). It is well-suited for studying the culture and social practices of a specific community or group in another country. Researchers can gain a deep understanding of the local context, beliefs, and behaviors.

In-depth Interviews Conducting in-depth interviews allows researchers to explore the perspectives, experiences, and opinions of individuals from different cultural backgrounds. This method is valuable for cross-cultural studies as it provides rich, contextualized data. Conducting person-to-person interviews in foreign countries can be a rewarding but challenging endeavor for academic researchers. These challenges can stem from various factors, including cultural, logistical, and ethical considerations. Following are some of the key challenges associated with conducting interviews in foreign countries:

- One of the most common and significant challenges is the *language barrier*. Researchers may not be fluent in the local language, which can impede effective communication with participants. Translation services may be required, but this can introduce issues related to accuracy and interpretation, suggesting the need for a back translation.
- Researchers must be *culturally sensitive* and aware of local customs, norms, and taboos. Failure to do so can lead to misunderstandings or offense, which can hinder the research process and damage relationships with participants.
- Finding and *gaining access* to suitable participants can be challenging, especially in countries where there may be legal or bureaucratic hurdles to research. Building trust within the local community is often necessary to secure participants.
- Arranging interviews in foreign countries involves *logistical challenges* such as securing appropriate venues, transportation, and accommodations. These logistics can be particularly complex in remote or less-developed regions.
- *Ethical considerations* may differ from those in the researcher's home country. Researchers must navigate local ethics review boards and ensure that their research complies with local ethical standards and regulations.
- International research often requires more *time and resources*. Travel, accommodation, and translation services can significantly increase the cost of the research project.
- Researchers from different cultural backgrounds may inadvertently introduce *bias into their interviews*, affecting the quality and validity of the data collected. It is important to be aware of and address these potential biases.
- Participants may feel *uncomfortable or hesitant* to share sensitive information with foreign researchers, particularly on topics that are culturally sensitive or politically charged.

Focus Groups Focus groups are useful for exploring collective viewpoints and cultural norms. When conducting focus groups in other countries, it is important to consider cultural dynamics and language differences. Nevid and Maria (1999) discuss factors that affect qualitative research, with emphasis on focus-group research, suggesting the cultural values that can affect the selection of research design, recruitment of focus-group participants, and ability to obtain information in group settings. They suggest the importance of demonstrating sensitivity and rapport with informants or members of focus groups, and other factors, such as the language of the moderator or the interviewer, can be factors in obtaining accurate information.

Case Studies Case studies can be based on an individual, a group, an organization, an event, or any phenomenon of interest. This method can be adapted to cross-cultural research by selecting cases from different countries and comparing them to identify similarities and differences. Case studies are a valuable research method in cross-cultural studies, allowing researchers to delve deeply into specific instances or contexts to gain a comprehensive understanding of how culture influences various phenomena. They often involve comparing findings across different cases or cultural contexts. This comparative approach helps identify cultural patterns, variations, and potential universalities. Case studies are particularly useful in exploring cultural variations, similarities, and differences in various aspects, such as communication, decision-making, and leadership, and they can generate rich, context-specific data that can provide insights into broader cultural patterns and theories.

Cross-cultural case studies typically involve qualitative data collection methods such as interviews, observations, and document analysis. They can contribute to the development or refinement of cross-cultural theories and models. By examining specific cases in detail, researchers can extend existing theories or propose new ones to explain cultural phenomena.

Finally, cross-cultural case studies can provide not only theoretical but also practical insights for various fields, including business, education, healthcare, and international relations. This method can be used to investigate topics such as leadership styles in multinational organizations, the impact of culture on healthcare practices, and cross-cultural negotiations in international business. Findings can inform policy decisions, cultural training programs, and cross-cultural communication strategies.

In sum, case studies are a valuable research method in cross-cultural studies because they allow for in-depth exploration of specific cultural contexts and provide insights into how culture influences various aspects of human behavior and society. However, sampling can be a challenge in cross-cultural case studies. Researchers must carefully select cases that represent the cultural diversity they aim to study. Language and translation issues may arise, requiring careful attention to ensure accurate data collection and interpretation. And ethical concerns related to informed consent, confidentiality, and cultural respect may arise when conducting cross-cultural case studies (see Chap. 12). Through careful data collection and analysis, cross-cultural case studies can contribute to our understanding of the complex interplay between culture and human experiences.

Other Methods Additional methods that can be used in cross-cultural research include: (1) *Content analysis*, which involves analyzing textual, visual, or audio materials to uncover patterns and themes, can be applied to cross-cultural research by examining media, literature, or other cultural artifacts from different countries. (2) *Narrative analysis*, which focuses on the stories people tell to make sense of their experiences, can help researchers understand cultural narratives and identity constructions. (3) *Visual methods*, such as photo-elicitation or video diaries, allow participants to express themselves in ways that may not be captured through traditional interviews. And (4) *historical analysis*, which involves the examination of historical documents, archives, and records, can help researchers understand historical aspects of a culture or country.

When conducting research in other countries, it is crucial to consider ethical aspects, including informed consent, cultural sensitivity, and ethical guidelines specific to the host country. Additionally, involving local researchers or collaborators who are familiar with the cultural context can enhance the quality and validity of one's research.

9.3.2 Cultural Coding and Interpretation

Cultural coding and interpretation are fundamental concepts in the field of cultural studies, anthropology, sociology, and semiotics. *Cultural coding* is the practice of assigning specific meanings and symbols to various elements within a culture. These elements can include language, symbols, rituals, art, clothing, gestures, and more. It is a way in which a society imparts information, beliefs, and customs. Language is a prime example of cultural coding. Words and phrases are used to convey complex ideas and emotions within a culture. Symbols, whether they be religious, political, or cultural, are also important forms of coding. For example, the American flag is a symbol deeply coded with meaning related to patriotism and national identity. Cultural coding also extends to social norms, which dictate what behaviors are considered acceptable or taboo within a society. These norms are typically transmitted through socialization and can vary greatly from culture to culture. Cultural coding involves the construction of meaning within a cultural context. It helps individuals and groups make sense of the world around them and shapes their perception of reality.

Cultural interpretation refers to the process of understanding and making sense of cultural codes. It involves analyzing and making sense of data or observations collected from different cultural groups or contexts, focusing on decoding the symbols, signs, and meanings embedded within a particular culture. Interpretation is subjective and can vary based on an individual's background, experiences, and perspectives, and it is often interdisciplinary, drawing from fields such as anthropology, sociology, literature, and art history, helping to uncover the layers of meaning embedded in cultural artifacts. Cultural interpretation acknowledges *cultural relativism*, the idea that one should approach other cultures without imposing one's own values and beliefs. Instead, it seeks to understand a culture on its own terms. Cultural interpretation often draws from *hermeneutics*, a philosophical approach to understanding texts and symbols. Hermeneutics emphasizes the importance of context and the interpreter's engagement with the material being interpreted. Lastly, it is worth mentioning that different *interpretive communities* exist within a society, each with its own set of beliefs and interpretations. For example, a religious community may interpret sacred texts differently from a secular one, leading to distinct understandings of the same cultural symbols.

In summary, cultural coding and interpretation are essential components of the study of culture. They involve the creation and understanding of meaning within a cultural context, encompassing language, symbols, norms, and the diverse ways different individuals and communities interpret and make sense of their cultural environment. These concepts are crucial for fostering cross-cultural understanding and addressing issues related to cultural diversity and identity.

9.4 Indigenous Research Methods in Cross-Cultural Research

Using indigenous research methods in cross-cultural research is an approach that recognizes and respects the cultural diversity of the world's indigenous peoples while conducting research across different cultures. This methodology is rooted in the idea that traditional Western research methods may not always be appropriate or effective when studying indigenous communities or conducting research in culturally diverse contexts. Instead, it emphasizes the importance of incorporating indigenous perspectives, values, and methodologies into the research process. The following facts and observations have implications for conducting indigenous studies:

- Indigenous research methods prioritize cultural sensitivity and respect for the customs, traditions, and worldviews of the communities being studied. Researchers should approach indigenous communities with humility and a willingness to learn from and collaborate with community members.
- Indigenous research methods often involve close collaboration with the community being studied. This means engaging community members in the research process, seeking their input and consent, and ensuring that research benefits the community in some way.
- Many indigenous cultures have rich oral traditions and storytelling practices. Researchers may incorporate these methods into their work, using narratives and storytelling as a way to gather and convey information.
- Indigenous research often takes a holistic approach, considering the interconnectedness of all aspects of life, including the environment, spirituality, and culture. Researchers may need to broaden their research questions and methods to encompass this holistic perspective.
- Indigenous communities often have specific cultural protocols and rituals that should be respected during the research process. Researchers must be aware of and adhere to these protocols.
- Indigenous research methods are guided by specific ethical principles, including reciprocity (giving back to the community), respect for intellectual property and traditional knowledge, and the right to control and interpret research findings.
- The gift of multiple perspectives, known as "two-eyed seeing," developed by Mi'kmaw Elder Albert Marshall, emphasizes the importance of viewing the world through both Indigenous and Western perspectives, as a way to promote the idea of approaching issues with a balanced perspective that respects and integrates both ways of knowing.
- Indigenous research methods aim to challenge and decolonize traditional Western research paradigms that may have historically marginalized indigenous voices and perspectives. This involves acknowledging and rectifying past injustices in research.
- Whenever possible, researchers should work in the local language and incorporate local knowledge systems. This can help bridge communication gaps and foster a deeper understanding of the research context.

- Indigenous research often emphasizes that data belongs to the community. Researchers should work with the community to determine how data will be used and shared, with the aim of empowering the community and avoiding exploitation.

Incorporating indigenous research methods into cross-cultural research is not only a matter of ethical research practice but also a way to enrich the depth and quality of research by drawing on the diverse perspectives and knowledge systems of indigenous communities. However, it is essential to approach this process with cultural humility, collaboration, and a commitment to upholding indigenous rights and values.

9.5 Challenges and Issues

Academic research is a global endeavor that often requires scholars to conduct studies in foreign countries to advance knowledge and address research questions. While international research can be intellectually rewarding, it also presents unique challenges. This section explores the complexities of conducting academic research in foreign countries, shedding light on the hurdles researchers may encounter and offering strategies to overcome them.

Conducting research in foreign countries necessitates a deep understanding of local cultures, customs, and social norms. Researchers must be sensitive to cultural differences that can impact interactions with study participants, data collection methods, and ethical considerations. Failure to account for cultural nuances can lead to misunderstandings or biased research outcomes.

9.5.1 Ethical and Legal Compliance

Different countries have ethical standards and regulations governing research. Compliance with local research ethics boards and regulations is essential. These can differ significantly from one country to another and may require extensive paperwork and approvals.

9.5.2 Access to Participants and Data

Gaining access to research participants and data sources can be a complex process, particularly when research involves vulnerable populations or sensitive topics. Recruiting participants for research can be more difficult in certain countries due to cultural, social, or logistical reasons. Researchers must establish trust within the local community, collaborate with local institutions, and navigate bureaucratic hurdles to secure access.

9.5.3 Cultural and Language Barriers

One of the foremost challenges researchers encounter when conducting consumer studies in foreign countries is navigating cultural and language differences. These differences can affect everything from survey design and question wording to data interpretation. Researchers must be culturally sensitive, ensuring their surveys and research methods are appropriate for the target culture, and they often require translation services to eliminate language barriers. Language can be a significant barrier to effective communication and data collection. Researchers may need to work with interpreters or translators, which can introduce potential issues related to translation accuracy and bias. Additionally, language barriers may limit access to certain segments of the population. Language can be a significant barrier, particularly when conducting fieldwork or collaborating with researchers from different linguistic backgrounds. Translation and interpretation services may be necessary.

9.5.4 Resources and Funding

Conducting research in foreign countries often demands additional resources, including travel expenses, personnel, and translation services. Securing funding can be a challenge, as grant applications may require demonstrating the significance of international research and the potential impact on the academic community. Access to funding and research resources can vary greatly between countries. Some countries may have robust funding mechanisms and well-equipped research facilities, while others may struggle to provide adequate support for research.

9.5.5 Data Quality

Ensuring the quality and reliability of data collected in foreign countries can be challenging due to language barriers, cultural differences, and varying research practices. Researchers must implement rigorous data validation and quality control measures to maintain research integrity.

9.5.6 Cultural Bias and Ethnocentrism

Researchers must be aware of their own cultural biases and avoid ethnocentrism, the tendency to view one's own culture as superior. This bias can affect research design, data collection, and interpretation of findings.

9.5.7 Collaboration Challenges

Collaborating with researchers in different countries can be challenging due to differences in time zones, work cultures, and communication styles.

9.5.8 Sampling and Generalizability

Achieving a representative sample is challenging in cross-cultural research. The selection of participants or groups for cross-cultural studies is challenging. Ensuring that samples are representative of the populations being studied is difficult, and small sample sizes can limit the generalizability of findings. Culture can be defined in numerous ways, and there can be substantial variation within a single culture. Ensuring that findings can be generalized beyond the studied group can be complex.

9.5.9 Measurement Equivalence

Many standard psychological and sociological measures have been developed in Western cultures. These may not be valid or reliable when used in different cultural contexts, leading to measurement bias. It is essential to ensure that the measures used in cross-cultural research are equivalent across cultures. This involves not only translation but also cultural adaptation to maintain the integrity of the data.

9.5.10 Data Analysis and Interpretation

Analyzing cross-cultural data can be complex. Researchers must decide whether to use a universal framework or account for cultural differences in their analysis. Both approaches have their advantages and challenges. Researchers must choose appropriate statistical techniques and consider how cultural factors may interact with one another. Understanding cultural nuances in data and interpreting findings accurately can be challenging for researchers who are not intimately familiar with the local context. The researcher's own background, experiences, and biases can influence data collection and interpretation. It is essential to acknowledge and address these potential sources of bias.

9.5.11 Publication Bias

Researchers' ability to publish cross-cultural research in reputable journals or gain recognition for their research can be challenging, especially if they are based in countries with less established research traditions. There is often a bias toward publishing research from Western, English-speaking cultures, which can limit the visibility of cross-cultural studies from non-Western contexts.

9.5.12 Ethnographic Research Challenges

In ethnographic research, where researchers immerse themselves in a culture, building trust and rapport with the studied community can be challenging, and maintaining objectivity can be difficult.

Conducting academic research in foreign countries offers invaluable opportunities for cross-cultural collaboration and the expansion of knowledge. However, these opportunities come with a unique set of challenges. Researchers must be well-prepared, culturally sensitive, and adaptable to navigate the complexities of international research successfully. By addressing these challenges, scholars can contribute meaningfully to their respective fields and foster global research collaborations that advance our understanding of complex issues.

9.5.13 Use of Measurement Instruments in Other Countries

Should a measurement instrument be used in other countries? This is one of the most frequently asked questions by early career researchers. The decision to use a measurement instrument developed in one country in another country depends on several factors, and it should be made after considering the following: First, if the measurement instrument is in a language different from that spoken in the country of the research study, it may need a back translation to ensure that the instrument measures what it intends to measure consistently. Second, it is advisable to adapt the measurement instrument for the new context through a process called *cross-cultural validation*. This involves making cultural and linguistic adjustments and testing the instrument's psychometric properties in the new population. The characteristics of the population in the target country should be similar to the population in which the scale was developed. If there are substantial differences in demographics or cultural factors, the scale's performance may vary.

Third, if the research goal is to make cross-country comparisons, using the same instrument can be advantageous. However, it is crucial to ensure that any differences observed are not due to measurement bias. Thus, assessing measurement invariance through confirmatory factor analysis is required (Steenkamp and Baumgartner, 1998). Fourth, different countries may have varying norms, standards, and practices in the domain being measured. Researchers should consider whether the instrument aligns with local standards and whether any adjustments are necessary. If the scale is not a good fit for the new context, consider cross-cultural adaptation methods such as translation, back-translation, and cognitive interviews. These methods can help ensure the scale's cultural equivalence. Collaboration with researchers from the target country can provide valuable insights into cultural appropriateness and help with adaptation. Finally, the use of the measurement instrument in a different country must comply with local ethical guidelines and legal regulations, and it may require permissions and approvals, if necessary.

In summary, while it is possible to use scales developed in one country for research in another, it requires careful consideration and adaptation to ensure the validity and reliability of one's research findings.

9.5.14 Generalizability of Findings to Other Countries

Can research findings in one country be generalized to others countries? The generalizability of research findings to other cultures and contexts is a critical consideration in academic research. It refers to the extent to which the results of a study conducted in one culture or context can be applied or extended to other cultures or contexts. This issue is particularly important in fields such as psychology, sociology, anthropology, and even in some areas of the natural sciences, where cultural and contextual differences can significantly impact the validity and applicability of research findings.

Researchers should be aware of factors that can affect the generalizability of their findings, and they need to be cautious about assuming that findings from one culture will apply universally because of the following reasons: First, different cultures have their own norms, values, beliefs, and behaviors. To enhance generalizability, it is often necessary to conduct cross-cultural studies that compare findings across multiple cultures. Second, the context in which a study is conducted can have a profound influence on the results. For example, economic, political, and social factors can vary widely between countries or regions. Researchers should carefully consider whether their findings are context-specific or have broader applicability. Third, the composition of the sample used in a study can affect generalizability. If a sample is not representative of the population or culture of interest, it may limit the extent to which findings can be generalized. Efforts should be made to obtain diverse and representative samples.

Fourth, the tools and measures used in a study should be culturally and contextually appropriate. Instruments that work well in one culture may not be valid or reliable in another. Researchers may need to adapt or develop new measures to ensure validity across cultures. Fifth, replicating studies in different cultures or contexts is a robust way to test the generalizability of findings. If similar results are obtained across diverse settings, it strengthens the case for generalizability. Sixth, developing theories that are grounded in cross-cultural or cross-contextual understanding can enhance generalizability. These theories can provide a framework for explaining why certain findings may be applicable across cultures or contexts. In a similar vein, meta-analysis, which involves synthesizing findings from multiple studies, can help researchers assess the consistency and magnitude of effects across different cultures and contexts.

In conclusion, researchers must carefully consider the cultural and contextual factors that may influence the generalizability of their findings. While some findings may have broad applicability, others may be context-specific. Conducting research that explicitly addresses cross-cultural and cross-contextual differences is essential for advancing our understanding of human behavior and phenomena in a globalized world.

9.6 Assessing Cultural Effects: The Case of Religion

The use of several definitions of culture in the literature and variables that define it present challenges to researchers who wish to assess cultural effects. Because religion can be used to define a culture and the strength of one's religious beliefs or religiosity is a variable often employed to assess cultural effects, this section illustrates how researchers can design a study to investigate such effects. To illustrate the examination of cultural effects, this section employs the example of religious orientation as a defining cultural variable to address disparities in selected behaviors and values across cultures. Select sections and materials from one of our earlier studies (Moschis and Ong, 2011) are used as illustrations. Specifically, four sections are presented in a condensed format for these illustrations: Introduction, Theory and Hypotheses, Method, and Findings and Implications. They are used to place relevant information, briefly describing in *italics* the information contained in each of these sections, to help researchers see how to craft and report a study of cultural effects.

Introduction *This section describes the importance of the topic, the problem, and the proposed research to address it. Text with references is used to illustrate the purpose of each subsection—importance of topic (A), problem (B), and purpose and objectives (C).*

A. ***Importance of topic.*** The topic of religious orientation has captivated social scientists for more than a century, with scholars like Durkheim (1912) delving into it. This fascination arises from the belief that religion plays a pivotal role in shaping an individual's conduct, well-being, and overall existence, as illustrated by the works of Ebaugh (2002), Francis and Kaldor (2002), Poloma and Pendleton (1990), and Woods et al. (1999). Moreover, there is compelling evidence indicating that religion can also exert an influence on specific aspects of consumer behavior, as demonstrated by the research of Burroughs and Riedfleisch (2002), Delener (1990, 1994), Hirschman (1981), McDaniel and Burnett (1990), Mokhlis (2006), and Wilkes et al. (1986). Consequently, there is a call for further exploration into how religious orientation impacts certain facets of an individual's life, encompassing their life satisfaction and consumption-related preferences.

B. ***Problem.*** *This section places existing knowledge in context and states the problem.*

   Research into religiosity and consumer behavior can be broadly categorized into two groups: the first group explores the connection between an individual's level of religiosity and their consumer choices, while the second group compares consumer behaviors among people from different cultures or subcultures. In the first category of studies, the focus primarily centers on examining how religiosity impacts consumer behavior within a particular culture, often without delving into the underlying factors that mediate the link between religion and consumer choices. However, it remains unclear whether religiosity itself is the causal factor or if other associated variables play a more significant role. For example, several studies have revealed that religious individuals tend to be older (who are also less educated as indicated; e.g., Moschis, 1992), and age exhibits an inverse relationship with materialism (as found in studies by Burroughs and Rindfleisch, 2002; LaBarbera and Gurhan, 1997). Could it be that the connection between religiosity and consumer behavior is influenced more by age-related factors rather than religiosity as the sole determinant?

Conversely, when examining consumer behavior across different cultures, studies often draw conclusions about the impact of religiosity based on differences between countries and cultures while paying minimal attention to country-specific variables such as economic and social factors, as well as other nonreligious elements that could influence behavior. These studies assume that variations in levels of religious orientation among people in different cultures or countries lead to disparities in consumption patterns, as demonstrated by research like that of Sood and Nasu (1995) and Wong et al. (2003). However, they often overlook alternative explanations for these differences, which could stem from a multitude of variables aside from religion, encompassing broader environmental influences, mediating processes, and variances in how individuals from different countries respond to questions and measurement instruments, as seen in the studies of Schwarz (2003) and Wong et al. (2003).

C. ***Purpose and objectives.*** *This section derives the study's purpose and objectives from materials in preceding paragraphs.*

In our study, we investigate whether the associations between religiosity and various behaviors observed in prior cross-country studies were a result of religious values themselves or other factors. We investigate how religiosity influences an individual's well-being and consumer preferences within a sample sourced from Malaysia, a culturally diverse country. The aim is to confirm the results of prior research, which utilized samples from various countries and regions, along with diverse measures of religiosity and well-being (Ebaugh, 2002; Francis and Kaldor, 2002; Poloma and Pendlenton, 1990; Wong et al., 2003; Woods et al., 1999). To ensure the accuracy of our findings, we carefully control for potential effects of factors linked to religiosity. Specifically, we control for the possible effects of age-related factors by using a sample of older consumers (age 50+). Furthermore, our research examines how religious beliefs within various ethnic and religious subcultures influence consumer behavior in Malaysia, a country renowned for its diverse religious subcultures. In doing so, we aim to account for other potential country-related influences, including gross national product, the extent of westernization, and broader cultural or environmental factors like exposure to advertisements, brand availability, and language, as suggested in previous studies (Kelley and de Graaf, 1997). Additionally, we take steps to minimize the impact of systematic errors that may affect responses from Asian consumers due to considerations of social desirability, drawing insights from the research of Schwarz (2003) and Wong et al. (2003).

Background and Hypotheses *This section focuses on explanations of the effects of religion, offering theories for the link of religiosity to our variables of interest in different cultural and subcultural contexts. Such explanations focus on mechanisms* *or processes that characterize development and change, serving in the formulation of hypotheses.*

While past research has identified positive associations between religiosity and an individual's well-being, we have relatively limited understanding of the mechanisms or processes that establish the link between religiosity and one's emotional or physical states and general behavior. Furthermore, there is scant knowledge regarding the reason(s) religiosity correlates with specific types of consumer behaviors among older consumers residing in countries outside of the United States. Some researchers have leaned on stress theory to explain the observed relationships between religiosity and well-being (e.g., Burroughs and Rindfleisch, 2002). They argue that individuals with higher religiosity tend to experience greater happiness because they turn to God for solace when facing everyday stresses, while those with lower religiosity may be more vulnerable to life stressors that negatively affect their well-being, a notion illustrated by Lazarus and Folkman (1984). Thus, we hypothesize that religiosity would positively contribute to an individual's well-being, defined by criteria frequently suggested in prior studies, including self-esteem, life satisfaction, and physical and emotional health (as reported in research by Amato and Sobolewski, 2001; Larson, 1978; Thoits and Hewitt, 2001; Uhlenberg and Mueller, 2003).

***Hypothesis 1**: In comparison with less religious persons, those who are more religious are more likely to exhibit higher levels of well-being; they (a) have higher self-esteem, (b) are more satisfied with their lives, and (c) are in better health.*

***Hypothesis 2:** Stress mediates the effects of religiosity on (a) self-esteem, (b) satisfaction with life, and (c) health.*

Due to their unwavering commitment to their belief systems, religious individuals are often perceived as having a dogmatic disposition, a notion supported by research conducted by Delener (1994), Mokhlis (2006), and Stark and Glock (1968). This strong commitment is believed to extend to other forms of commitment and relationships, including family and consumption, as suggested by Larson and Goltz (1989), and further explored in the context of consumer behavior by Fournier (1998) and Mokhlis (2006). Studies indicate that religious commitment correlates positively with a preference for nationally recognized or well-established brands, as shown in the research by Mokhlis (2006) and Wilkes et al. (1986). It is also associated with lower risk tolerance during shopping, as indicated in Delener's work (1990, 1994), and places a greater emphasis on product quality when making selections from among products and stores, a phenomenon observed in studies conducted by McDaniel and Burnett (1990) and Mokhlis (2006).

***Hypothesis 3**: There is an inverse relationship between religiosity and (a) changes in brand preferences and (b) changes in-store preferences.*

Method *This section briefly discusses the context of the study (Malaysia), which has diverse religious and ethnic subcultures, enabling us to disentangle the effects of religion from other country- and age-related factors that are intertwined in the results of previous studies.*

The present study involves a large-scale survey using face-to-face interviews with a total of 645 Malaysians aged 50 and older. The Malays made up about 40% of the sample, and the Chinese and Indians constituted about 35% and 26%, respectively. About 40% of respondents in the sample were Muslims, 28% Buddhists, and 21% Hindus. We implement controls to account for effects associated with individual countries, such as socioeconomic and environmental factors, as well as cultural variations in social desirability, by restricting our analyses to a single nation. Additionally, we control for age-related factors, specifically generational disparities in values, by focusing our research on older consumers.

Findings and Implications *This section reports the study's main findings and major contribution to knowledge; it offers explanations of the reason for the emerged relationships between religiosity and our variables of interest.*

The motivation behind this study was to evaluate the influence of religiosity on consumer preferences and well-being while considering potential alternative factors and explanations that might have contributed to the findings of prior research. Our investigation encompasses an exploration of the effects of religiosity within each of Malaysia's three primary subcultures. It is worth noting that religiosity holds different meanings, beliefs, and socially acceptable ways of expressing religious values within each ethnic subculture. One intriguing discovery arising from our study is the variations in the strength of the relationships between religiosity and indicators of well-being across these three subcultures. This suggests that the beneficial effects of being a religious individual may depend on the specific religion one adheres to. The reasons for these variations could be rooted in the doctrines and teachings of different religions. For instance, a religion that emphasizes abstinence from material possessions may indirectly contribute to the enhanced well-being of its followers by serving as a coping response to stress (Baker et al., 2013b; Moschis, 2007), given that materialism has consistently exhibited a negative correlation with an individual's well-being in numerous studies reported in the academic literature (e.g., Burroughs and Rindfleisch, 2002). The study helps explain the mechanisms that may account for the negative relationship between materialism and life satisfaction reported in previous studies conducted in many countries.

In contrast to previous studies that report significant associations between religiosity and various consumer behaviors, our study does not uncover significant differences attributable to an individual's religious beliefs among older adults. This observation stems from our study finding that religiosity is positively associated with age but does not exhibit a connection with changes in consumer preferences. Given that earlier studies indicate an inverse relationship between age and both religiosity and changes in consumer preferences, it is conceivable that the causal variables for these consumer behaviors, as identified in prior research, may be related to other age-related factors (e.g., education) rather than religiosity *per se*.

9.7 Suggestions for Conducting Cross-Cultural Studies

The following suggestions are offered to early career researchers interested in cross-cultural research:

- Develop competence in doing research in single cultures before embarking on cross-cultural research.
- Embrace cultural relativism, which means understanding that behaviors, norms, and values are shaped by specific cultural contexts. Avoid making value judgments or assuming one culture's perspective is superior to another.
- Always consider the cultural and historical contexts when interpreting findings. What may be true in one culture at a specific time may not apply universally.
- Be aware of potential biases in research methods and instruments. Ensure that they are culturally appropriate and sensitive. Biased measures can lead to incorrect conclusions.
- Language nuances can significantly impact findings. Ensure accurate translation and consider that certain concepts may not have direct equivalents in other languages. *Always* use back translation of scales in quantitative studies in other countries.
- Familiarize yourself with cultural dimensions frameworks like Hofstede's cultural dimensions or the GLOBE study's cultural dimensions (e.g., Ollier-Malaterre and Foucreault, 2018). These frameworks can provide a structured way to understand cultural variations.
- Engage in comparative analysis to identify patterns or differences across cultures. This often involves statistical analysis to determine if findings are statistically significant.
- In addition to quantitative data, qualitative research can provide deeper insights into cultural nuances. Interviews, focus groups, and participant observation can be particularly valuable.
- Use multiple sources of data and methods to validate your findings. This can help ensure that your conclusions are robust and not overly influenced by a single source or method.
- Develop cultural competence by immersing yourself in the culture you are studying or by collaborating with experts from that culture. This can help you gain a more nuanced understanding of the findings.
- Recognize the role of historical and socioeconomic factors in shaping cultural behaviors and attitudes. These factors can have a profound influence on cross-cultural findings.
- Be cautious about generalizing findings to an entire culture. Cultures are diverse, and individuals within a culture may have varying beliefs and behaviors.
- Be mindful of ethical considerations, including informed consent and the potential harm or benefit of your research to the studied cultures. Consult relevant ethical guidelines.
- Involve experts in the cultures you are studying, and seek peer review from scholars with expertise in cross-cultural research.

- Consider the practical implications of your findings for international business and policy.
- In quantitative studies, *always* include a social desirability scale (e.g., Strahan and Gerbasi, 1972) in your data collection instruments, and use it as a control variable in hypothesis or model testing.

9.8 Emerging Trends and Implications for Research

Cross-cultural academic research is a dynamic and evolving field that continues to adapt to societal changes and technological advancements. Researchers who are interested in cross-cultural research should build their programmatic research in emerging areas which have yet to be adequately explored and are likely to receive attention for many years or decades. Over the years, several trends have emerged in cross-cultural research, reflecting shifts in research methodologies, theoretical frameworks, and societal developments. The following notable trends have implications for future cross-cultural research:

1. *Migration and Diaspora.* As migration patterns continue to change, there is growing interest in understanding how individuals and communities adapt to new cultural contexts and maintain connections with their home cultures. This research often involves examining issues of identity, acculturation, and cultural preservation.
2. *Cultural Neuroscience.* This interdisciplinary field explores the neural basis of cultural differences in cognition, emotion, and behavior. Researchers are increasingly using neuroimaging techniques to investigate how cultural experiences shape the brain and influence perception and decision-making.
3. *Indigenous Knowledge and Perspectives.* Indigenous cultures are gaining recognition for their unique knowledge systems and perspectives on various issues, including the environment, health, and social justice. Cross-cultural research is increasingly engaging with indigenous communities to better understand and respect their worldviews.
4. *Cross-Cultural Psychology and Well-Being.* Research in this area explores how cultural factors influence well-being, mental health, and happiness. It considers the role of cultural values, norms, and practices in shaping individuals' psychological well-being.
5. *Globalization and Transnationalism.* Globalization has led to increased interconnectedness among cultures. Researchers have been examining how globalization affects cultural identities, practices, and communication patterns. They can also investigate the emergence of transnational identities and hybrid cultural expressions.
6. *Multidisciplinary Approaches.* Cross-cultural research has become more multidisciplinary, drawing from fields such as anthropology, psychology, sociology, linguistics, and economics. This multidisciplinary approach allows researchers to gain a broader perspective on cultural phenomena, and it suggests the employment of multi-theoretical conceptual frameworks in future studies. The

conceptual life course model based on the life course paradigm offers such a multi-theoretical approach to cross-cultural research (See Chap. 15, Sect. 15.3.2).

7. *Cross-Cultural Marketing and Consumer Behavior.* In an increasingly globalized marketplace, understanding how culture influences consumer preferences, advertising effectiveness, and brand loyalty is crucial for businesses.
8. *Digital and Technological Advances.* The digital age has transformed cross-cultural research. Researchers are utilizing online surveys, social media, and big data analytics to collect and analyze cross-cultural data more efficiently. This trend creates opportunities for the study of online communities and their impact on cross-cultural interactions.
9. *Cultural Intelligence.* Understanding how individuals can develop cultural intelligence or cultural competence is vital for people working in diverse environments. Research can explore the development of cultural sensitivity, empathy, and effective cross-cultural interactions.
10. *Cultural Influences on Environmental Attitudes and Behaviors.* Understanding how culture shapes attitudes and behaviors toward the environment can inform efforts to address global environmental challenges. Research in this area can explore eco-cultural values and their impact on conservation efforts.

The trends in these areas reflect the ongoing evolution of cross-cultural research as it responds to the challenges and research opportunities presented by our increasingly interconnected world, and they suggest areas requiring further exploration. Given the ever-evolving nature of societies and cultures, cross-cultural researchers have an ongoing responsibility to explore and understand the intricacies of human behavior and societies worldwide.

References

Amato, P. R., & Sobolewski, J. M. (2001). The effects of divorce and marital discord on adult children's psychological Well-being. *American Sociological Review, 66*, 900–921.

Baker, A., Moschis, G. P., Benmoyal, S., & Pizzutti, C. (2013a). How family resources affect materialism and compulsive buying: A cross-country life course perspective. *Journal of Cross-Cultural Research, 47*(4), 335–362.

Baker, A., Moschis, G. P., Ong, F. S., & Pattanapanyasat, R. (2013b). Materialism and life satisfaction: The role of stress and religiosity. *Journal of Consumer Affairs, 47*(2), 1–14.

Berry, J. H. (1992). Acculturation and adaptation in a new society. *International Migration, 30*(1), 69–85.

Berry, J. W. (2017). Theories and models of acculturation. In S. J. Schwarz & J. B. Unger (Eds.), *The Oxford handbook of acculturation and health* (pp. 15–28), Oxford University Press.

Berry, J. W., Poortinga, Y. H., Segall, M. H., & Dasen, P. R. (1992). *Cross-cultural psychology: Research and applications*. Cambridge University Press.

Burroughs, J. E., & Rindfleisch, A. A. (2002). Materialism and Well-being: A conflicting values perspective. *Journal of Consumer Research, 29*, 348–370.

Cheng, S.-T., & Hamid, P. N. (1997). Dispositional optimism in Chinese people: What does the life orientation test measure? *International Journal of Psychology, 32*(1), 15–22.

Colby, A. (1998). Foreword: Crafting life course studies. In J. A. Giele & G. H. Elder (Eds.), *Methods of life course research: Qualitative and quantitative approaches*. Sage.

Delener, N. (1990). The effects of religious factors on perceived risk in durable goods purchase decisions. *Journal of Consumer Marketing, 7*, 27–38.

Delener, N. (1994). Religious contrasts in consumer decision-making patterns: Their dimensions and marketing implications. *European Journal of Marketing, 28*(5), 36–53.

Diamantopoulos, A., Reynolds, N., & Simitras, A. (2006). The impact of the response styles on the stability of cross-cultural comparisons. *Journal of Business Research, 59*(2006), 925–935.

Diener, E., Emmons, R. A., Larsen, R. J., & Griffin, S. (1985). The satisfaction with life scale. *Journal of Personality Assessment, 49*(1), 71–75.

Durkheim, E. (1912). *The elementary forms of religious life*. Allen and Unwin.

Eastman, J. K., Fredenberger, B., Campbell, D., & Calvert, S. (1997). The relationship between status consumption & materialism: A cross-cultural comparison of Chinese, Mexican & American students. *Journal of Marketing Theory & Practice, 5*(Winter), 52–66.

Ebaugh, H. R. (2002). Presidential address 2001, return of the sacred: Reintegrating religion in the social sciences. *Journal of the Scientific Study of Religion, 41*(3), 385–395.

Elder, G. H., Johnson, M. K., & Crosnoe, R. (2003). The emergence and development of life course theory. In J. T. Mortimer & M. J. Shanahan (Eds.), *Handbook of the life course* (pp. 3–19). Plenum Publishers.

Fournier, S. (1998). Consumers and their brands: Developing branding theory in consumer research. *Journal of Consumer Research, 24*, 343–373.

Francis, L. J., & Kaldor, P. (2002). The relationship between psychological Well-being and Christian faith and practice in an Australian population sample. *Journal of Religion, 41*(1), 179–184.

Ger, G., & Belk, R. W. (1996). Cross-cultural differences in materialism. *Journal of Economic Psychology, 17*(February), 55–77.

Hall, E. T. (1976). *Beyond culture*. Anchor.

Hirschman, E. C. (1981). American Jewish ethnicity: Its relationship to some selected aspects of consumer behavior. *Journal of Marketing, 45*(summer), 102–110.

Hofstede, G. (1980). *Culture's Consequences*. Sage.

Iwata, N., Roberts, C. R., & Kawakami, N. (1995). Japan-US comparison of responses to depression scale items among adult workers. *Psychiatry Research, 58*(October), 237–245.

Kelley, J., & Graaf, N. D. (1997). National context, parental socialization, and religious beliefs: Results from 15 nations. *American Sociological Review, 62*, 639–660.

LaBarbera, P. A., & Gurhan, Z. (1997). The role of materialism, religiosity, and demographics in subjective Well-being. *Psychology and Marketing, 14*(January), 71–97.

Larson, R. (1978). Thirty years of research on subjective Well-being of older Americans. *Journal of Gerontology, 33*, 109–125.

Larson, L. E., & Glotz, J. W. (1989). Religious participation and marital commitment. *Review of Religious Research, 30*, 387–399.

Lazarus, R., & Folkman, S. (1984). *Stress, appraisal, and coping*. Springer.

Livermore, D. (2015). *Leading with cultural intelligence: The real secret to success*. AMACOM.

Markus, H. R., & Kitayama, S. (1991). Culture and the self: Implications for cognition, emotion, and motivation. *Psychological Review, 98*(2), 224–253.

Mathur, A. (2019). George P. Moschis tribute special issue: His philosophy and contributions (part I). *Journal of global scholars of. Marketing Science, 29*(4), 359–371.

Mathur, A. (2020). George P. Moschis tribute special issue: His philosophy and contributions (part II). *Journal of Global Scholars of Marketing Science, 30*(1), 1–3.

McDaniel, S. W., & Burnett, J. J. (1990). Consumer religiosity and retail store evaluative criteria. *Journal of the Academy of Marketing Science, 18*(Spring), 101–112.

Mokhlis, S. (2006). The effects of religiosity on shopping orientations: An exploratory study in Malaysia. *Journal of the American Academy of Business, 9*(1) March, 64–74.

Moschis, G. P. (1992). *Marketing to older consumers*. Quorum.

Moschis, G. P. (2007). Stress and consumer behavior. *Journal of the Academy of Marketing Science, 35*(3), 430–444.

Moschis, G. P. (2019). *Consumer behavior over the life course: Research frontiers and new directions*. Cham, Switzerland: Springer.

Moschis, G. P. (2021). The life course paradigm and consumer behavior: Research frontiers and future directions. *Psychology & Marketing, 38*(11), 2034–2050. https://doi.org/10.1002/mar.21586

Moschis, G. P., & Ong, F. S. (2011). Religiosity and consumer behavior of older adults: A study of subcultural influences in Malaysia. *Journal of Consumer Behavior, 10*(1), 8–17. https://doi.org/10.1002/cb.342

Moschis, G. P., Ong, F. S., Ambassi, M., Yamashita, T., & Mathur, A. (2011). Cultural and age-related differences in reliability. *Journal of Targeting, Measurement and Analysis for Marketing, 19*(3/4), 141–151.

Nakano, K. (2001). Psychometric evaluation of the Japanese adaptation of the aggression questionnaire. *Behavior Research and Therapy, 39*(July), 853–858.

Nevid, J. S., & Maria, N. L. S. (1999). Multicultural issues in qualitative research. *Psychology & Marketing, 18(4*, 305–325.

Ollier-Malaterre, A., & Foucreault, A. (2018). GLOBE's cultural dimensions: Implications for global work–family research. In K. Shockley, W. Shen, & R. Johnson (Eds.), *The Cambridge handbook of the global work–family interface* (Cambridge handbooks in psychology) (pp. 69–86). Cambridge University Press.

Poloma, M. M., & Pendelton, B. F. (1990). Religious domains and general Well-being. *Social Indicators Research, 22*, 255–276.

Richins, M. L. (2004). The material values scale: Measurement properties and development of a short form. *Journal of Consumer Research, 31*(1), 209–219. https://doi.org/10.1086/383436

Rosenberg, M. (1965). *Society and the adolescent self-image*. Princeton University Press.

Schwarz, N. (2003). Self-reports in consumer research: The challenge of comparing cohorts and cultures. *Journal of Consumer Research, 29*, 588–594.

Schwarz, S. J., & Unger, J. B. (Eds.). (2017). *The Oxford handbook of acculturation and health*. Oxford University Press.

Sood, J., & Nasu, Y. (1995). Religiosity and nationality: An exploratory study of their effects on consumer behavior in Japan and the United States. *Journal of Business Research, 34*(September/October), 1–9.

Stark, R., & Glock, C. Y. (1968). *American piety: The nature of religious commitment*. University of California Press.

Steenkamp, J., & Baumgartner, H. (1998). Assessing measurement invariance in cross-national consumer research. *Journal of Consumer Research, 25*(1), 78–90.

Strahan, R., & Gerbasi, K. R. (1972). Short, homogeneous version of the Marlow crow social desirability scale. *Journal of Clinical Psychology, 28*(2), 191–193.

Suzuki, T., Tsukamoto, K., & Kazuhiro, A. (2000). Characteristic factor structures of the Japanese version of the state-trait anxiety inventory: Coexistence of positive-negative and state-trait factor structures. *Journal of Personality Assessment, 74*(3), 447–458.

Tajfel, H., & Turner, J. (1979). The social identity theory of intergroup behavior. *Psychological Review, 86*(3), 220–238.

Thoits, P. A., & Hewitt, L. N. (2001). Volunteer work and well-being. *Journal of Health and Social Behavior, 42*(2), 115–131.

Trompenaars, F., & HampdenTurner, C. (1997). *Riding the waves of culture: Understanding diversity in global business*. Nicholas Brealey Publishing.

Uhlenberg, P., & Mueller, M. (2003). Family context and individual well-being. In J. T. Mortimer & M. Shanahan (Eds.), *Handbook of the life course* (pp. 123–148). Kluwer Academic/Plenum Publishers.

Wilkes, R. E., Burnett, J. H., & Howell, R. D. (1986). On the meaning and measurement of religiosity in consumer research. *Journal of the Academy of Marketing Science, 14*(Spring), 47–56.

Wong, N., Rindfleisch, A. A., & Burroughs, J. (2003). Do reverse-worded items confound measures in cross-cultural consumer research? The case of material value scale. *Journal of Consumer Research, 30*, 72–91.

Woods, T. E., Antoni, M. H., Ironson, G. H., & Kling, D. W. (1999). Religiosity is associated with affective and immune status in symptomatic HIV-infected gay men. *Journal of Psychosomatic Research, 46*, 165–176.

Writing Manuscripts for Academic Journals 10

Writing a paper for publication is not very different from producing a product and trying to market it to the target market. This means that it is important for researchers to understand the criteria journals use to accept or reject a manuscript, in much the same way consumers decide whether to buy or not buy a product. They must understand the articles that appeal to specific journals because they are relevant and potentially interesting to the journal's readers or "customers." To the extent articles satisfy their readers' "consumption" needs and are credible (e.g., peer-reviewed), they contribute to their knowledge. Therefore, the main requirements for getting a paper published include the following: understanding the needs of the journals in one's field, knowing the type of research that contributes to a specific area, and addressing the criteria journals and their reviewers use to accept or reject a manuscript.

This chapter focuses on these factors. It begins with tips on how to identify your paper's intended contribution. Next, the chapter discusses the types of research and articles that make significant contributions because they help advance knowledge for theory development and practice. Information on your paper's contribution and journal preference for types of articles help in selecting the most appropriate journal for submitting your manuscript, and it suggests ways to position the manuscript for the greatest impact on the journal's readership. The chapter also discusses the criteria journals and reviewers use to decide whether to accept or reject a manuscript. Finally, the chapter's main focus is on the preparation of the manuscript for the purpose of satisfying reviewers by offering tips and guidelines for constructing its major components (sections) and suggesting information to include in them, and it also provides guidelines for revising conditionally accepted manuscripts and for handling reviewers' concerns and suggestions. This chapter should be particularly relevant and helpful to those researchers who have yet to fully master the art of crafting and positioning articles.

G. P. Moschis, *Academic Research in Business and the Social Sciences*,
https://doi.org/10.1007/978-3-031-56548-9_10

10.1 Identify the Intended Contribution

Research is typically done in order to address a problem or issue, understand a phenomenon, or answer a question, and the researcher decides how to best accomplish research objectives. If the reader is not aware of the problem or issue, he or she needs to be informed about it and its relevance to him or her. And once the reader is informed, he or she expects to learn what was done about it, what the researcher found that helps answer the research question or understand the phenomenon, and the reason the findings are relevant to him or her. Therefore, writers of research projects must decide how to best tell readers their "story," or "sell" their product (research) to their target consumers, who are interested in satisfying their information needs.

Readers of research articles may have a wide variety of information needs depending on contexts in which they are embedded. While the large majority of them are likely to be other researchers who are looking for answers to their research questions or are trying to develop more effectual studies, other readers are likely to be interested in the results of research that informs decision-making outside academics. Therefore, it is important for early career researchers to understand potential users of the research studies in order to best address and satisfy their needs. As such, first and foremost, they should try to understand the intended contribution of their article.

Academic articles typically attempt to make one or more types of contributions. They aim at making an empirical, theoretical, conceptual, or methodological contribution.

Empirical Researchers typically make empirical contributions by offering answers to research questions. Answers to empirical questions have implications for theory development and practice or policy decisions. For example, one may want to answer the question: "Are women more compulsive buyers than men?" "Are older car drivers more likely than younger drivers to have car accidents?" If a research study shows that women are more compulsive buyers than men, this finding would have implications for the development of intervention programs, and it could have implications for theory development, as this finding would serve as a reason for offering different explanations for the emerged differences (e.g., biological, psychological, social; e.g., Moschis, 2017). Similarly, if research shows that older car drives are more prone to having car accidents, this finding may serve as the basis for charging older car drivers higher insurance premiums, and it could have implications for theory development, as researchers may offer different explanations for the observed age differences in car accidents (e.g., changes in the perceptual system, declining abilities to process information; e.g., Moschis, 2022).

In these two examples, questions that are raised imply the existence of some prior knowledge or evidence for expecting gender and age differences, but insufficient bases for drawing conclusions. They imply a statement of directional hypotheses or pointing to the characteristic most likely to exhibit the behavior of interest.

However, empirical questions can also be framed in an exploratory format, such as the following: "Are there gender differences in people's compulsive buying tendencies?" "Are there age differences among car drivers who have car accidents?" Regardless the manner in which the questions are framed, the emerged differences can contribute to theory development and practice, prompting researchers to seek and offer explanations, while absence of significant differences would not inform decision making or provide bases for theoretical formulation.

Theoretical Theoretical contributions focus on providing a satisfactory explanation for a phenomenon and any observed or emerged relationships between variables. As mentioned in Chap. 3, a satisfactory explanation of a phenomenon or research question under investigation is provided when a theory can explain *what* happens, *how* it happens, and *why* something happens (Salthouse, 1991), and it can further explain *when* the phenomenon occurs—i.e., under what conditions. Therefore, theoretical contributions can be made by providing answers to these questions. For example, in the absence of a theory, one can develop a new theory or propose a competing one used in another discipline that explains a phenomenon or answers a research question, such as why something happens. The theoretical question suggests the presence of empirical evidence and seeks an answer (Alford, 1998).

Fournier's (1998) theory of consumer relationships with brands exemplifies this type of contribution. If a theory exists that explains a phenomenon, the researcher can make a contribution by proposing a competing theory available in other fields of social sciences that can improve or replace an existing theory. For example, early developmental explanations of children's consumer behavior based on Piaget's theory of cognitive development predicts the age at which young people will be able to complete a purchasing transaction. However, Ausabel's theory predicts that children can develop consumer skills at a much younger age than predicted by Piaget's theory, if they are given the opportunity to go through a simulated shopping trip. Results of experiments conducted by the author and his associated (Moschis et al., 1980; Stampfl et al., 1978) at the University of Wisconsin's lab facilities for studies of kindergarten children help improve Piaget's theory of cognitive development.

Theoretical contributions can also be made not only by explaining the reason for a phenomenon—i.e., why something happens, but also *how* it happens, by offering insights into the process(es) or mechanism(s) that link(s) context to outcome. The study of process or mechanism is a much more difficult proposition, as it entails the investigation of change that takes place over time. Positivist researchers attempt to explain change mechanisms and their effects by using mediating variables. For example, life course studies on the development of materialistic attitudes and compulsive buying habits in more than 10 countries highlight the mediating role of parents and peers (e.g., Baker and Chan, 2020; Moschis, 2017, 2019). In contrast, humanist researchers infer change processes by studying the sequence of events experienced by informants over time (e.g., Belk et al., 2013).

Researchers also can contribute to theory development by studying the circumstances or conditions under which a given theory helps explain a phenomenon—i.e., when or under what conditions something happens. Those who attempt to make such a contribution tend to focus on moderating variables. Moderating variables take different forms driven by agency and contextual factors. Given the multitude of factors that can affect outcome, several theories can help explain a phenomenon or help answer a research question. In addressing a research question or problem, in most cases, the question is not whether a theory is relevant in helping understand the phenomenon. Rather, the question is about which theory is most relevant in providing a satisfactory explanation in a given context and for certain population characteristics. For example, in two of our studies in Malaysia, a country with large and diverse subcultures (Malays, Chinese, and Indians), we assessed the direct and moderating effects of religiosity and ethnicity on the relationship between materialistic values and well-being. We found the effects of religiosity differ not only on the basis of the strength of one's religious beliefs but also on the type of religion the person adheres to (Baker et al., 2013; Moschis and Ong, 2011).

Finally, a theoretical contribution can be in the form of the development of an overarching theoretical framework that encompasses more than one theory. Such frameworks are increasingly becoming popular for three main reasons: First, no single theory is likely to provide a complete explanation of a phenomenon, and different theories are useful in explaining different types of phenomena or answering different research questions. Second, although some theories within a particular field may be viewed as competing (e.g., personality, attitude, motivation), most theories in different disciplines can be viewed as complementary (e.g., social, psychological). Third, the increased collaboration among researchers from different disciplines is likely to promote the development of multi-theoretical frameworks. For example, working with members of the gerontology faculty who had backgrounds in several fields of social science, and attending research seminars on trends in different disciplines helped me better understand the life course paradigm, which formed the foundation for the development of the multi-theoretical life course conceptual framework (Moschis, 2019).

Conceptual A conceptual contribution is usually in the form of a new measure. The new measure applies to a phenomenon or concept that needs to be investigated, but for which there are no existing or satisfactory measures. For example, the phenomenon of interest could be people's new forms of behavior that they have developed as a result of the introduction of artificial intelligence (AI). It could apply to the way(s) they use ChatGPT to perform new tasks that they could not perform in the past, such as writing various documents, paraphrasing, and planning comprehensive travel itineraries, and it could include the ways they use this platform as a search engine, replacing the use of other search engines (e.g., Google, Travel Advisor). Thus, the researcher's contribution could be the development of a conceptual definition and subsequently a measurement instrument that captures a person's "relationship" with the new technology in the form of behavioral and psychological attachment, even as a new form of addiction. A literature review for conceptualizing this phenomenon could be conducted for explication purposes (see concept explication, Chap. 3), aiming at developing a conceptual definition that would suggest an appropriate operational definition. An example of this contribution can be seen in the development of a consumer uniqueness scale (Tian et al. (2001).

Alternatively, the researcher can make a contribution by improving an existing conceptual definition of a phenomenon that has been investigated in previous studies. He or she would have to follow the same process for constructing a new conceptual definition by explicating the concept to identify the necessary and sufficient conditions that would help define it. For example, if the researcher's literature review suggests that necessary conditions (characteristics) that define a person as a compulsive buyer include "excessive buying," "uncontrollable behavior," and "uninterrupted/continuous" pattern over prolonged time, the researcher's new conceptual definition should clearly state these, and the operational definition (e.g., statements to be included in the measure) should tap the excessiveness, uncontrollability, and continuity of the behavior. The contribution would be in the improvement of the definition of compulsive buying in that previous definitions do not include all three conditions. An example of an improved definition of compulsive buying can be seen in the work of Ridgeway, Kukar-Kinney, and Monroe (2008) scale. Their conceptual definition captures both the obsessive-compulsive and impulse-control dimensions of compulsive buying, and their resultant six-point measure of compulsive buying overcomes limitations of other previously used scales, distinguishing compulsive buying behaviors from the consequences of those behaviors.

Methodological The last type of contribution a researcher can make is methodological. This typically involves the introduction of a new methodology to solve an existing problem that researchers in a discipline either do not know how to solve or cannot solve more efficiently (see Table 4.1, cell C, in Chap. 4). For example, a common problem researchers who use cross-sectional data often encounter is the reciprocal influence between the two variables, such as the relationship between attitudes and behavior—i.e., attitudes affect behavior, and vice-versa. Correlational data would indicate a strong positive relationship between the two variables, but it would be unclear the relative influence of each of these variables on the other. The data I had collected for my dissertation helped demonstrate the appropriate methodology for partitioning the variance accounted for by each hypothesized causal relationship (Churchill and Moschis (1979).

Methodological contributions can also be in the form of proposing a new method that would lead to improvement in relevant outcomes, such as profits, performance, efficiency, well-being, etc. When proposing a new method, it is imperative that you demonstrate the superiority of the new method over the existing or commonly used. When I founded the Center for Mature Consumer Studies (CMCS) and started interacting with colleagues who were teaching gerontology courses and studying the aged and aging, I would hear that age is a "worthless" variable because it merely measures the passage of time. However, as I was also talking to marketers concurrently, I would hear them saying that age is a useful variable because people in different age groups respond differently to their offerings.

In our first large-scale national study at CMCS, I collected information that showed the type of aging our study's participants had experienced, as aging is multidimensional—i.e., biophysical (e.g., functional), psychological (e.g., cognitive age), and social (e.g., old-age roles experienced). I used this information to place my sample of older consumers into categories based on these measures that tapped their aging experiences and formed four segments that I called "gerontographic" clusters (e.g., Moschis, 1992, 1996). This segmentation tool could better explain older consumers' responses to marketing offerings of companies in various industries than segmentation based on age or other factors companies were using at that time (Moschis, 1992, 1996, 2022; Moschis et al., 2000). As aging is universal, the gerontographic segmentation model produced similar results in several countries (e.g., Moschis et al., 2020; Nimrod, 2013; Sthienrapapayut et al., 2018).

To summarize, it is extremely important for early career researchers to understand the kinds of contributions that their research studies make to knowledge (theory and practice). And it is of equal importance to learn to match the various types of contributions with journal readers' needs, discussed in the next section.

10.2 Journal Selection and Manuscript Positioning

Before drafting a manuscript, it is important to determine the appropriate publication venue. Based on the study's design and results, the researcher should have a fairly clear idea of the most suitable outlet. The choice of the appropriate outlet relies on the nature of the scholarly work being developed. While there are no universally accepted guidelines for selecting an outlet, certain journals provide guidance regarding the kinds of manuscripts they prefer to publish. For instance, if the researcher or team of collaborators believe that the study's findings significantly contribute to a specific field within business or the social sciences, then the manuscript should be directed toward the top-tier journals. Another factor to consider is the manuscript's content. Specialized journals like the *Journal of Advertising* and *Journal of Retailing* actively seek studies that make even modest contributions to highly specialized domains. In cases where the study presents "interesting" but not necessarily groundbreaking findings, or when researchers are introducing thought-provoking concepts that are yet to receive support, such papers may find a more suitable home at a conference.

Ideally, the process of positioning a manuscript should commence during the planning phase, where one can deliberate on the intended contribution and identify the relevant variables pertaining to that specific contribution. To illustrate, when I was devising the study for my dissertation, I determined the destination for the three most impactful manuscripts, followed by the subsequent three or four articles earmarked for lower-tier journals and conferences. More precisely, the paper containing the conceptual model with variables representing each component of the model found its fit in the *Journal of Marketing Research* (JMR) (Moschis and Churchill, 1978). Another article featuring variables with implications for marketing practice, such as those representing the firm's controllable factors (the so-called "four Ps"), was tailored for the *Journal of Marketing* (JM) (Moschis and Churchill, 1979). The third article that expounded on a particular methodology relevant to consumer studies was well-suited for the *Journal of Consumer Research* (JCR) (Churchill and Moschis, 1979).

Subsequently, the fourth article, encompassing variables of relevance to retailers, was submitted to the *Journal of Retailing* (JR) (Moschis, 1978–1979), while the fifth article, appealing to a broad audience, was directed toward the *Journal of the Academy of Marketing Science* (JAMS) (Moschis, 1981). Four other papers were developed based on residual findings from exploratory data analyses. They were suitable for presentation at conferences organized by the American Marketing Association (AMA) and the Association for Consumer Research (ACR) and were published in their respective conference proceedings (Moschis, 1979; Moschis and Churchill, 1977a; Moschis and Moore, 1979a, b). And one more manuscript as well as the entire dissertation were published as research monographs (Moschis, 1978; Moschis and Churchill, 1977b).

Through meticulous planning and dissecting a study, it becomes possible to craft multiple papers, each tailored to a distinct publication venue. For instance, if the study encompasses (a) theory testing, (b) the introduction and utilization of a novel methodology, and (c) the revelation of unforeseen findings, potential papers arising from this study can be suitable for journals that emphasize theoretical and methodological contributions for (a) and (b), respectively, and for conferences (c). In cases where the study's scope exceeds the capacity of a single article, it may be prudent to prepare two separate manuscripts, each reporting a portion of the findings. It is worth noting that journals typically discourage publishing multiple articles based on the same dataset or having more than one manuscript on the same topic from the same dataset under review simultaneously.

Early career researchers should undertake certain preliminary steps before selecting a journal. Firstly, they ought to compile a list of journals approved by their department as suitable publication targets. Many departments maintain a tiered list of journals based on their relative publishing difficulty (e.g., level A, level B) and may even implement a point system to reward authors whose articles are published in these journals. Secondly, researchers should assess the relevance of their research topic to these journals and rank them accordingly. Utilizing this 2 × 2 matrix, researchers can categorize selected or relevant journals into four groups: (a) very challenging but highly relevant, (b) very challenging but less relevant, (c) less challenging but highly relevant, and (d) less challenging and less relevant. Priority should be assigned to journals in category (a), followed by those in category (c). Assuming their department classifies journals into four levels (A, B, C, D), category (a) would encompass A- and B-level journals, while category (c) would encompass

C- and D-level journals. Several online sources provide a classification of journals, although the journal classifications differ across sources (e.g., Scopus, ISI). Other sources allow you to search for specific journals and see their classification quartile and impact factor (e.g., https://journalsearches.com).

Early career researchers should be aware of the quality of the different types of journals in their field, because the outlets used for their research affect the perceived quality of their work, evaluations by their institution, and the image they portrait to the academic community (see "metrics" in Chap. 11). Journal quality may differ even when journals claim the same impact factor. Presently, there are two types of journals most appropriate for academic publications: traditional or subscription-based and open-access journals. The first type reaches subscribers who pay an annual rate for their membership, although separate articles from journal issues are also available to nonsubscribers for a fee. Open-access journals, in contrast, do not have subscription fees, but charge those authors whose article is published usually between $1000 and $2000. And they make every article available to anyone for free or for a small fee. These journals always tout short review times, usually a couple of weeks, which raise issues about the quality of reviewers they use and their reviews.

Generally, open-access journals are not viewed as favorably as subscription-based journals, based on my experience and anecdotal evidence. These journals aggressively seek out high-profile authors, inviting them to publish their articles free of charge. They hope these contributions by widely known scholars will elevate their status and increase journal citations. A similar strategy is used quite often by lower-level or lesser-known subscription-based journals.

Before selecting a journal, make sure you know how your department evaluates publications in these journals, including the acceptable percentage of the relative contribution of coauthors, or credit for articles co-authored by several researchers in certain order (e.g., lead, second, third authorship), and make sure you understand how these factors affect promotion and tenure decisions, as well as salary supplements and merit raises. It has been my experience that departments do not view favorably journals that accept manuscripts for a fee. And the ranking of journals within your field is more important than the ranking of journals outside your field. Therefore, before you consider sending your manuscript to any journal, you should have adequate information about the journals on your target list. Normally, department heads should be able to provide you with such information.

The choice of publication outlet also influences one's writing style and terminology used in the paper. Demonstrating that the work is of interest to the target audience of the selected journal or conference is of outmost importance. Furthermore, for each paper developed, researchers should always have one or two alternative publication venues in mind in case of rejection by the initial journal. As a general guideline, it is advisable to avoid submitting a paper to a conference if it has not been previously considered by at least a B-level journal.

10.3 Manuscript Preparation

10.3.1 Understand Your Readers

Before you start writing, consider who your target audience is. Tailor your language, tone, and style to suit their needs and expectations. Learn to write for meeting reader expectations. Gopen and Swan (1990) provide one of the best discussions of the reader's expectations in the context of academic prose. They assert that readers expect to have their beliefs considerably changed as a consequence of reading the writer's manuscript. Mick (2008) summarizes readers' expectations by stating that "Readers have expectations that writers must know and honor. These expectations range from the levels of sentence, paragraph, and section structure up to the level of knowledge structure;" and "readers expect to be taught as a result of their efforts" (p. 18).

Mick (2008:20) offers a summary list of additional suggestions for exceptional writing:

- Start the process by identifying only one or two mega-themes for knowledge contribution (usually reflected or condensed in the title), stick very closely to them throughout the entire manuscript, and explain how all sub-themes fit precisely within the mega-themes.
- Strive overall to write a manuscript that any neighbor or relative could understand.
- Work especially hard on the opening and the closing of a manuscript because these are decisive for attracting and catapulting the reader into enthusiastic judgments about the manuscript's insights.
- Keep the links between ideas short and direct, with few detours or complicated routes of logic.
- Accept the fact that persistent cycles of revision work are almost always more consequential than the construction of the first draft.
- Read a nearly completed manuscript aloud in order to find the more subtle, but still important, glitches to be fixed.
- And last but hardly least, seek the counsel of a professional copyeditor whenever the magnitude and the difficulty of the writing necessitates.

10.3.2 Manuscript Outline and Sections

Before the researcher starts preparing a manuscript, he or she should first develop a rough outline while having in mind the target outlet. This helps you organize your thoughts, maintain focus, and create a logical flow. Organize your manuscript into clear sections with descriptive headings. Each section should have a purpose, and it should be structured in such a way so that it accomplishes its purpose, and the paragraphs of the section should serve that purpose. For example, the purpose of the "Introduction" section is to provide the rationale for the research reported in the manuscript. The purpose of the "Background" section is to put the research reported in the manuscript in proper context by presenting relevant theory and research, which justify hypothesis development. Use subheadings, bullet points, and numbered lists to break up text and improve readability. For example, subheadings in the "background" sections could include a "literature review" or "previous research" subsection that presents research findings about the topic, a "theoretical perspectives" subsection that discusses previous theories offered as explanations of the topic or phenomenon under investigation, and a "hypothesis" section. A compelling headline and an engaging opening paragraph are crucial to grab readers' attention and encourage them to continue reading.

The various sections of this outline can be progressively elaborated by inserting content. My approach involves augmenting and, if necessary, modifying the preliminary outline. Although there are diverse methods for structuring and composing manuscripts, I favor what I term the "assembly line process." This means that one can work on any section of the manuscript at any time, not necessarily following the order proposed by the outline.

When writing, it can be beneficial to bear a few considerations in mind. Authors should refrain from expecting their initial draft to be perfect or to match their ultimate vision for the final manuscript. Instead, they should jot down their ideas and focus on refining the text later, much like applying "cosmetics." Any potentially relevant content can be placed anywhere within the paper initially, with subsequent refinement and organization adjustments as needed. Additionally, authors should be mindful of the key factors that can lead to manuscript rejection. Reviewers anticipate certain essential elements and their proper placement, such as stating the paper's purpose in the introduction.

However, two primary factors significantly influence a reviewer's assessment of a manuscript and recommendation to the editor: the method(s) employed and its contribution to knowledge. It is crucial to note that the manuscript's contribution can only be evaluated once the methods have been deemed acceptable. Therefore, after articulating the intended contribution early in the paper, the remainder of the manuscript, including the stated conclusion regarding its contribution, is often evaluated based on its methodological rigor. Hence, authors should prioritize an understanding of the bases for manuscript rejection. Consequently, when crafting a manuscript, it is advisable for the researcher to embrace a Machiavellian philosophy metaphorically, which suggests that "The best way for a person to get to Heaven is to get to know the roads that lead to Hell and learn to avoid them." If a paper offers a reasonable contribution and reviewers cannot identify significant flaws or if the researcher has proactively addressed potential methodological concerns satisfactorily, the manuscript's prospects for publication are greatly enhanced. Therefore, in the subsequent discussion of the primary manuscript components, I endeavor to remind the reader of potential reasons for manuscript rejection on a section-by-section basis, including some previously mentioned points, while offering suggestions to mitigate criticism.

10.3.3 Suggested Manuscript Structure and Contents

Manuscript structure is likely to vary depending on factors such as the nature of the intended contribution and research approach used (e.g., theoretical/conceptual, quantitative, qualitative). Every manuscript reporting results of an *empirical* study should have at least six sections: Introduction, Background (conceptual framework and hypotheses), Methodology, Results, Discussion, and Implications and/or Directions for future research.

Introduction In the introductory section, the author plays a pivotal role in making a compelling case for the manuscript. It is crucial to recognize that many reviewers form their initial judgments based on the opening pages or paragraphs. This section should comprise a minimum of three paragraphs, with an emphasis on brevity and clarity, avoiding lengthy paragraphs.

The first paragraph's primary purpose is to grab the reader's attention by underscoring the significance of the chosen topic. In the second paragraph, the focus should shift to highlighting the current timely problem, issue, or knowledge gap. This can be achieved by briefly summarizing the existing body of knowledge, effectively setting the stage for the study's objectives. The third paragraph is instrumental in informing the reader about the study's objectives and what unique insights they will gain from the article that are not already known, essentially defining its contribution to the specific field.

Background The background section's structure can vary, contingent on factors like the study's nature, intended audience, and length requirements. If it delves into previous research, it will encompass a presentation of prior studies and a summary of existing knowledge. Additionally, this section should introduce and discuss the conceptual framework employed in the study, preferably in the form of a visual representation.

Incorporating a conceptual framework is often advantageous as it justifies the choice of specific variables, illustrating that they stem from a broader conceptual model. Visual aids, such as figures depicting variables, can assist readers in grasping proposed relationships and facilitate their comprehension of the rationale behind the hypotheses. The absence of a robust conceptual framework can be a primary reason for paper rejection.

Alternatively, the background section can focus on hypothesis development, drawing from relevant theory and research findings that support the theory across diverse contexts, thereby substantiating each of the proposed hypotheses. Thorough research is essential, necessitating the gathering of information from reputable sources and proper citation. Accurate and well-researched content enhances the credibility of your manuscript.

Methodology When crafting research papers in general, and especially when composing the methodology section, it is crucial to keep in mind that reviewers are actively seeking flaws in the study that could justify rejecting the paper. In essence, most reviewers are inclined to search for reasons to reject rather than accept a manuscript. It would greatly benefit the researcher to provide justifications for every aspect of his or her work, even if briefly. By doing so, the researcher can proactively address potential objections from reviewers.

The methodology section is particularly susceptible to criticisms. While some reviewers may not be well-versed in the content of the preceding sections, the methodology is an area that tends to draw close scrutiny from most reviewers. This is because they frequently identify issues related to the sample, nonresponse rate, measurement with focus on reliability and validity, demand artifacts, common method biases, and more. When crafting this section, researchers should be proactive in addressing potential criticisms related to their decisions on various tasks, ranging from sample selection to the choice of measures and analytical methods. It is advantageous to attempt to reframe what might initially seem like a limitation as a strength. For instance, in anticipation of criticism for utilizing students as study participants, one might state: "Utilizing students as participants serves as a means to control for factors that contribute to variations in responses attributed to differences in age and educational levels (e.g., Diamantopoulos et al., 2006)." Additionally, one could mention that "college students have frequently been considered the 'backbone of much of scientific research in psychology' (Kasser, 2002:7) and have been widely employed in studies published in leading scientific journals (e.g., Rindfleisch et al., 1997)."

Similarly, when foreseeing a potential negative response to the use of Amazon's Mechanical Turk panel, the researcher could explain: "While it cannot be assumed that a sample drawn from Amazon's Mechanical Turk worker panel is representative of the entire US population, prior research has indicated that samples from this panel exhibit sufficient diversity and suitability for substantive hypothesis testing across various aspects of behavior (Buhrmester et al., 2011)."

Under this heading in a manuscript, reviewers focus on variable definition and measurement. They are likely to look at the way variables in the hypotheses are defined and measured. Therefore, for each variable stated in the hypotheses, the investigator should try to include its conceptual definition, operational definition, and measure. In the "Variable Measurement" subsection of the methodology section, one must use the same label or wording of the variable that is used in the hypotheses. For example, if the variable label "social responsibility" is used in a hypothesis, the conceptual and operational definitions and measures of this variable would be as follows, respectively: "A firm's social responsibility refers to a philosophy that promotes the welfare of society (conceptual definition). It is operationally defined by the firm's level of support of activities and organizations that exclusively benefit the general public (operational definition). It is measured by the percentage of annual profits spent on activities and organizations that benefit the general public (measure)." The words "refers to," "operationally defined," and "measured" should be included in the description of these three categories (for additional examples of differences among these categories, see Moschis and Churchill, 1978, Appendix). If the investigator has followed every step in the concept explication process (described in Chap. 3), he or she should not have difficulty with this task.

Critiques of a study's measures are prone to arise, particularly when these measures are unfamiliar to reviewers or when they raise questions regarding validity and reliability. In the former scenario, it is advisable for the researcher to apprise the reviewers of the measure's validity, as exemplified by the measure of "childhood environment" with the statement: "We relied on the well-established measure of childhood environment" (Mittal and Griskevicius, 2016: 640). Likewise, if the alpha reliability coefficient falls below the 0.70 threshold, it is liable to be flagged as a limitation, and this should be addressed by citing authoritative sources to mitigate this concern. For instance, one could assert: "Although the scale reliabilities do not reach particularly high levels, scales yielding alpha values in the 0.60 to 0.70 range are still considered acceptable for research purposes, especially when dealing with constructs that are difficult to measure (Lance et al., 2006), and even within the 0.50 to 0.60 range during the exploratory stages of research (Nunnally, 1967)."

It is crucial to consistently convey to reviewers that the researcher acknowledges methodological challenges or issues and has employed the best available approaches to address them. For example, in response to concerns about data quality from MTurk panel members, one might state: "Some scholars have expressed reservations about the data quality stemming from MTurk panel participants (cf. Goodman and Paolacci, 2017). However, we have followed the recommended steps outlined by other scholars to minimize potential data degradation attributable to respondent misrepresentation or dishonesty (cf., Goodman and Paolacci, 2017; Wessling et al., 2017)." Similarly, to tackle concerns related to common method bias arising from responses to sensitive questions (Podsakoff et al., 2003), one could declare: "Due to the sensitive nature of the inquiry, we incorporated the Marlow-Crow social desirability scale (Strahan and Gerbasi, 1972) to mitigate this form of response bias."

When the researcher chooses a specific method for data analysis from various available options, it is imperative to provide a rationale for this choice by referencing a reputable source. If the decision to employ a less-than-optimal or suitable method cannot be justified, it is advisable, at the very least, to apprise the reviewers of the researcher's awareness of alternative methods. For instance, in justifying the utilization of Baron and Kenny's (1986) mediation testing method, one might elucidate: "Given that there exists a repertoire of 14 methods for assessing mediation effects, each possessing its own set of advantages and drawbacks (MacKinnon et al., 2002), we opted for Baron and Kenny's (1986) approach. This choice is predicated on its wide acceptance and extensive use in studies published in leading scientific journals (e.g., Rindfleisch et al., 1997)."

Results Many reviewers anticipate that the paper will encompass descriptive statistics and correlations among study variables, partly because these are essential for potential meta-analyses of similar studies. Hence, the initial table should encompass these statistical details. Reviewers may also seek clarification regarding the methodologies employed to generate these statistics. It is vital for the researcher to elucidate the methods used to derive his or her findings. If there were alternative methods available, the researcher should articulate the rationale for not utilizing them. For example, if the results are rooted in a straightforward regression model, researchers can proactively address potential critiques for not employing regression mixture models by explaining: "We refrained from using regression mixture models as we lacked theoretical underpinnings suggesting distinct participant groups would respond differently to the questions (e.g., Van Horn et al., 2009)."

Moreover, researchers should preemptively address findings that tend to be perceived as limitations by less experienced reviewers, such as low R-squared values. In instances where R-squared values are low, researchers can state, for instance: "Although our analysis yielded low R-squared values, Duncan (1975: 65) contends that researchers should prioritize the observed relationships among hypothesized variables rather than fixating on the R-squared values within the equation." Similarly, if the results deviate from the researcher's expectations, they should provide some elucidation (e.g., "The observed non-significant relationships may be attributable to the presence of moderator variables"). It is advisable to suggest any unexpected or insignificant findings, along with other unresolved weaknesses, as avenues for future research (e.g., "Hence, future research endeavors should explore theory-based moderators...").

In cases where a limitation arises from the analysis and there are limited means to rectify it, the researcher should openly acknowledge this limitation. To convey awareness to the reviewers, the researcher should cite relevant sources that discuss methods previously employed to address such limitations. For instance, when faced with highly correlated independent measures, the researcher should recognize the challenge and mention that there are limited remedies available. They can then demonstrate their awareness of previously suggested methods, such as mean-centering, which may not completely alleviate the multicollinearity problem (e.g., Echambadi and Hess, 2007).

It is highly probable that reviewers may raise methodological issues that are not specific to the researcher's study but are commonplace among researchers employing the same methodology, such as concerns about the external validity of laboratory experiments. These issues or limitations should be proactively acknowledged. For example, the researcher can state: "An inherent limitation in the current study, as well as in studies utilizing a similar methodology, is..." By informing the reviewers of their awareness of the issue and their efforts to mitigate its impact, the researcher can potentially earn a more favorable reception from understanding reviewers.

Results The results section in many manuscripts often suffers from poor organization and presentation, based on my experience. This issue likely arises from the way researchers tend to structure their writing, often opting to initially present their key findings rather than arranging them in accordance with the stated hypotheses or research questions. To enhance reader comprehension, it is beneficial when writers begin a paragraph with an introductory sentence that recalls the expectation or hypothesis established beforehand.

Discussion Moving on to the discussion section, its significance lies in the opportunity it provides for researchers to delve deeper into their findings. This section should elaborate on the primary contribution of the study and establish connections between the study results and the research question or problem. When a hypothesis is supported, it can be helpful to elucidate why this discovery holds significance. The discussion should weave a narrative, commencing with the study's rationale and concluding with an exploration of what readers have gleaned from the research that was previously unknown to them. It should "tell a story." It should elucidate the relevance of this new information to the issue raised in the manuscript's introduction and study objectives.

Additionally, for hypotheses that were not supported, the researcher should speculate about the possible reason(s) (e.g., presence of moderating variables, sample characteristics). These reasons should be suggested as opportunities and directions for future research for theory validation, improvement, or modification (preferably in the "Implications" section of the manuscript). Finally, this section should encompass the study's limitations or constraints. Personally, I prefer addressing limitations early in the discussion section rather than relegating them to the very last paragraph of the manuscript, using credible sources to mitigate each limitation whenever feasible. I believe that it is better to inform readers of study's limitation early and suggest they consider findings in the light of these limitations, rather than ending the manuscript by creating doubts about the validity of the findings presented.

Implications The final section holds significance as it offers an opportunity for researchers to extract meaning from their findings. It should suggest the implications of the study's insights, particularly regarding theory development and practical applications for various interested parties, such as educators, marketers, policy makers, and fellow researchers. Moreover, it should indicate potential avenues for further investigation and future research directions by, for example, offering propositions for rigorous testing. Novice researchers often have a tendency to overstate the significance of their findings by asserting that statistically significant results also hold substantial managerial importance. They sometimes make definitive claims about the relevance of their discoveries. Researchers can certainly draw conclusions based on their results, but they must exercise caution in the phrasing of implications for theory and practice. It is advisable to provide context by acknowledging that the study's findings are derived from a single investigation and that additional studies are necessary to replicate them in diverse contexts, such as different countries and sample sizes, while addressing the reported limitations. The stated implications should be contingent on the validation of the findings. Therefore, when discussing implications, authors should employ cautious language that implies a need for prudence in considering a course of action, using terms like "suggest" and "may" rather than making strong recommendations.

Assuming the manuscript successfully addresses reviewer concerns regarding its conceptual and methodological aspects, the primary criterion for determining its acceptance or rejection becomes its contribution. At this stage, the editor plays a central role in the final decision, as he or she must evaluate the manuscript's contribution relative to that of other manuscripts deemed acceptable for publication by reviewers. It is rare to find an editor rejecting a manuscript that reviewers strongly recommend for publication. However, when a manuscript's contribution is unclear or marginal, the evaluation may involve additional criteria. These criteria include the paper's length-to-contribution ratio and its contribution compared to that of other manuscripts in the same category. While researchers have limited control over manuscripts competing for journal space, reducing the paper's length can enhance its appeal to the editor and improve its competitive edge.

In addition to condensing the manuscript's text where possible, two effective methods can be employed to reduce its length. A significant portion of the paper's methods can be omitted from the manuscript and instead made available on a website, with a citation link provided in the paper for readers to access detailed information (as also demonstrated by Netemeyer et al., 2018). Secondly, researchers can eliminate unnecessary references. By creating two alphabetical lists of references—one for references cited alone in the text, in absence of other references, and another for all remaining references—researchers can remove references from the second list that are cited in conjunction with those from the first list. Many authors tend to overuse references, and in most cases, citing a few recent references suffices.

Guidelines for conducting and reporting *qualitative* research are offered by Belk and associates (2013). An excellent and detailed set of guidelines for crafting manuscripts for scholarly journals is also offered by Summers (2001).

10.4 Improving Writing Quality: Revising and Editing

Skills at writing and revising manuscripts are usually acquired over a long time. Three factors appear to immensely help improve writing quality: knowing what to write, absence of alternative interpretations of what is written, and conciseness in writing, according to good writers' opinion (e.g., Mick, 2008; Summers, 2001). "Writing quality is often a reflection of the author's thoughts" (Summers, 2001: 411), because if authors do not understand what they want to communicate, they are likely to have difficulty writing. Therefore, when authors have difficulty writing, they should first question the clarity of their thoughts on the topic they are writing about. Second, simply writing to get one's ideas across is not enough, if alternative interpretations of the written text are possible. As one of Robert Stevenson's quotes about writing states, "Don't write merely to be understood. Write so that you cannot possibly be misunderstood" (Summers, 2001). This suggests the need for thorough examination of possible alternative meanings of words and sentences the author puts together in his or her effort to communicate a specific message to readers. Third, the ability to write concisely is a virtue, as it affects manuscript length that affects editors' decision whether or not to publish a manuscript. Long and awkward wording of sentences tends to distract from the main point the author intends to get across, and using terminology known only to some readers tends to lead to ambiguity and affects comprehension.

10.4.1 Paragraphs

A well-structured paragraph is a fundamental building block of effective writing. It should convey a single main idea or point clearly and coherently. For example, the Introduction section should have a minimum of three paragraphs, as mentioned earlier in this chapter, with each having a purpose. The first paragraph should highlight the importance of the topic or issue. The second paragraph should focus on the problem related to the topic, such as insufficient knowledge about the topic, conflicting or inconclusive findings regarding our current state of knowledge, and justifying the need for the proposed study that should be clearly stated in the third paragraph. The following is a guide on how each paragraph should be structured:

Topic Sentence:

- Start your paragraph with a clear and concise topic sentence. This sentence should introduce the main idea or point you want to convey in the paragraph.
- The topic sentence serves as a roadmap for the reader, providing a preview of what the paragraph is about.

Supporting Sentences:

- Follow the topic sentence with a series of supporting sentences. These sentences provide evidence, examples, explanations, or details that support and develop the main idea.
- Each supporting sentence should relate directly to the main idea expressed in the topic sentence.

Transitions:

- Use transitional words and phrases to connect sentences within the paragraph. Transitions help maintain the flow and coherence of the paragraph. Examples of transitions include "furthermore," "in addition," "however," and "for example."

Order and Organization:

- Organize your supporting sentences logically. You can use chronological order, spatial order, order of importance, or cause-and-effect order, depending on the nature of your paragraph's content.
- Ensure that there's a natural progression from one idea to the next. Avoid sudden jumps or shifts that might confuse the reader.

Concluding Sentence:

- End the paragraph with a concluding sentence that summarizes the main point and, if necessary, provides a transition to the next paragraph.
- The concluding sentence should not introduce new ideas but should rather wrap up the discussion in a way that reinforces the paragraph's main point.

Unity, Coherence, and Flow:

- Maintain unity by ensuring that all sentences within the paragraph relate to the main idea expressed in the topic sentence.
- Ensure coherence by using logical connections between sentences and avoiding abrupt shifts in tone or topic.
- Ensure that each paragraph logically connects to the previous one and leads to the next. This creates a coherent and easy-to-follow narrative.

Length:

- While there is no strict rule about the length of a paragraph, it is generally recommended to keep paragraphs concise. Aim for around three to five sentences, but adjust as needed based on the complexity of your ideas.

Purpose and Focus:

- Consider the purpose of your paragraph. Is it to provide information, argue a point, describe a process, or tell a story? Tailor the structure to align with your paragraph's purpose.

Revision and Editing:

- After writing a paragraph, review it for clarity, coherence, and relevance. Make necessary revisions to improve the structure and content.
- Check for grammatical errors and ensure that your sentences are clear and well-constructed.

Context:

- Consider how your paragraph fits into the larger context of your manuscript. Ensure that it contributes to the overall flow and progression of your ideas.

Remember that the structure of a paragraph is a flexible framework that can be adapted to suit the specific needs of your writing. Well-structured paragraphs not only make your writing more readable but also enhance the overall clarity and effectiveness of your communication.

10.4.2 Sentences

Transition Sentences Use transition sentences to smoothly guide readers from one point to the next. These sentences help maintain the flow of your manuscript.

Clarity and Simplicity Use clear, concise language. Avoid jargon or overly complex vocabulary unless it is necessary for your audience. Aim for simplicity and readability.

Vary Your Sentence Structure Use a mix of sentence lengths and structures to keep your writing interesting. Avoid using overly long or complex sentences consistently.

Grammar and Punctuation Brush up on grammar and punctuation rules. Pay attention to common trouble spots like subject-verb agreement, punctuation marks, and sentence structure. Strong grammar and punctuation skills are essential. Proofread your work carefully and, if needed, use grammar-checking tools or seek assistance from a copy editor.

Proper structuring of sentences enhances comprehension. Mick (2008) summarizes Gopen and Swan's (1990) seven principles related to writing structure:

1. Verbs should follow their grammatical subjects as soon as possible.
2. The end of a sentence is the key stress position where the reader anticipates what the writer is drawing attention to.
3. The beginning of the sentence is the topic position where the reader anticipates the main person or chief thing in the story of the sentence to be identified.
4. Information provided earlier in the discourse should also be placed in the topic position for linkage backward and for contextualization forward.
5. Verbs of active voice should be regularly preferred over those of passive voice.
6. The reader needs context before being asked to consider something new.
7. The importance of the substance of the sentence should coincide with the relative expectations for the emphasis raised by the sentence structure. (p.18)

Finally, the services of a professional copy editor could significantly enhance the manuscript's quality, making it easier for reviewers to read through the sections and understand with less effort the material the author attempts to communicate to the reader. Reviewers often judge the writer's competency and experience in writing by factors that may not be considered important, such as the use of acronyms and the frequency of mentioning the same name or word in a set of sentences. For example, after the first time an acronym is mentioned next to the words it represents, such as the American Medical Association (AMA), only the acronym AMA should be mentioned throughout the remaining of the manuscript, except at the beginning of a sentence where the words should be spelled out. And if a series of sentences refer to a noun (e.g., name of a person, object, organization, etc.), only every other sentence must use its pronoun (he, she, it)—i.e., nouns and pronouns must be used in every other consecutive sentence.

10.5 Spelling, Grammar, and Plagiarism Checking

The last step in preparing and finalizing the manuscript is to run it through software programs to correct any errors in spelling and grammar. Besides Microsoft Word, there are several software tools available for checking spelling, grammar, and plagiarism, helping users identify whether a piece of text has been copied or closely paraphrased from another source. Turnitin is probably the most widely used in educational institutions; it compares submitted papers to a vast database of academic content, journal articles, and other written material to identify potential plagiarism. WriteCheck is a service offered by Turnitin, allowing users to check their writing for plagiarism, and offers a grammar and style check as well. Grammarly has grammar and spelling checking features, in addition to plagiarism checker that compares your text to billions of web pages to detect potential matches. Other software programs are also available that offer plagiarism-checking features, including Copyscape, Quetext, Plagscan, and Unicheck.

Before using any plagiarism-checking tool, it is important to review and understand the terms of service and any associated costs. Additionally, if you are using such tools for academic purposes, make sure you comply with your institution's policies regarding plagiarism detection and prevention. Finally, you should know the possible source(s) of similarity scores you might see in the report. Similarity scores from the "Internet" could include your documents that you shared with others via commercial platforms. Once uploaded and shared, these apparently remain on the system and inflate similarity scores, often forcing you to paraphrase your own work.

10.6 Seek Critical Feedback Before Submission

Most researchers spend a considerable amount of time working on a research project that leads to the first draft of a manuscript. During this time, they are intimately involved with every stage of the research process, knowing what they are doing and often the reason for every decision they make. The same holds when writing the manuscript concerning their research project. When they use certain words, they know their meaning; when they cite results, they know how they were obtained; and when they discuss the implications of their findings, they know the bases for their statements. Researchers have immersed themselves in their project that they often have difficulty noticing omissions and ambiguities in their writing, leading to ineffectual communication of their ideas to others. And many are aware of this problem because one often hears researchers saying, "I cannot edit my own writing." However, it is imperative that authors make an effort to self-edit their manuscript in order to reduce these problems.

John Summers (2001) offers three sound suggestions to help authors edit their own work. First, authors should set aside their manuscript for a few weeks to reduce familiarity with their paper. Second, they should try to evaluate the manuscript from the point of view of a person who knows nothing or little about the research topic. Lastly, authors should consider the extent to which their students would be likely to understand most of what they say in their manuscript, and they should revise areas of concern, based on their perceptions of students' inability to do so.

However, there is no better substitute for critical feedback that authors can receive from colleagues serving as informal reviewers, or journal reviewers, after the manuscript has been submitted. Informal reviewers who are familiar with the topic are those likely to provide the most helpful and constructive criticisms. And even those informal reviewers who are not familiar with the research area can provide comments helpful in improving writing quality. Because critical feedback from journal reviewers can be a basis for manuscript rejection, eliminating the journal from the list of potential targets for the manuscript, it is in the researcher's best interest to first request the feedback of informal reviewers interested in and knowledgeable about the topic, as well as those who could help improve writing quality.

It is not advisable for early career researchers in general, doctoral students in particular, to work in isolation (Summers, 2001). Researchers in general can benefit immensely by working with others and receiving constant feedback on their projects. Early career researchers should make a concerted effort to develop or join an existing network of researchers who have an interest in specific areas. These individuals can usually be identified and approached at conferences, where researchers have opportunities to meet and interact with colleagues attending presentations of papers on highly specialized areas. Alternatively, researchers can join formal or informal networks. For example, in my efforts to promote academic research at Thailand's Mahidol University, I established the Consumer Life-course Studies Group (CLSG), which is a network of dozens academic researchers from several countries around the world. These researchers have opportunities to collaborate on multicountry studies, coauthor manuscripts, participate in funded research within countries, share resources (e.g., articles, books, databases), review papers of other members, and attend the annual CLSG conference.

Early career researchers should be aware of the fact that their submitted manuscript competes for journal space with dozens of manuscripts written by many researchers who have had a great deal of experience and have worked as a team to develop their manuscript. More important, experienced researchers in specific areas likely have had their manuscripts reviewed by other expert colleagues who not only have published on the same topic but also serve as reviewers of journals. And quite often, those who provide informal feedback to authors of a paper are also the same "anonymous" reviewers of a journal who are asked to review the submitted manuscript.

Once a colleague has provided valuable feedback as to how authors can improve their paper and this feedback has been incorporated into the submitted manuscript, the same colleague who is asked by the journal editor to evaluate the revised manuscript is likely to find few additional flaws and recommend to the editor acceptance of the paper. And while reviewers are expected (and often asked) by editors to indicate whether they have previously seen the manuscript they are asked to review, it is totally left up to the reviewer's professionalism to do so, knowing that the authors of the manuscript might be asked by the editor to review their own work on a later date.

It is unknown how widespread such practices are in various fields, but I have witnessed several of such "abnormalities" during my academic career. For example, it is not uncommon for an author to send a draft of the paper to a dozen potential reviewers of a journal, as authors often acknowledge the contribution of a large number of individuals who commented on drafts of their published article. What should the novice researcher do, in view of such inequalities that put them at disadvantage? Two general strategies are recommended: First try to work in the area of your interest with one or more well-known researchers in the same area. If you are able to do so, you will likely benefit from their skills and experience, which will increase publication possibilities in higher-tier journals. In the event one cannot collaborate with the more experienced researchers, his or her second option is to work with others who can provide complementary resources.

Early career researchers should never hesitate to ask well-known researchers to collaborate, as long as they know how these collaborators plan to contribute to a project. Their contribution could be in the form of, for example, labor (e.g., interviewing participants) or data analysis. The more resources an early career researcher can contribute, the greater the attraction to potential collaborators. For example, a novice researcher may propose a study that would replicate research published by a well-known researcher, offering to collect, process, and analyze data in a different context (e.g., another country). Generally, researchers should welcome opportunities for collaborative studies, to the extent these projects do not deviate from their main research streams. Collaborative projects increase research productivity and lead to additional rewards, such as invitations to campuses.

The second strategy involves working with a team of individuals who have special skills or resources that they could apply to performing various research tasks. Doctoral students in particular have such opportunities due to the circumstances in which they are embedded (e.g., taking the same classes) that facilitate frequent interaction. And they can also collaborate with faculty, providing them with opportunities to develop additional skills outside the classroom. For these individuals, it is the learning experience with the different stages of academic research, from conceptualization through the review process, that is important, not the output or the tier-level target journals; they do not have to aim at top-tier journals.

References

Alford, R. R. (1998). *The craft of inquiry*. Oxford.

Baker, A., & Chan, K. (2020). The effects of life events on the development of materialism and compulsive consumption: A life course study in the United States and Hong Kong. *Journal of Global Scholars of Marketing Science, 30*(1), 88–104. https://doi.org/10.1080/21639159.2019.1613904

Baker, A., Moschis, G. P., Ong, F. S., & Pattanapanyasat, R. (2013). Materialism and life satisfaction: The role of stress and religiosity. *Journal of Consumer Affairs, 47*(2), 1–14.

Baron, R., & Kenny, D. (1986). The moderator-mediator variable distinction in social psychological research. *Journal of Personality and Social Psychology, 51*, 1173–1182.

Belk, R., Fischer, E., & Kozinets, R. V. (2013). *Qualitative consumer & marketing research*. Sage Publications.

Buhrmester, M., Kwang, T., & Gosling, S. D. (2011). Amazon's mechanical turk: A new source of inexpensive, yet high-quality data? *Perspectives on Psychological Science: A Journal of the Association for Psychological Science, 6*(1), 3–5.

Churchill, G. A., & Moschis, G. P. (1979). Television and interpersonal influences on adolescent consumer learning. *Journal of Consumer Research, 6*(1), 23–35.

Diamantopoulos, A., Reynolds, N., & Simitras, A. (2006). The impact of the response styles on the stability of cross-cultural comparisons. *Journal of Business Research, 59*, 925–935.

Duncan, O. (1975). *Introduction to structural equation models*. Academic Press.

Echambadi, R., & Hess, J. D. (2007). Mean centering does not alleviate collinearity problems in moderated multiple regression models. *Marketing Science, 26*(3), 438–445.

Fournier, S. (1998). Consumers and their brands: Developing branding theory in consumer research. *Journal of Consumer Research, 24*, 343–373.

Goodman, J. K., & Paolacci, G. (2017). Crowdsourcing consumer research. *Journal of Consumer Research, 44*(1), 196–210. https://doi.org/10.1093/jcr/ucx047

Gopen, G. D., & Swan, J. A. (1990). The science of scientific writing. *American Scientist.*, 78, (November-December), 550–558.

Kasser, T. (2002). *The high price of materialism*. MIT Press.

Lance, C. E., Butts, M. M., & Michaels, L. C. (2006). The sources of four commonly reported cutoff criteria: What did they really say? *Organizational Research Methods, 9*, 202–220.
MacKinnon, D. P., Lockwood, C. M., Hoffman, J. M., West, S. G., & Sheets, V. (2002). A comparison of methods to test mediation and other intervening variable effects. *Psychological Methods, 7*(1), 83–104.
Mick, D. (2008). Inklings: From mind to page in research. *Design Research Quarterly, 3*(4), 16–20.
Mittal, C., & Griskevicius, V. (2016). Silver spoons and platinum plans: How childhood environment affects adult. *Journal of Consumer Research, 43*(4), 636–656.
Moschis, G. P. (1978). *Acquisition of the consumer role by adolescents*. Georgia State University, Business Publishing.
Moschis, G. P. (1978–1979). Teenagers' response to retailing stimuli. *Journal of Retailing, 53*(Winter), 80–93.
Moschis, G. P. (1981). Patterns of consumer learning. *Journal of Academy of Marketing Science*, (Spring), 110–126.
Moschis, G. P. (1992). Gerontographics: A scientific approach to analyzing and targeting the mature market. *Journal of Services Marketing, 6*(3), 17–26.
Moschis, G. P. (1996). *Gerontographics: Life-stage segmentation for marketing strategy development*. Quorum.
Moschis, G. P. (2017). Research frontiers on the dark side of consumer behaviour: The case of materialism and compulsive buying. *Journal of Marketing Management*. https://doi.org/10.1080/0267257X.2017.1347341
Moschis, G. P. (2019). *Consumer behaviour over the life course: Research frontiers and new directions*. Springer Publishing, Inc.
Moschis, G. P. (2022). *Marketing to the aging population: Strategies and tools for companies in various industries*. Springer.
Moschis, G. P., & Churchill, G. A. (1978). Consumer socialization: A theoretical and empirical analysis. *Journal of Marketing Research, 15*(4), 599–609.
Moschis, G. P., & Churchill, G. A. (1979). An analysis on the adolescent consumer. *Journal of Marketing, 43*(3), 40–48.
Moschis, G. P., & Churchill, G. A., Jr. (1977a). *Formal consumer education: An empirical assessment* (Vol. No. 6-77-25). University of Wisconsin.
Moschis, G. P., & Churchill, G. A., Jr. (1977b). Mass media and interpersonal influence on adolescent consumer learning. In B. A. Greenberg & D. N. Bellenger (Eds.), *Contemporary marketing thought* (pp. 68–71). American Marketing Association.
Moschis, G. P., & Moore, R. L. (1979a). Family communication and consumer socialization. In W. Wilkie (Ed.), *Advances in consumer research* (Vol. VI, pp. 359–406). Association for Consumer Research.
Moschis, G. P., & Moore, R. L. (1979b). Family communication patterns and consumer socialization. In *Educators' conference proceedings* (pp. 226–230). American Marketing Association.
Moschis, G. P., & Ong, F. S. (2011). Religiosity and consumer behavior: A study of subcultural influences. *Journal of Consumer Behavior, 10*(1), 8–17.
Moschis, G. P., Lawton, J. T., & Stampfl, R. W. (1980). Preschool children's consumer learning. *Family and Consumer Sciences Research Journal, 9*(1), 64–71.
Moschis, G. P., Lee, E., Mathur, A., & Strautman, J. (2000). *The maturing marketplace: Buying habits of baby boomers and their parents*. Quorum Books.
Moschis, G. P., Mathur, A., & Sthienrapapayut, T. (2020). Gerontographics and consumer behavior in later life: Insights from the life course paradigm. *Journal of Global Scholars of Marketing Science*. issue 1: George P. Moschis tribute special issue, part two, *30*(1), 18–33.
Netemeyer, R. G., Warmath, D., Fernandes, D., & Lynch, J. G., Jr. (2018). How am I doing? Perceived financial Well-being, its potential antecedents, and its relation to overall Well-being. *Journal of Consumer Research, 45*(1), 68–89. https://doi.org/10.1093/jcr/ucx109
Nimrod, G. (2013). Applying gerontographics in the study of older internet users. *Journal of Audience & Reception Studies, 10*(2), 46–64.
Nunnally, J. C. (1967). *Psychometric theory*. McGraw Hill, 1967.

Podsakoff, P. M., MacKenzie, S. B., Lee, J. Y., & Podsakoff, N. P. (2003). Common method biases in behavioral research: A critical review of the literature and recommended remedies. *Journal of Applied Psychology, 88*(5), 879–903.

Ridgway, N. M., Kukar-Kinney, M., & Monroe, K. B. (2008). An expanded conceptualization and a new measure of compulsive buying. *Journal of Consumer Research, 35*(4), 622–639.

Rindfleisch, A., Burroughs, J. E., & Denton, F. (1997). Family structure, materialism and compulsive consumption. *Journal of Consumer Research, 23*(4), 312–325.

Salthouse, T. A. (1991). *Theoretical perspectives on cognitive aging*. Lawrence Erlbaum Associates.

Stampfl, R. W., Moschis, G. P., & Lawton, J. T. (1978). Consumer education and the preschool child. *Journal of Consumer Affairs, 12*(Summer), 277–291.

Sthienrapapayut, T., Moschis, G. P., & Mathur, A. (2018). Using gerontographics to explain consumer behavior in later life: Evidence from a Thai study. *Journal of Consumer Marketing, 35*(3), 17–27.

Strahan, R., & Gerbasi, K. R. (1972). Short, homogeneous version of the Marlow Crow social desirability scale. *Journal of Clinical Psychology, 28*(2), 191–193.

Summers, J. O. (2001). Guidelines for conducting research and publishing in marketing: From conceptualization through the review process. *Journal of the Academy of Marketing Science, 29*(4), 405–415.

Tian, K. T., Bearden, W. O., & Hunter, G. (2001). Consumers' need for uniqueness: Scale development and validation. *Journal of Consumer Research, 28*(1), 50–66. https://doi.org/10.1086/321947

Van Horn, L., Masyn, K., Jaki, T., & Ramey, S. L. (2009). Assessing differential effects: Applying regression mixture models to identify variations in the influence of family resources on academic achievement. *Developmental Psychology, 45*(5), 1298–1313.

Wessling, S. K., Huber, L., & Netzer, O. (2017). MTurk character misrepresentation: Assessment and solutions. *Journal of Consumer Research, 44*(1), 211–230. https://doi.org/10.1093/jcr/ucx053

Evaluating, Accepting, and Rejecting Manuscripts

11

11.1 Manuscript Evaluation

When a manuscript is submitted to a journal, the Editor will make the initial evaluation, usually based on factors such as the paper's suitability for the journal, its length, and other factors that are often stated in the Journal's "guidelines for authors." In recent decades, journal editors are increasingly using the manuscript's potential impact factor in deciding whether to put the manuscript through the review process or reject it. This factor is based on the editor's perceived likelihood that the article will be cited widely by future researchers, which would affect his or her journal's impact factor (score). Although editors are likely to consider the number of publications cited from their own journal, it is important to understand that the number of citations of articles that have been published in the editor's journal is not the sole determinant of whether a manuscript will be accepted or rejected.

11.1.1 Editor's Evaluation Criteria

A journal editor's decision to accept or reject a manuscript is based on a comprehensive evaluation of multiple factors, including:

1. *Quality of Research.* The most critical factor is the scientific quality of the manuscript. Editors and peer reviewers assess whether the research is well-designed, is conducted rigorously, and contributes meaningfully to the field.
2. *Originality.* Manuscripts should present novel findings or provide a unique perspective on existing knowledge. Repetitive or redundant research may not be accepted, even if it has numerous citations of articles that have appeared in the editor's journal.
3. *Clarity and Presentation.* Manuscripts should be well-written, logically structured, and adhere to the journal's formatting and style guidelines. Poorly presented work may be rejected.

G. P. Moschis, *Academic Research in Business and the Social Sciences*,
https://doi.org/10.1007/978-3-031-56548-9_11

4. *Relevance to the Journal's Scope.* The research should align with the focus and scope of the journal. Manuscripts that are outside the journal's scope may be rejected.
5. *Ethical Considerations.* Editors may consider ethical issues, such as plagiarism, data manipulation, or conflicts of interest. Manuscripts that violate ethical standards can be rejected.
6. *Peer Reviewer Comments.* Peer reviewers' evaluations and recommendations are crucial in the decision-making process. Editors weigh their feedback heavily.
7. *Citations.* The number of citations of manuscripts published in the editor's journal is increasingly becoming an important factor. However, high citation counts alone do not guarantee acceptance. Editors also consider the quality and relevance of the citing articles.
8. *Balance and Diversity.* Editors may aim for a balanced and diverse selection of manuscripts in each issue or volume, which can influence their decision-making.

It is worth noting that different journals and editors may prioritize these factors differently, and the decision-making process can vary across journals. A manuscript should be evaluated comprehensively to ensure that it meets the journal's standards for scientific quality, novelty, and relevance. Quite often, the editor evaluates the manuscript on factors such as sources of data, its authors, and its perceived contribution. For example, since the publication of the article by Wessling and associates (2017), many marketing journals would not accept manuscripts that used Amazon's MTurk panel for data collection. The editor may also look at the names of the authors, and he or she would be more likely to process manuscripts written by persons who are widely published than unknown authors.

Editors make every effort to select manuscript that stand a good chance to be favorably evaluated by reviewers for the main reason that he or she may not be able to find enough suitable reviewers to evaluate the large number of manuscripts that are submitted. And once a reviewer is assigned a manuscript for review, it is unlikely that he or she will be asked to review another manuscript before the review for that piece is completed. There are no accurate statistics about the number of manuscripts that are not put through the evaluation process or are "desk rejected," but one source cites 80% of the papers submitted to major journals (Summers, 2001), mainly because of the large number of manuscripts that are submitted in one's field. For example, in conversations I have had with journal editors over the years, I was informed that in recent decades, major marketing journals have been receiving in excess of 1000 manuscripts annually and had acceptance rates in single digits. This underscores the importance of doing everything possible for the authors to avoid desk rejections and give their manuscripts a chance to be evaluated by reviewers.

When journal editors cannot find reasons not to put a manuscript through the review process, they look for potential reviewers of the manuscript. The first place most likely they will look is the journal's editorial board. If there are no members of the editorial board available or able to review the manuscript, editors are likely to look for qualified reviewers elsewhere. Some editors use the key words that authors are asked to place on the front page of their manuscript to identify qualified reviewers, while other editors look at the manuscript's list of references, hoping to find persons who have been doing research on the topic. Many journals maintain a list of ad hoc reviewers who have a wide variety of skills and interests in areas of business and the social sciences (e.g., qualitative research, information and communication technologies, well-being) that editors frequently call upon for evaluating a manuscript. Because the manner in which manuscripts submitted to journals are scrutinized nowadays, those that are put through the review process are more likely to be favorably evaluated than in the past when a much larger percentage of manuscripts was put through the review process.

Early career researchers should keep in mind that a manuscript they submit to a journal might not be evaluated by the most knowledgeable and competent reviewers in the area related to their manuscript, especially if the manuscript has been submitted to a low-tier journal. Although editors try to find the most qualified reviewers to evaluate a manuscript, they are not likely to have those most qualified review manuscripts for lower-tier journals. This is because those most qualified are likely to be interested in spending time reviewing for the most prestigious journals, leaving little time to review for lower-level journals. And they might not see many benefits associated with reviewing manuscripts for such journal because they might think that they are not going to learn much from reviewing a manuscript that does not deserve consideration by a higher-level journal.

What all these mean to early career researchers is that, as they are submitting manuscripts to increasingly lower-tier journals, the likelihood of manuscript acceptance increases because the reviewers for lower-tier journals might not be sufficiently knowledgeable to evaluate the manuscript; and, as a result, they might also be receiving lower quality evaluations from these journals. Therefore, they should be compassionate, especially when they realize that the editor and reviewers' comments and suggestions are baseless. In such cases, the author(s) should try to "educate" the reviewers without offending them. An effective way to do this is by acknowledging the reviewers' concern as a "valid" point and, in turn, providing justification for their decisions.

11.1.2 Reviewer's Evaluation Criteria

Experienced reviewers normally evaluate a manuscript on two broad bases: (a) its contribution to one's discipline and (b) the credibility of the reported findings. With respect to the manuscript's contribution, reviewers want to know what they and the readers are going to learn from reading the article that is not already known and how or why this new knowledge is important to the readers. And the article's credibility is judged on the basis of absence of flaws in the research process employed that may have affected the validity of the reported findings.

Type(s) of Contribution The types of contribution articles typically attempt to make have been discussed in Chap. 10. They are briefly discussed here as well for the purpose of providing further clarification and offering examples of contributions. Reviewers are likely to evaluate a manuscript that reports the results of *quantitative* research based on its contribution to knowledge it intends to make in one or more of the following four areas: theoretical, conceptual, methodological, and empirical.

Theoretical contribution can be made by introducing and applying a new theory to an existing problem. The new theory may supplement an existing theory, or may be a competing or alternative theory; and theoretical contribution could even be made by helping improve an existing theory. In the latter case, the existing theory could be improved by, for example, specifying the conditions under which the theory will hold (e.g., by suggesting one or more moderators) and the process(es) that explain(s) the occurrence of the phenomenon in the form of mediating variables—i.e., the underlying mechanisms that explain how one variable affects another. This type of contribution is very common and it can be seen in several studies (e.g., Genau et al., 2022; Shin and Damon Aiken, 2012; Tarman and Sari, 2023).

Conceptual contribution can be in the form of improved definition of constructs by, for example, adding or replacing construct domains. This contribution normally involves the expanded conceptualization of a variable and the development of a new measurement instrument. The reader can see examples of conceptual contributions in studies that entail the development of, for example, improved measures of materialism (Richins, 2004) and compulsive buying (Ridgway et al., 2008).

Methodological contribution can be in the form of demonstrating the use of a new method for solving an existing problem. The new method is expected to demonstrate how to solve a problem for which there is not a known method or how it improves explanation and prediction over existing methods. In the latter case, the research should show evidence the new method is improvement over existing methods. Example of the first type of contribution can be seen in the work of Churchill and Moschis (1979) and Laisawat et al. (2012), which show how to solve the problem of reciprocal causality between two variables. An example of the second contribution can be seen in the development of a model for segmenting the older consumer market that can explain and predict older consumer behavior better than alternative models such as age-based and cognitive age-based segmentation models (Sthienrapapayut et al., 2018; Moschis et al., 2020).

Empirical contribution can be seen in the results of exploratory quantitative studies, as well as in the results of analyses for hypothesis testing; and it is present in studies aimed at answering empirical questions, such as "Are women heavier users of mobile phones than men?" Reported correlations between variables without explanation for the observed relationships, as in correlation matrixes, patterns of observation, and nonrandomly occurring phenomena are considered empirical or empirical regularities (Hunt, 1983).

Reviewers are likely to evaluate the contribution of a manuscript that reports *qualitative* research based on interpretation of new data gathered from various sources (e.g., depth interviews) and the literature review of published studies. Belk and associates (2013) suggest contributions of qualitative research: (a) The "observed" phenomenon should be broken down into mutually exclusive and exhaustive categories of elements that represent its wide range and numbers of meanings (dimensions) that researchers have assigned to codes in "mapping" the phenomenon as a construct; (b) the identification of the process theory that links antecedents to outcomes in the form of temporal sequence of events (or cluster of events) that explain their "temporal bracketing" and their causal interdependence; (c) "conditions that give rise to a phenomenon or the consequence precipitated by a phenomenon" (p. 152); and (d) relationships among elements and processes that are not fully understood are cast into propositional statements. These writers give examples of the types of contributions reviewers are expecting to see in qualitative studies, and additional specific examples of contribution in each of the four areas such as conditions that give rise to a phenomenon (Hirschman, 1992).

Literature Reviews Reviewers are likely to evaluate a manuscript that is based on existing data from published studies based on its incremental contribution to knowledge. This is not to say that manuscripts that simply summarize key findings from previous studies on a particular topic do not make a contribution, as they inform readers by identifying gaps in knowledge and suggesting directions for further research; and they also facilitate meta-analyses. Churchill and Perrault (1982: 287) suggest that a review should "advance the field by virtue of its insightful, integrative, and critical evaluation of the state of work in a subject area." And Summers (2001) asserts that a good review should "provide a *synthesis* (emphasis his) of the literature and make clear what is 'known' with a fair amount of certainty and where are the gaps are" (p. 411). Thus, a review manuscript should organize, integrate, and interpret data to provide new insights into an issue or problem and also develop a new theory or conceptual framework.

If reviewers apply these criteria for evaluating articles that review literature using the methods discussed in Chap. 8, they are not likely to favor those types of reviews that are merely reporting what has been found, or how and by whom, as their main objectives. Rather, they are likely to look at reviews that use the findings of studies as bases for creating new knowledge, develop new theory, offer novel interpretations of previous findings, and generally report fresh ideas that advance theory and practice in a field or discipline. Thus, most likely, reviewers will see merit in literature reviews, such as integrative, grounded theory, and meta-ethnography; they may see value in a systematic or narrative review that reports state-of-the-art knowledge and identifies gaps which suggest future research directions; and they are likely to see relatively little value in reviews that are simply descriptive or void of valid interpretations with questionable implications for practice, as in the cases of scoping and bibliometric reviews that report the articles published over time in a journal or on a particular topic. This in not to say that the latter have no value. Editors generally favor review articles because such articles tend to be frequently cited, affecting the journal's impact factor (see "Metrics" in this chapter). I suspect that editors of most journals, especially those who require authors to cite articles that have been published in their journal, are likely to publish articles that report bibliometric analyses of author and journal citations. There appears to be an inherent risk in writing review manuscripts that merely report what other researchers have found. Specifically, articles that fall short of making valid interpretation of the reported findings, such as bibliometric reviews, are likely to create the impression that the author is a "reporter" rather than a researcher.

Another issue in writing a review manuscript relates to the method employed by the researcher(s). When the purpose of a review is to accomplish certain objectives, such as build a new theory or conceptual framework, and there is more than one method to review literature, a host of questions might be raised, such as: Why use this method and not others that have similar objectives? Would other methods have led to different outcomes or conclusions, leading to a different theory or model? What evidence can be offered in support of the validity of the conclusions? The main problem with the use of a specific review method is that the results are not compared to an alternative method, as in the case of introducing a new segmentation method where one can use objective criteria to show the superiority of one method over alternative and commonly used methods. For example, when a model was developed to help segment the older consumer market based on measures of aging, the efficacy of this model was compared to those previously used segmentation models (e.g., age-based) in their ability to predict a variety of consumer behaviors (e.g., Moschis, 1996; Moschis et al., 2020). Thus, the researcher cannot claim that the chosen review method was the most appropriate, impactful, or useful.

Research Credibility A manuscript that appears to meet the reviewers' criteria when it is evaluated for its contribution might not be accepted for publication, if the research process that led to its results and conclusions is flawed. Therefore, researchers should be familiar with factors that both contribute and undermine the study's credibility as well. Most reviewers who examine a manuscript are likely to look for content that will either satisfy them or will "raise flags" about the manuscript's weaknesses that they are likely to use when they write their evaluation report to its authors and the journal's editor. Several of criteria reviewers use to evaluate a manuscript are presented chronologically below, including several in the form of questions reviewers might ask.

First, when reading the "introduction" section, reviewers are trying to determine not only the manuscript's intended contribution, but also the extent to which the research topic is important, timely, interesting, and mainly appropriate and relevant to the journal's readers. The reviewers might ask questions such as follows: Are the manuscript's objectives realistic and doable? Who would be interested to know about the results or conclusions of the study and why? This section is perhaps the most important part of the manuscript and some reviewers might decide not to read further, if the introduction is not convincing enough to stimulate interest in the project.

Second, a manuscript that does not employ a sound theoretical or conceptual framework is not likely to be accepted. When reading the "background" section of the manuscript, the reviewers are likely to look for a sound theoretical or conceptual framework that supports the study contained in the manuscript. They are also likely to see whether the literature reviewed is well integrated within the theoretical or conceptual framework and provides sound bases for derivation of the study's hypotheses or the selection of variables to be included in a model. The reviewers are likely to ask: Why is this theory relevant? Are the hypothesized relationships derived from the theory(ies) presented? If there is more than one theory used, a reviewer might ask: Why is the theory employed more relevant than another theory (that can be mentioned by the reviewer)? Is there an overarching multi-theoretical conceptual framework appropriate in subsuming the proposed theories?

Third, reviewers are likely to look closely at the research design used and, generally, the research process, from the selection of participants to the methods of analysis used. And they may decide to reject the manuscript due to methodological flaws of the study, despite merit in its conceptualization. Reviewers of respectable journals *very likely* will ask questions about common method bias and any steps taken to minimize it (Podsakoff et al., 2003). Reviewers might ask specific questions about the conceptualization and measurement of constructs, their reliability and validity, and scales used from previous studies (if more than one is available). They might ask for information about methods of selection of participants, sample size or non-sampling errors, and how these were handled. Reviewers are also likely to question the method's suitability in accomplishing the study's objectives and, in some cases, ask for explanation for not using more than one method or a more appropriate method of data analysis.

Fourth, when reading the results and the discussion of the study finding reported in the manuscript, reviewers are likely to pay attention to (a) the significance of the emerged findings and (b) the manner in which these are reported or stated in the text. Authors have a tendency to over-state the significance of any findings and downplay the emerged insignificant relationships. For example, they assert causality when two variables are correlated, or a unidirectional influence between the variables when a reciprocal influence might exist. Authors know that trivial findings are not going to help "sell" the manuscript, but reviewers can see this in the way results are reported and discussed. Reviewers are likely to notice the superficiality of the emerged findings, which is not going to be to the authors' best interest.

Finally, the reviewers might judge the manuscript based on its implications for theory and practice *relative* to its length. They might ask: What is that we have learned from this study that we didn't already know? What is the importance and relevance of the findings for theory and practice? Are the findings likely to change the way researchers think about studying a phenomenon, or business practitioners make policy and business decisions? Findings of studies which are statistically significant and helpful in theory development might not be significant for practice because developing policy and business strategies is not cost-free and likely to be evaluated on expected outcome of decisions relative to their costs.

Most leading journals or their editors provide valuable suggestions to authors for enhancing the manuscript's chances of acceptance and avoiding rejection. For example, Churchill and Perreault (1982) provide guidelines for empirical and conceptual articles. Similarly, Varadarajan (1996) discusses many of the weaknesses in manuscripts reported by reviewers and suggests guideposts for authors. Early career researchers, especially doctoral students, should familiarize themselves with the criteria journals use to evaluate manuscripts, as many such criteria are also relevant in preparing dissertation proposals that will be evaluated by members of their dissertation committees.

11.2 Revising the Manuscript and Responding to Reviewers' Comments

Once the manuscript is submitted to a journal, the editor will make the initial evaluation. If this evaluation is favorable, he or she will look for qualified reviewers to evaluate the manuscript. If reviewers perceive that a manuscript either already offers or has the potential to make a significant contribution, the editor may recommend revision. The extent and complexity of the required revisions can vary, and editors might suggest revisions with a cautionary note, indicating potential challenges and the possibility of an unsatisfactory outcome. However, as a general guideline, the likelihood of acceptance for a revised manuscript is typically higher than the likelihood of acceptance when it is initially submitted, as authors have greater control over the manuscript's destiny—i.e., what they have to do to satisfy the reviewers. While revisions can be time-consuming, many researchers find them to be the most rewarding and intellectually stimulating aspect of the academic research process.

This section provides guidance on how authors should approach an editor's invitation or request for manuscript revision and how to handle reviewers' comments.

11.2.1 Responding to Editor and Reviewers

Immediately upon notification of the required revisions, the author(s) should notify the editor of their plans to undertake the revision and the approximate date by which they plan to complete it, unless the editor gives them a deadline. Next, they should make the revision one of their highest priorities. As the editor and the reviewers normally expect to see a Revision Notes document that would explain how the researchers have responded to their comments and suggestions, the authors should start drafting this document from the first day they start working on the revision. In most cases, there is no required format for the revision notes, but only the expectation that the author(s) will address each reviewer's comment or concern by indicating what was done, or the reason for not accommodating the reviewer's suggestion.

In the Revision Notes document, the authors should outline and number each reviewer's substantive comment and criticism and then try to address it. In addressing these comments on a reviewer-by-reviewer basis, they should first state each of the reviewer's request, suggestion or concern, and any reviewer suggestion(s) as to how to handle each; and, in turn, they should state what was done to address it. For example, "Reviewer A suggests that …" (They should state the reviewer's request or suggestion verbatim) and then, after they have stated each, they should state (in different font) the steps they have taken to undress it. Appendix 11.1 illustrates this response format, showing excerpts from a set of revision notes prepared in response to reviewer comments and the editor's invitation for revision.

For each of the comments addressed by the authors in accordance with the reviewers' recommendations, they should transparently communicate the nature of the concern, the suggestions made by the reviewers, and the steps taken to address these concerns. In cases where the authors are unable to address specific comments for various reasons, they should endeavor to present a strong case in favor of their stance without causing offense to the reviewers. For instance, they might express agreement with the reviewer's perspective, acknowledge consideration of the suggested option, and subsequently explain the rationale behind their chosen method, often citing precedents from previous studies as justification. However, it is advisable not to assert the superiority of their method or choice over that suggested by the reviewer. It can be a practical approach to compile a list of responses to numbered reviewer comments, or alternatively, create a list encompassing all suggestions along with explanations regarding their handling. For any comments or criticisms that cannot be addressed, authors should provide a reason and frame them as potential opportunities or suggestions for future research.

When the authors begin revising their paper, it is suggested they start working on the easiest revisions first, while spending several days thinking about the major ones. Major revisions usually involve the re-writing of sections and possibly re-analysis of data. Taking extra time to address reviewer comments and suggestions gives authors more time to think about the best way to handle them. However, addressing each of the reviewers' comments and suggestions satisfactorily does not guarantee acceptance, even after the reviewers recommend acceptance.

11.2.2 Handling "Difficult" Reviewers

Although the vast majority of reviewers make accurate and reasonable assessment of the manuscripts assigned to them by the editor, there are occasions when a reviewer writes a review which makes it difficult for authors to handle. These are reviews which contain comments and suggestions that make authors do unnecessary work to address them. Because, on the one hand, the authors cannot ignore reviewer comments, but on the other hand they have to respond quite often by "educating" the reviewer in a tactful and professional way. There are several types of reviewer comments and suggestions that make a reviewer difficult to handle. The paragraphs that follow outlines six types of comments along with suggestions for responding, with examples illustrated in Appendix 11.2.

1. In evaluating a revised version of the manuscript, the reviewer raises concerns about issues which he or she thinks that were not addressed when these were addressed in a prior revision (remain unanswered) (Appendix 11.2, item 1).The authors should respond by providing evidence that contradicts his or her statement.
2. The reviewer may infer the presence of flaws because he or she has not read the manuscript carefully (Appendix 11.2, item 2a). In this case, the authors should

provide evidence to satisfy the reviewer's concern, without explicitly stating his or her oversight.

3. The reviewer brings up new issues that he or she could or should have raised in the initial review (Appendix 11.2, item 2b). The authors should respond by indicating that the reviewer may have raised this issue because the explanation was not clear, without offending the reviewer for his or her omission.
4. The suggestions for revision are extraordinary and unrealistic, making them impossible to address. Most likely, the reviewer has vested interest in not seeing the manuscript published for numerous reasons (e.g., results are not in line with his or her own research or views) (Appendix 11.2, item 2c). The authors should state that the request is unreasonable and impractical due to constraints beyond their control, providing a long list of reasons in support of their answer. But the author(s) may also acknowledge the pertinence of the reviewer's suggestions by providing a reasonable alternative.
5. The reviewer criticizes the method (theories and models) without offering suggestions for overcoming or improving them; and he or she suggests the presentation of information that does not exist (Appendix 11.2, item 3a). In this case, the authors should inform the reviewer that the requested information is neither available to address his or her suggestion, nor would it had been possible to present. And they could also ask him or her to recommend better or more appropriate models.
6. The reviewer suggests revisions or additions that are not in line with existing or state-of-the-art knowledge. He or she apparently has not read the front part of the manuscript thoroughly and assumes the research is theory-based, requiring hypothesis development and testing, when the research question posed is an empirical one (Appendix 11.2, item 4a). The authors should provide details for their decision.

Lastly, authors should keep in mind that it is up to the editor's discretion to accept or reject a manuscript that has been favorably evaluated, as editors use additional criteria for evaluating a manuscript, such as its contribution relative to other manuscripts that have been evaluated favorably. Favorable evaluation of a manuscript normally leads to its acceptance, which can create an issue when there is limited journal space. The backlog of accepted manuscripts might affect the editor's decision to accept additional manuscripts that have been evaluated favorably by the reviewers. In sum, favorable evaluations of manuscripts do not always guarantee acceptance. And there have been cases where the backlog of manuscripts that were accepted by an editor were not published by the new editor. For example, when a new editor of a major marketing journal "inherited" 42 manuscripts that had been accepted by the previous editor, he notified the authors of the 39 manuscripts that their work did not meet his journal's standards and did not publish them.

11.2.3 Withdrawing a Manuscript from the Review Process

After submitting a manuscript to a journal, certain events could make the author(s) consider withdrawing their manuscript from the review process. While it is not very likely that the author(s) will experience events that would lead to the manuscript's withdrawal from the journal's consideration, early career researchers should be aware of possible reasons and how to handle them. First, authors might discover that there were errors in reporting the results of their study. These errors could have occurred for any number of reasons, including human or mechanical errors in data processing, analysis, and reporting of results; and they may include inaccuracies in statements made that are not supported with evidence. In such a case, the authors have the responsibility to notify the editor of the nature of errors or inaccuracies and apologize. If these errors significantly change the conclusions reached and reported in the manuscript, the authors should inform the editor and request the manuscript be withdrawn from the review process and the reason for their decision. However, if the errors do not change the reported findings, as in the case of differences only in the sizes statistical figures (e.g., size of correlations, significance levels), the authors should let the editor know of these inaccuracies in the data reported and offer to make the changes, if a revision is requested by the editor, leaving it up to him or her to decide.

Second, the author(s) may also decide to withdraw their manuscript after receiving reviewer and editor feedback from the first round of their manuscript's review. This is most likely to happen because of two main reasons: Either the author(s) does not find it practical to address the requested revision due to the effort and resources that would be required (e.g., additional skills, time), which the authors are not able or willing to provide, or because the authors do not want to comply and make revisions in line with the editor's request or suggestions. The latter could happen for various reasons. For example, the author(s) might think that the reviewer and editor's suggestions are not valid because of their lack of knowledge or competence in their evaluations. Additionally, the authors might think that the revisions could lead to a publication inconsistent with their previously published works. I am using the example below to illustrate these points from a request for a manuscript revision I recently received from an editor of a B-level international journal.

> Ideally, the method section should start with the following paragraphs to convince editor and reviewers about your awareness of classic outstanding review papers…develop your methodology section with the following paragraph:
>
> "Systematic review papers can be of several types, namely – Structured review focusing on widely used methods, theories and constructs (Rosado-Serrano et al., 2018; Paul & Singh, 2017; Kahiya, 2018), Framework based (Paul & Benito, 2018), Hybrid-Narrative with a framework for setting future research agenda (Kumar et al., 2019; Dabić et al., 2020), theory-based review (Gilal et al., 2018; Paul & Rosado-Serrano, 2019), a meta-analysis (Knoll & Matthes, 2017), bibliometric review (Randhawa et al., 2016), Review aiming for model/framework development (Paul & Mas, 2019; Paul, 2019)."

> Add above in the methodology section of the paper and report what type of review you have chosen and why you have chosen your specific type of review?
>
> The main purpose of a review article is to critically analyze the literature published under the theoretical lens-specific theory and then identify what methods, contexts, independent variable, dependent variable, mediating variables, and moderating variables were used.

Based on my knowledge at that time, I did not agree with anything the editor stated in his email to me for various reasons: (a) The types of reviews he considered "systematic," because the list was not exhaustive and included types that were not systematic (e.g., bibliometrics); (b) some suggested types could not have been "widely used," because I was not aware of them (even could not find their developers on the Internet by author or type); (c) I did not agree with the Editor's statement about the "main purpose of a review article" because I was aware of additional review types and methods; and (d) I didn't think it would be appropriate to use the Editor's suggested/requested write-up verbatim in my work, citing the types of reviews and references that were not consistent with my knowledge of established conventions, as such a statement would have conveyed to the academic community deficiency in my knowledge about the subject matter.

I concluded that either the Editor and reviewers were "off-base" or their definition of (or expectations for) a review article announced in the Journal's annual "call for papers" for the special issue on "Systematic Reviews in Consumer Studies" was inconsistent with my knowledge. As I had reviewed, and had received reviews for, hundreds of manuscripts during the previous four decades, and also had published dozens of review articles, several in respectable journals, I reminded myself of my experiences and the need to be compassionate when considering reviewer and editor's feedback on my manuscripts. These individuals are trying to do a job the best way they can. And early career researchers should know that in some instances authors know more than journal reviewers and editors; and their manuscripts often help educate reviewers as well. The job of reviewers is often described as "thankless," with the only main benefits they receive for their time are the opportunity to learn about recently published research and, in some cases, ask the authors to cite their own work, which would help their citation score or h-index (as described later in this chapter).

As I was confident that my review article would see publication light in another journal, I did not see merit in investing time to revise my manuscript in line with the Editor's suggestions. I therefore responded politely as follows:

> It appears that the paper's present main goal—i.e., to present a review of research on an emerging novel approach to study a wide variety of topics of interest to consumer researchers—does not make the contribution intended for the special issue. Therefore, I apologize for taking up your and the Reviewers' time, and I am requesting the withdrawal of the paper.

11.3 After Manuscript Acceptance

The editor's notification of manuscript acceptance often comes with a number of requests that authors must satisfy in order to see their manuscript published. Depending upon the journal and its editor, as well as the condition of the authors' manuscript, these requests can vary from very simple or easy tasks to time-consuming endeavors. Appendix 11.3 shows some of the so-called "minor revisions" that the editor or journal staff might request as conditions for publishing your manuscript.

Most of the items on this list are standard requirements across journals, and it is to the author(s)' best interest to attend to as many as possible prior to submission, especially format, consistency of citations, and copy editing; and others are unusual requests, like developing multiple-choice questions. As I mentioned in Chap. 10, almost every editor would like to see articles from his or her journal cited in your manuscript. And some of them make this a condition or requirement for publishing your article, as shown in Appendix 11.3. Some editors would suggest the articles he or she would like to see cited, while others do not mind which articles the author sites, as long as they are from their journal; and most often the extra citations do not relate to any elements of the author's manuscript. This creates extra work for the authors, who have to try accommodating the editor's request; and it undermines the credibility and professionalism of the author, who is forced to accommodate irrelevant publications into his or her manuscript. Such practices are most common among lower-tier journals, as the one on Appendix 11.3, where the editor clearly states the reasons for his request—i.e., to elevate the journal's impact factor and the author's citation numbers, hence the reason these scores are becoming increasingly artificial Koltun and Hafner (2021) (see also "Metrics" in this chapter).

Although editors can recommend citation of articles that would improve a manuscript, and most of them along with their reviewers may do so even if the articles they recommend have not been published in their journal, it is not uncommon to see suggested articles that are either from the editor's journal or have been written by the editor, as it can be seen in the editor's suggestion/request in Sect. 11.2.3 and Appendix 11.3. And because the editor recommends citation of his work, as seen in Sect. 11.2.3 and Appendix 11.3, it does not necessarily mean that the editor is trying to increase the impact of his research. He or she may truly believe that his articles would be the most beneficial for the authors to read and cite. However, by recommending citation of his or her articles that have not appeared in highly regarded journals in one's field, especially when the editor urges the authors to cite articles from his or her own journal for raising journal and author visibility (Appendix 11.3), he or she runs the risk of creating the wrong impression in the academic community. Further, if editors create the perception that they are trying to increase their own citation scores by requesting the authors to cite their articles, reviewers might also be motivated to do the same, and authors could engage in more self-citation as well, adding to the artificiality of metrics used by universities to make important decisions that affect faculty members' well-being.

Early career researchers must be aware of these additional requirements and conditions, which entail additional work on their part. They must be prepared to navigate the "post-manuscript acceptance" process required, even when they think they have a legitimate reason to believe that the additional tasks are time-consuming, unnecessary, and unfair because they require time and promote interests of other parties.

11.4 Handling Rejected Manuscripts

Early career researchers should take comfort that there is an outlet for everything they write, I would often tell my students based on my experience. If one can write a paper that gets an idea across, eventually this paper will see publication light in some outlet, whether in the form of an article, or a book chapter, or a conference proceedings paper. But the strategy is to first aim at a reasonably higher-level outlet, before considering lower-level options. Therefore, for every paper authors prepare, they should make a list of 3–4 outlets or journals, starting with the higher-tier one(s) and ending with the lowest level journal that their university or department considers acceptable. If the manuscript is not judged suitable for publication in the first journal, they should send it to the next journal on the list, *after* they revise it by incorporating substantive comments and addressing criticism of reviewers. I do not recommend submission to the next journal without these revisions, in part because a revision that addresses reviewer comments is likely to strengthen the manuscript, proactively addressing similar criticisms in the future; and there is always the possibility of having the same reviewer in the next journal who would be very unhappy to find out that the authors ignored his or her comments and suggestions that took time to write. Every rejection should be viewed as opportunity to develop a better manuscript, and the paper's chances are increasingly enhanced because comments are incorporated into subsequent revisions, proactively addressing reviewer concerns and concurrently targeting less demanding journals with each rejection. As the manuscript improves and evaluated increasingly by lower level and less demanding journals, it will eventually be accepted by a lower-tier journal.

11.5 Reviewing for Scholarly Journals

Reviewers provide invaluable service to the discipline. They help the editor make decisions about the types of manuscripts that should be published, helping advance one's discipline. Reviewers on editorial boards are normally very qualified to evaluate the suitability of a manuscript for publication. The same can be said about ad hoc reviewers. The reasons reviewers perform this service vary. Some do it because they enjoyed the reviewing process, others do it because they have a benefit from it, such as keeping up with the state-of-the-art knowledge in their field, and others do it for the mere prestige of being a reviewer. They have a motive in common for being reviewers. They all serve as reviewers because they want to advance their discipline.

Although the quality of the reviews is so important to the discipline, reviewers normally receive very little training in reviewing manuscripts. It is frequently left up to the journals to inform reviewers on how to perform manuscript reviews. In certain occasions, some reviewers (ad hoc reviewers in particular) perceive the reviewing task as a chore in part because they see little benefit from reviewing other than keeping up with the literature in their area of research interest. And journals often have to remind reviewers of the due date of their reviews. However, regardless of their status or motivation for reviewing, they should all attempt to make a good review not only to help advance their discipline but also to help the authors.

Because reviewers can remain anonymous, and some of them feel that reviewing is a thankless task, they take a little time to improve their skills at reviewing when they have the opportunity to do so. And some of them may not even perform an adequate or fair review. Yet, their decision to recommend or not recommend a manuscript for publication can be crucial to the authors' careers and might even affect their entire lives, as it was the case with me when I was told that in order to get my doctoral degree I would have to publish two sole-authored articles in the top journals in my field. To help reviewers improve their skills at reviewing and sensitize authors to the criteria reviewers are using to evaluate their manuscripts, this chapter ends by providing two sets of guidelines: One that lists the information good reviewers are looking for in evaluating a manuscript (stated as questions); and some guidelines that can help not only some editors perform their duties but also authors can find helpful in improving their manuscripts as well as their responsibilities as future reviewers.

11.5.1 What Reviewers Are Looking for and Should Be Asking

The following questions may be asked when evaluating any manuscript:

- Is the title appropriate? Does it reflect the content accurately?
- Does the abstract allow reader to understand what the article is about?
- Is the author's stance on the research topic made clear within a first few paragraphs or within the first page?
- Does the introduction give a succinct overview of the article? Does the content have appeal for diverse audiences?
- Does the work add to the existing knowledge in the field? What have we learned from the manuscript that we did not already know?
- Do the results lead to a new theory or framework? Are the results innovative?
- What source of citations does the author use? Is the literature review accurate, up-to-date, and cited from leaders in the field and scholarly sources?
- Is the format/structure of the manuscript appropriate for the article type?
- Which style of writing does the author use? Is it appropriate?
- Is the research design used in the study appropriate for the research question?
- Were appropriate methods or procedures (e.g., statistical tests, models, or analytical frameworks) used to analyze or synthesized the data?
- Does the discussion or conclusion relate to the objectives of the manuscript?

- Are there places in the manuscript where the meaning is ambiguous?
- Is the quality of the writing good? Does the manuscript flow seamlessly?
- Are illustrative materials such as tables and figures used effectively?
- Is the manuscript error free? Is there any spelling or typing errors that show signs of hasty preparation?
- Are the references in the proper format?
- Have study limitations been acknowledged?
- Are all ideas tied together and related to the study's objectives in the conclusion?
- Are the study's design and methods sufficiently transparent and well-documented to allow for replication by other researchers?

The following questions could be asked in evaluating quantitative studies:

- Were the hypotheses derived from a theoretical or conceptual framework?
- If more than one theoretical or conceptual framework is appropriate for addressing a research question, why was the framework that used most appropriate for the study?
- Could characteristics or size of the sample that was used have affected the results?
- Have the authors provided evidence that the variables used were valid and reliable?
- What steps were taken by the authors to address issues of common method bias (in cross-sectional studies)?
- What steps were taken to account for possible demand artifacts (in experimental studies)?
- What have we learned from the study that we did not already know?
- What is the significance of the implications of the study findings (if any) for theory, practice or directions for future research?

The following questions could be asked in evaluating qualitative studies:

- Do the authors use criteria applicable to evaluating results of qualitative studies.
- (credibility, transferability, dependability, and confirmability)?
- Do the study results help develop theory about the phenomenon under investigation?
- Is the research tradition employed in the study appropriate for its research objectives?
- Did the researcher use any sound bases (e.g., existing theories) for making data interpretations and/or building a new theory?
- What have we learned from the study that we did not already know?
- What is the significance of the implications of the study findings (if any) for theory, practice or directions for future research?

Additional considerations in evaluating ***cross-national*** *studies.*

Evaluating a cross-national study involves assessing its quality, validity, and relevance. The following are questions a reviewer should ask in evaluating a cross-national study:

- Are methods employed culturally and contextually appropriate for the countries under study?

- Are issues of instrument back translation applicable?
- Are measurement instruments validated or adapted for cross-national use?
- Is there consistency of data collection methods across different countries?
- How are potential sources of bias or error addressed in the analysis?
- Have appropriate statistical techniques or control variables been used to account for cultural or contextual differences (e.g., metric invariance, social desirability)?
- Have the authors acknowledged potential sources of bias, challenges in cross-national research, and the generalizability of findings.
- Do interpretations of study findings take into account the cultural, historical, and political contexts of the countries involved?

11.5.2 Preparing Manuscript Review/Evaluation Reports to Editors and Authors

Comments for Editors Editors expect reviewers to make a recommendation and provide justification for their decision. The comments to the editor are confidential and normally are not shared with the authors. Reviewer comments to editors should state the main reasons for the reviewer's decision to recommend revision, and whether the reviewer thinks the authors will be able to address his or her concerns and suggestions satisfactorily; and he or she should mention the main areas where revisions are needed to make the manuscript publishable. When recommending rejection, the reviewer should specifically state the flaws that justify rejecting the manuscript.

Comments for Authors There is no agreed upon format for preparing reviewer comments for authors. Unless a specific format is requested by the editor, some reviewers prefer to group their comments on manuscript limitations or flaws into those that are correctable or minor and those that cannot be corrected, according to their opinion. However, in my view, determining whether a limitation or problem is or is not correctable is a subjective decision, as the reviewer is not aware of authors' capabilities, resources, and the like. Conceivably, every limitation is correctable, if the researcher is told how to revise a study or manuscript and has time and resources to do so. My advice is to list comments and suggestions chronologically and label them so that they apply to major sections of the manuscript (e.g., conceptual, methodological). Below are some guidelines for reviewers (see also Summers, 2001):

- Be tactful when criticizing the work of authors. Some of the authors could be even doctoral students who are yet to develop "immunity" to harsh criticism by reviewers.
- Begin the review by stating any positive features of the manuscript before mentioning its limitations.
- Avoid attacking the authors and their work using negative words (e.g., confused, disappointed, frustrated).

- When mentioning limitations, explain the reason for each and what needs to be done to fix it.
- Show impartiality to the research approach (qualitative, quantitative) used to study the research question, and avoid commenting on areas outside your expertise. Try to demonstrate a neutral and objective stance by using facts to support your concerns and suggestions.
- If you think that for any reason the manuscript cannot be published in this journal, recommend other suitable outlets.
- Show that you want to help the authors improve their manuscript by suggesting revisions that would make it publishable. And provide them with tools (e.g., references) that would help them.
- For those aspects of the manuscript that you find problematic (e.g., conceptual, theoretical, methodological, writing quality), be specific about the reason(s) and give examples; and, in turn, suggest better alternative(s) (e.g., conceptual framework, theory, measure), if possible.
- If uncorrectable flaws and unexpected findings do not overshadow the positive aspects of the manuscript, recommend their inclusion as directions for future research.
- Observe the due date of your review.

11.6 Metrics

Scientometrics is the field of study that involves the quantitative analysis of scientific literature and scientific impact. It employs statistical methods and metrics to analyze patterns of publication, citation, and collaboration within the scientific community. Scientometrics aims to provide insights into the structure and dynamics of scientific research, as well as the impact and influence of individual researchers, institutions, and academic journals. Scientometric studies often examine trends in scientific publications, such as the growth of research output over time, and co-authorship analysis to identify research networks and collaborative trends.

In the field of scientometrics, citation metrics are commonly used to assess the impact of scientific works. This includes metrics like the h-index, impact factor, and citation counts for individual papers, authors, or journals. Bibliometrics (discussed in Chap. 8) is a subset of scientometrics that specifically focuses on the quantitative analysis of bibliographic information, such as publication and citation data. The field of scientometrics provides valuable tools for assessing the productivity, impact, and trends within the scientific community. Researchers, institutions, and policymakers use scientometric analyses to make informed decisions about resource allocation, research priorities, hiring new faculty, and promotions.

11.6.1 h-index

The h-index, or Hirsch index, is a metric that quantifies both the productivity and impact of a researcher's scientific output. It was proposed by physicist Jorge E. Hirsch (2005) as a way to measure the cumulative impact of a researcher's work over time. It is calculated by arranging a researcher's publications in descending order based on the number of citations each publication has received; the h-index is the highest number, h, such that the researcher has at least h publications with h or more citations. For example, if a researcher has an h-index of 10, it means that he or she has at least 10 publications, each of which has been cited at least 10 times.

The i10-index is part of Google Scholar citations, a freely available Web search engine that indexes the full text or metadata of scholarly literature across an array of publishing formats and disciplines. It is a metric used to measure the impact of scholarly publications by providing a simple way for researchers to track citations to their work. Specifically, the i10-index is the number of academic papers that a researcher has authored or co-authored that have received at least 10 citations each. In other words, if a researcher has an i10-index of 20, it means that he or she has at least 20 publications that have each been cited at least 10 times. While the h-index considers the highest number of publications with at least the same number of citations, the i10-index is more focused on the number of papers with at least 10 citations. It is a quick way to gauge the impact of a researcher's work, particularly in terms of the number of papers that have achieved a moderate level of citation attention.

Researchers often include both the h-index and the i10-index in their academic profiles to provide a more comprehensive view of their scholarly impact. The h-index has become a widely used metric in academia for assessing the impact of researchers, and it is commonly used for evaluation and comparison purposes during academic hiring, promotions, tenure, and grant applications. Although it is a widely used metric for evaluating the impact of a researcher's scientific output, its effectiveness as a measure of impact has been a subject of debate (e.g., Bornmann et al., 2011; Schubert, 2009). The index has limitations, which are frequently mentioned (e.g., Ding et al., 2020; Gingras and Khelfaoui, 2020; Kotov, 2010; Spicer, 2015), because it:

- Tends to favor established researchers who have been active for a longer period. Early career researchers may not have had enough time to accumulate a high h-index.
- Does not consider the quality of the journals in which publications are cited. It treats all citations equally, regardless of whether they come from high-impact or low-impact journals; and tends to measure quantity not quality of publications.
- Can be inflated as a result of self-citations and misuse, as evidence have been reported involving regular cross-citations between good friends (Kotov, 2010) or a small circle of people who routinely cite each other's work that have been called "citation soviets" (Spicer, 2015).

- Does not consider a researcher's contribution to co-authored publications. The index treats every co-author the same, regardless of number of co-authors or name sequence on an article.
- Does not account for citation practices across academic disciplines that may differ in average citation counts and may be influenced by the size of the research community or fields where researchers may have different pools of potential citations.
- Is primarily based on citations to journal articles, and it may not adequately capture the impact of conference papers or books, which can be significant in certain disciplines.
- Does not account for different levels of accessibility to articles, especially by researchers in foreign universities, limiting opportunities for citation of articles in certain subscription journals compared with open-access journals.
- Tends to underestimate the achievement of scientists with a "selective publication strategy"—those who do not publish a high number of documents but who achieve a very important international impact.

Upon my retirement from Georgia State University (GSU) in 2020, I endowed the "George P. Moschis Influential Researcher Award," which is aimed at promoting and rewarding impactful research of faculty in the GSU's Mack Robinson College Business. Recipients of this award are expected to meet the criteria that are presented very early in Chap. 13 of this book. The 2023 winner of this annual award was a former 35-year colleague in our Department of Marketing. Frankly, this was a pleasant surprise because he did not meet any of the four criteria for the award, as I was very familiar with his work and his ad hoc research "style" that is more likely to produce high h index scores than impactful research. Specifically, although he had virtually no sole- or senior-authored publications in the Department's list of top journals and was not well-known for anything in particular, he had a very large number of publications in low-impact outlets on just about any topic of marketing where he had found the opportunity to collaborate with others, largely as a junior co-author. Apparently, the selection committee members were impressed by his high h-index scores, as those in a field of business are not likely to be able to assess the quality of many journals in every other business field. Perhaps this is the main reason the h-index makes it easy for non-experts in a field to evaluate a researcher's contribution to his field (Spicer, 2015).

11.6.2 Impact Factor

The impact factor is a metric used to assess the influence or prestige of a scholarly journal within a particular academic field. While primarily associated with journal evaluation, the impact factor is a scientometric metric that measures the average number of citations received by articles published in a particular journal over a specific time period. It is calculated based on the average number of citations that articles published in a journal receive over a specific time period, usually two years. For example, the 2023 impact factor might be based on citations of articles published in the journal in 2021 and 2022. The number of citations received by all articles published in the journal during the calculation period is tallied and divided by the total number of citable articles published in the journal during the same period. For example, a journal's impact factor for 2023 would be the total citations in 2023 divided by the total citable articles published in 2021 and 2022.

The impact factor is often used as an indicator of the relative importance of a journal in its field, in much the same way the h-index is used as a measure of a researcher's impact. The impact factor is widely used as a tool for evaluating and comparing the "impact" or visibility of different journals. Journals with higher impact factors are often considered more prestigious, and researchers may use this metric when deciding where to submit their manuscripts for publication. Thus, impact factors can be used as a quick reference to assess the perceived quality or impact of a journal. This can be useful for researchers, institutions, and funding agencies to gauge the relative importance of journals. It can be particularly relevant for academic evaluations and tenure decisions of institutions, and researchers may use impact factors for benchmarking and ranking purposes, aiding in the comparison of research output and productivity.

However, it is important to note that the impact factor has its limitations. It may not be a comprehensive measure of the quality of individual articles or the impact of specific research contributions. Impact factors are based on citation counts, which can be influenced by various factors, including self-citations, review articles, and citation practices that may not necessarily reflect the true quality of research. Some journals may engage in practices to boost their impact factor, such as publishing review articles, which tend to attract more citations, or engaging in excessive self-citation by requiring authors to cite publications from their journals. Additionally, it can be influenced by factors such as the journal's publication frequency, citation practices, and the types of articles it publishes.

As an early career researcher, you might consider the impact factor when assessing potential journals for publication. Journals with higher impact factors are often considered more prestigious. But I would also likely take into account other factors such as the target audience of the journal, the relevance to your research area, and the overall reputation of the journal within my academic community. There are journals that claim high impact factors but have relatively lower reputation in part because they frequently announce special issues of review articles that tend to inflate journal impact scores and h-index of contributors, factors which have questionable value for practitioner's (Stremersch et al., 2007). For example, one international journal that focuses on publishing articles in the field of consumer behavior has been announcing a special issue of literature reviews on various consumer topics annually.

As journal impact factors are inflated, some journals benefit more than others, especially open-access journals. Furthermore, it is becoming increasingly difficult to assess journal quality based on impact factor. For example, recently the *International Journal of Consumer Studies* (IJCS) has been touting a 10.0 impact factor, which is nearly twice as large as the 6.1 impact factor recently reported by the *Journal of Marketing Research* (JMR), perhaps the most prestigious journal in the marketing field. However, I doubt that you will find any marketing professors who will tell you that they would rather have a publication in IJCS than JMR.

Thus, early career researchers should consider more than a journal's impact factor. The best source of information about the journal's quality are perceptions of colleagues in your department. Most departments have lists of journals that show the desirability of publishing in each. As promotion and tenure decisions within university departments and colleges are greatly influence by your department's senior colleagues, who are the first group who decides about your future in that department or institution. For this reason, it is not the name of the impact factor of journal in which you have published that matters, but the journal's quality as perceived by your senior colleagues. And knowing how your department in general evaluates these journals, especially senior colleagues who are likely to vote on your promotion and tenure before they can make a recommendation to other college and university evaluators, is what mostly counts.

The journal impact factor has become an "epidemic" in academics because it tends to affect the evaluations of journals and faculty who publish in them, although it is increasingly recognized in academia that sizes of impact scores can be artificial. For example, I have been advised by journal editors in recent years to cite articles that appeared in their journals as a condition (stated as " a strong suggestion") for accepting my manuscript. One editor even asked me to cite specific articles, and another associate editor asked me to cite several of his articles, although these publications had no clear relevance to my manuscript! (See also Appendix 11.3.) Apparently, this is a widespread practice, because a recent survey of researchers, which I was also asked to complete, attempted to investigate this "phenomenon." As this practice increasingly becomes known in academia, the importance of journal impact factor is likely to decline because impact scores will lose validity.

Another issue surrounding the impact factor is in reference to the journal's impact on readers who would benefit most from applying the findings of a study reported in articles published in the journal. A journal's score merely shows impact on academics, not on practitioners or those for whom implications of research findings are suggested as contribution. Unfortunately, there are no good metrics to show the impact of an article reported in an academic journal on decisions of policy makers and practitioners who are expected to benefit from a researcher's findings, much less on the quality of the information used in decision-making (Stremersch et al., 2007).

Appendix 11.1 Revision Notes

(Ref.: Ms. No. JAR Paper2151)

Title: "The Value of information Sources in Shaping Political Views: A Comparative Study of Party Supporters and Undecided Potential Voters".

We thank the Editor and the two Revivers for their comments and suggestions. We are stating each verbatim and, in turn, we show (in italics) the revisions and additions made to accommodate each.

Editor's Suggestions

R1-there are major issues with the lack of a clear and convincing theoretical foundation here, which affects all aspects of the paper.

A new section on mass communication theories has been added (pp.5–6), helping to interpret many of study findings in the context of these theories.

Reviewer #1

1. The main problem of the article is its lack of theoretical anchoring, which translates into a lack of explanation of the results obtained. Why, for example, are "loyal democrats" more sensitive to traditional sources of information than the other two categories?

   We have added a "Background" section that contains two subsections: One that summarizes research on media effects, and another that briefly presents communication theories. The former includes research showing media party bias.
2. Statistically speaking, the methodologies are relatively simple. Would it not be possible to study mediation and moderation effects? The limits of the study are not sufficiently deepened as well as the avenues of research.

   As mass communication theories tend to assume direct media effects (with the exception of the two-flow theory), we had no bases for using mediating and moderating variables. Further, we had no way of identifying "influentials" and "followers" in our sample, but only infer their status based on their relative responses to sources of information (influence of personal vs. *media). We felt such an analysis would have been exploratory and would have add little to the paper, whose length already increased substantially as a result of the additions suggested by the reviewers.*

   6b- Using an online survey, isn't there a self-selection bias since people who use the web the most are more likely to be selected and have a particular profile in terms of age and political orientation?

   We agree with the Reviewer about self-selection bias, which is likely to be present in every survey (regardless of data collection method used due to suboptimal response rates), and keeps researchers from using random samples. However, because our main goal was to test relationships between variables rather than estimate parameters of variables, our interest was in obtaining adequate variable variance that allows testing of relationships. We provide means and standard deviations of the main variables, while variance for additional variables, such as age, is shown in the table that has been added.

Reviewer #2

1a-the gap of the research is not clearly stated.

The intro+sed (end of third par. and middle of fourth par.). Additional gaps are identified end of section "Research on media effects" (p. 4) and in the last paragraph of "Models of communication effects" section (p.8–9).

1b-Often, the expected theoretical contributions are explained in the introduction section. At this stage, it seems that the theoretical contributions are limited.

The research is not really counterintuitive, replicating past results different sources may influence political beliefs and values.

We have revised the "Introduction" section, identifying gaps in knowledge that are addressed in the present study, as suggested by the questions raised and outlined in the study's research objectives.

1c-At this stage, we cannot see what is the distinctive contribution of the paper.

The paper's contribution can be better seen after the results of the study are presented. In the "Discussion" section, the reader can see several contributions of this research, both theoretical and practical. Specifically, the results show:

(a) *contributions to theory by showing (third and fourth par.) how the results support one or more theories that are now presented in a new section early in the paper (pp.5–6),*
(b) *contribution to research in this area by answering questions regarding the effects of political sources of consumer information on potential voters and pointing out directions for further research (second and fifth par.),*
(c) *practical implications of interest to political campaign managers (sixth and seventh par.), and,*
(d) *public policy (end of fifth par.).*

Appendix 11.2 Revision Notes

(Ref.: Ms. No. JAR Paper2151R1)
(Third revision—June 2021)

We thank the Reviewers for their comments. We found the suggestions of Reviewer 1 helpful and constructive. However, although we found several of Reviewer 2 suggestions helpful, we also found the main bases of two of his/her criticisms and suggestions—i.e., that we have done something which we have not done, and that for this paper we should conduct one or more studies to replicate our study findings—rather extraordinary and impractical. We have responded to the Reviewers' comments on a point-by-point basis, explaining in detail the revisions/additions we have made in our efforts to accommodate their suggestions.

Reviewers' comments: We are restating each of their comments verbatim and, in turn, we explain (in *italics*) how we have addressed each.

Reviewer #2

1. I am thankful to the authors for their intent to answer our remarks even if most of them remain unanswered.

   We don't understand the Reviewer's comment that most of his/her remarks remain unanswered because we had addressed each. We have attached the previous set of our point-by-point responses to his/her previous remarks, which suggest that most of his/her suggestions in the recent review are new.
2. Regarding the positioning and the Introduction section.
   (a) I understand now that the authors have made a choice to position their research within a deductive approach, justifying an absence of conceptual model and hypotheses.

*The Reviewer indicates that we "have made the choice to position their research within the deductive approach," but he/she next quotes the statement from our paper which says that we "...**use of the inductive rather than deductive approach to knowledge development...**" (emphasis ours). S/he thinks that we used the deductive approach, making this statement throughout his/her comments to the very last paragraph. Because we don't understand why the Reviewer states something that we have not said or done, we cannot respond to this comment.*

(b) However, I am not convinced by the arguments they have developed. In the Introduction section, they state: "The lack of consensus on the effects of media in general and social media in particular suggests the use of the inductive rather than deductive approach to knowledge development for the purpose of producing evidence of empirical regularities and conclusively describe the nature of the phenomenon that should explained by theory, a research process consistent with Hunt's (1983) notions of "logic of discovery" and "logic of justification," respectively."

Unfortunately, this observation is not made in the context of our previous statement:

"To summarize, the present state of knowledge on the effects of media on voters is not sufficient to conclusively describe a phenomenon that would lend itself to theoretical explanation." (p.4).

What we are saying in these two statements is that we simply don't know whether and how the various media affect voters and, therefore, we cannot explain a phenomenon that has not been empirically verified.

(c) However, the paper focuses only on one study. There is then a need to conduct at least one additional study to check if the results presented can be replicated.

Although we completely agree with the Reviewer that an additional study would be useful in replicating the study findings, we don't think that this suggestion is reasonable or practical for the following reasons:

(a) *The present version of the paper is already 44 pages long and has 8 tables. A replication study would add at least 20 more pages of text and 8 additional tables, making the paper too long for any journal.*
(b) *It is not a common or acceptable practice to conduct a study followed by a second in order to replicate the results of the first study. If the Reviewer is aware of an article that does this, we would like the benefit of knowing how this is done efficiently.*
(c) *Even an additional study might not satisfy the Reviewer, judging from his comment in the last paragraph that* "additional studies replicating the established results are still needed to give credit to this positioning."
(d) *We had no reason to believe that a second study using the same type of sample and analyses would not produce similar results.*

However, the Reviewer's comment on the need for validation of the study findings are well-taken, and we have done three things to accommodate her/his suggestion:

(a) *We have acknowledged the limitations of the findings based on cross-sectional studies, and have suggested further research for validation of our findings using multiple methods (pp.).*

As we always include in our surveys a question that taps social desirability, we re-analyzed the data controlling for this factor, as suggested by Podsakoff et al. (2003). *We state this on page 25.*

(b) *Rather than conducting a second study to validate our findings regarding relationships between dependent variables (measures of political views—*i.e., *knowledge, ideology,* etc.*) and information sources, we performed analyses using two sub-samples. We randomly divided the total samples of potential voters used in each regression into two sub-samples (Tables 6 and 7). And for those sub-samples containing a sufficient number of observations to satisfy the assumptions of multiple regression analysis, we performed tests of equivalence of the regression coefficients. We tested the hypotheses that the effects of the various sources of political information differ across the two samples, using the Chow's F-test of equivalence of the coefficients in each regression. The emerged sizes of the F values for these regressions were not large enough to conclude that respondents in the two sub-samples responded (or were impacted) differently by the various sources of political information, providing evidence of validity of our results. And we have added a couple of sentences about this test and results (p. 23).*

3. The literature review and method

(a) Here again, I am not convinced by the collection of model and theories. Additionally, the authors have stated that there is limited empirical evidence regarding the effects of main stream and social media on voters and political views.

One way to help improve the literature review can be with a table of extant research on the topic and findings/takeaway and then use this to clarify any gaps and help show where this adds the contribution. This comprehensive table will be helpful to understand the variables (and their status: moderator, mediator, control variables and so on) that have been studied so far to explain the effects of information sources on political decisions and views. As a result, this table may help to identify the variables that have been studied so far to explain the influences of information sources on political views.

Although the Reviewer has been informed (and states our observation) that there is limited evidence to support allegations regarding media effects, she/he recommends the construction of a comprehensive table "to understand the variables (and their status: moderator, mediator, control variables and so on) that have been studied so far to explain the effects of information sources on political decisions and views". This suggestion raises several questions:

(a) *How do we present findings regarding the presumed relationships that have **not** been previously studied and reported?*
(b) ***If such information were available**, would it have been possible to develop one table based on the number of relationships between the 10 information sources and the large number of dependent variables we investigated in our study? (we counted 160 reported relationships!).*
(c) *How many tables would be needed, if we could report mediators, moderators, and control variables for each of these relationships?*

(b) As underlined in my previous review, I do not understand how the authors have selected the constructs they measured. In addition, I do not see how they measured the "political views" construct. The authors have measured a set of variables (public affairs knowledge, opinions, issue importance) without any justification. Are those constructs used as a proxy measure of "political views"?

*We thank the Reviewer for his/her comment. Indeed, we cannot assume that every reader is familiar with the possible effects of information sources on audience—*i.e., *cognitive, affective, conative or behavioral responses. Therefore, we have added a sentence to explain the meaning of the general construct of "political views" and its components (variables) used (p.6).*

(c) In the method section, it will be more convenient to have a table with the constructs measured, a clear identification of the source of the scale used (which was not systematic) along with the reliability and convergent and discriminant validities of the scales. Scales' validities are missing.

*We appreciate the Reviewer's observations and concerns. Unfortunately, we found no canned scales or constructs of the measures of political views. We think this is because the field of politics is dynamic, with new and different issues being relevant at different times. Actually, we used one main psychological construct (political ideology), for which we have presented evidence of reliability and validity (p. 12) because it is a new measure that we developed. The other two measures of independent variables (knowledge and change in beliefs) are indexes, where validity is time/period specific (*e.g., *different issues are relevant at different times) and reliability assessment is meaningless, as each topic/issue does not necessarily have much in common with other issues/ topics to justify treating the composite indexes as psychological constructs (Herbert and Cohen,* 1996*).*

However, the Reviewer's concern is well-taken, especially with respect to single-item measures of information source usefulness. And we have addressed his/her concern by:

(a) *adding a sentence with a reference to justify the absence of evidence of validity and reliability for the two indexes of the dependent variables (p.17),*

(b) *highlighting the limitation of single-item measures of information sources (p.), and,*

(c) *commenting on the need for better measures of information sources in future studies (p.).*

4. The literature review and method

(a) The presentation of the results is somehow disturbing. While the use of correlations is in line with the "deductive positioning" of the paper, why then using a multiple regression analysis which supposes to have clear hypotheses behind the tested links.

We used regression analysis in the recent revision because it was suggested by Reviewer 1. In the initial version, we had used Pearson and partial correlations, instead of multiple regression coefficients, as the independent variables (sources of information) are theoretically intercorrelated, leading to multicollinearity. Yet, the information on variance accounted for (R squared) across groups is useful and could not have been produced by correlation analyses.

(b) The authors seem to control for age and income. On which literature do they focus on to assume that those two variables may impact political views. In that case, what about the other socio-demographic variables such as sex and social status? What other confounding variables should impact political views.

We controlled for age and income because it was suggested by Reviewer 1 (please see previous Revision Notes, R 1 comment #4). As this study was exploratory, and there was evidence that use of social media and their effects are likely to be inversely related to age, we have presented on p. 16 (last par.). Based on these cohort-related differences, Reviewer 1 correctly suspected that age could bias the study findings and suggested analyses controlling not only for age but also for income, as shown in Tables 6 & 7.

The main purpose of our study was to uncover relationships between sources of political information and political views, rather than uncover variables that have confounding effects on these relationships, we did not explore the effects of variables other than those suggested by Reviewer 1.

(c) I understand that this review is probably not what the authors expected when re-submitting their manuscript. I commend the authors on their effort to better explain their deductive positioning, but additional studies replicating the established results are still needed to give credit to this positioning. I hope my remarks and suggestions can take their manuscript forward and I wish them good luck with the pursue of their interesting current research topic.

We thank the reviewer for his/her constructive comments that helped improve our paper. And we hope that we have adequately explained the reasons we could not address some of his/her criticisms and suggestions.

Appendix 11.3 Suggestions for Minor Revisions

1. **Submission requirements**: Please use MS Word or a compatible software to prepare the new version. Please submit a clean version of your paper (without track changes). Use Times New Roman font size 12. Please submit a revised version of the paper and a point-to-point response file. Please submit these files by the due date indicated in the email message.
2. **Format.** We use APA style for the format and following level headings. Please use the latest edition of Publication Manual of the American Psychological Association to prepare the new version. If you don't have the manual, you may use resources online at: https://apastyle.apa.org/
3. **Consistency of the citations.** Please double check the consistency of in-text citations and entries in the reference list. A source cited in the text should be found in the reference list. An entry in the reference list should be cited in the text and years in text and in the references should match.
4. **JFCP citations.** Please cite more recent, relevant papers from JFCP, at least 3 published in 2021 or later, including accepted papers posted on the AFCPE website. It is very important to raise the visibility of JFCP in indexing/abstracting services, which will benefit you, the authors too. You may use the key word search to locate papers at the JFCP website (http://www.afcpe.org/publications/).
5. **Review questions.** Please prepare 3 multiple choice questions based on the final version of your paper and submit it as a separate file. This file should include the paper's title and names of all authors. The questions will be used by AFCPE for continuing education purposes. Please follow the attached sample file to prepare the questions.
6. **Title page file.** In the title page file, include all authors' names, job titles, departments, universities, mailing addresses, and emails. Also indicate who is the corresponding author. If this study is funded by any organizations, disclose the funding sources under Acknowledgement.
7. **Copy editing**. Please carefully copyedit the paper before the new version is submitted. We put some editorial suggestions in the file. Please review them carefully and see if they represent what you mean.
8. **Language**. Please set US English as the default language in the Word file.
9. **Keywords.** Please include a list of 4–6 keywords following the abstract in alphabetical order.
10. **Headings.** Please follow the APA style for headings. Please use only three levels of headings.
11. **Tables and Figures.** Include all tables and figures at the end of the text file, after the reference page.
12. **Literature review.** Need to pay attention to recent literatures on financial socialization, financial behavior, and financial capability. For financial socialization, see Norvilitis (2023) and relevant papers published in JFCP, especially since 2021. For financial behavior, see Goyal et al. (2022). Financial competence is a concept similar to financial capability. For the discussion of financial capability, see Xiao et al. (2022).

Goyal, K., Kumar, S., & Xiao, J. J. (2021). Antecedents and consequences of Personal Financial Management Behavior: a systematic literature review and future research agenda. *International Journal of Bank Marketing, 39*(7), 1166–1207.

Norvilitis, J. M. (2023). Financial socialization and financial behavior. In J. J. Xiao & S. Kumar (eds.). A research agenda for consumer financial behavior (pp 47–58). Edward Elgar.

Xiao, J. J., Huang, J., Goyal, K., & Kumar, S. (2022). Financial capability: A systematic conceptual review, extension and synthesis. *International Journal of Bank Marketing, 40*(7), 1680–1717.

References

Belk, R., Fischer, E., & Kozinets, R. V. (2013). *Qualitative consumer & marketing research. Thousand Oaks*, CA: Sage Publications.

Bornmann, L., Schier, H., Marx, W., & Hans-Dieter, D. (2011). Does the *h* index for assessing single publications really work? A case study on papers published in chemistry. *Scientometrics, 89*, 835–843. https://doi.org/10.1007/s11192-011-0472-0

Churchill, G. A., & Moschis, G. P. (1979). Television and interpersonal influences on adolescent consumer learning. *Journal of Consumer Research, 6*(1), 23–35.

Churchill, G. A., Jr., & Perrault, W. D., Jr. (1982). JMR editorial policies and philosophy. *Journal of Marketing Research, 19*(August), 283–287.

Dabić, M., Vlačić, B., Paul, J., Dana, L. P., Sahasranamam, S., & Glinka, B. (2020). Immigrant entrepreneurship: A review and research agenda. *Journal of Business Research, 113*, 25–38.

Ding, J., Liu, C., & Kandonga, G. A. (2020). Exploring the limitations of the h-index and h-type indexes in measuring the research performance of authors. *Scientometrics, 122*, 1303–1322. https://doi.org/10.1007/s11192-020-03364-1

Genau, H. A., Blickle, G., Schütte, N., & Meurs, J. A. (2022). Machiavellian leader effectiveness: The moderating role of political skill. *Journal of Personnel Psychology, 21*(1), 1–10. https://doi.org/10.1027/1866-5888/a000284

Gilal, F. G., Zhang, J., Paul, J., & Gilal, N. (2018). The role of self-determination theory in marketing science: An integrative review and agenda for research. *European Management Journal, 37*(1), 29–44.

Gingras, Y., & Khelfaoui, M. (2020). Why the h-index is a bogus measure of academic impact *the conversation* published: July 8, 2020 7.52pm BST updated: July 10, 2020 3.17pm BST.

Herbert, T. B., & Cohen, S. (1996). Measurement issues in research on psychosocial stress. In Kaplan, H.B. (Ed). *Psychosocial stress: Perspectives of structure, theory, life course, and methods* (295–332). San Diego: Academic Press.

Hirsch, J. E. (2005). An index to quantify an individual's scientific research output. *Proceedings of the National Academy of Sciences of the USA., 2005*(102), 16569–16572. https://doi.org/10.1073/pnas.0507655102

Hirschman, E. C. (1992). The consciousness of addiction: Toward a general theory of compulsive consumption. *Journal of Consumer Research, 19*(2), 115–179.

Hunt, S. D. (1983). *Marketing theory: The philosophy of marketing science*. Irwin Publishing Company.

Kahiya, E. T. (2018). Five decades of research on export barriers: Review and future directions. *International Business Review, 27*(6), 1172–1188.

Knoll, J., & Matthes, J. (2017). The effectiveness of celebrity endorsements: A meta-analysis. *Journal of the Academy of Marketing Science, 45*(1), 55–75.

Koltun, V., & Hafner, D. (2021). The h-index is no longer an effective correlate of scientific reputation. *PLoS One, 16*(6), e0253397. https://doi.org/10.1371/journal.pone.0253397. PMID: 34181681; PMCID: PMC8238192.

Kotov, N. A. (2010). Fraud, the h-index, and Pasternak. *ACS Nano, 4*, 585–586. https://doi.org/10.1021/nn100182y

Kumar, A, Paul, J & Unnithan, A. (2019). Masstige Marketing: A Review, Synthesis and Research Agenda. *Journal of Business Research 113* (issue C), 384–398.

Laisawat, S., Jantara, A., Ong, F. S., & Moschis, G. P. (2012). Clarifying the relationship between materialism and Well-being: Testing for reciprocal and third-variable effects. *Journal of Global Scholars of Marketing Science, 22*(1), 1–25.

Moschis, G. P. (1996). *Gerontographics: Life-stage segmentation for marketing strategy development*. Quorum.

Moschis, G. P., Mathur, A., & Sthienrapapayut, T. (2020). Gerontographics and consumer behavior in later life: Insights from the life course paradigm. *Journal of Global Scholars of Marketing Science, 30*(1), 18–33.

Paul, J. (2019). Marketing in emerging markets: a review, theoretical synthesis and extension. *International Journal of Emerging Markets, 15*(3), 446–468.

Paul, J., & Benito, G. R. (2018). A review of research on outward foreign direct investment from emerging countries, including China: what do we know, how do we know and where should we be heading? *Asia Pacific Business Review, 24*(1), 90–115.

Paul, J., & Mas, E. (2019). Toward a 7-P framework for international marketing. *Journal of Strategic Marketing*, published online https://doi.org/10.1080/0965254X.2019.1569111

Paul, J., & Rosado-Serrano, A. (2019). Gradual Internationalization vs Born- Global/International new venture models: A review and research agenda. *International Marketing Review, 36*(6), 830–858.

Paul, J., & Singh, G. (2017). The 45 years of foreign direct investment research: Approaches, advances and analytical areas. *The World Economy, 40*(11), 2512–2527.

Podsakoff, P. M., MacKenzie, S. B., Lee, J. Y., & Podsakoff, N. P. (2003). Common method biases in behavioral research: A critical review of the literature and recommended remedies. *Journal of Applied Psychology, 88*(5), 879–903.

Randhawa, K., Wilden, R., & Hohberger, J. (2016). A bibliometric review of open innovation: Setting a research agenda. *Journal of Product Innovation Management, 33*(6), 750–772.

Richins, M. L. (2004). The material values scale: Measurement properties and development of a short form. *Journal of Consumer Research, 31*(1), 209–219.

Ridgway, N. M., Kukar-Kinney, M., & Monroe, K. B. (2008). An expanded conceptualization and a new measure of compulsive buying. *Journal of Consumer Research, 35*(4), 622–639.

Rosado-Serrano, A., Paul, J., & Dikova, D. (2018). International franchising: A literature review and research agenda. *Journal of Business Research, 85*, 238–257.

Schubert, A. (2009). Using the h-index for assessing single publications. *Scientometrics, 78*, 559–565. https://doi.org/10.1007/s11192-008-2208-3

Shin, S., & Damon Aiken, K. (2012). The mediating role of marketing capability: Evidence from Korean companies. *Asia Pacific Journal of Marketing and Logistics, 24*(4), 658–677. https://doi.org/10.1108/13555851211259070

Spicer, A. (2015). Explainer: what is an H-index and how is it calculated? *The Conversation*, (May 21) https://theconversation.com/explainer-what-is-an-h-index-and-how-is-it-calculated-41162

Sthienrapapayut, T., Moschis, G. P., & Mathur, A. (2018). Using gerontographics to explain consumer behavior in later life. *Journal of Consumer Marketing, 35*(3), 17–27.

Stremersch, S., Verniers, I., & Verhoef, P. C. (2007). The quest for citations: Drivers of article impact. *Journal of Marketing, 71*(3), 171–193. https://doi.org/10.1509/jmkg.71.3.171

Summers, J. O. (2001). Guidelines for conducting research and publishing in marketing: From conceptualization through the review process. *Journal of the Academy of Marketing Science, 29*(4), 405–415.

Tarman, G. Z., & Sari, B. A. (2023). The mediating role of mindfulness on social anxiety and procrastination. *International Journal of Mental Health and Addiction, 21*, 1013–1024. https://doi.org/10.1007/s11469-021-00637-5

Varadarajan, P. R. (1996). From the editor: Reflections on research and publishing. *Journal of Marketing, 60*(October), 3–6.

Wessling, S. K., Huber, J., & Netzer, O. (2017). MTurk character misrepresentation: Assessment and solutions. *Journal of Consumer Research, 44*(1), 211–230.

12 Ethics in Research

There are numerous articles and writings in relation to scientific and medical publishing, but surprisingly less written on the ethics of academic publishing. This chapter presents the importance of knowing and understanding the issues dealings with ethics in academic research. It identifies major issues and the possible penalties for failing to observe the formal and informal codes that exist. The purpose of dealing with this subject is to ensure that early career researchers who are involved in academic writing can readily identify expectations and adhere to them.

While it may be tempting to assume that scientists possess a well-developed sense of ethics and that contemporary scientific research is mostly free from wrongdoing, research indicates otherwise. A survey conducted by Swazey and associates (1993), which involved both faculty members and students, discovered that 43% of students and 50% of faculty were aware of instances of scientific misconduct. Furthermore, the survey revealed that a significant portion of students, as well as 26% of faculty members, hesitated to report academic misconduct due to potential adverse consequences. Evidently, there is a pressing need for ethical discussions within today's academic community.

This chapter is structured as follows. First, it contrasts two fundamental approaches to ethics. Next, it discusses ethical considerations in three main parts of the research process, the planning and participant recruitment phase, the execution phase, and the reporting phase. Last, it examines how ethical principles are (and should be) enforced today. The primary sources of information used in this chapter come from published research (e.g., Aguinis & Henle, 2002; Hughes et al., 2010), anecdotal evidence, and my personal experiences.

The author thanks Kris Babicci and Carl Lindwall for providing the materials for this chapter.

G. P. Moschis, *Academic Research in Business and the Social Sciences*,
https://doi.org/10.1007/978-3-031-56548-9_12

12.1 Background on Ethics

Let's commence by clarifying the actual meaning of ethics. The English term "ethics" has its linguistic roots in the Greek word "ethos," which signifies an individual's character or disposition. In contemporary usage, ethics has a comprehensive definition and is often regarded as a branch of philosophy. It pertains to the manner in which people should behave; and it involves evaluating these behaviors (often in terms of good versus evil, just versus unjust, right versus wrong), and aims to formalize principles and rules for actions deemed "ethical." Virtually every human endeavor can be examined through the lens of ethical philosophy. More specifically, research ethics is focused on establishing guidelines for the execution, assessment, and validation of scientific research. In this chapter, I will elaborate on widely-accepted principles for conducting scientific research in a manner that aligns with what most members of the scientific community would consider as "ethical."

12.1.1 Perspectives on Ethics

When examining ethics from a philosophical standpoint, it can be approached through two distinct lenses: the utilitarian perspective and the deontological perspective, with the latter being rigid and the former being adaptable. Deontological ethics views ethical and moral principles as universal and separate from practical real-world considerations.

Deontological ethical frameworks often employ absolute terms, such as "always" or "never" (e.g., it is never permissible to lie; one should always exhibit neighborly love), regardless of practical outcomes. In contrast, utilitarian ethical approaches entail a cost-benefit analysis, where an action is generally considered ethical if it results in greater benefits than harm or provides the greatest overall good for the largest number of individuals. The societal benefits (e.g., increased knowledge, a cure for a disease, a more efficient algorithm) must outweigh the associated costs (often involving wasted time, invasion of privacy, energy, or potential mental and physical harm). In adapting the initial statement to align with a utilitarian perspective, it would read as follows: "It is generally not acceptable to tell a lie, unless…". Most contemporary scientific research predominantly follows the utilitarian approach to ethics.

12.1.2 Ethics in Academic Research

Ethics, in essence, is a branch of philosophy concerned with human morality. It carries the implication that, when addressing ethical matters in a general sense, there exists a right course of action, as well as a wrong one. Consequences for wrongdoing can be significant, with potential repercussions applied to the work itself, the author, or both. Coats (2008) introduces the idea that ethics are governed by a set of principles. In the realms of business and government, there is an increasingly emphasized focus on codes of conduct, many of which encompass ethical considerations as their core. Consequently, it is logical to argue that ethics in the context of academic writing should also adhere to a code, albeit informally recognized without concrete evidence, audits, or registration. At a minimum, authors should strive to write with a sense of "respectfulness," and there is already an established foundation for values (Dahl, 2009).

Right from the outset of academic courses involving any form of written work, be it assignments, manuscripts, theses, dissertations, or publications, prospective students are advised and later educated about the crucial dimensions of ethics. This is particularly critical in the context of academic writing. Throughout their academic journey, spanning studies that entail writing and publishing, as well as their professional careers, authors continuously receive reminders about these ethical considerations. They undergo scrutiny from various quarters, including peers, instructors, lecturers, reviewers, editors, and publishers. Occasionally, misunderstandings may arise regarding the subject, but breaches can be intentional, or authors may simply be unaware of the nuances of ethical perception. However, as is the case in law, ignorance is not a valid defense (Benos et al., 2005). Upholding the highest ethical standards is indispensable for preserving the credibility and trustworthiness of academic research. In many instances, universities and research institutions have their own specific codes of ethics and guidelines that researchers are expected to adhere to in order to prevent misconduct. This chapter delves into several codes of ethics as they pertain to three primary stages of the research process: planning, conducting, and reporting research.

12.2 Ethics When Planning Research

Planning research studies involves a critical phase where ethical considerations play a fundamental role in ensuring the responsible conduct of research. The following are some ethical issues to consider when planning research studies.

12.2.1 Competence Assessment

First and foremost, it is crucial to highlight that researchers must confirm their own ability to conduct the research they intend to undertake. Research conducted by individuals lacking sufficient expertise or knowledge in the chosen research design can yield erroneous conclusions and, in extreme cases, pose risks to participants and society at large. It is essential to underscore that ignorance—i.e., not being aware of ethical considerations in a particular research design—is never an acceptable excuse. The onus is squarely on researchers to ensure their own competence in adhering to relevant ethical guidelines. Additionally, ethical dilemmas may arise if researchers lack the essential skills and qualifications to develop or employ specific research instruments. The utilization of poorly designed instruments can result in results that are either invalid or unreliable. Thoughtfully planned research is more likely to meet ethical standards, as it is more likely to yield well-founded conclusions that contribute meaningfully to knowledge advancement.

12.2.2 Informed Consent

One of the fundamental pillars of research involving human subjects is the principle of informed consent. Informed consent signifies that it falls upon the researcher to guarantee not only the participant's willingness to partake in the study but also their comprehension of the implications of their participation. It is crucial in this context that the study description is conveyed in plain, easily understandable language rather than in academic jargon that might pose difficulties for individuals not well-versed in the field. In certain research contexts, the requirement for informed consent may be waived, as in historical research scenarios primarily utilizing archival data or in the case of naturalistic observation commonly employed in the natural sciences. When seeking informed consent for research involving human subjects, researchers should address the following:

1. Participants should be informed about the fundamental purpose of the study. This entails explaining what is expected of participants in terms of their involvement, time commitment, and any potential incentives for participation. It is important to note that providing specific details about the study, such as specific hypotheses, is not necessary to avoid potential bias in respondents.
2. Participants have the right to decline participation or withdraw from the study at any point without facing any penalties. This is particularly crucial, and potentially problematic, when the researcher holds a position of authority over the participants (e.g., as a teacher or supervisor).
3. Participants have the right to be informed about the implications of their withdrawal. Certain studies, such as long-term longitudinal research spanning several years, may involve varying incentives over the course of the study. For instance, a participant might receive a small cash incentive at the beginning of the study and a larger one upon completion several years later. In such cases, participant withdrawal is common, and participants should be informed about the compensation they are entitled to if they choose to withdraw before the study's conclusion.
4. While more prevalent in fields like psychology or medicine than in management research, some studies may elicit negative emotions in participants, such as stress, fatigue, or anxiety. In medical research, there is also a minimal risk of physical harm. It is imperative that potential participants are informed about all potential risks, as well as benefits, before agreeing to participate.

12.2.3 Privacy and Confidentiality

Individuals participating in scientific research should possess the autonomy to control the extent of personal information they disclose. They must always have the option to decline to answer any study-related questions without the obligation to provide an explanation. While privacy pertains to the individual, confidentiality pertains to the data pertaining on the individual. A research participant should always retain the right to consent to the sharing of their data with specific parties. Additionally, they should receive information on how their data and measures used, such as data coding, will be stored to ensure anonymity.

Researchers carry an ethical responsibility to safeguard the privacy and confidentiality of participants, which encompasses protecting their personal details and implementing anonymization or de-identification procedures when necessary. Participants are entitled to knowledge about how their confidentiality and anonymity will be upheld. This holds paramount importance, both ethically and practically, to counteract respondent bias, as later discussed in this chapter. Researchers should establish rigorous protocols for preserving participants' privacy and confidentiality, encompassing secure data storage, anonymization processes, and safeguards for sensitive information.

12.2.4 Protection from Deception and Harm

The practice of using deception has become less common in contemporary research and is now typically considered a last resort. Researchers employing deception must demonstrate that the value of their research significantly outweighs any potential harm and that there are no feasible alternative methods to address the research question. Regarding informed consent, participants should also be informed that they may not receive complete information about the study. One way to mitigate the potential harm of deception is by conducting a debriefing session, as elaborated upon later in this chapter.

Ethical researchers should make every effort to minimize harm to participants. This entails a thorough evaluation of potential risks and benefits and the implementation of measures to mitigate any harm that may arise during the study. In certain research contexts, particularly in community-based or participatory research, involving the community or relevant stakeholders in the planning phase is crucial. Researchers must respect community values, concerns, and priorities. Similarly, researchers planning studies involving diverse cultures should exhibit cultural sensitivity and show respect for local customs, norms, and beliefs.

12.2.5 Using Students as Subjects

While it is generally preferable to recruit participants from a completely random sample of the population, practical constraints often make this challenging. Many scientific researchers, particularly those affiliated with or employed by universities, find students to be a particularly accessible group due to their proximity. In certain fields, such as psychology, student populations are the most frequently used samples. In many areas of social science, student samples are commonly employed in experimental and exploratory research designs.

Researchers often recruit students for research experiments by offering extra credit within a course they are enrolled in. In this situation, researchers must assess the level of coercion associated with the incentive for participation. While researchers may argue that participation provides an opportunity for extra credit, students might perceive that not participating will negatively impact their grades, effectively making participation seem obligatory. However, if research participation can be presented as a valuable learning experience related to the course's learning objectives, it may be ethically justified. Additionally, as undergraduate students may not have reached the legal age of majority, researchers may need to obtain parental consent in addition to the minor's consent. In this context, it is crucial for the researcher to communicate the research's objectives using language suitable for the target audience.

12.2.6 Minority Participants

In countries characterized by significant diversity, such as the United States, it is prudent to take specific precautions when conducting studies involving minority populations. Minority groups with a history of discrimination, such as African-Americans in the United States, the burakumin minority in Japan, or the untouchable caste in the old Indian varna system, may tend to view academic research less favorably, often with suspicion, and sometimes even as a tool for suppressing minorities. In studies involving minority populations, it is of paramount importance to clearly articulate how and why the research can be advantageous for the well-being of minority members. Additionally, it may be advisable to collaborate with researchers who belong to the focal minority or to utilize assistants from within that community.

When devising research that encompasses vulnerable populations like children, the elderly, individuals with cognitive impairments, or marginalized groups, special ethical considerations must be taken into account. Researchers are obligated to establish additional safeguards and implement informed consent processes to protect the rights and welfare of these vulnerable participants.

12.2.7 Ethics in Sampling

Decisions with respect to sampling should attend to the following:

- *Ensuring Fair and Unbiased Sampling.* Researchers are obligated to employ impartial and equitable methods when selecting samples. It is essential to avoid any biases that might favor specific groups or individuals. Techniques like stratified sampling and randomization can be employed to promote fairness in sample selection.

- *Composing the Sample.* Researchers should not deliberately include or exclude participants based on certain characteristics when forming "randomized" groups.
- *Accurate Reporting of Sample Size.* Researchers should accurately report the actual sample size they have collected. There have been instances where manuscripts initially reported a relatively small sample size for one journal, but after rejection (partly due to the small sample size), the same manuscript was later reviewed for another journal with a tripled sample size while retaining the same statistical results.
- *Sampling from Online Sources.* When gathering data from online sources or social media, researchers must address privacy and consent concerns. It is crucial to respect individuals' digital footprints and obtain appropriate permissions when necessary.

12.2.8 Ethics in Designing and Using Data Collection Instruments

Developing instruments to obtain results that serve the researcher's views of reality or the "marketability" of research findings, rather than discovering the truth or objective reality, is unethical. Here are examples of instrument development and use that can be considered unethical:

- *Placement of Questions.* Manipulating question sequencing to get certain responses. For example, survey participants are likely to provide more favorable responses to the sequencing of scales where, for example, a scale that measures satisfaction with life is followed by a scale that measures satisfaction with material possessions, than when the two scales are presented in reverse sequence.
- *Changing the Location of Scale Items.* Using the same items of a scale, but changing their order of presentation could affect scale reliability. For example, changing the location of positively worded and negatively worded items, by placing all five positively worded items of a 10-item scale in sequence, followed by all five negatively worded items can increase scale reliability.
- *Placing Measures of Variables within the Same Question.* Placing items of scales measuring a dependent and an independent variable in the same question, such as measures of attitudes toward a brand and purchase of the brand, can inflate the relationship between the two variables due to common method bias.
- *Leading Questions.* Using leading questions to affect responses. For example, the question "Should the United States imposed sanctions on the Chinese government for claiming that the Covid-19 virus originated in bats?" assumes that all scientific investigations have led to the same conclusion.
- *Framing Questions.* Stating questions where answers are influenced by context, such as the consequence(s) of their response(s), can be unethical. For example, response to a question, such as "Do you think President Biden should be

impeached" (rather than "Do you think President Biden committed an impeachable offense?"), could be influenced by the respondent's perceived desirability of having the Vice-President as President.

- *Issues of Intellectual Property*. Using another researcher's published or unpublished data collection instruments (e.g., questionnaires, scales) without asking permission or giving credit. This is a potential ethical issue, particularly for unpublished work.
- *Improperly "Adapting" Scales Developed in Other Countries*. Scales developed in certain countries, such as United States, often need to be adapted to better fit the cultural context of a particular country. Adapting a scale developed in one country by purposely deleting items that are likely to help increase the reliability of the scale (e.g., by decreasing the ratio of the number of negatively-worded to positively-worded items) would be unethical and could bias results.

12.2.9 Ethical Review

Numerous institutions mandate that research involving human subjects undergo an ethical evaluation, typically conducted by institutional review boards (IRBs) or ethics committees. Prior to commencing their studies, researchers should actively seek ethical approval from these IRBs or ethics committees. These entities rigorously assess the ethical facets of research protocols to ascertain their adherence to established ethical standards. Researchers are obliged to engage in these processes and effectively address any concerns raised.

In summary, ethical considerations constitute a foundational aspect of research study planning. Researchers are duty-bound to adhere to ethical principles, safeguarding the rights and well-being of participants, upholding the research process' integrity, and fostering responsible and substantial contributions to knowledge.

12.3 Ethics in Conducting Research

In conducting research, researchers have the responsibility to protect participants from harm. It is further important to note that the choice of research design has different implications to ethical considerations. The basic rights of participants discussed earlier, namely, informed consent, privacy, confidentiality, and protection from deception, are relevant to empirical studies. A qualitative research design (e.g., naturalistic observation) is inherently very different from a cross-sectional or an experimental research design, where the former has a higher level of researcher-participant interaction.

12.3.1 Fabrication and Falsification

Research misconduct at this stage of research includes fabrication and falsification. The Office of Research Integrity (ORI) at the United States Department of Health and Human Services defines each of these:

Fabrication "Fabrication is making up data or results and recording or reporting them. It involves inventing data, measurements, or experiments that did not occur, and presenting them as if they are real." In simple words, it means the making up data or results. In research ethics, fabrication is considered a serious violation because it involves intentionally creating false information and presenting it as genuine research findings. Researchers are expected to maintain the highest standards of integrity by accurately reporting their methods and results and refraining from inventing or falsifying data.

Falsification "Falsification is manipulating research materials, equipment, or processes, or changing or omitting data or results such that the research is not accurately represented in the research record. It can involve altering or misrepresenting data, images, or other research findings." Altering research results is a grave ethical violation. This not only misleads the academic community but can also have real-world consequences if the research informs public policy or industry practices. In research ethics, falsification is considered a serious breach of integrity because it involves deliberately altering or misrepresenting research data or results in a way that distorts the accuracy of the research record. Researchers are expected to maintain the highest standards of honesty and transparency in reporting their findings, and falsification undermines the credibility and trustworthiness of scientific research.

12.3.2 Working with Doctoral Students

Another common misconduct of faculty is their use of research assistants for non-research tasks, such as teaching and grading. Assignment of doctoral students to faculty for assisting them with their research projects is a part of student's training. It benefits the student who, in the processes of helping the faculty research, also becomes familiar with the various task required for project completion and publication. Therefore, to the extent doctoral students spend their time on non-research assignments, such activities that do not serve the students' best interests because the doctoral program normally prepares students for academic research rather than a teaching career; and the students are deprived of learning opportunities and exposure to various faces of the research process faculty are working on and need assistance. Doctoral students are more likely to benefit from tasks related to research, such as interview transcriptions, rather than non-research tasks such as grading students' assignments and exams.

Working with students on their dissertations is an area where ethical issues can be raised. As part of their normal responsibilities or work load, faculty members are expected to guide students by supervising their dissertations and serving on dissertation committees. Some university assign faculty members to doctoral students as soon as the student is accepted into the program, ensuring fair and equitable distribution of work load. In such universities, the faculty member serves multiple roles throughout the student's program, including the role of advisor and dissertation chairperson; and in most cases, he or she becomes a co-author of the student's dissertation, either because of the supervisor's substantial contribution to the student's project or because the student is coerced by the advisor to accept co-authorship (often as a condition for successful completion of the dissertation and assistance with publications from it).

Dissertations are typically expected to demonstrate the student's "independent" work and contribution to their discipline. Through their dissertations, students are expected to demonstrate their ability to conceptualize a research problem or question, as well as executing their project with minimum assistance from their dissertation supervisor and committee members. Ethical issues are raised when the supervisor, who has vested interest in the successful execution of the study, makes a "substantial' contribution when the student's dissertation project is an extension of the advisor's stream of research. I know of universities where their faculty evaluation committees for hiring, promotion or tenure junior faculty do not place much weight on the faculty member's co-authored publications based his on her dissertation, even when the articles out of the dissertation are single-authored.

In other universities, especially in the United States, doctoral students may be assigned an advisor but are given the choice to select a dissertation supervisor when they are ready to embark on their dissertation project. The faculty member who is approached by the student is free to accept or decline this request, depending on several factors. A major consideration is the number of dissertation projects that person has already been supervising, as additional projects would involve additional work load and lost opportunities for that individual to pursue more attractive projects. Another consideration is the extent the proposed dissertation project aligns with that faculty member's research interests and expertise. Under such circumstances, he or she may specify conditions for his or her role as a dissertation advisor or chairperson, often in a form of a contract, ranging from co-authorships to data sharing/ownership. The faculty member's vested interest in the dissertation may lead to his or her greater than normal involvement and level of contribution to the project; and the student's project has a potential of becoming a joint rather than an "independent" study.

12.3.3 Ethical Issues in Humanistic Research

Ethics is one of the most problematic issues in humanistic research. Willful misrepresentation or false documentation by the humanist researcher can be of ethical concern, as such misconducts may not be detected by auditors (e.g., Hirschman,

1986). And while results emerged from positivistic studies can be verified by others who have access to the same data, the high level of subjectivity involved in the process of knowledge development in humanistic studies makes it difficult to detect such unethical practices. Hirschman (1986) discusses additional ethical issues that can arise from three types of the researcher's interaction with participants: participant observation, limited role-playing, and researcher's active and complete participation in the subject population. Distanced observation might not create much of ethical issue. However, partial participation or role-playing, especially complete participation, where the researcher can have a direct contact with subjects, may create more serious moral and ethical issues in research.

Humanistic research, which explores the subjective experiences, values, and meanings of individuals and communities, presents its own set of ethical challenges and considerations. I can highlight some of the ethical problems that researchers in the field of humanistic research may encounter:

1. *Reflexivity and Bias.* Humanistic research often involves the researcher's interpretation of participants' experiences. Researchers must be aware of their own biases, assumptions, and subjectivity and make efforts to minimize these influences. Transparent reflexivity and rigorous analysis techniques are essential.
2. *Power Imbalance.* There can be a power imbalance between the researcher and the researched, especially if the researcher has more education, resources, or privilege. Researchers must strive to minimize this imbalance, foster collaboration, and empower participants in the research process.
3. *Authenticity and Representation.* Humanistic research aims to provide an authentic representation of participants' experiences. Researchers must ensure that their interpretations are faithful to participants' voices and perspectives, avoiding distortions or misrepresentations.
4. *Exploitation and Tokenism.* Researchers should avoid exploiting vulnerable individuals or communities by extracting information without providing appropriate benefits or reciprocity. Similarly, tokenism—superficially including participants to fulfill diversity requirements without meaningful engagement—should be avoided.
5. *Researcher-Participant Relationships.* Researchers should establish and maintain transparent, respectful, and reciprocal relationships with participants. Clear boundaries and expectations should be communicated to avoid any harm or misunderstandings.
6. *Post-Study Support.* In some cases, participants in humanistic research may be left with emotional or psychological impacts due to the research process. Researchers should provide appropriate post-study support and referrals to mental health professionals, if needed.
7. *Dissemination of Findings.* Ethical considerations extend to the dissemination of research findings. Researchers should ensure that participants' voices are accurately represented in publications, presentations, or other forms of communication, and they should obtain additional consent if necessary.

Overall, conducting ethically-sound humanistic research requires a deep commitment to respecting the dignity and autonomy of participants while striving to represent their experiences authentically and responsibly. Researchers in this field should be prepared to engage in ongoing reflection, dialogue, and ethical decision-making throughout the research process to address these and other ethical challenges effectively.

12.3.4 Debriefing

Following the completion of a study, especially an experimental and qualitative study, it is essential to invite participants to a debriefing session where the researcher provides additional information about the study, including details such as the tested hypotheses and the comprehensive study design. The primary purpose of the debriefing session is twofold: to ensure that participants gain access to the scientific knowledge often touted as a benefit of study participation and, equally important, to alleviate any potential adverse effects while fostering a sense of dignity and satisfaction with their time spent as subjects. In cases where deception was employed, the debriefing process should place special emphasis on dehoaxing (clarifying the deception and rectifying any misinformation provided) and desensitizing (addressing any negative feelings or harm that may have arisen from the study).

Debriefing holds significance not only in experimental research but also in qualitative and humanist research settings. It plays a crucial role in various research paradigms, especially in humanistic studies. Below are some considerations to keep in mind when conducting debriefing in humanistic studies:

- *Ethical Considerations.* Debriefing is essential in humanistic studies to ensure that research participants are treated ethically and with respect. This is particularly important when studying sensitive topics or when participants may be vulnerable.
- *Informed Consent.* Debriefing can help clarify the nature of the research to participants after their involvement. This is especially important when informed consent procedures may not have provided a complete understanding of the study's objectives or when the research evolves during the study.
- *Clarification and Feedback.* Debriefing provides an opportunity for participants to ask questions, seek clarifications, and provide feedback about their experiences in the study. This can lead to a deeper understanding of the participants' perspectives and the research findings.
- *Managing Emotional Impact.* In humanistic studies, participants may engage with emotionally charged or challenging subject matter. Debriefing can help participants process their emotions and experiences and ensure they are not left in a state of distress after their involvement in the research.
- *Participant Empowerment.* Debriefing empowers participants by allowing them to reflect on their involvement and contribute to the research process. It can foster a sense of agency and collaboration between researchers and participants.

- *Data Validation.* Debriefing can also serve as a method of data validation in qualitative research. Researchers can confirm their interpretations with participants, helping to enhance the validity of the study's findings.
- *Reflexivity.* Researchers in humanistic studies can also benefit from debriefing themselves. Reflecting on their interactions with participants, their own biases, and the evolving nature of the research can lead to deeper insights and methodological improvements.

In summary, debriefing is not only relevant but highly valuable in humanistic studies. It contributes to ethical research practices, participant well-being, data quality, and researcher reflexivity. However, the specific format and content of debriefing will vary depending on the nature of the study, the research questions, and the characteristics of the participants. Researchers should carefully plan and conduct debriefing in a manner that is sensitive to the unique features of their humanistic research.

12.3.5 Ethics in Collaborative Research

Ethics in collaborative research is of paramount importance to ensure the responsible and ethical conduct of research when multiple researchers from different backgrounds, institutions, or disciplines work together on a project. Ethical considerations in collaborative research help maintain trust among collaborators, protect the rights and welfare of research participants, and uphold the integrity of the research process. The following are key ethical principles and issues to consider in collaborative research:

1. *Informed Consent.* All collaborators should obtain informed consent from research participants, ensuring that they fully understand the research purpose, procedures, risks, and benefits. Clear procedures for obtaining and documenting consent should be established.
2. *Authorship and Contributorship.* Collaborators must agree on authorship criteria and roles in developing the research project at the outset of the project. Authorship should be based on substantial intellectual contributions, and roles and responsibilities should be clearly defined.
3. *Transparency.* Open and transparent communication among collaborators is crucial. Information sharing should include data, methodologies, protocols, and any potential conflicts of interest. Transparency promotes accountability and ensures that all collaborators have access to the necessary information to evaluate and validate the research.
4. *Data Sharing and Ownership.* Collaborators should agree on data sharing and ownership arrangements. Decisions about who owns the data, how it will be managed, and who has access to it should be made collaboratively and documented.
5. *Research Integrity.* Collaborators are collectively responsible for upholding research integrity. This includes honesty, accuracy, and adherence to ethical standards throughout the research process.

6. *Conflict Resolution.* A mechanism for resolving conflicts or disagreements among collaborators should be established. It is essential to address issues promptly and fairly to maintain a productive working relationship.
7. *Equitable Resource Allocation.* Collaborators should ensure that resources, including funding, equipment, and personnel, are allocated equitably based on contributions and needs. Fair resource allocation minimizes the potential for conflicts.
8. *Ethical Review.* Collaborative research may require ethical review by multiple institutions or ethics committees, depending on the project's scope. Researchers should adhere to the ethical review processes of all involved institutions.
9. *Cross-Cultural Sensitivity.* Collaborative research that spans different cultural contexts should demonstrate sensitivity to cultural norms, values, and practices. Respect for local customs and traditions is essential.
10. *Data Privacy and Security.* Collaborators should establish robust data privacy and security measures to protect research participants' confidentiality and sensitive information. Compliance with data protection regulations is crucial.
11. *Timeliness and Accountability.* Collaborators should meet agreed-upon timelines and milestones, taking responsibility for their tasks. Delays or deviations from the research plan should be communicated and addressed promptly.
12. *Communication of Results.* Collaborators should collectively decide how research results will be communicated, including authorship order for publications and presentations. All collaborators should have the opportunity to review and provide input on research outputs.
13. *Responsible Conduct.* Collaborators should uphold responsible conduct in research, including proper citation of others' work, avoiding plagiarism, and avoiding any form of research misconduct.

Ethical considerations in collaborative research require ongoing attention, open dialogue, and a commitment to ethical principles throughout the research process. Clear agreements and guidelines can help ensure that the collaboration is conducted ethically, fostering trust and the successful achievement of research goals.

12.4 Ethics in Reporting Research

This chapter has covered ethical considerations in planning and conducting research, including how to interact with human subjects and collaborators in executing research. It now turns its focus to ethical considerations when conveying findings to the scientific community. Specifically, it covers ethics in writing and serious forms of misconduct, such as (mis)representation of results, censoring, plagiarism, collaborators authorship, and data provision for replication.

12.4.1 Censoring

In research, there is an inherent risk that the collected data may diverge from the researcher's initial expectations or hypotheses. It is considered unethical to manipulate or censor data that contradicts prior beliefs, hypotheses, or research objectives. Data obtained from a study with a robust research design holds intrinsic value for the scientific community, particularly when it challenges established conventions. Ethical breaches can occur in any of the three primary phases of the research process: planning and recruitment, execution, and reporting. However, the reporting stage has traditionally received the most scrutiny, as researchers often face significant pressure to publish noteworthy results to advance their academic careers. It is also likely that most misconduct takes place during this phase.

12.4.2 Plagiarism

In simple terms, the subject of ethics is intricate, and it can also be perplexing. Numerous practitioners, researchers, scholars, and publishers hold varying perspectives on the constituents of ethics. However, there appears to be a common consensus among most, with plagiarism being regarded as a key element (King et al., 1997). The Office of Research Integrity (ORI) at the United States Department of Health and Human Services defines plagiarism as follows: "Plagiarism is the appropriation of another person's ideas, processes, results, or words without giving appropriate credit. Researchers and scholars must always properly acknowledge the contributions of others to their work to avoid plagiarism." In essence, plagiarism, according to the ORI, involves using someone else's intellectual or creative work, whether it be ideas, processes, results, or verbatim text, without providing the proper attribution or credit to the original source. Properly acknowledging and citing the contributions of others is a fundamental ethical practice in research and scholarship. Plagiarism also includes self-plagiarism, which means that writers should not copy or reuse their own works, without adequate reference to where that work was originated.

There are tools like Draft Coach that can provide feedback in real-time that helps guide us towards proper citation so that researchers can focus on writing better manuscripts. This is the best kind of feedback, one that actually helps, telling us specifically what we need to improve.

12.4.3 Data Sharing

Contrary to certain beliefs, scientific research fundamentally relies on trust. When individuals engage with published research, they typically have no viable option but to place trust in the reported results. To ensure the accuracy and objectivity of research reporting, it is advisable for researchers to make their primary data available to fellow members of the scientific community who seek to replicate or validate the study. Unfortunately, this practice is not consistently observed. In a study that attempted to contact authors of previously published scientific articles to request access to primary data, fewer than 5% of authors had access to such data and were willing to share it (Aguinis and Henle, 2002). A more recent study by Stieglitz and associates (2020) found one-third of academic researchers indicated willingness to share their datasets with others. Ethical researchers should consider the importance of sharing data and research materials as a means to enhancing transparency, reproducibility, and the progress of scientific knowledge. However, data sharing must also be conducted with due consideration for confidentiality and privacy concerns. Regarding colleagues who seek to utilize the data of others, ethical responsibilities come into play.

Authors may not be open to making their data, research procedures, and materials used available to the editor or others. This can raise concerns about the author's integrity and the credibility of the reported research findings. Ethical researchers should consider sharing data and research materials to promote transparency, reproducibility, and the advancement of science. However, data sharing must also respect confidentiality and privacy concerns, especially when data and methods constitute intellectual property of the researcher.

12.4.4 Other Forms of Misconduct

Reporting research results is a critical aspect of the research process, and it comes with several ethical considerations. Ensuring the accuracy, transparency, and responsible dissemination of findings is essential. The following are areas where ethical issues relevant to reporting research results can arise:

Conflict of Interest Academic studies are frequently funded by organizations whose objectives and policies may not be well-aligned with general public's perceptions or best interests, as in the case of cable TV networks and political organizations. And some academic studies may "produce" data biased in favor of the funding agency. Researchers should disclose any financial, personal, or professional conflicts of interest that could bias their research or the interpretation of results. They should acknowledge the sources of funding for their research. Failure to disclose funding sources can raise questions about bias or conflicts of interest. However, tentatively stating (manufacturing) credentials of the study (e.g., giving credit to well-known funding sources), for the purpose of manipulating editor and reviewer perceptions, is unethical. Several journals require and publish author(s)' statement of conflict of interest. Transparency is crucial to maintain trust in the research.

Respect for Intellectual Property Researchers should respect intellectual property rights, including copyright and patents, when reporting their findings and using others' work. For example, when researchers request the complete scale that was used in an author's study, they should give credit to the person who constructed the scale, as that instrument is considered the intellectual property of the person who developed it.

Improper Citations Researchers should avoid citing sources to support a statement they make, when there is no information in these sources to support their view. I have been surprised several times to review and read articles that cite my work incorrectly (purposely, I assume) to give credence to a statement made.

Reporting Results Not Emerged from Analysis Quite often, researchers make statements about findings that did not emerge from the analysis. This is more likely to be an ethical issue when reporting results from quantitative studies, compared to qualitative studies where statements made are based on the researcher's interpretations and subjective judgment.

Making Unsubstantiated Claims Early career researchers tend to make (unintentionally) a relatively larger number of claims that cannot be substantiated. This is often the case when they discuss their research findings and their implications for practice. The most common claim is in regard to causality. For example, based on results of cross-sectional studies, they are likely to state that variable X affects variable Y. What appears more dangerous and unethical is making recommendations for policy and intervention based on emerged findings, without putting these finding in their proper context. For example, statistically significant relationships do not necessarily demonstrate managerially significant relationships, where other factors play a role (e.g., costs of applying findings). Similarly, applying the emerged findings could best serve one segment but alienate other segments.

Inclusion of Acknowledgments Researchers should acknowledge every form of assistance they have received from individuals who have helped the authors develop and publish an article. It is not clear the type of assistance that deserves acknowledgement. However, those who have provided input that helped produce a better article (e.g., comments on earlier drafts, suggestions of colleagues that were incorporated into the manuscript) deserve recognition. Contributors who do not meet the criteria for authorship but have made significant contributions (e.g., data collection, technical support, or administrative assistance) should be acknowledged in the acknowledgments section of the manuscript. Conversely, giving undeserved credit to individuals in "acknowledgements" merely for the benefit of these individuals is considered unethical.

In conclusion, ethical reporting of research results is essential to maintain the integrity of the scientific process and the trust of the public, fellow researchers, and institutions. Researchers should adhere to established ethical principles and guidelines throughout the reporting process.

12.4.5 Authorship

For professional academic researchers, a top priority is the publication of their research in reputable scientific journals. This is because the quantity and quality of their publications directly impact their career, influencing factors such as respect, status, salary, promotions, and tenure. A general guideline is that authorship credit should be extended only to individuals who have made significant contributions to the research endeavor. The challenge lies in defining the somewhat elusive concept of "significant" contribution. Typically, conceptualizing the research, designing the study, conducting data analysis and interpretation, and writing the research paper are considered sufficient grounds for authorship credit, while routine tasks do not meet this criterion. It is advisable to avoid honorary or ghost authorship, where someone is credited as an author without making a substantial contribution. However, individuals involved in routine or secondary tasks should be recognized in the acknowledgments section of the publication.

12.4.6 Order of Authorship

When there are multiple authors, determining the order in which their names should appear can be a challenging issue, especially when the number of researchers is very large (e.g., Wranik et al., 2016). The general guideline is that authorship order should reflect the actual intellectual contributions to the study and should not be based on status or power dynamics. This issue can become particularly sensitive when a senior faculty member collaborates with a graduate student. In such cases, credit for a research paper based on a student's dissertation should primarily be attributed to the student, even though the support of the senior researcher may have been instrumental in the research's success. Nonetheless, senior researchers should be cautious about granting unearned credit to the student, such as placing the student's name first in cases where their contribution was minimal. This could unfairly benefit the student over his or her peers and other junior researchers in advancing their careers. To mitigate such issues, authorship considerations should be discussed early in a research project, with roles and expected contributions of all team members clearly defined. It is also feasible to establish a qualitative points-based framework to assess each individual's contribution. In cases of disputes, third parties, such as colleagues or department management, should be engaged for resolution.

A recent trend in academic publishing is for journals to require co-authors to state their relative contribution. Specifically, authors state the nature of their contribution—i.e., whether they contributed in the conceptualization of the study, data analysis, writing the manuscript, etc. (e.g., Wranik et al., 2016). Other journals require the relative (%) contribution of the co-authors. This is typically the information used by an increasing number of universities when they evaluate their faculties. Traditionally, if there were two co-authors, for example, one (usually the senior) would report to the junior author's unit their relative (%) contribution. This tends to be subject to change and bias, often reflecting each co-author's needs and raising ethical issues. By publishing the nature and relative contribution of each co-author, journals are helping promote fairness and academic honesty, helping institutions make an objective and fair assessment of co-authors' contribution to an article.

Ethical guidelines for co-authorship in research are crucial to ensure fairness, transparency, and accountability in collaborative research efforts. The following are some key ethical principles and guidelines for co-authorship, many of which are suggested by journals:

1. *Substantial Contribution.* Co-authors should have made a substantial intellectual or practical contribution to the research. Authorship should not be granted merely for nominal or administrative roles.
2. *Authorship Criteria.* Authors should meet the criteria outlined in the journal's or institution's authorship guidelines. These criteria often include contributions to the conception, design, data collection, analysis, interpretation, and drafting of the manuscript.
3. *Drafting and Revising.* Authors should participate in drafting the manuscript and revising it critically for intellectual content. All authors should have the opportunity to review and approve the final version before submission.
4. *Acquisition of Funding.* Those who have contributed to securing funding for the research should be acknowledged but not automatically granted authorship, unless they meet authorship criteria (outlined on the top of this list).
5. *Data Analysis and Interpretation.* Authors who conduct data analysis and contribute to the interpretation of results should be considered for authorship. Researchers who solely provide data or technical assistance may be acknowledged but not listed as authors. However, if the data provided to researchers is based on an unpublished research instrument that is considered one's intellectual property, making data collection possible, co-authorship should be given to the developer of the instrument.
6. *Reviewing and Editing*: Peer reviewers and editors who review and provide feedback on the manuscript should not be automatically considered co-authors. However, they can be acknowledged for their contributions.
7. *Consent and Agreement.* All authors should agree to their authorship position and order, and they should give their consent for publication. Disputes about authorship should be resolved through open and transparent communication.
8. *Corresponding Author.* The corresponding author is responsible for handling communication with the journal, addressing revisions, and ensuring compliance with ethical and publication guidelines. This role should be clearly defined among co-authors.
9. *Order of Authors.* The order of authors should reflect their relative contributions to the research. Common practices include listing authors in order of decreasing contribution or specifying their roles in a contributorship statement.
10. *Guest, Gift, and Ghost Authorship.* Guest authorship (adding authors who did not contribute substantially) and ghost authorship (excluding contributors from authorship) are unethical practices and should be avoided. Authors should be transparent about their roles.

11. *Changes in Authorship.* Any changes to the list of authors or authorship order should be justified and agreed upon by all affected parties. Journal editors should be informed of changes, and they may require explanations.
12. *Ethical Conduct and Research Integrity.* Co-authors are collectively responsible for the ethical conduct of the research. They should adhere to research integrity standards, including honesty, data accuracy, and compliance with ethical guidelines.
13. *Disclosure of Conflicts of Interest.* Authors should disclose any financial, personal, or professional conflicts of interest that could influence the research or its interpretation. Transparency is essential for maintaining trust.
14. *Responsibility for Errors.* All authors share responsibility for the accuracy and integrity of the research. If errors or misconduct are discovered, they should be promptly addressed and corrected.
15. *Retraction and Correction.* Authors should cooperate with the journal and follow its guidelines for retractions or corrections when necessary due to errors or ethical concerns.

In summary, ethical co-authorship in research requires clear criteria, transparency, open communication, and a commitment to fairness and accountability among all contributors. Researchers should adhere to established guidelines and standards in their respective fields and journals while ensuring that authorship accurately reflects each author's contributions to the research.

12.5 Submitting the Manuscript

12.5.1 Submitting to Multiple Outlets

Some early career researchers may consider submitting the same manuscript to more than one journal in order to expedite publication of their work. They hope to receive favorable evaluations from one or more journals and withdraw the manuscript from a journal's review process, if it is evaluated favorably by more than one journal by, for example, not making the required revisions; and to have a publication in a desirable outlet within a relatively short time. Early career researchers usually have limited time to demonstrate to their university that they can publish in academic journals or are worth of promotion and tenure. However, the practice of submitting the same manuscript to more than one outlet simultaneously or while it is under review by another journal, it is unethical, unprofessional, and risky. Researchers should be considered of the time and efforts of editors and reviewers. And in the event one of the reviewers is asked by different journals to evaluate the same manuscript, it is highly likely this reviewer will also inform the editors accordingly. This could be damaging to the researcher's academic integrity. Many journals have explicit policies that do not allow submission of the same manuscript to another journal while it is under review.

12.5.2 Request to Exclude Reviewers

Some journals or editors allow authors to request exclusion of certain reviewers from the review process. In most cases, the authors have a legitimate reason for not having a reviewer evaluate their work, as in the case where author's work challenges the reviewer's published research. However, when the author requests the editor not to allow a qualified reviewer to evaluate his or her manuscript because that reviewer possesses skills and knowledge about the topic that jeopardize the manuscript's chance for publication, such a request is unethical.

12.5.3 Co-Authors Without Their Consent

Placing one's name on a manuscript without their consent is unethical. Novice researchers may see benefit in having as a co-author someone who is well-known in their field, but they should not put other researchers' names on their manuscripts, even when they have a reason to believe that the co-author would not object to it. As a general rule, every co-author should have the chance to see the manuscript they are co-authoring before it is submitted for review. Nowadays, almost every journal expects co-authors to provide their email address, which is used to notify all co-authors about manuscript submission. If a co-author's name appears on the manuscript without their consent and the journal editor is notified to this effect, the editor likely will not process the manuscript.

12.5.4 Manipulating the Review Process

Deliberate attempts to undermine the peer review process are unethical. A common strategy that is often used to eliminate the most informed and likely critical reviewers is to send the manuscript to several experts in an area before submitting the manuscript to a journal, knowing that some of them will be asked by the target journals to review the manuscript. As these experts would have seen the manuscript, they will have to inform the journal(s) accordingly. Another strategy often used by the author is to prepare two manuscripts on the same topic. He or she may submit to a journal the weaker manuscript as a decoy, knowing that the editor is likely to request experts on the topic to review it, and submit the stronger article weeks later, knowing that the reviewers are not as likely to be as informed or critical as the more expert reviewers. Another strategy authors may use to eliminate potential reviewers is intentionally avoiding the citation of experts' work, although it is relevant to their own research, knowing that editors often use researchers who are cited in the manuscript as reviewers because they have previously published on a topic.

12.5.5 Inflating the Number of References from Target Journals

Editors prefer publishing manuscripts that cite articles that have appeared in their journals, as such citations contribute to the journal's impact factor. I am aware of a major journal in my field that for years would not publish articles which did not mention studies published in that journal. And editors often will even suggest the articles that should be cited in a manuscript before it can see publication light. Researchers are aware of the importance editors attach to the references of articles that have appeared in their journal, and they may purposely inflate the number of such reference to gain an edge over other submitted manuscripts. Artificially inflating impact factor scores harms the credibility of the journal and the authors who publish in it and undermines the objective and fair evaluation of faculty members' research performance by their institutions.

12.6 Enforcement of Ethical Principles

Although research has indicated that ethical violations may be more frequent than commonly perceived, there are specific mechanisms in scientific research that serve as safeguards for ethical compliance. These include ethics codes, institutional review boards, peer review, and, as previously mentioned, mandates for data provision to enable the replication of previously published research.

12.6.1 Ethics Codes

In most scientific disciplines, there exists a de facto authoritative body that holds sufficient influence to establish and guide ethical standards within the field. In the realm of psychology research, for example, the American Psychological Association (APA) has garnered significant influence, shaping ethical considerations on a global scale. The APA upholds a document known as the "Ethical Principles of Psychologists and Code of Conduct." Similarly, the American Medical Association (AMA) has developed its "AMA's Code of Medical Ethics." As another example, the American Marketing Association, also known as AMA, maintains a "Statement of Ethics," albeit less comprehensive in detail. These ethical codes effectively serve as the widely accepted benchmark for determining ethical conduct within their respective fields.

12.6.2 Institutional Review Boards

While primarily observed in the United States, many universities establish Institutional Review Boards (IRBs) with the primary purpose of evaluating potential risks and ethical quandaries in research involving human subjects, especially in the realms of biomedical and behavioral studies. These IRBs typically adopt the utilitarian philosophical approach to ethics, which assesses the balance between costs and benefits, as discussed earlier in this chapter. In the United States, the presence of an IRB is essentially mandatory for universities that receive federal funding. In technical terms, all research proposals involving human subjects should undergo IRB approval. However, there are exceptions, and exemptions are typically granted in cases where the research falls into one of the following categories:

1. Examination of educational practices.
2. Utilization of tests, surveys, or interviews that are inherently non-sensitive.
3. Observation of public behavior.
4. Analysis of historical data.

12.6.3 Peer Review and Data Provision

Nearly all contemporary published research undergoes a peer review process in which an editor from a scientific journal seeks the input and recommendations of respected experts within the specific field covered by the manuscript. These experts may opt to either reject the manuscript, accept it, or request revisions, which can range from major to minor, prior to recommending acceptance. Reviewers typically evaluate various aspects of the manuscript, including its theoretical framework, methodology, data analysis, and conclusions.

While peer review offers substantial advantages and often enhances the overall quality of academic research publications, it also introduces its own ethical considerations. These include the potential for reviewer bias toward significant findings or the pressure to provide lenient critiques of manuscripts authored by close colleagues. Instances have also arisen where reviewers have appropriated ideas or data from manuscripts they were evaluating.

Furthermore, as previously mentioned, numerous journals and professional associations establish requirements concerning data provision, aimed at facilitating objective examination of the validity of conclusions derived from primary data by independent third-party researchers.

12.7 Reviewing and Evaluating Manuscripts

Reviewing and evaluating research studies is a crucial aspect of the scientific process, and it also carries its own set of ethical considerations. Peer reviewers and evaluators play a pivotal role in maintaining the quality and integrity of research. The following guidelines can be used for ethical evaluation of manuscripts by reviewers, who should:

- Take their assignment seriously, as their decision can affect the careers and well-being of manuscript authors. If they are not willing to devote adequate time and attention to reviewing the manuscript requested by the journal editor, they should decline the editor's invitation.

- Disclose any potential conflicts of interest that could bias their evaluation of the research. This includes financial, personal, or professional conflicts related to the study or its authors.
- Maintain the confidentiality of the manuscripts they review. They should not disclose any details about the study to unauthorized individuals or use the information for personal gain; and they should provide an impartial and fair assessment of the research. And they should not let personal biases or preconceived notions influence their judgment.
- Complete their evaluations in a timely manner, respecting the deadlines set by the journal or institution. Delays in the review process can impact the publication timeline, the careers of authors, and the progress of science.
- Provide constructive and well-founded feedback to authors. Criticisms should be specific and objective; and they should aim at improving the quality of the research by suggesting actions that need to be taken by the author(s).
- Be vigilant about detecting plagiarism or any form of unethical practices in the manuscript under review. If plagiarism is suspected, it should be reported to the journal editor.
- Avoid making prejudiced or inflammatory remarks. If the research involves sensitive or controversial topics, reviewers should approach the evaluation with sensitivity and respect for diverse perspectives.
- Ensure that authors properly cite relevant previous work. They should also alert editors if they suspect that the authors have omitted citations to unfairly undermine the work of others.
- Have the necessary expertise to evaluate the research effectively. If a reviewer feels inadequately qualified to assess certain aspects of a manuscript, they should inform the editor.
- Respect the intellectual property rights of authors and not use or share unpublished research findings without their permission.
- Report any concerns about the ethical conduct of the journal's editorial process to the appropriate authorities, such as the journal editor or ethics committee.
- Disclose to the editor your knowledge about manuscript author(s), if you know who they are. And do not give their manuscript a favorable review, hoping that the authors will do the same for your manuscript.
- Evaluate whether research involving human or animal subjects adheres to ethical guidelines and has received proper ethical approval.
- Consider how research findings may be used and whether they have the potential for misuse, particularly in fields with ethical implications, such as biotechnology or social sciences.

In summary, ethical considerations in reviewing and evaluating research studies revolve around transparency, fairness, impartiality, and adherence to established ethical principles. Reviewers should be diligent in upholding these principles to ensure the integrity of the peer review process and the quality of published research.

12.8 Ethical Responsibilities of Journal Editors

Ethical conduct for journal editors is critical to ensure the integrity, fairness, and credibility of the publication process. Editors play a pivotal role in maintaining the quality and trustworthiness of academic journals. Journal editors should uphold the following ethical principles:

1. *Impartiality and Fairness*. Editors should treat all submitted manuscripts fairly and impartially, regardless of the authors' identity, affiliation, nationality, or other characteristics. Manuscripts should be evaluated based on their academic merit and scientific quality.
2. *Confidentiality*. Editors must maintain strict confidentiality regarding the content of submitted manuscripts. Manuscripts and related information should only be shared with reviewers, editorial board members, and other relevant parties on a need-to-know basis.
3. *Disclosure of Conflicts of Interest*. Editors should disclose any potential conflicts of interest that could affect their impartiality in handling a manuscript. This includes personal, financial, or professional relationships with authors, reviewers, or institutions associated with the submitted work.
4. *Transparency*. Editors should ensure transparency in the editorial process. This includes providing clear and detailed instructions to authors regarding manuscript submission, peer review, and publication procedures. Editors should also communicate decisions and feedback to authors and reviewers promptly and transparently.
5. *Peer Review Integrity*. Editors should select qualified and unbiased reviewers who can provide constructive and objective feedback on manuscripts. They should also ensure that the peer review process is conducted fairly and without any manipulation or favoritism.
6. *Plagiarism and Ethical Misconduct*. Editors should actively address issues of plagiarism, data fabrication, and other forms of research misconduct. At the very minimum, they should use appropriate software programs to check the submitted manuscript for duplication/plagiarism before putting it through the review process. Suspicious cases should be thoroughly investigated, and appropriate actions, such as retraction or correction, should be taken if ethical violations are confirmed.
7. *Quality Control*. Editors should work to maintain and enhance the quality of the journal. This includes regularly assessing and improving the journal's peer review process, publication standards, and editorial board and its policies.
8. *Publication Ethics*. Editors should adhere to established publication ethics guidelines, such as those set forth by organizations like the Committee on Publication Ethics (COPE) and the International Committee of Medical Journal Editors (ICMJE). These guidelines cover issues like authorship, citation, and handling of ethical concerns.
9. *Authorship and Authorship Disputes*. Editors should ensure that authorship is based on substantial contributions to the research and that all listed authors

have approved the final version of the manuscript. Editors should also be prepared to mediate authorship disputes if they arise.

10. *Correction and Retraction.* Editors should be willing to correct errors or inaccuracies in published articles and, when necessary, retract articles that are found to be seriously flawed or ethically problematic.
11. *Editorial Independence.* Editors should maintain editorial independence from the journal's ownership or funding sources. They should not allow external pressures to influence editorial decisions.
12. *Continuous Professional Development.* Editors should engage in ongoing professional development to stay updated on best practices, ethical standards, and emerging issues in academic publishing.
13. *Transparency of Co-authors' Contribution.* Editors should request co-authors to state the nature of their contribution and relative effort on an accepted manuscript. This information should be placed on the manuscript.
14. *Abstain from Inflating Their Journal's Impact Factor.* Editors should not request authors to cite publications that appear in their journal, if such publications serve no purpose other than artificially raising their journal's impact factor score.
15. *Abstain from Inflating Their Own h-index Score.* Editors should not request authors to cite their own work or suggest the use of methods that are likely to benefit the editors' visibility, if such citations or works are not relevant to, or contradict, the authors' research.

In summary, journal editors should act with integrity, transparency, and fairness throughout the editorial process to ensure the quality and credibility of the journal and to uphold the trust of the academic community and the public in the dissemination of scientific knowledge.

12.9 Avoiding Problems and Penalties

Having a solid understanding of potential ethical pitfalls and maintaining constant awareness of the responsibility and accountability associated with writing is an excellent starting point for avoiding any potential consequences that may be imposed on an author. There is an increasing focus on identifying ethical lapses in writing, as illustrated earlier and by the findings of Benos and associates (2005). It is crucial to recognize that ignorance is not a valid excuse and can lead to significant penalties, even when the wrongdoing was unintentional. Sharma and Singh (2011: 149) remind authors of the seriousness of plagiarism in particular by stating that:

> Most of the time, plagiarism is an unintended behavior. But plagiarism can tarnish the image of an author very badly. Reputed journals consider plagiarism as a highly unethical practice and they strongly depreciate such behaviors. Concern about plagiarism in the international community has led to the development of guidelines by Committee on Publication Ethics (COPE).

Authors can undertake certain tasks to prevent issues by maintaining well-organized records of their research, readings, and references. They bear responsibilities that align with ethical writing, including the essential duty of taking charge of their own writing and editing. Allowing others to write on one's behalf is not considered acceptable, and it is even less acceptable to disown the consequences of such actions. Authors must compile comprehensive reference lists and ensure that citations adhere to established standards and norms. Additionally, problems can occasionally arise when an article has the same or different author(s) in multiple outlets, potentially leading to embarrassment and strained professional relationships, as noted by King and associates (1997).

Penalties for ethical violations can range from the withdrawal of an article from publication to placing the author on a watch-list for future submissions. They may also involve bans on authors submitting to specific journals for a defined period or indefinitely. In severe cases, particularly involving students, expulsion from the academic course or doctoral program can be the most significant punishment. These consequences can be harsh and, in all instances, have the potential to lead to embarrassment and varying degrees of damage to one's reputation, affecting not only the researchers themselves but also academic faculty and other authors associated with them.

Authors must quickly grasp the importance of proper citation. This means that whenever they use another person's work, ideas, processes, results, or words, they must acknowledge the source by providing references to the authors and the publication year in their own articles. In the case of direct quotations, these should be enclosed in quotes, with the page number of the quoted source also referenced. When quoting more than a few lines or sentences directly, specific formatting techniques such as indentation, grouping, and the use of a distinct font are necessary.

12.10 Responsibilities and Obligations

Authors bear distinct roles and responsibilities in addressing ethical considerations. These responsibilities encompass ensuring that their research is consistently innovative and original. All authors must possess awareness of any submission bearing their name or work, and they must provide their consent for all aspects of the submission. It is imperative that the manuscript is open to evaluation by anonymous reviewers, and proper acknowledgment and citation practices must be strictly observed whenever quoting or paraphrasing.

Referees also carry responsibilities in detecting and reporting ethical violations, which can be identified at various stages in the research-to-publication process. It is not in any author's best interest to leave such breaches for reviewers to discover, as highlighted by Benos et al. (2005). These authors outline clear obligations, emphasizing that authors must uphold the trust of their colleagues and demonstrate self-responsibility in their writing. Furthermore, authors have a duty to serve the public through their publications, considering the perspective and comprehension of their readers.

Documentation concerning academic ethics is notably lacking, and it appears that this concept has become deeply ingrained in the culture of research and authorship. Researchers and authors are generally expected to possess an innate understanding of ethical principles, without the need for extensive investigation. Nevertheless, existing literature primarily focuses on the most prevalent ethical issues of plagiarism, fabrication, and falsification. However, as I have mentioned, numerous other ethical considerations that should be taken into account when engaging in academic writing across all disciplines.

There exists a set of inherent responsibilities and obligations that must be routinely followed, as the potential penalties for failing to do so have been shown to be quite severe. It is in the best interests of all participants in the writing process, including researchers, authors, co-authors, reviewers, editors, and publishers, to ensure that ethical codes, whether formal or informal, are rigorously adhered to.

In conclusion, several ethical considerations that have been presented are fundamental aspects of planning, conducting, and reporting research studies. Researchers must uphold ethical principles to protect the rights and well-being of participants, ensure the integrity of the research process, and promote responsible and meaningful contributions.

References

Aguinis, H., & Henle, C. A. (2002). Ethics in research. In S. G. Rogelberg (Ed.), *Handbook of research methods in industrial and organizational psychology* (pp. 34–56). Blackwell Publishing.

Benos, D. J., Fabres, J., Farmer, J., Gutierrez, J. P., Hennessy, K., Kosek, D., Lee, J. H., Olteanu, D., Russell, T., Shaikh, F., & Wang, K. (2005). Ethics and scientific publication. *Advances in Physiology Education, 29*, 59–74.

Coats, A. J. S. (2008). Ethical authorship and publishing. *International Journal of Cardiology, 131*, 149–150.

Dahl, G. (2009). Sociology and beyond: Agency, victimization and the ethics of writing. *Asian Journal of Social Science, 37*(3), 391–407.

Hirschman, E. C. (1986). Humanistic inquiry in marketing research: Philosophy, method, and criteria. *Journal of Marketing Research, 23*(August), 237–249.

Hughes, J., Hunter, D., Sheehan, M., Wilkinson, S., & Wrigley, A. (2010). *European textbook on ethics in research*. Publications Office of the European Union.

King, C. R., McGuire, D. B., Longman, A. J., & Carrol-Johnson, R. M. (1997). Peer review, authorship, ethics, and conflict of interest. *Journal of Nursing Scholarship, 29*(2), 163–168.

Sharma, B. B., & Singh, V. (2011). Ethics in writing: Learning to stay away from plagiarism and scientific misconduct. *Lung India, 28*(2), 148–150.

Stieglitz, S., Wilms, K., Mirbabaie, M., Hofeditz, L., Brenger, B., López, A., et al. (2020). When are researchers willing to share their data?—Impacts of values and uncertainty on open data in academia. *PLoS ONE, 15*(7), e0234172. https://doi.org/10.1371/journal.pone.0234172

Swazey, J. P., Anderson, M. S., & Lewis, K. S. (1993). Ethical problems in academic research. *American Scientist, 81*, 542–553.

Wranik, W. D., Hayden, J. A., Price, S., et al. (2016). How best to structure interdisciplinary primary care teams: The study protocol for a systematic review with narrative framework synthesis. *Systematic Reviews, 5*, 170. https://doi.org/10.1186/s13643-016-0339-9

13 Research Over the Course of Academic Life: Goals, Strategies, and Tactics

It is my contention that academic research that serves the researcher's best interest should change in scope over one's academic career. This chapter builds on my earlier article (Moschis, 2019a) to suggest research goals and effectual research strategies that should be employed at different stages of the person's academic life.

13.1 Stages of Academic Life

Research goals and strategies are suggested for five main stages, each having a different focus: preparation stage, high-output stage, identity-development stage, high-impact stage, and retirement stage. Viable research goals and strategies are highlighted at each specific stage of the person's academic career, along with tactics and required resources that would facilitate goal accomplishment.

Further, it is my contention that *regardless of stage*, researchers should pursue the following goals and strategies:

(a) Demonstrating leadership and research independence that can be evidenced through publications in top-tier journals within their field, either as the sole author or in a senior co-authorship role.
(b) Engaging in programmatic research that entails focusing on specific research streams, with a concentration on contemporary or emerging topics. This commitment should be reflected in lead-authored publications.
(c) Efforts to influence others in their primary field that can be gauged by the development of theories, models, or methods that can contribute to the advancement of knowledge in their discipline. This influence is demonstrated through the presence of relevant citations in globally recognized and reputable journals.
(d) The impact of their research on practice that can be assessed by publications in journals widely read by practitioners, covering topics relevant to their research streams.

G. P. Moschis, *Academic Research in Business and the Social Sciences*,
https://doi.org/10.1007/978-3-031-56548-9_13

For each stage below, recommended goals are delineated first, followed by effectual strategies for their accomplishment; and specific tactics related to these strategies are suggested along with the types of resources that would be needed to support them.

13.1.1 Preparation Stage: Learning the "Nuts and Bolts" of Academic Research

The initial phase involves preparing for a career in academia, where having a Ph.D. degree is now a standard requirement at accredited universities. Doctoral programs are where aspiring academics receive the bulk of their training. Therefore, individuals considering a Ph.D. degree should thoroughly assess various aspects of doctoral programs, not only entry prerequisites but also program structure, available faculty, and financial support. Drawing upon my extensive experience as director for a major marketing doctoral program in the United States, I suggest that prospective students evaluate these programs by seeking answers to the following critical questions: What unique skills can I develop at this institution that may not be available elsewhere? Who are the faculty members responsible for imparting these skills, and how esteemed are they in their respective fields? What is the faculty-to-student ratio in the department offering the program, and will I have access to the faculty I intend to work with? How can I finance my studies during the doctoral program? What is the typical duration for completing program requirements? What levels of financial support, such as assistantships and scholarships, are provided annually, and how many students receive them (e.g., the percentage of doctoral students receiving financial support)? Are the expectations for earning a doctoral degree reasonable compared to other institutions? Many of these inquiries can be addressed by consulting the coordinator or director of the department's Ph.D. program. Additionally, seeking input from current doctoral students and faculty members can offer valuable insights into the program's culture and expectations. Guidelines for choosing doctoral programs are also offered in Chap. 2.

Goals To select an institution that would provide the best opportunities to receive the training necessary for. conducting and publishing effectual academic research.

Objectives There are several key objectives that individuals should strive for during their doctoral program, including:

1. Acquiring a diverse range of methodological skills, as discussed by Summers (2001).
2. Developing the ability to critically analyze existing literature and identify its shortcomings, as emphasized by Summers (2001).
3. Cultivating conceptual skills, such as the capacity to propose alternative explanations for relationships between variables observed in the literature, address inconsistencies across studies and consider the influence of unobserved variables.
4. Enhancing both written and oral communication skills.

Strategies At this stage, strategies should revolve around the exploration of topics of interest and finding a balance between personal interests and practical constraints. By exploring various potential research areas, encompassing both methodological and substantive aspects, doctoral students can evaluate their own passions and capabilities. This exploration can help individuals identify areas that truly resonate with them. An effective approach involves reviewing recent research conducted by the faculty within their own department. It is advisable to focus on areas aligned with the research interests of potential dissertation advisors to avoid difficulties in finding suitable supervision. It is recommended that students compile a short list of general areas of interest that overlap with the research interests of available advisors. During this phase, research opportunities, as depicted in Chap. 4 (Table 4.1), often depend on availability rather than personal preferences. Therefore, students should make an effort to be physically present in their departments on a daily basis, engaging with faculty and fellow students, rather than working remotely.

Tactics Tactics to employ at this stage should encompass the following:

1. Engaging in coursework that covers a wide spectrum of methodological areas, encompassing both quantitative (e.g., structural equations modeling, experimental design) and qualitative (humanistic) research methods.
2. Exploring the potential to collaborate with faculty members on ongoing projects, whether as a research assistant or through voluntary contributions.
3. Investigating opportunities to join forces with faculty and fellow doctoral students on research endeavors with the potential for publication.
4. Enrolling in courses focused on writing and editing, studying the writing styles of successful authors in academic articles, conducting self-guided study, and actively seeking feedback on writing assignments from professional copy editors.

Resources Most students embarking on their doctoral program journey soon realize that the requirements for a doctoral program are significantly distinct from those in a master's program, demanding substantial lifestyle adjustments. Balancing doctoral program requirements with employment is often unfeasible, with many individuals needing to temporarily suspend work or withdraw from their jobs. Successfully completing doctoral program requirements while maintaining regular employment is exceedingly rare. Unless students possess financial independence or have allocated sufficient funds for their education, the level of support offered by the university becomes a critical factor in selecting a doctoral program. Key resources that students should be concerned with include the following:

1. Sustained financial assistance.
2. Access to technical support, including consultants and specialized software.
3. Support for attending conferences, including travel funding.
4. Availability of programs facilitating interactions with external experts, such as invited speakers.
5. Other forms of support, such as access to research center databases.

13.1.2 High-Output Stage: Focusing on Productivity and Efficiency

This marks the initial formal phase in the academic journey of individuals typically employed as assistant professors. It is during this stage that early career researchers face the highest workload in terms of preparing new courses while having relatively fewer service responsibilities. Faculty research productivity plays a pivotal role in decisions related to promotion and tenure. As most academic institutions anticipate junior faculty members to meet stringent standards for research output within a relatively short timeframe for promotion and tenure considerations, researchers at this juncture should prioritize building their publication track record. When seeking their first academic position, they should seek out educational institutions that provide sufficient support and time for research and writing endeavors. As early career researchers prepare to transition into this stage, several crucial factors should influence their choice of workplace. When evaluating potential universities, they should look beyond salary and fringe benefits and inquire about matters such as the number of courses assistant professors are expected to teach annually, the availability of summer research support, whether research funding is guaranteed or competitive, and if competitive, the ratio of summer research awards to the number of applicants. Additionally, they should explore incentives for contract research or bringing external funds to the university, such as course release or extra compensation.

Goals To demonstrate significant promise for a successful academic career through the establishment of an exemplary track record, warranting consideration for tenure and elevation to the position of associate professor, or an equivalent rank.

Objective The primary objective is to establish a publication record that aligns with, and ideally exceeds, the promotion and tenure criteria set by the researcher's institution.

Strategies During this phase, the quantity of published articles and the quality of the journals where they are published take precedence over the specific content of the articles. While evidence of leadership and independence in research is important, it is not an absolute prerequisite, as long as the researcher's name does not consistently appear after senior authors or among the last co-authors in most publications. Key strategies should involve the following:

1. Exploring research opportunities primarily within sets A and C (as outlined in Chap. 4, Table 4.1)
2. Cultivating research networks
3. Devoting research time exclusively to projects that have the potential to yield publications in A- and B-level journals, as opposed to other types of projects like conference papers or book chapters

Tactics

1. Delegating straightforward, labor-intensive research tasks (e.g., transcribing in-depth interviews) to research assistants
2. Submitting manuscripts to journals known for short review times
3. Establishing an efficient filing system for publications that have been read or referenced
4. Initiating or taking a leading role in new projects likely to result in sole- or senior-authored publications
5. Avoiding projects with high opportunity costs, such as textbooks or conference papers

Resources

1. Access to research assistants
2. Opportunities for course releases
3. Availability of extramural and university funds dedicated to research

13.1.3 Developing Identity and Expertise

This stage typically characterizes the researcher's role as an associate professor. During this phase, it becomes crucial for the researcher to concentrate on one or two specific areas or topics for two primary reasons: (a) to cultivate a reputation as an expert in a particular field and (b) to construct a publication record that can either lead to promotion to the rank of full professor or facilitate the acquisition of a more favorable position at a different academic institution. In most universities, associate professors at this stage have obtained tenure, and while many continue enacting their current roles without interruption, others explore alternative career opportunities, including various forms of business consulting.

Goals For researchers aspiring to attain the position of full professor or to become candidates for prestigious titles, as well as those aiming to remain competitive for positions at other academic institutions, it is imperative to provide concrete evidence of leadership and independence in their research endeavors to secure promotion to full professor. Equally vital is the demonstration of having achieved a recognized status or reputation as a nationally recognized authority in at least one area of research or scientific inquiry.

Key Objectives

1. Attain recognition as an authority in one (preferably two) relatively specialized research area(s) at the (inter)national level.
2. Demonstrate leadership and research independence through sole- and senior-authored publications in top-tier journals within one's field of expertise.

Strategy Conducting programmatic research emerges as a crucial strategy for achieving goals. Vigorous pursuit of activities contributing to goal attainment is recommended, while endeavors that might compromise the desired outcome (such as ad hoc research) should be steered clear of. It is advised to concentrate all research endeavors solely on one or two specific topics or areas.

- Concentrate your research activities on exclusively one or two areas.
- Learn as much as possible about the chosen topic(s) or area (s).
- Confine collaborative research to one's select topic(s) or area (s).
- Invest time in activities that help develop the image of an expert in an area.

Tactics

- Write a research book on your select topic.
- Establish a research center that does studies in your chosen area (see Sect. 13.2 in this chapter).
- Publish articles on a select topic or area in a wide variety of journals and other outlets (e.g., conference proceedings, books).
- Develop and teach a course on a select topic or research area.
- Edit a journal issue on your select topic.
- Complete a continuous education course or program on a select topic or area.

Resources

- Research assistants
- Course releases
- Extramural and university funds for research
- Support for writing proposals for external funding

13.1.4 Shifting the Emphasis to Research That Matters

At this stage, assuming the researcher has attained the rank of full professor, there are relatively few concrete rewards associated with research productivity. This phase of the researcher's academic journey places the least demands on him or her in terms of expectations for research output. This is primarily because one's career at the current institution is no longer contingent upon promotion and tenure decisions. This phase typically distinguishes researchers who engage in research out of genuine enjoyment from those who view research as a means to achieving other career objectives. Those in the former category are unlikely to cease their research and publishing activities, often delaying retirement or seeking opportunities at other universities to continue their academic pursuits. Most often, researchers who remain active at this stage are seeking research opportunities to make meaningful contributions to their field without the pressure of meeting specific research goals within predefined timeframes.

Researchers who have successfully built a reputation for their expertise in a particular research area, especially if their knowledge holds significant implications for policy and practice, will find themselves presented with a wide array of opportunities. These opportunities can take various forms, including employment offers from other institutions, securing research grants, involvement in long-term projects such as book writing and consulting, and invitations for visiting appointments at other academic institutions. The time dedicated to pursuing these opportunities often competes with research activities, impacting research productivity and necessitating a selective approach when choosing projects to undertake.

Goals For those who have no intentions of retiring and aim to remain actively engaged during this phase, their primary objective often shifts toward making a substantial and meaningful contribution to their field. This shift involves moving away from research solely driven by expediency or self-interest and toward research that holds the potential to significantly impact their discipline. In my opinion, the most impactful contribution one can make to their field involves enhancing the methodologies employed by researchers. Such contributions could manifest as the development of novel theories or the introduction of innovative research approaches that fundamentally alter how researchers approach and address research questions.

The primary goals for researchers who have no intentions to retire at this stage should be to:

1. Develop theories, models, or methodologies that can be adopted by others to advance knowledge within their discipline. An exemplar of this objective can be found in the section titled, "Conceptual model development: The case of the life course paradigm," later in this chapter.
2. Continue research within the few specific, narrow areas or topics chosen by the researcher.

Strategies Researchers who do not plan to retire at this stage often favor shifting their focus from research geared solely toward self-promotion and image-building to research that holds the potential for significant disciplinary impact. This shift involves placing a greater emphasis on research quality over quantity, even when recognizing that projects aligned with their goals may be time-consuming and entail a degree of risk.

Tactics for these researchers should include the following:

1. Identifying emerging trends that could have implications for research in their select area(s).
2. Engaging in projects with the potential to significantly advance knowledge.
3. Exploring research opportunities within Set D (as outlined in Chap. 4, Table 4.1).

Those who have plans for imminent retirement while thinking of staying active are likely considering two main options: either seeking full-time or part-time positions at other institutions or pursuing independent activities like book writing and consulting. It is crucial for them to develop strategies that ensure the availability of, or accessibility to, resources necessary for their post-retirement research, writing, and consulting endeavors. These strategies could involve building networks of fellow researchers, engaging in more collaborative projects, and exploring short-term employment opportunities at different locations, including foreign institutions.

Tactics for those individuals contemplating retirement but wish to remain engaged in their field:

1. Prior to retirement, it is essential to secure adequate resources, such as databases derived from surveys or electronic archives of published documents. These resources will be indispensable for continuing research and writing endeavors after retirement.
2. Foster and nurture global networks of researchers who can potentially collaborate on future studies by offering essential resources and complementary skills.
3. Investigate opportunities at other universities for part-time employment that emphasizes research and provides support for research initiatives and assignments. This might include involvement in funded research projects, supervision of dissertations, or affiliation with a research center.
4. Search for recent review articles in different scientific disciplines, such as trends in neuroscience, to stay informed and inspired.

Resources For individuals who plan to continue researching and writing after their formal retirement, they will need resources that can be provided by a university, if they secure a part-time or full-time position that has research expectations. Alternatively, these resources and opportunities would need to be provided by potential collaborators. Resources that would enable a person to remain active after retirement, whether employed at another institution or collaborating with colleagues, include the following:

- Access to research assistants
- Access to libraries
- Course releases
- Extramural and university funds designated for research
- Assistance with writing proposals for external funding opportunities

13.1.5 Beyond Retirement

Retired professors often lack substantial research support, except for potential access to their university's library. Those who secure short-term positions at other institutions typically continue their research with support stipulated in their contracts and their new institution's research expectations. For the majority of retired professors seeking continued engagement, common options include book writing and business consulting, as academic research holds a lower priority. Those still interested in publishing often focus on co-authored articles and, to a lesser extent, books. This shift is partly due to retirees placing greater value on activities like travel and socializing and encountering limited resources and colleagues supporting their writing. Nevertheless, some retirees plan for research and writing, ensuring they have access to necessary resources. As an example, Peter Drucker, when asked about his numerous books, revealed that he wrote the first third before retiring and the rest afterward.

Goal: Continuous engagement in research and writing
Strategies: Shift emphasis from academic research to book writing, continue collaborating with colleagues.
Tactics: Activities that promote research collaboration.
Resources: Databases for research (e.g., surveys, interviews) and book writing (e.g., library, labor).

13.2 The Role of Research Centers in Research Goal Accomplishment

University research centers are established for several reasons, the two main being (a) to attract resources and (b) to support their faculty's research. Secondary reasons include university publicity via various forms of mass media aimed at enhancing the university/college/department's image, attract additional funds to support the university's staff and administrative activities, and provide service to the community. The purpose of this section is to make the reader aware of the functions and activities of research centers, from their missions and goals to evaluation of their accomplishments, including factors that are likely to help a center succeed. As I was the founding director of a very successful research center, Center for Mature Consumer Studies (CMCS), I use my 33-year-long experience in directing the center's activities as a basis for my observation and suggestions.

13.2.1 Requirements for Establishing a Research Center

Several conditions are likely to favor the establishment of a university-based research center. Favorable conditions must exist within the university and in the university's environment. These conditions are first outlined below and discussed in detail in the sections that follow.

Conditions within the university that favor the establishment of a center include the following:

- At least one individual within the department or college must be familiar with the research topics and issues that would be the focus of the center's activities.
- At least one individual within the same department must be willing to serve as the center's first director.
- Research-oriented faculty, preferably from several areas of business and social sciences, must be available and willing to support the center's activities.
- The department and college within which the proposed center is to be housed must be willing to support its establishment.
- Financial support for the center's start-up costs must be available.
- A university- or college-based public affairs department must exist to publicize the center's establishment and its research.

Conditions outside the university that favor the establishment of a center include the following:

- The center's research focus must be on a timely topic that is increasing in importance because of its commercial, government, and social implications.
- Absence or scarcity of centers similar to the one proposed.
- Journals in various fields must be willing to process manuscripts on topics the proposed center is to focus on.
- Potential funding agencies should be willing to evaluate and fund proposals for research.
- Sufficient number of potential "consumers" of center's research must exist or increasingly rises.

13.2.2 Two Types of Research Centers

Academic research centers can be classified into service-oriented and research-oriented, depending on the types of research they conduct and their purpose. *Service-oriented* research centers focus on applied or practitioner-oriented research, while *research-oriented* research centers focus on research suitable for academic publications. This is not to say that research produced by service-oriented centers are not suitable for academic publications, and research produced by research-oriented centers is of no interest or relevance to practitioners. It is the center's mission and main goals of its research that determines their status.

Because of differences in main goals, the strategies and tactics employed by the two types of centers also differ. Research and other activities of service-oriented are primarily aimed at increasing the center's visibility and credibility for the purpose of attracting corporate and government funds for applied research. In contrast, the main activities of researcher-oriented center focus on trying to secure funds for conducting research of primary interest to readers of academic journals. The differences in goals, strategies, and tactics between the two types of research centers can be illustrated by describing the activities of CMCS, which functioned as both service-oriented and research-oriented center for several years, as I was intimately involved with its activities as director (Appendix 13.1).

13.2.3 Research Centers and Early Career Researchers: An Assessment

Because CMCS operated about half of the time as a service-oriented and as a research-oriented center, generating applied and theoretical research, respectively, the reader may be able to see the wide scope of research centers. In sum, a research center can serve as a vehicle for accomplishing a wide variety of goals. It can help attract resources, promote the name of an institution or department that houses it, and enhance the expertise of its researchers. However, the extent to which a research center benefits academic researchers appears to depend on its main focus—i.e., whether it is a service-oriented, emphasizing applied research, or a research-oriented, emphasizing academic research.

Generally, a service-oriented research center makes it easier to attract corporate and government funds for research, but the data suitable for the needs of its sponsors are rarely compatible with the needs of academic researchers; they are most suitable for lower-level and practitioner-oriented journals. One can see in Appendix 14.3 (Chap. 14) a sample of journals that published studies based on data generated by CMCS while operating as service-oriented research center. In contrast, research-oriented centers can better address the needs of the academic audience and higher-level journals but have limited opportunities for attracting funds for projects. Researchers in these centers usually have more time to devote to research projects, compared to researchers in service-oriented centers who must also spend time administering funded projects (e.g., hiring and supervising staff).

This brief assessment suggests that earlier career researchers who contemplate working with or through research centers should consider the research center's orientation. They should avoid service-oriented research centers, although they may find the availability of funds and data attractive. Service-oriented research centers, generally, can be of greater benefit to mid-career researchers who wish to enhance their image as experts on a few topics—i.e., stage of "Developing identity and expertise." These individuals also are likely to have been at that stage for some time and have developed a research record on a topic compatible with the mission and goals of the center, making it easier to attract funding.

13.3 An Illustration of Conceptual Model Development

As an example of strategies that are suitable for researchers at the stage of their academic career (prior to retirement), "Shifting the emphasis to research that matters," this section illustrates my goal to make a contribution by developing a conceptual model that helps researchers study consumers over the course of their lives. It represents an effort to improve previous approaches that attempt to study consumers over time by explaining changes in their behaviors from observed age- or stage-related differences. Specifically, this section provides the background material relevant to the development of a general conceptual model, followed by studies that have used the conceptual research framework to examine a wide variety of research topics.

13.3.1 A Life Course Conceptual Research Framework

While the life course approach to research has gained widespread acceptance in various fields and is lauded as a significant achievement in social science (e.g., Elder et al., 2003; George, 2003), it has not yet made inroads into the realm of consumer behavior. Furthermore, a critical gap exists in the absence of a comprehensive, multi-theoretical conceptual life course model that synthesizes previous research across disciplines, serving as a roadmap for future studies. Existing life course models are limited and tend to rely on assumptions rooted in specific disciplinary theories. Despite considerable discussion of the multi-theoretical life course approach in literature, which is known as the life course paradigm (LCP), there are no conceptual models that effectively integrate the assumptions and tenets of this paradigm. The following section presents an ambitious attempt to fill this void by developing a conceptual life course model.

The development of this conceptual life course model draws upon life course paradigmatic principles, relevant theories, and results of empirical studies from existing literature (e.g., Moschis, 2019b). It integrates these conceptual notions and supportive evidence to develop a model that consists of mainly six types of variables and their interrelationships. These variables can be categorized into two broad groups, which together form the foundational elements of the LCP and serve as the basis for the general conceptual model presented in this chapter (as depicted in Fig. 13.1). (For a more in-depth exploration of the theoretical and empirical support for this model, please refer to Moschis, 2019b).

The first group of elements encompasses three primary types of variables, highlighted within the shaded area of the model. These variables constitute the core components of the model. The first type encompasses events or changes experienced by individuals, whether expected (e.g., retirement) or unforeseen (e.g., chronic illness), occurring at specific stages or times (T1) in their lives. The second type encompasses three interrelated adaptation processes triggered by these events or changes, illustrated as egg-shaped figures. These processes include socialization mechanisms (e.g., family communication), stress responses (both acute and chronic stress), and coping strategies (primary and secondary), as well as changes in human capital (knowledge and mastery). The third category within the shaded area involves outcomes, which consist of variables in the form of events, changes, or patterns of thoughts and actions that manifest at later points in time (T2). These events and outcomes can take the form of individual choices or shifts in thoughts and behaviors, ranging from sudden to gradual transformations, or they may manifest as patterns of thoughts and actions. Many of these life events and experiences are interconnected and referred to as "transactional" events because the likelihood of one event occurring at T2 depends on the occurrence of another event at T1 (as shown in Fig. 13.1).

The second group of elements encompasses three distinct categories of contextual factors (displayed outside the shaded area in Fig. 13.1), collectively shaping the diverse circumstances in which individuals are situated. These contextual factors include the following: (a) the timing of events (the age at which individuals experience them) and the temporal extent of experiences (Ts); (b) factors associated with human agency, encompassing earlier life experiences (at T-1) and attributes like events/changes, socio-cultural contexts, choices, conditions, and traits (Ps); and (c) structural factors defined at varying levels of aggregation and stability (Ss) relevant to the timeframe spanning T1 to T2. These contextual elements exert influence on variables and relationships (depicted within the shaded area of Fig. 13.1), which encompass both experienced and anticipated events at T1, the adaptation processes

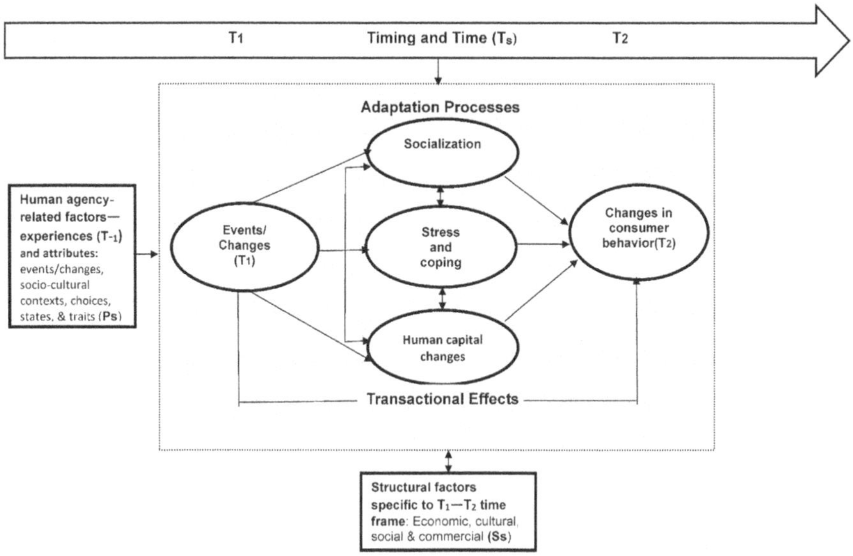

Fig. 13.1 A conceptual life course model. (Source: Adapted from Moschis (2019b))

instigated by these events, and their outcomes at T2, all within the T1 to T2 timeframe. Over time, certain structural factors (Ss) may themselves be influenced by events and individual actions, resulting in reciprocal effects (as illustrated in Fig. 13.1).

Therefore, the outcomes in the form of changes or patterns of thoughts and behaviors at T2 are the consequences of events, changes, or transitions previously encountered, the adaptation processes, and the contextual factors relevant to the specific T1 to T2 timeframe in an individual's life. The influence of these sets of factors leads to distinct outcomes during various timeframes across an individual's lifespan, as they undergo different life changes (viewed as events) and are situated within different temporal contexts.

The timeframe (T1 to T2) denotes a period between the event or change experienced at T1 and the event or change that occurs (or experienced) at T2, which can be measured in various units of time, such as the number of years.

In line with the core premise of the LCP, the development, stability, and alterations in patterns of thoughts and actions do not transpire arbitrarily in isolation but are systematically linked to evolving life circumstances, which are perceived as life events. These events encompass choices made by individuals, as well as anticipated and unanticipated biological, psychosocial, and environmental changes. These life events that individuals encounter throughout their lives necessitate adaptations to new life conditions and influence their thoughts and actions. The absence of such events tends to foster stability in thoughts and behaviors, as outlined by Elder and Johnson (2002). How individuals experience, interpret, and respond to these changes (events) at a given moment in time (T1) and adapt to them over time (T1 to T2) hinges on the timing and duration of these events (Ts), the individual's earlier life circumstances (at T-1) and attributes (Ps), as well as the structural contexts (Ss) in which one is embedded during a particular timeframe (i.e., during T1 to T2). The resulting outcomes, which can assume various forms (outcomes/events at T2), are the product of both the direct and indirect effects of life events and adaptation processes, as well as the direct and moderating impacts of contextual variables (as depicted in Fig. 13.1).

A person's reactions and adjustments to life events and evolving life circumstances over time, including the decisions made at T1, are guided by five foundational principles within the LCP, as detailed by scholars like Elder et al. (2003) and George (2003). These principles primarily pertain to the role of contextual factors situated outside the shaded area of Fig. 13.1 and the connections among variable sets within that shaded area throughout an individual's entire lifespan. The first principle, concerning the "timing of events" (Ts in Fig. 13.1), focuses on when in a person's life a specific life event occurs. The "time and place" principle asserts that an individual's life course is deeply embedded in and shaped by the historical contexts and locations experienced over their lifetime. The "linked lives" principle highlights the interdependence between an individual and their social spheres throughout their life, encompassing family, friends, and colleagues. The "life-span development" principle posits that individuals continually develop and adapt to changes, such as those occurring between T1 and T2 in Fig. 13.1, throughout their lives. Lastly, the "human agency" principle suggests that individuals actively shape their life course by making choices (e.g., marriage, retirement) and responding to experienced events at T1 based on personal constraints and life circumstances (e.g., biological, financial; Ps in Fig. 13.1). They also engage with evolving environments (Ss in Fig. 13.1), resulting in behavioral outcomes and societal changes.

When examining consumer behavior within the context of the LCP, as illustrated in the model (Fig. 13.1), the various changes, responses, and choices made by individuals manifest as events they experience. Adaptations to these events and evolving life conditions dictate alterations and continuities across different life domains (e.g., work, family, education) that collectively constitute an individual's life course trajectory, as described by Elder et al. (2003). By applying these concepts to the field of consumer behavior, many consumer choices become events that signify transitions into new consumption states and define specific consumption trajectories (e.g., education, housing, financial). These trajectories, in turn, shape an individual's overall consumption path as an integral component of their life course trajectory.

Therefore, I contend that the principles relevant to studying an individual's adaptation to life events throughout their life can also be applied to understanding adaptations to consumer roles and events, such as becoming a homeowner or investor. Consumers adapt to different consumption states in a manner akin to their adaptation to other shifting life circumstances. Consequently, the continuity and change observed in consumer behavior, encompassing patterns of thoughts and actions, likely result from responses and adaptations not only to evolving life conditions (life events, roles) but also to consumption-related events that occur over the course of a consumer's life.

Within the framework of the LCP illustrated in Fig. 13.1, I introduce research in consumer behavior that can be contextualized within this comprehensive conceptual framework (Moschis, 2019b, 2021). Following the structure of this framework, I elucidate life course conceptual and theoretical concepts to offer fresh perspectives on the examination of consumer behavior. And I reference and interpret consumer research that aligns with these perspectives, illustrating how disparate theories and previous findings can be harmonized within the LCP. This synthesis leads to the development of general propositions for the relationships depicted in Fig. 13.1, devoid of specific variables, thereby providing conceptual guidance for future research endeavors. These propositions, in turn, serve as the foundation for demonstrating elsewhere (e.g., Mathur, 2019, 2020; Moschis, 2019b; Yingwattanakul and Moschis, 2017) how the LCP can be applied to specific domains of consumer research, enhancing and advancing prior studies. Additionally, they offer a template for research in specialized fields, such as personal finance (Moschis, 2019b) and preventive healthcare (Yingwattanakul and Moschis, 2017).

The conceptual model introduced in this section represents an expansion of an earlier life course model I initially formulated (Moschis, 2007). It remains open to revision and further development, evolving as our knowledge deepens and environmental conditions change. For instance, it can accommodate the inclusion of additional contextual variables and the delineation of specific adaptation processes, such as those involving socialization agents and mechanisms (e.g., social media, online learning). The aim is to encourage researchers to contemplate new approaches to studying consumers throughout their lifespans.

13.3.2 Life Course Studies of Consumer Behavior

In a recent review article (Moschis, 2021), I categorize life course studies of consumer behavior into two main groups: those that suggest life course explanations and those that are grounded in the LCP, including the original conceptual model developed in 2007 and its later expansion and revision (2019b) (Fig. 13.1).

Studies Implying Life Course Explanations Studies exploring consumers' behaviors throughout their lives, which presume life course explanations, emerged in the literature during the final two decades of the twentieth century. Although these investigations are not explicitly labeled as "life course" studies, they incorporate elements and assumptions reminiscent of the LCP. Notable examples include Andreasen's influential 1984 study, which connects life events in the form of life status changes to shifts in consumer preferences through changes in lifestyles. Other studies with implicit life course explanations focus on narrow theoretical perspectives like socialization, human capital, and stress (e.g., Moschis in 2021). Despite these perspectives being integral to the multi-theoretical LCP, studies applying them in the latter part of the last century are not considered authentic life course inquiries. Even when researchers use the term "life course" in studies examining consumer transitions across different life stages that link life events to shifts in consumption activities, they rely on limited theoretical lenses within the LCP to elucidate behavioral changes at various stages or ages, such as role theory, stress theory, or cognitive theory (Moschis, 2021).

In a similar vein, we see additional studies from the last two decades of the twentieth century that presume life course explanations for consumer behavior. These studies are primarily descriptive in nature, providing minimal theoretical insights into the origins, progression, and alterations in consumption patterns, often inferred from observed age or age-group differences. The review article (Moschis, 2021) also points out that the few studies attempting to establish links between consumption at a specific point in an individual's life and their past experiences and future expectations fall short in several ways. They either do not attempt to adequately address the processes of change associated with earlier times and contexts, or they neglect to examine the influence of consumers' prior experiences within the context of time and history.

In the same review article, the reader sees studies akin to Andreasen's work from 1984, which are grounded in limited life course explanations and incorporate variables derived from the LCP. However, despite these investigations offering various models to elucidate shifts in consumer behavior over time, they all fall short of fully incorporating the comprehensive elements, principles, and axioms of the multi-theoretical LCP in a manner that would advance consumer life course research.

Studies Based on the LCP To demonstrate the value of applying the life course approach in consumer research, the original conceptual model was developed based on the relevant tenets of the LCP, specifically focusing on the development materialistic values and compulsive buying tendencies (Moschis, 2007). This model has served as a foundation for integrating prior research on these subjects and interpreting empirical findings. Furthermore, it has facilitated research on materialism and compulsive buying across a dozen countries (e.g., Mathur, 2019, 2020; Moschis (2019b). However, these studies, which employ this conceptual life course model for hypothesis formulation or data interpretation, have primarily centered on the mechanisms promoting the development of these two consumption orientations, largely overlooking contextual variables beyond country-related influences. Subsequently, this life course model underwent revision and expansion by its creator, incorporating variables and assumptions suggested by the LCP, not only to explain materialism and compulsive buying but also a wide range of behaviors of interest to consumer researchers (e.g., Moschis, 2019b, 2021).

The review article (Moschis, 2021) demonstrates the application of the LCP's tenets and axioms as depicted in the conceptual life course model (Moschis, 2007, 2019b) across various aspects of consumer behavior. It provides an overview of studies examining the development of materialism and compulsive buying in 11 and nine countries, respectively. Additionally, the same review presents findings from three studies on financial habits in five countries and results from two studies on preventive healthcare using data from another five countries. Two more studies, involving samples from the USA and Thailand, employ life course concepts to explain diverse consumer behaviors. Furthermore, the article underscores the advantages of utilizing qualitative methods in life course research, exemplified by Minowa and Belk (2020) in a study on gift-giving among mature consumers, showcasing how qualitative data can be interpreted within the conceptual life course model shown in Fig. 13.1.

In the same review article (Moschis, 2021), the results of a longitudinal study employing life course theoretical perspectives to illustrate how older consumers' decisions are influenced by experiences earlier in life and future expectations are discussed. Similar theoretical concepts are applied in another article within the same review to clarify the relatively low percentage of hearing-impaired individuals who purchase hearing aids and the reasons behind the prolonged delay in purchase, shedding light on the life course paradigmatic principles of timing, time, and place.

The review article also delves into studies that have utilized the LCP to enhance existing models, as detailed in Moschis (2021). These include a study employing samples from Germany, the USA, Thailand, and Turkey, illustrating how stage models like the Family Life Cycle (FLC) can be enriched by integrating theoretical concepts derived from the LCP. Additionally, the article presents further applications of the life course conceptual model in two studies examining consumer responses to natural disasters, both discussed in the same review article. Lastly, the article addresses the issue of generalizing the efficacy of the LCP across different contexts and provides the outcomes of two cross-cultural studies, demonstrating the LCP's usefulness as a research framework for studying consumer behaviors in diverse cultural settings.

The life course conceptual model has been employed in recent years to explain consumer behavior in response to threats, such as Covid-19—viewed as a life event (Suttharattanagul et al., 2022), financial well-being in later life (Prakitsuwan et al., 2022), responsible or mindful buying (Mathur and Moschis, 2023), financial socialization (Moschis et al., in press; Prakitsuwan et al., in press), sustainable food consumption (Moschis et al., 2020), and consumer well-being in general (Moschis and Mathur, 2024); and it has been offered as a viable conceptual framework for studying the formation of consumption habits in early life (Moschis and Mathur, 2024).

Appendix 13.1 Service and Research Foci of the Center for Mature Consumer Studies (CMCS)

CMCS: Service-Oriented (Years 1987–2002)

(a) *Mission/Goals: Emphasis on applied (practitioner-oriented) research.* CMCS' mission was to generate and disseminate information useful in improving the efficiency of various organizations and the well-being of older adults. Specific goals included:

1. Achieve national recognition for the Marketing Department, Robinson College of Business (RCB) and Georgia State University (GSU).

2. Become self-supporting in securing resources and data for academic research.

(b) *Strategies*

1. Conducted research to determine the effectiveness of business strategies.
2. Generate credible information of interest to policy and business decision makers
3. Disseminate information via a variety of academic journals, trade publications and other mass media.

(c) *Summary of Tactics (Activities)*

1. Conducted studies of main interest to practitioners and mass media
2. Disseminated information to thousands of organizations, including corporations, government agencies, nonprofit organizations, and media.
3. Prepared and published books and articles in academic and practitioner journals
4. Presented research findings at business forums and academic conferences
5. Developed a national network of CMCS affiliates from academia and industry
6. Hosted visiting professors and doctoral students from U.S. and abroad
7. Provided opportunities to dozens of graduate students to gain experience in conducting research studies.

(d) *Main Accomplishments*

1. Thirty-six (36) refereed publications in academic outlets
2. Five (5) books
3. Sixteen (16) papers presented at inter/national business conferences
4. Six (6) papers presented at inter/national academic conferences
5. Developed seventeen (17) lengthy industry reports for sale, which generated revenues in the range of $50000 to $100000 (accurate figure could be calculated based on available receipts)
6. Grants & contract from the industry, government and foundations, totaling $85000
7. Wide national and local media coverage by hundreds of newspapers, trade publications, magazines, TV and radio stations.
8. CMCS was recognized by *American Demographics* magazine for five consecutive years as one of the best sources of marketing information in the U.S.
9. Several recognitions of CMCS and its director's research by businesses and academia
10. Supported an average of two (2) graduate research assistants (GRAs) (masters and doctoral) per quarter
11. Funded the dissertations of four (4) students, totaling approximately $25000
12. Paid for one of director's summer course releases.
13. Generated and secured databases, which were used in the development of academic manuscripts and the training of doctoral students; and contributed to faculty development by facilitating research and interaction across disciplines and departments. Dozens of faculties and doctoral students directly or indirectly benefited from CMCS activities.

14. Provided salary supplements to Marketing Department staff ($1000 to $2000 annually)

(e) *Sources of Funding*

1. Grants & contracts
2. Book royalties
3. Fees for consulting services provide by CMCS director
4. Revenues from sale of industry reports
5. Small donations

(f) *Center Personnel*

Only its director received RCB/Department support (one course release annually) on a continuous basis. However, several dozen individuals, both faculty and doctoral students from different GSU colleges and RCB departments, worked on CMCS-funded projects, used CMCS data for publication and directly or indirectly contributed to, or benefited from, the Center's activities

CMCS: Research-Oriented (Years 2003–2020)

(a) *Mission/Goals*

CMCS mission changed in 2003 in response to new RCB mandate. Its mission was to generate and disseminate information for the purpose of enhancing the well-being of older adults in the marketplace.

CMCS goals were driven by research issues of primary interest to academicians that had potential for publication in top marketing journals, with little concern about the needs of practitioners and policy makers.

(b) *Strategies*

a. Expanded CMCS research scope to help understand older consumers by studying consumers over the course of their lives by establishing the Consumer Life-course Studies Group (CLSG) in 2011 at Mahidol University's College of Management (Thailand)
b. Diffused the life course approach as a conceptual framework for studying consumer well-being in general, and older consumers in particular.
c. Integrated CMCS goals and activities within the CLSG's broader mission and goals for greater efficiency and impact.

(c) *Summary of Activities*

1. Developed a life course conceptual model to help guide academic research.
2. Initiated research projects that had the potential for academic publications in top marketing journals, engaging less in activities aimed at raising funds for CMCS (e.g., commercial research)
3. Engaged in cost-effective and time-efficient activities to help do more academic research in light of reduced financial resources by, for example, collaborating
4. with researchers from other universities who had the skills and resources to support academic research.
5. Formed alliances with researchers from countries all over the globe to support collaborative research aimed at producing refereed publications.

6. Activities aimed at building CMCS satellite units around the globe to enhance GSU/RCB's name globally and secure resources needed for academic studies
7. Increased emphasis on the training of marketing doctoral students.
8. Mentoring of faculties and doctoral students in foreign universities around the globe, and promoting the Department, RCB and GSU

(d) *Major Accomplishments*
   a. Substantial increase in the number of refereed publications co-authored with faculty and doctoral students. The record shows more than twice as many co-authored publications with 52 colleagues and doctoral students from all over the globe from 2003 to 2020 than from 1987 to 2002.
   b. Sixty-six (66) refereed publications in academic outlets, with four (4) in the top five journals that are on RCB's list of premier marketing journals.
   c. One (1) research book
   d. Four (17) papers presented in academic conferences
   e. Four (7) chapters in books
   f. Generated enough funds to support an average of two (2) GRAs annually.
   g. Established three CMCS satellite units, two within universities (Sejong University, Korea, and University of Malaya)
   h. Formed research alliances with 35 researchers from 20 countries around the globe (Japan, Korea, Italy, Hong Kong, Thailand, Malaysia, France, Germany, Holland, Greece, South Africa, Vietnam, India, Indonesia, Australia, Brazil, Pakistan, Turkey, United Arab Emirates, and USA) for the purpose of conducting cross-cultural research using the author's life course conceptual model.
   i. Secured a wealth of databases for academic research at no cost by collaborating with and mentoring researchers in foreign countries
   j. Expanded/promoted CMCS name globally via mass media, presentations at conferences and business forums, and collaboration with foreign scholars on various projects.

(e) Sources of Funding
   a. Funds from Director's Research Professorship
   b. Book royalties
   c. Fees from limited customized commercial research
   d. Fees from incremental sale of commercial reports (developed prior to 2003)
   e. Small donations

(f) *CBA/Department Support:* One course release annually to CMCS Director

(g) *CMCS Personnel*

Formally, CMCS has a Director (George Moschis) and an Associate Director (Carolyn Curasi). Other marketing faculty and doctoral students are involved, depending on their needs and interest. CMCS makes itself and its resources (e.g., data) available to those in RCB and other colleges of GSU who wish to collaborate on academic projects that have potential for publication in premier marketing journals.

References

Elder, G. H., & Johnson, M. K. (2002). The life course and aging: Challenges, lessons, and new directions. In R. A. Settersen (Ed.), *Invitation to the life course: Toward new understanding of later life, Part II*, (pp. 49–81). Amityville, NY: Baywood.

Elder, G. H., Johnson, M. K., & Crosnoe, R. (2003). The emergence and development of life course theory. In J. T. Mortimer & M. J. Shanahan (Eds.), *Handbook of the life course* (pp. 3–19). Plenum Publishers.

George, L. K. (2003). Life course research: Achievements and potential. In J. T. Mortimer & M. J. Shanahan (Eds.), *Handbook of the life course* (pp. 671–680). Plenum Publishers.

Mathur, A. (2019). George P. Moschis tribute special issue: His philosophy and contributions (Part I). *Journal of Global Scholars of Marketing Science, 29*(4), 359–371.

Mathur, A. (2020). George P. Moschis tribute special issue: His philosophy and contributions (Part II). *Journal of Global Scholars of. Marketing Science, 30*(1), 1–3.

Mathur, A., & Moschis, G. P. (2023). Antecedents and outcome of mindful buying. *Journal of Consumer Affairs, 57*(4), 1684–1713. https://doi.org/10.1111/joca.12565

Minowa, Y., & Belk, R. W. (2020). Qualitative approaches to life course research: Linking life story to gift giving. *Journal of Global Scholars of Marketing Science, 30*(1), 60–75.

Moschis, G. P. (2007). Life course perspectives on consumer behavior. *Journal of the Academy of Marketing Science, 35*(2), 295–397.

Moschis, G. P. (2019a). Pathways to successful academic research: A life course perspective. *Journal of Global Scholars of Marketing Science*. George P. Moschis tribute special issue, part one, *29*(4), 372–408.

Moschis, G. P. (2019b). *Consumer behavior over the life course: Research frontiers and new directions*. Springer Publishing, Inc.

Moschis, G. P. (2021). The life course paradigm and consumer behavior: Research frontiers and future directions. *Psychology & Marketing, 38*(11), 2034–2050. https://doi.org/10.1002/mar.21586

Moschis, G. P, & Mathur, A. (2024). Children and adolescent consumer behavior: Insights from the life course paradigm. *Journal of Consumer Behavior*, published online: 18 February 2024 https://doi.org/10.1002/cb.2314

Moschis, G. P., Mathur, A., & Shannon, R. (2020). Toward achieving sustainable food consumption: Insights from the life course paradigm. *Sustainability, 12*(13), 1–18.

Moschis, G. P, & Mathur, A. (in press). Seeking profits by enhancing consumer well-being; A life course perspective. In Faith Sonmez (Ed.) Consumer psychological wellbeing. Springer.

Moschis, G. P, & Mathur, A. (2024). Children and adolescent consumer behavior: Insights from the life course paradigm, Journal of Consumer Behavior. published online: 18 February 2024 https://doi.org/10.1002/cb.2314

Moschis, G. P., Prakitsuwan, P., & Mathur, A. (in press). Financial socialization: Insights from the life course paradigm. *Journal of Financial Counseling and Planning.*

Prakitsuwan, P., Moschis, G. P., & Mathur, A. (in press). A study of financial socialization in life course context. *Journal of Financial Counseling and Planning.*

Prakitsuwan, P., Moschis, G. P., & Shannon, R. (2022). Using the life course paradigm to study financial well-being in late life. *Asia Pacific Journal of Marketing and Logistics, 34*(1), 60–74. https://doi.org/10.1108/APJML-06-2020-0415

Summers, J. O. (2001). Guidelines for conducting research and publishing in marketing: From conceptualization through the review process. *Journal of the Academy of Marketing Science, 29*(4), 405–415.

Suttharattanagul, S. L., Cai, Y., & Moschis, G. P. (2022). Life course explanations of consumer responses to threats: The case of COVID-19. *Cogent Business & Management, 9*, 1. https://doi.org/10.1080/23311975.2022.2151193

Yingwattanakul, P., & Moschis, G. P. (2017). Life course perspectives on the onset and continuity of preventive healthcare behaviors. *The Journal of Primary Prevention, 38*(5), 537–550.

14 Writing Proposals

A research proposal is a formal document that outlines a plan for a research project. It serves as a blueprint or roadmap for conducting a research study and is typically submitted to funding agencies, academic institutions, or research review committees for approval and financial support. Proposals are in different formats depending on their intended targets and agency formal requirements. They can be broadly classified into (a) proposals used within institutions for approval and financial support and (b) those used for external funding of research projects or other services. Common proposals in the first category include the following: proposals submitted by doctoral students for approval of their research project as partial fulfillment of their program requirements and proposals submitted by faculty to their institutions for research support, which is usually in the form of reduced teaching load in order to devote extra time to research. The structure of both types of internal proposals, including research goals, is predominantly driven by the policies of the proposer's institution and the proposer's needs, research skills, and interests.

In contrast, the formats of proposals for external funding are driven by the needs of funding government agencies and corporations or nonprofit organizations. Proposals that address the needs of funding agencies are either solicited or unsolicited. The first category entails the development of proposals according to specific requirements of the funding agency, which specifies the types of proposals it would consider for funding in a request-for-proposal (RFP) announcement. Unsolicited proposals provide some flexibility in their structure, although they must contain the same basic elements as RFP. Finally, proposals prepared for corporate support are primarily driven by the needs of the intended user of the project's results. This chapter discusses these four types of proposals, focusing on the relative importance of their components, as these are likely to be of greatest interest and relevance to early career researchers, including doctoral students.

G. P. Moschis, *Academic Research in Business and the Social Sciences*,
https://doi.org/10.1007/978-3-031-56548-9_14

14.1 Thesis or Dissertation Proposal

Graduate students often need to write a thesis or dissertation proposal as part of their academic program requirements. These proposals outline the research topic, objectives, methodology, and expected contributions to the field. But the specific format and requirements may vary by academic institution and discipline. It is essential to follow the guidelines provided by the proposer's institution and seek guidance from their advisor or dissertation supervisor when preparing a dissertation proposal. Dissertation proposals typically contain the (a) main research question or problem a proposed study will address in a specific area or topic, (b) a review of the literature relevant to the research question or problem that justifies the employment of certain research approach(es), (c) the research design or plan that specifies how the research will be conducted, (d) data collection methods and analyses, and (e) the expected contribution(s) of the proposed investigation relevant to the research question or problem. These five elements are present in nearly every thesis or dissertation proposal, but they differ in content for items (b), (c), and (d), depending on whether the proposed study is quantitative or qualitative; and elements (b) and (c) are often combined, as shown in the sample dissertation proposal in Appendix 14.1.

14.1.1 Quantitative Research Proposal

Quantitative research proposals focus on collecting and analyzing numerical data to answer research questions or test hypotheses. These proposals typically include details about how specific hypotheses are derived from reviewing relevant theories and research. A great deal of emphasis is placed on the relevant theoretical or conceptual framework that justifies the selection of variables for hypothesis development; and it provides rationale for the proposed research design, which typically takes the form of a cross-sectional survey or an experiment, depending on whether the proposed study attempts to falsify relationships or infer cause-and-effect between variables. The quantitative research proposals also include details on data collection methods, measurement of variables mentioned in hypotheses, and statistical analysis techniques. Finally, these proposals explain how the proposer plans to obtain ethical approval from the relevant ethics review board, if required.

Survey Research Proposal If a proposed study involves the administration of surveys or questionnaires, the proposal should state the rationale for the survey with regard to the main research question. And it should emphasize methods of data collection (e.g., online, telephone, mail), sampling (e.g., sampling method, sample size), and analysis, focusing on statistical tests appropriate for testing each hypothesis.

Experimental Research Proposal Experimental research proposals detail the design and implementation of controlled experiments to investigate causal relationships between variables. They often include information about type of experimental design, participants, randomization, experimental variables, control groups, experimental procedures, and data analysis (see also Chap. 7). The following types of information are often required to be included in an experimental research proposal:

- The type of experimental design you plan to use (e.g., pretest-posttest control group, Solomon four-group design).
- The experimental variables, independent variable(s) (the factor(s) you will manipulate or experimental treatments), and dependent variable(s)—the outcome(s) you will measure.
- Any control variables or factors that you will hold constant or control for in your experiment.
- Information about your study participants, including the sampling method, the anticipated sample size, and their characteristics, including demographics (e.g., age, gender) and any specific criteria for inclusion or exclusion.
- A step-by-step description of how the experiment will be conducted, including any materials or equipment used.
- Explanation of how participants will be assigned to different experimental conditions (randomization or matching).
- Explain the debriefing method you plan to use.

14.1.2 Qualitative Research Proposal

Creating a strong dissertation proposal for a qualitative study is crucial to gain approval and guidance from your academic institution. This is because qualitative research requires a great deal of experience on the part of the doctoral student, who acts subjectively and "alone" throughout most of the data collection, analysis, and interpretation stages; and he or she might not be able to receive as much assistance from others at these stages as students who conduct a quantitative study, where feedback and help tend to be in a more objective form (e.g., reliability coefficients, appropriate software). Using the general structure discussed earlier and illustrated in Appendix 14.1, the proposer should pay particular attention to the methodological component of the proposal as it relates to qualitative methods. Specifically, you should:

- Describe the qualitative research methodology you plan to use (e.g., grounded theory, phenomenology, case study, ethnography, content analysis, etc.).
- Explain why this methodology is appropriate for your research questions and objectives.
- Detail your data collection methods (e.g., interviews, focus groups, observations, document analysis) and justify their selection.

- Discuss your approach to data analysis, including coding techniques, thematic analysis, or other qualitative analysis methods.
- Address issues of validity and reliability in qualitative research and how you plan to enhance the trustworthiness of your findings.
- Provide a clear description of your sampling strategy, including how you will select informants or sources of data.
- Explain how you will gain access to your informants and any ethical considerations, including informed consent and confidentiality.
- Outline your data analysis process, including how you will code and categorize data, identify themes or patterns, and draw conclusions.
- Discuss the software tools, if any, that you will use for data management and analysis.
- Address ethical issues related to your research, including informed consent, participant anonymity, and any potential harm.
- Explain how you plan to obtain ethical approval from the relevant ethics review board if required.
- Provide a rough timeline for the various stages of your research, from data collection to final write-up. This helps demonstrate the feasibility of your project.
- Describe debriefing procedure.

Remember that the level of detail required may vary depending on the specific requirements of your institution, funding agency, or the nature of your research. Be sure to follow any guidelines or templates provided for research proposals in your academic context.

14.1.3 Mixed-Methods Research Proposal

In some cases, researchers may combine both quantitative and qualitative approaches within a single study. Mixed-methods research proposals must include elements of both quantitative and qualitative research proposals described earlier. In addition, these research proposals outline how these different methods will be integrated to provide a comprehensive understanding of the research question.

14.2 Proposal for Institutional Research Support

Faculty regularly submit proposals to their department, college, or university, requesting support in the form of reduced teaching load or compensation for not teaching one or more courses, and sometimes even extra compensation. Such proposals are normally prepared according to guidelines, and support is typically awarded to proposers on a competitive basis. The basic structure of such a proposal is not very different from the structure seen in Appendix 14.1, with three major exceptions. First, proposals for research support are substantially shorter, usually no more than 5–10 pages. Second, they state how the data are to be secured and any costs for obtaining them. Third, these proposals normally include an additional section that shows the proposer's record of journal publications from previous awards, as well as his or her intended target journal(s) for the proposed research. This section is one of the major factors in the evaluators' decision whether to recommend the proposal for funding or support. Proposers who show that they have made effective use of previous research awards in the form of publication in quality journals normally have better chances for receiving future awards.

Awarding extra time or compensation for not teaching is often not sufficient for conducting the proposed study, which normally involves data gathering expenses. The recipients of these research award who do not want to use their own funds to pay for the study's expenses customarily adopt one of the following strategies: They propose a study for which they have already secured data, completed the study, and even had a publication accepted or likely to be accepted; or they collaborate with colleagues who have the resources necessary for this study, usually agreeing to co-author publications from their data; or they work closely with students on their dissertation, with the expectation of joint publications from the student's dissertation. The latter is usually a mutually satisfying arrangement but highly questionable, as it is not often clear if the student's work represents his or her "independent" contribution, even when the student is the lead co-author. This is perhaps one of the reasons articles based on dissertations that are co-authored by one or more of the student's committee members (anecdotally) "do not count as much" for the student.

14.3 Proposal for External Funding

Learning to write research proposals for external funding is not only important but often essential for a professor's career. It not only provides the financial means to conduct research but also offers numerous professional and personal benefits that can significantly contribute to a successful and fulfilling academic career. Here are several reasons why this skill is crucial:

- *Funding is Essential.* Research projects often require financial resources for data collection, analysis, equipment, and hiring research assistants. Without funding, it is challenging to conduct meaningful research.
- *Career Advancement.* Securing research funding can lead to career advancement. Many universities and institutions consider a professor's ability to attract research grants as a key factor in promotion and tenure decisions.
- *Independence and Academic Freedom.* Research funding can provide a level of independence, allowing professors to pursue their research interests and questions without being overly constrained by departmental or institutional priorities.
- *Professional Development.* The process of writing research proposals teaches valuable skills, such as project management, budgeting, and clear communication. These skills are transferable and can benefit a professor's overall career.

- *Networking*. Preparing grant proposals often involves collaboration with colleagues, both within and outside the institution. This can lead to valuable networking opportunities and partnerships that can enhance a professor's research and teaching.
- *Contribution to Knowledge*: Funded research contributes to the body of knowledge in a particular field, which is a fundamental aspect of academia. It allows professors to make meaningful contributions to their discipline.
- *Student Engagement*. Research projects funded by grants can often involve students, providing them with valuable research experience and mentoring. This can enhance the professor's reputation as an educator.
- *Institutional Reputation*. Successful grant acquisition can enhance the reputation of both the professor and the institution. It reflects positively on the professor's ability to secure external support and the institution's research capabilities.
- *Sustainability*. Continuous research funding helps sustain a professor's research program over the long term, ensuring he or she can pursue a research agenda that spans years or even decades.
- *Competitive Advantage*. In an increasingly competitive academic environment, the ability to secure research funding can set a professor apart from their peers. It demonstrates a commitment to research excellence.
- *Extra Compensation*. In order to encourage faculty to submit proposals for external funding, many universities have policies which allow extra compensation for the proposer who can obtain resources from funding agencies and organizations. This is typically is the form of percentage of the total funding, or fixed amount equivalent to teaching a number of courses, usually stated in the institution's policies.
- *Support University's Infrastructure*. Externally secured funds for research help pay for the proposer's university infrastructure that supports the proposer at various stages, from proposal writing to technical support. Payment is usually in the form of "overhead" expenses, usually between 10% and 50% of the estimated cost of the proposed study that the proposer must include in the proposal.

The importance of writing good proposals is attested to by the efforts of universities to teach their faculties proposal writing skills and the support they offer to them for proposal writing in various forms (e.g., workshops, seminars, online).

14.3.1 Solicited Proposal

Solicited proposals are submitted in response to a specific solicitation issued by a sponsor. Such solicitations, typically called Request for Proposal (RFP), or Request for Quotation (RFQ), are usually specific in their requirements regarding format and technical content and may stipulate certain award terms and conditions. Such proposals normally have fixed timelines for submission and project completion. Major consideration of the agency's evaluators includes the proposer's competence and reputation related to the topic of the proposal, the institution's infrastructure (e.g., proposer's support team), requested budget, and completion timeline.

14.3.2 Unsolicited Proposal

Unsolicited proposals are submitted to a sponsor that has not issued a specific solicitation request but is believed by the investigator to have an interest in the subject. The structure of such proposals varies, but they all include the basic elements of a proposal: The importance of the problem or research question and its relevance to the funding agency, the purpose of the proposed investigation, the research approach and methods appropriated for the research question, and expected findings and their importance to the funding agency. As with the solicited proposals, the competence of the investigator(s) is critical and so is the credibility of their supporting institution. The unsolicited proposal should also include the proposed study's "deliverables" (e.g., report, presentation, data), expected time required for completion, and detailed budget. An example of such a proposal is shown in Appendix 14.2.

14.4 Corporate-Sponsored Proposal

A corporate-sponsored proposal is typically for applied research rather than an academic study, although applied research in some cases can also be of interest to academic journals. Applied research aims to address practical problems or issues and produce solutions or actionable recommendations. It is often used in fields such as engineering, medicine, and business to solve real-world problems. A proposal for such research is funded either by a single corporation, and usually takes the form of a proprietary research study, or by several companies that share the results of the proposed study that is commonly known as "syndicated study." A syndicated study, also referred to as a syndicated research or syndicated market research, is a type of research study conducted by a market research company or organization with the goal of gathering and analyzing data on a specific industry, market, or topic. Unlike proprietary research, which is commissioned and conducted for a specific client or organization, syndicated studies are conducted independently and made available to multiple clients or subscribers.

Corporate-sponsored studies are rarely conducted by individual faculty members interested in using the study's data and findings for academic purpose. This is in part because data from such studies tend to be unsuitable for publication in academic journals or because academic investigators cannot receive permission from the study's sponsor(s) to use these data for publication. However, academic institutions often conduct corporate-sponsored studies through specialized units, such as research centers and institutes, in much the same way commercial research firms provide research services for a fee.

14.4.1 Proprietary or Customized Research Proposal

Institutions and professors who develop expertise in conducting certain types of research are likely to be approached by organizations that want to use their services.

They are invited to submit a proposal for research, usually after they are informed about the research problem or purpose of the study; and they frequently must discuss extensively the research study needed with company staff and even sign a "nondisclosure" statement prior to such discussions. And professors or centers can conduct the study either by using company resources (e.g., employees, data collection), in which case the investigator(s) act(s) as consultant(s), or do so independently. In either case, a proposal needs to be prepared by the investigator(s) that should include the following:

- The scope of the study
- Research objectives, with great detail and specificity
- Type of study or studies (if more than one type—e.g., focus groups, online survey, telephone survey), including details on sample(s) (size, type, sampling frame, etc.)
- Costs, broken down by activity (e.g., data collection, editing, processing, analyses) and unit (e.g., per focus group, completed interview)
- Fee for the investigator(s)' services and out-of-pocket expenses (e.g., travel), and payment schedule (payment for costs of the study upon acceptance of the proposal); for investigator's fee upon delivery/presentation of the final report/results
- Timeline for completing the study
- Date of interim or progress report
- Study "deliverables" (e.g., report, presentation, data)
- Timeline for follow-up questions/clarification of study findings
- Date the data will be available to the investigator(s) for academic publications (optional)
- Expiration date of the proposal

Suggestions (a) Offer to the sponsor(s) option to negotiate investigator(s)' fee by allowing them to include extra questions for academic study (e.g., extra questions, pages or minutes).
(b) Negotiate the use of data for academic purposes after a number of years, if suitable for publications, for a lower fee.
(c) **NEVER** recommend course of action in the form of policy or strategy based on research findings of your study.

Early career researchers who decide to undertake a proprietary or *any* corporate-funded study on their own while employed by a university must consider their university's policies and potential conflict-of-interest issues before developing a proposal. First, they normally must request from their units (e.g., department, college) permission to engage in outside activities; and they must describe these activities and their duration, as well as the recipient(s) of these services. Second, they must be careful to avoid using any university resources for a study their university is not formally involved with, such as students assigned to them by their units for research assistance. Universities may allow their faculty to pay for using their facilities and resources for "personal" reasons, but this should be approved prior to proposal development. Third, in instances where the researcher would be allowed by the sponsor of the study to use the data for publication on a later date, this should be formally stated and accepted by the sponsor of the study and the researcher's unit. Finally, early career researchers should keep in mind that studies that do not lead to publications in respected journals can be time-consuming and take away time the investigator could have spent on academic projects; and they can have adverse effects on the researcher's productivity and progress toward promotion and tenure.

14.4.2 Multi-sponsor or Syndicated Research Proposal

Syndicated studies are normally conducted by research firms and sometimes by university specialized research units such as research centers. Nearly every research firm can do a market study on any topic (there is no license requirement) and the vast majority of them do not specialize on any particular topic. As such, university-based centers that specialize on researching particular topics have an edge in terms of expertise and credibility. And professors who are affiliated with research centers also enjoy such benefits. However, research firms have the required resources to conduct studies prior to finding companies to pay for them. This is not the case with university centers, which must have the resources to pay for required research expenses before they conduct a syndicated study.

With costs of research studies rising, research service providers are trying to ensure syndicated research studies are profitable before they conduct or propose them. To this end, they become increasingly selective and focus on studies that are likely to be purchased or funded by a large number of clients. Specifically, they spend time examining market trends and needs of the potential users of findings of these studies before committing resources. This section discusses an effective approach to proposal development for a syndicated study by a university center, as early career researchers are relatively more likely to be involved in such a study via a center rather than commercial firm. I draw upon my lengthy experience in conducting syndicated studies by working as consultant for a commercial research firm and as the founding director of the Center for Mature Consumer Studies (CMCS).

During my early years of my academic career, I was retained by an Atlanta-based research firm, Payment Systems, Inc. (PSI, a subsidiary of American Express at that time), to assist with studies of interest to financial institutions and retailers in general. I and my co-researcher, late Thomas J. Stanley, both Associate Professors of Marketing at Georgia State University (GSU), would develop proposals for, and direct, syndicated research studies of affluent American consumers' financial habits. We would use published and proprietary data compiled by PSI staff to identify market and financial industry trends, as well as trends in technologies used in delivering such services (e.g., early stages of the Internet); and we would assess information needs of potential users of such information for developing research proposals. These proposals would be sent by PSI to potential users, inviting them to participate in the proposed studies by paying a substantially lower price than the actual cost of the national mail surveys. Once PSI would secure enough sponsors to cover all costs and target profit, the study would commence. The reports on the results of the studies would be made available to additional companies, at a higher price shortly after completion of the study and at a gradually decreasing prices as the data were becoming dated. If there were not enough sponsors of the proposed study by a specified date, PSI would return the funds to those who had paid. My co-researcher and I had an arrangement with PSI, allowing us to use the large databases for academic publications after a certain number of years.

I applied this model of syndicated research proposal as soon as I founded CMCS. With limited funds from donations and book loyalties, I first did a mail survey of several hundred marketing managers of US companies in a dozen major industries, asking them to indicate their needs for information when marketing to older consumers. Based on results of these surveys, I developed proposals for potential sponsors of national surveys in each industry. The main information needs of the marketing managers were incorporated into a few questionnaires. The results of the surveys were widely publicized via mainstream media and industry publications and were used to develop more than a dozen industry reports on the consumption habits of older Americans; and they were sold to a large number of organizations, generating funds to support doctoral dissertations, pay for the director's time, hire research assistants, and provide salary supplements to my Department's staff.

Potential sponsors of syndicated studies are not likely to be as demanding as those in academics with respect to basic elements of a standard research proposal. These individuals normally want to know three things: What they are going to learn from the study that they don't already know, when they will know (study completion), and how much will cost. With these parameters in mind, early career researchers who are interested in working alone or with others who support research activities of centers should develop proposals using the guidelines below.

Problem and Objectives

- State the problem or research question within a narrow context, as narrow as possible (as it may apply only to a particular industry).
- Specify the research objectives in the form of knowledge to be gained that can help in policy or strategy development.
- For objectives where the value of information is not clearly related to policy or business decision, briefly explain why the knowledge to be gained is important and how it could be used

Method

- Keep in mind that the proposal likely will be read only by individuals who are not researchers.
- Avoid the use of academic jargon and technical terms.
- Keep this section brief and to the point; and state what you are going to do to accomplish your objectives (e.g., survey, focus groups), not how you are going to do it and why.

Expected benefits

- State exactly what the reader will learn from this study—i.e., the specific types of information, which should relate to the study's objectives.
- Elaborate on the final report and its contents that you will prepare, in a way easy for a person who is not a researcher to understand.
- Describe other "deliverables," such as oral presentation of results to all sponsors during a conference upon the completion of the study (certain date and place), data availability, and access to the Center's researchers for a reasonable period after the study.

Cost (estimate the study's average cost if conducted by a consulting or research firm):

- Before completion of the study—30% of the estimated average cost
- Within 1 year after completion—50% of the estimated average cost
- Within 2–3 years after completion—30% of the estimated average cost
- Within 4–5 years after completion—10% of the estimated average cost

Personnel and resources (names, titles, and positions of the Center's staff who will be working on the study; for each state their credentials and experience with previous similar studies and a possible link to their CVs):

- Director
- Associate Director(s)
- Data analyst(s)
- Writer(s) and copy editors (s)
- Technical support team (University's staff)

Timelines

- *Study to begin on or before:*
- *Progress report on or before:*
- *Estimated completion of the study by:*
- *Post-study period for clarification of study results ends on:*

Note: Proposers of corporate-sponsored applied research should be cognizant of the value of the data generated by these studies. They normally do not generate data suitable for publications in highly theoretical and methodological journals. A sample of publications is shown in Appendix 14.3 to help the early career researcher determine the desirability of using data from corporate-funded studies.

Appendix 14.1: Suggested Outline and Length of Dissertation Proposal

Introduction (6–10 pages, about 2–3 pages per section below)

(a) A write up on the importance of the topic and its relevance to various audiences.
(b) Identify gaps in knowledge and needed research
(c) Purpose and objectives

Background (10–12 pages, should contain at least 1–2 pages on each of the following sections below). It includes literature review.

(a) Brief discussion of your concept (a condensed version of your concept explication—see Chap. 4)
(b) Conceptual or theoretical framework and how/why it is relevant to your proposed study; and it should relate to your concept and purpose of your study (for quantitative proposals). Literature review related to your topic may serve as a source for theory development and data interpretation (in proposed qualitative studies).
(c) Focus on select variables derived from theory as potential explanatory factors for your topic (concept) of interest (for quantitative proposals).
(d) Statement of some key hypotheses (for quantitative proposals). If possible, state your hypotheses in the context of a graphic figure/model.

Methods (12–15 pages)

(a) Research approach and design (see Chap. 6)
(b) Methods and procedures: Sampling/informants, data collection methods used, designing experiments, manipulation checks, pre-tests, etc. (see Chap. 7).
(c) Variable measures (cite sources for using existing measures)—validity & reliability; and coding procedures (see Chap. 7)
(d) Analyses and results or data interpretation (analytic tools, such as regression, ANCOVA, MANOVA).
(e) Statistical tests of significance to be used for hypothesis testing (for quantitative studies, tests such as F-test).
(f) Method of data integration (for mixed method research design (see Chap. 7).

Expected contribution (about 4–5 pages should summarize what is to be learned from this study that is not already known). Identify your proposed study's intended contribution, if it is going to be (see Chap. 10):

(a) Theoretical (like offering new or competing explanation to existing problem, specify the conditions an existing theory explains a phenomenon—e.g., the role of mediating or moderating variables?).
(b) Conceptual (would it be an improved conceptual definition, which usually involves the development of a new measure?)
(c) Empirical (Are you going to offer answer to a research question?)
(d) Methodological (Are you proposing a new method/approach to address a new or existing problem, if so, how do you propose to show the superiority of your proposed method?).

Research ethics. The proposal should include details on steps the proposer will take to ensure s/he will follow the institution's required procedures (e.g., receiving permission to use students as subjects) and professional standards for conducting the prosed study and writing articles for publication in academic journals (e.g., proper citation).

References, figures, tables., appendixes (about 10-12 pages)

Note: Ensure that your dissertation proposal is well-structured, free of grammatical errors, and aligned with the guidelines provided by your academic institution. Seek feedback from your advisor or committee members to refine your proposal before submission.

Appendix 14.2: Sample of Unsolicited Research Proposal

Social Sustainability: Preserving and Enhancing the Well-Being of Present and Future Generations

A new type of thinking is essential if mankind is to survive and move toward higher levels—Albert Einstein

by

1. Dr. Randall Shannon, Assistant Professor of Marketing, CMMU, Mahidol University.
2. Dr. George P. Moschis, Adjunct Professor and director of the Consumer Life-course Studies Group, CMMU, Mahidol University; and Alfred Bernhardt Research Professor, Georgia State University, USA.

Research Rationale

Since the 1980s, the concept of sustainability has shifted towards a focus on human sustainability on Earth. The most widely cited definition of sustainability, proposed by the United Nations' Brundtland Commission on March 20, 1987, emphasizes that sustainable development meets the present needs without compromising the ability of future generations to meet their own needs. A concise interpretation suggests that sustainability involves enhancing "the quality of human life while staying within the carrying capacity of supporting ecosystems." Beyond this, sustainability entails responsible and proactive decision-making and innovation to minimize negative impacts and maintain a balance between ecological resilience, economic prosperity, political justice, and cultural vibrancy, ensuring a desirable planet for all species both now and in the future. This concept is encapsulated by three dimensions: environmental sustainability, focusing on the capacity to sustain rates of renewable resource harvest, pollution creation, and non-renewable resource depletion indefinitely; economic sustainability, addressing the ability to support a defined level of economic production indefinitely; and social sustainability, concerning the ability of a social system, such as a country, to function at a defined level of social well-being indefinitely.

Challenges like sustainability have persistently eluded resolution across generations. The inability of problem solvers to address issues of this nature stems from a lack of root cause analysis. This oversight has resulted in solutions that may seem plausible intuitively but, in practice, prove ineffective as they do not tackle the fundamental causes of a problem. Despite the dedicated efforts of numerous activists, the global ecological footprint continues to escalate year after year, decade after decade. The prospect of achieving environmental sustainability is continually questioned in the face of environmental degradation, climate change, and excessive consumption.

Intuitively, the three dimensions of sustainability are interconnected and mutually influential. For instance, economic development contributes to societal overconsumption, which in turn impacts the environment. Consequently, to effectively address sustainability issues, attention must be directed towards all three dimensions. However, the predominant focus of previous endeavors aimed at addressing sustainability has been limited.

In this proposed research, we take a more comprehensive approach to tackling sustainability challenges. Rather than viewing the problem solely as a matter for corporations or governments, we recognize it as a societal issue. Human beings, acting as consumers and decision-makers in various capacities, bear significant responsibility for their behaviors, which impact not only their present and future well-being but also that of future generations. Moreover, these individual actions influence the actions of governments and corporations, thereby having implications for sustainability. Our perspective aligns with others who address sustainability issues, although we go beyond by proposing concrete actions. For instance, Thwink.org contends that the objective of Homo sapiens is, or should be, to optimize the quality of life for current and future generations. Implicit in this perspective is the idea that individuals should take responsibility for their own welfare and that of their descendants. This raises two important questions:

What actions should humans take to accomplish this goal?

How do we instill, or go about changing, behaviors that optimize the quality of life of present and future generations?

The need for every country to address these questions is pressing and timely, especially considering the Earth's population growth. The current global population of 7.3 billion is projected to increase to 8.5 billion by 2030, 9.7 billion in 2050, and 11.2 billion in 2100, as per the United Nations report, World Population Prospects: The 2015 Revision. It is crucial that we comprehend the anticipated demographic changes in the coming years and recognize the challenges and opportunities they pose for achieving sustainable development, utilizing our planet's resources efficiently, and preserving or enhancing the quality of life.

These challenges are gaining significance due to the Earth's aging population—the most significant demographic shift in human history. Currently, around 650 million people are over the age of 60 globally, a number expected to nearly quadruple to over 2 billion by 2050. The older age brackets will experience an even more rapid increase. While the rise in the percentage of older individuals over the next decades is a global trend, developing countries are anticipated to undergo more pronounced changes in age composition. The older population in developing nations is predicted to grow by 200–300% over the next 30 years. For instance, in China, the older population (aged 60 and over) is expected to double to nearly 400 million in about 30 years. In certain developing countries like Thailand, the rate of increase in the older population is projected to be seven to eight times higher than in industrialized nations like the United Kingdom and Sweden, according to United Nations estimates. In Asia, the population is expected to shift from having 11% to 12% of people over 60 years old today to more than 25% by 2050. Asia, with greater declines in fertility, has smaller percentages of children (24%) and youth (16%).

These demographic shifts are impacting the governments, institutions, and individuals of every country. They are placing strain on pension funds and healthcare systems and are resulting in economic ramifications that influence economic growth, savings, and investments. Furthermore, they are influencing families and giving rise to concerns such as elderly caregiving, family structure, living arrangements, and the quality of life in old age.

In summarizing our argument and rationale for the proposed research, addressing issues related to the quality of life for present and future generations within the confines of limited resources necessitates considering human agency. People must take greater responsibility for their own well-being and that of future generations. Successfully tackling such a formidable challenge involves understanding individuals as consumers of increasingly scarce resources, educating and motivating them to adopt behaviors that discourage overconsumption, and enhancing their well-being as well as that of future generations over an extended lifespan. This argument forms the fundamental theme of the recent research orientation in academia known as "transformative consumer research."

Research Objectives

To propose corporate and public policies fostering values and habits promoting sustainability across generations with longer lifespans, it is essential to comprehend the development and transformation of behaviors.

Consequently, the primary goal of the suggested research is to address two key questions:

1. How do consumers cultivate socially responsible consumption habits that sustain and enhance well-being throughout their lives?
2. What factors contribute to the transition from undesirable consumer habits at various life stages to socially desirable ones that enhance well-being over a lifetime?

Given the multitude of socially desirable habits pertinent to sustainability and well-being, ranging from general lifestyles (e.g., preventive healthcare) to socially responsible consumption activities (e.g., recycling), it is impractical for a single study to cover all relevant behaviors. Initially, we propose two studies concentrating on areas pertinent to personal well-being: one on preventive healthcare and another on financial habits. This choice is grounded in the following reasons:

(a) Health and financial independence are pivotal contributors to an individual's sense of well-being, particularly in later life stages.
(b) With the increasing life expectancy of people, a larger percentage will contend with chronic conditions that impede physical independence. Adopting preventive healthcare habits enables an older person to function independently, especially given the declining numbers of caregivers due to changing demographics and social values (e.g., a decrease in multi-generational living arrangements).
(c) The diminishing availability of future caregivers for aging individuals, rising healthcare costs due to increased life expectancy, and the desire for a well-lived later life (e.g., recreation) necessitate financial habits throughout one's life to enhance overall quality of life.
(d) In contrast to values and behaviors established early in life that change little over time (e.g., overconsumption, materialism), the adoption and alteration of preventive healthcare behaviors and financial habits can occur at any stage during adulthood, facilitating their study across multiple generations.
(e) Because similar studies are being planned concurrently on these topics in 10 other countries around the globe, the results from the proposed study in Thailand would allow comparison with those in other countries and allow for validation of the study findings.

Methodology

To accomplish our objective, the study of a wide range of consumers would be necessary. The study of younger respondents would be necessary in order to uncover the reasons for the onset of socially desirable habits (preventive healthcare and financial habits) in early life that promote wellbeing in later life. The study of older respondents would allow us to assess the wellbeing (life satisfaction) of those who engaged in socially-desirable behaviors over a longer time in their lives, and validate our assumptions that these habits enhance quality of life in later years. The study of middle-aged would allow us to examine reasons that lead to the onset or change in preventive healthcare and financial habits. Such information would be useful in designing programs that promote the onset and continuity in such behaviors.

To achieve these objectives, we suggest adopting the life-course approach, offering a unified methodological framework for individual country research projects. The life-course approach presents a sophisticated framework for empirical research without imposing specific substantive queries on researchers whose regional and national contexts may differ significantly. Consequently, individual researchers can formulate specific questions tailored to their local circumstances while still sharing a common and broader perspective on the relationship among key variables. The life-course approach also promotes the utilization of diverse data collection techniques and analyses, spanning from traditional life-history and qualitative approaches to some of the most advanced and newly developed methods of longitudinal data gathering and statistical analysis.

Scope of the Project/Study Population/Study Site

We are proposing 2 (two) large-scale surveys in Thailand, surveying adult respondents, ages 20 and older.

Online Survey 1: The onset and changes in preventive healthcare habits of three generations/cohorts: Cohort A, ages 20–40; cohort B, ages 41–60; and cohort C, ages 61 and over. A total of 900 adults will be surveyed, 300 from each age cohort.

Online Survey 2: The onset and changes in financial habits of three generations/cohorts: Cohort A, ages 20–40; cohort B, ages 41–60, and cohort C, ages 61 and over. A total of nine hundred (900) adults will be surveyed, 300 from each age cohort.

Name of Researchers

Randall Shannon, CMMU (a.randall@gmail.com

George Moschis, CMMU & GSU, gmoschis@gsu.edu

Benefits/Indicators

The proposed project would have several tangible benefits:

1. The findings of the proposed research will be used to provide the bases—i.e., a blueprint or prototype of methods—for developing of a research program in Thailand that would begin to generate information on a continuous basis and

serve as a source for novel corporate and public policy. Such information could provide the foundation for developing educational materials (e.g., courses, curricula) at schools and universities to help instil values and behaviors in young people; and it could help companies in developing strategies for rewarding socially-desirable behaviors of employees and customers, as well as for promoting the importance of consumer behaviors that enhance social sustainability and the quality of life of present and future generations.

2. The results would allow cross-country validations of our theories about the onset, continuity, and changes in socially-desirable behaviors that promote and enhance social sustainability. They will be compared with the results of similar surveys that are presently at the planning or implementation stage in other Asian countries (China, Korea, and Malaysia), as well as in other countries (USA, Holland, and Brazil).
3. Based on cross-country validation of the results of the proposed study of Thai adults, a blueprint for further studies will be made available (published in the form of modules) through CMMU's based Consumer Life-course Studies Group, to guide future studies by Thai educational institutions, government, and other interested parties on a variety of social sustainability issues or topics using similar populations as well as younger age groups.

Duration of the Project

We propose a duration of eight months from the date the project is funded. We can either run the project's surveys back to back, or we can run them concurrently.

Plan (Per Study)

Three focus groups, one from each cohort—three weeks in total

Questionnaire development, translation, back-translation, pilot testing—three weeks

Data collection, coding and data entry, data cleaning—three months

Data analysis—two months

Report and module—one month

Total: roughly eight months

Budget (Per Study)

We plan to hire a company to help facilitate data collection by providing email addresses. This involves helping find the potential respondents, facilitating the interviews, data collection, coding, data editing and processing. We will also need to translate and back translate the questionnaires into Thai and test for meaning equivalence, including pilot testing.

For each study, with a sample size of 900, we anticipate requiring a budget of approximately 600,000 baht, including incentive to participants.

Suggested fee for translation and back translation: 10,000 baht.

Focus groups among three cohorts, 20,000 baht for each, times three: 60,000 baht.

We propose hiring at least two research assistants to help with these projects, and would very much like to conduct focus groups before kicking off the large scale surveys. 15,000 per month for each assistant, times eight months. Total: 240,000 baht.

Ethics approval, anticipated 10,000 baht.

Development and printing of modules (1000 copies × 300 baht): 30,000.

Total budget requested: 955,000 baht per study.

Appendix 14.3: A Sample of Articles Based on Data from Corporate-Funded Studies

*Bellenger, D. N., Kennett, P., & Moschis, G. P. (1995). Marketing Financial Services to Mature Consumers. *Journal of Financial Services Marketing, 9*(2), 62–72.

*Foreman, J., Moschis, G., & Burkhalter, J. (2010). Gerontographics and Mass Media Preferences of Mature Consumers. In *4th International Conference Proceedings*. American Institute of Higher Education, Williamsburg, VA, March 17–19, 745–754.

Goldstucker, J. L., Moschis, G. P., & Stanley, T. J. (1986). Possible Effects of Electronic Shopping on Restructuring of Distribution Channels. *International Journal of Retailing, 1*(1), 20–32.

Goldstucker, J. L., Stanley, T. J., & Moschis, G. P. (1984). Will Consumer Acceptance of Videotex Services Affect Marketing? In *Proceedings of the Annual Educators' Conference*. Chicago: American Marketing Association, 200–204.

*Guillory, M., & Moschis, G. P. (2008). Marketing Apartments, Townhouses, and Condominiums to Seniors. *Senior Housing & Care Journal, 16*(1), 31–51.

*Kennett, P., Moschis, G. P., & Bellenger, D. N. (1995). Marketing Financial Services to Mature Consumers. *Journal of Financial Services Marketing, 9*(2), 62–72.

Korgaonkar, P., & Moschis, G. P. (1987). Consumer Adoption of Videotext Services. *Journal of Direct Marketing, 1*(4), 63–71.

Lumpkin, J. R., Gibler, K. M., & Moschis, G. P. (1992). Perceptions and Preferences of the Aged. *Australian Health and Aged Care Journal*, October, 66–68.

*Mathur, A., & Moschis, G. P. (1999). Exploring the Intergenerational Caregiver Market: A Study of Family Care Providers for the Elderly. *Journal of Marketing Theory & Practice, 7*(3), 76–86.

*Mathur, A., & Moschis, G. P. (1999). Socialization Influences on Preparation for Later Life. *Journal of Marketing Practice: Applied Marketing Science*, 163–167.

*Moschis, G. P. (2003). Marketing to Older Adults: An Updated Overview of Present Knowledge and Practice. *Journal of Consumer Marketing, 20*(6), 516–525.

*Moschis, G. P., Bellenger, D. N., & Curasi, C. (2005). Marketing Retirement Communities to Older Consumers. *Journal of Real Estate Practice and Education, 8*(1), 99–114.

*Moschis, G. P., Bellenger, D. N., & Curasi, C. (2003). Financial-Service Preferences and Patronage Motives of Older Consumers. *Journal of Financial Services Marketing, 7*(4), 331–340.

*Moschis, G. P., Bovell, L. (2013). Marketing Pharmaceutical and Cosmetic Products to the Mature Market. *International Journal of Pharmaceuticals and Healthcare Marketing, 7*(4), 357–373.

*Moschis, G. P., Burkhalter, J. (2007). Making Ends Meet: How Will the Elderly Manage their Finances and Post-Retirement Expenses? *Journal of Financial Services Marketing, 12*(3), 235–241.

*Moschis, G. P., Curasi, C., & Bellenger, D. (2003). Restaurant Selection Preferences of the Mature Market. *Cornell Hotel and Restaurant Administration Quarterly, 44*(4), 51–60.

*Moschis, G. P., Curasi, C. F., & Bellenger, D. N. (2004). Patronage Motives of Mature Consumers in the Selection of Food and Grocery Stores. *Journal of Consumer Marketing, 21*(2), 123–133.

*Moschis, G. P., Curasi, C. F., & Bellenger, D. N. (2003). What Influences the Mature Consumers? *Marketing Health Services*, 17–21.

*Moschis, G. P., Ferguson, J., & Zhu, M. (2011). Mature Consumers' Selection of Apparel and Footwear Brands and Department Stores. *International Journal of Retail and Distribution Management, 35*(10), 785–801.

*Moschis, G. P., Friend, S. (2008). Segmenting the Preferences and Usage Patterns of the Mature Consumer Health-Care Market. *International Journal of Pharmaceutical and Healthcare Marketing, 2*(1), 7–21.

*Moschis, G. P., Nguyen, H. V. (2008). Affluent Mature Consumers: Preferences and Patronization for Financial Services. *Journal of Financial Services Marketing, 13*(3), 259–267.

Moschis, G. P., Stanley, T. J. (1983). The ATM-Prone Consumer: Profile and Implications. *Journal of Retail Banking, 5*, 45–51.

Moschis, G. P., Stanley, T. J. (1984). Home Information Systems: Recent Developments and Implications. In *Proceedings of the Winter Educators' Conference*. Chicago: American Marketing Association.

Moschis, G. P., Stanley, T. J. (1984). America's Affluent. *American Demographics*, Spring 1984.

Moschis, G. P., Stanley, T. J. (1985). Will Consumers Let Computers Do the Walking? *Business Horizons, 28*(2), 22–29.

*Moschis, G. P., Unal, B. (2008). Travel and Leisure Services Preferences and Patronage Motives of Older Consumers. *Journal of Travel and Tourism Marketing, 24*(4), 259–269.

*Moschis, G. P., Weaver, T. (2010). Segmenting Demand for Long-term Care Services among Mature Consumers. *Services Marketing Quarterly, 31*(1), 106–115.

Stanley, T. J., Moschis, G. P. (1983). Flawed Surveys, Field Trials May Overstate Positive Consumer Acceptance of Videotex. *Marketing News, November 25, 1983*, 18–19.

Stanley, T. J & Moschis, G. P. (1984). America's affluent. *American Demographics*, 6(3), 28–33.

Stanley, T. J., Moschis, G. P., & Danko, W. D. (1987). Financial service segments: The seven faces of the affluent market. *Journal of Advertising Research*, 27 (4), 52–67.

Asterisk (*) denotes articles based on CMCS data.

15 Epilogue

A successful and satisfying academic career largely impinges on one's ability to conduct and publish academic research. In this book, I have maintained that successful academic publishing depends on two important sets of skill: ability to conduct credible research and ability to "package" your research for readers' consumption. I have argued that much of the formal training of academic researchers in doctoral programs focus on research methodologies, largely ignoring the training for academic publishing. Skills at publishing are likely to be developed through experience over relatively longer time. The main purpose for writing this book is to help close the gaps in research and publication skill disparities between early career researchers and those with experience, as well as among researchers with different levels of preparation for academic research and publishing.

Achieving greatness in academic research is a long journey that can last as long as one's academic career, especially if effectual strategies are employed at different stages of academic life and one keeps abreast and continuously capitalizes upon trends and developments that affect the researcher's ability to conduct and publish academic research. This last chapter is divided into two parts. The first part summarizes my views on how to achieve greatness in academic research, focusing on strategies for generating effectual research; and the second part presents my views on the present state and future of academic research, focusing on recent developments and trends that continuously present new opportunities and challenges to academic researchers for creating knowledge required to address new problems.

15.1 Book's Main Messages

This section summarizes some of the most pertinent recommendations that I want to get across to early career researchers. I emphasize the steps that can help you on your path to becoming an accomplished academic researcher. I am offering my most salient recommendations relevant to different stages in the person's academic

G. P. Moschis, *Academic Research in Business and the Social Sciences*,
https://doi.org/10.1007/978-3-031-56548-9_15

life, focusing on preparation and early stages, including effectual strategies and tactics.

If you contemplate pursuing a doctoral degree, keep in mind that doctoral programs tend to prepare researchers for an academic career. Assess your motivation for getting such a degree, as the process is very demanding and likely will change your lifestyle during your studies; and there is always a high likelihood you will not be successful at it, even after investing substantial time and financial resources. If you have doubts, take time to make a decision. As I served in the role of doctoral program director for my department for 15 years, I would try to make prospective applicants, as well as those at early stages in the program, aware of the requirements, demands, and sacrifices involved in the process of pursing this degree.

In the interest of the readers who are ambivalent about their decision or career goals, the book offers guidelines to help them make more informed decisions. One set of guidelines is relevant to those who are either contemplate entering a doctoral program or are at early stages and consider switching to another university. And another set of guidelines is relevant to those seeking employment upon graduation or are at early stages of their career and must decide whether to stay at their present position or seek a more desirable employment option.

I would often mention to my doctoral students not only the demands for the successful completion of the doctoral program, but also the requirements for a successful academic career. But I would also emphasize the benefits and frequently mention the results of a study of individuals in various occupations in half a dozen countries, where researchers asked them: "If you had to choose an occupation again, would you choose the same one?" College professors were by far the group that gave a positive answer to this question, with nearly 90% of them responding in the affirmative.

For those who make the commitment to pursuing a doctoral degree and have yet to choose a university or are already at early stages of a program, the suggestion is to ensure they choose, or transfer to, an institution that has a department whose faculty members have been publishing. It is extremely important for doctoral candidates to have access to a large number of faculty members who are not only well-known in the academic community for their research specialties and contributions, but also continue to be productive researchers. And most important is their accessibility to students, including the provision of opportunities to students to work with them in various roles (e.g., research assistants, advisees, collaborators on projects). In my experience, such opportunities are inversely related to faculty ranks, with more likely to be found in Assistant Professors and fewer in Full Professors. Yet, a faculty member's long-term availability is likely to be greater among senior than junior faculty members.

15.1.1 Need for Multifaced Preparation

Doctoral students preparing for an academic career that emphasizes research should benefit from taking courses in research methods and academic writing, to the extent they have access to such courses within their departments, institutions, or other universities. At a very minimum, they should be exposed to standard quantitative methods, including structural equation modeling (SEM), experimental research, and various traditions of qualitative methodologies. A course in writing and/or editing should also be included in the requirements. Beyond these courses, coursework in fields related to their major concentration, such as psychology, sociology, humanities, philosophy, statistics, and journalism or mass communication, would be helpful.

Besides formal training, preparation for an academic career that emphasizes research should include collaborative work with others in the same or different program, even in other disciplines, depending on opportunities. Working with productive faculty, observing and emulating their work habits, approaches to research, writing styles, and mindsets could be of great benefit. Also, of great benefit to the student would be writing *anything* for peer evaluation or submission to an academic outlet. It could be in the form of a short review of the literature in areas of interest to the student or a paper based on a small-scale quantitative or qualitative study (e.g., a case study). Exposure to the required tasks for crafting academic research papers and going through the manuscript submission, review, and revision processes would be a great learning experience for the student.

Early in the doctoral program, informal preparation should also include your personal assessment of your competencies, interests, and newly acquired skills. The goal should be to develop an understanding of your strengths and weaknesses and to do so by aligning your readings on topics parallel to those of interest to potential advisors or supervisors of your dissertation. Upon beginning their doctoral studies, students should be aware of the fact that they are frequently evaluated by faculty members of their department. Those who appear to show the greatest potential for successful completion of the program are the most likely to be sought after by faculty members of their department for various faculty supporting roles, such as research assistants and even collaborators on research projects. This suggests to first-year doctoral students the importance of creating favorable perceptions that underscore their dedication, commitment, interests, and abilities to completing their doctoral program requirements and being successful in their academic career. To many faculty members, doctoral students serve not only as potential co-authors of their dissertations but also as potential collaborators in future years. Active associate professors are those most likely stable in their position and most interested in serving on dissertation committees.

As doctoral students at late stages in their program, they should seek opportunities that allow them to understand the publication process by, for example, writing and submitting manuscripts to journals. They should familiarize themselves with the criteria reviewers use to evaluate a manuscript's contribution; and they should learn to conduct and position studies along these criteria. And they should also become familiar with common flaws that often form the bases for manuscript rejection, learning to proactively address them in conducting research and crafting their manuscripts.

15.1.2 Effectual Research Approaches and Strategies

Strategies during early career years should focus on producing a large number of publications (as discussed in Chap. 13), for the purpose of demonstrating potential for a successful research-based academic career. At this relatively short stage in the person's academic career, early career researchers should explore every possible opportunity for publication with collaborators. Also, as they are getting ready to make the transition into the "high impact stage" (discussed in Chap. 13), they should begin to evaluate research areas and topics for conducting programmatic research. They should be considering research areas and topics that:

(a) Are at a growth stage in their "life cycle," as shown by the relatively few publications in these areas.
(b) Are likely to have long "life cycles" due to sustainable trends in factors that are likely to promote the need for research for several years.
(c) Are under-researched, or topics where the present demand for information exceeds supply—i.e., several research questions remain unanswered.
(d) Are likely to be of interest to a wide range of groups of readers because they have potential to make substantial contributions to both knowledge and practice.
(e) Are aligned with the researcher's interests and expertise.

Another message this book has attempted to get across to readers has been the importance of programmatic research. As I mentioned earlier in this book, I would stress the importance of programmatic research in my research seminars to students and faculty by stating my belief that it is more important to have five sole- or senior-authored publications on a single topic in major journals in one's field than have 25 such publications on 25 different topics in the same journals in their *entire* academic career. Staying focused helps the researcher develop the image of an expert on a particular topic, while having a single publication on any topic does not project expertise in any particular area. You should also realize that a programmatic research strategy might not help you maximize your h-index, but I assume you want to be known as a scholar who is known for creating knowledge in some area rather than an ad hoc researcher who is not known for anything in particular because he or she prioritizes h-index maximization.

Although not easily achievable, early career researchers should strive to publish sole- and senior-authored articles in top journals in their respective fields. Such publications show qualities of leadership and independence in research. By contrast, having only co-authored publications, especially few sole-authored, conveys the image of a researcher who cannot do research or publish without the help of others. Anecdotally, some universities do not even put much credence to sole-authored articles out of one's dissertation, as the author likely received a great deal of assistance from several experts serving on his or her dissertation committee. Absence of sole-authored publications in top journals is not viewed favorably by evaluators in universities that have high standards in granting promotion and tenure to members of their faculty.

The importance of quality writing has been mentioned in several places of this book. Research findings and ideas that are not properly "packaged" are not likely to be appreciated by readers for their importance and relevance to theory and practice. Well-crafted manuscripts are easier for readers to enjoy reading; and they create the impression that something interesting is conveyed to them, although the information contained may not have much substance. Writing for academic journals is a skill that is developed with practice, and many suggestions for quality writing made in this book can help expedite its development.

Academic research is a global endeavor that often requires scholars to conduct studies in foreign countries to advance knowledge and address research questions. While cross-national research can be intellectually rewarding, it also presents unique challenges and risks in addition to those present in local or national studies. A chapter in this book has explored the complexities of conducting academic research in foreign countries, shedding light on the hurdles researchers may encounter and offering strategies to overcome them. Yet, based on the materials presented in this book and my experience in conducting dozens of cross-cultural studies, my recommendation to early career researchers is to avoid this type of research because of its potentially inherent risks. They should focus their research only on national studies, at least until they become confident that they have the necessary skills, knowledge, and resources for conducting effectual cross-cultural studies.

15.2 Keeping Abreast of Trends and Developments

A critical aspect of academic research is that it evolves in response to the changing landscapes of several factors, such as technology, data availability, and methodologies. These changes affect academic researchers in two important ways. First, they create opportunities for research to address new problems and issues; and in many cases they create opportunities for programmatic research as in the case of the Internet. Because research activities and publications tend to be demand-driven, researchers who are among the first to capitalize on research opportunities that are the result of changes or new developments have an advantage. Their manuscripts are likely to be well-received in part due to the relatively limited published research on the new topic, issue, or method, relative to the need for information; and they are likely to be evaluated favorably, as the reviewers familiar with the topic are likely to be limited in numbers or not as well informed as the manuscript authors. Manuscripts on new topics, methods, and developments often help inform reviewers, many of whom may not be very familiar with, or as knowledgeable as, the authors about the subject matter. One benefit of being a reviewer is to stay current on research in his or her area(s) of interest, without having to keep up with every publication on a particular topic.

Second, changes and new developments in many areas tend to affect the manner in which researchers conduct and publish research studies. Keeping abreast of changes enhances the likelihood of manuscript acceptance, while not keeping up with new developments can adversely affect publication likelihood. For example, the methods of testing for mediation and moderation proposed by Baron and Kenny (1986), which were widely accepted for several years, are considered outdated because of the development of more effectual methods (Clement & Bradley-Garcia, 2022; Hayes, 2018). These trends reflect the evolving nature of academic research. To stay up to date, it is essential to follow reputable academic journals, attend conferences, and engage with research communities in various roles, both online and in person.

15.2.1 Technological

New technologies are changing the landscape of academic research and publishing. They are affecting the way researchers conduct and assess literatures, collect and analyze data, and even write manuscripts. Several technological developments have been affecting academic researchers and their work, creating opportunities for innovative ways of conducting and publishing academic studies:

Crowdsourcing Technology has made it easier for researchers to engage the public in data collection and analysis, expanding the scope of research projects and involving a broader range of participants. The percentage of academic research studies that use Internet samples can vary significantly depending on the field of study, the research objectives, and the availability of appropriate samples. However, the use of Internet samples in academic research had been on the rise due to the increasing accessibility of online platforms and the potential for larger and more diverse samples. It is quite common in fields such as psychology, sociology, and marketing. For example, 43% of the studies that were published in the 2015–2016 volume of the *Journal of Consumer Research* used data collected online nearly 10 years prior to the publication of this book (Goodman & Paolacci, 2017). The exact percentage of studies using Internet samples would be difficult to quantify accurately without specific and up-to-date data. However, it is safe to say that the use of Internet samples has been a significant and growing trend in academic research.

When conducting surveys, experiments, or observational research in some areas of social and behavioral sciences, Internet samples can be a convenient and cost-effective way to gather data from a wide range of participants. This approach is particularly useful when studying online behaviors or when the research questions do not require a specific in-person or geographically constrained sample. The prevalence of Internet samples likely has been increasing due to the ongoing expansion of online research methods and tools. Researchers must always consider the advantages and limitations of using Internet samples in their studies and choose the most appropriate sampling methods for their research questions and objectives.

Use of AI-Generated Research Generative artificial intelligence (AI) is starting to produce research papers and articles. This technology is being used not only for data analysis but also for automating certain aspects of research, such as literature reviews, experimental designs, and even hypothesis generation. And it is being integrated into various academic fields, from healthcare to environmental science (e.g., Javidan et al., 2022; Jimma, 2023). Researchers are using these technologies to analyze vast datasets, make predictions, and discover new patterns. For example, data collection and analysis are facilitated by AI tools (ChatGPT, Otter.ai, Yabble and Atlas.ti) employed as research teammates (Mollick & Mollick, 2023). Similarly, researchers can use AI-based natural language processing (NLP) tools as a teammate (Mollick & Mollick, 2023) for audio-to-text interview transcription, translating non-English interviews and finally for auto-coding in thematic analysis. And Easterby-Smith et al.'s (2021) seven-step guide can be used in data analysis protocol. While this technology can be a valuable tool for data analysis, it also raises questions about authorship, quality control, and the future of researchers.

Other Technological Developments The Internet and digital libraries have made it easier for researchers to access a vast amount of information and research papers, enabling them to stay up to date with the latest findings in their fields. Online databases, journals, and open-access resources have revolutionized the way researchers gather information. Technology has facilitated the sharing of research findings and data through open-access journals, preprint servers, and collaborative platforms.

Technology has transformed the way researchers collaborate and communicate with their peers globally. Video conferencing, online collaboration platforms, and cloud-based tools have made it easier for researchers to work together and share their findings. Blockchain technology has been explored for ensuring the integrity and authenticity of research data, especially in fields where data provenance and security are critical.

The advent of big data technology has allowed researchers to analyze massive datasets, uncover patterns, and derive insights that were previously impossible to obtain. This has been particularly transformative in fields like social sciences and environmental science. And AI and machine learning techniques have been applied to various research areas, from natural language processing for text analysis to image recognition for medical diagnoses. These technologies help automate data analysis and discover hidden patterns in large datasets. Supercomputers and high-performance computing clusters enable researchers to perform complex simulations, run computationally intensive experiments, and solve intricate mathematical problems. Advanced lab equipment, such as DNA sequencers and mass spectrometers, has become more efficient and precise.

Specialized software tools and applications are available to aid researchers in various tasks, from data analysis and visualization to experiment control and data management. These tools enhance the efficiency and accuracy of research. Additionally, lab automation tools have improved the accuracy and reproducibility of experiments in fields like biology, chemistry, and materials science. Virtual reality (VR) and augmented reality (AR) have found applications in education and training, allowing researchers to create immersive simulations and environments for experimentation and data visualization.

These changes come with a host of ethical issues, which are increasingly becoming of concern to educational institutions, publishers, and the academic community as a whole; and they are likely to continue in the years to come, as they are driven by new technological developments, creating additional opportunities for research that could generate information useful in legislation and corporate policy.

15.2.2 Global Developments

Global Aging We are currently observing one of the most significant demographic transformations in human history: The aging of the global population. While developed countries presently have and will continue to have the largest share of elderly populations, it is worth noting that by 2050, 70% of the world's elderly will be residing in developing regions (Moschis, 2022). This demographic change is affecting virtually every individual on our planet, along with governments and institutions. All nations are starting to experience the consequences of the aging population as the increasing number of older adults strains pension and healthcare systems. This demographic shift is leading to economic implications that impact economic growth, savings, and investments. Additionally, this trend is influencing families and raising concerns related to elderly care, family structures, living arrangements, and the quality of life in one's later years. There are also considerations related to new business opportunities arising from the "maturing marketplace," resulting from shifts in the age composition of markets and their purchasing power. This demographic trend will continue to create opportunities for research on aging consumers.

Crisis Research Researchers are increasingly studying and developing strategies to address global crises, such as pandemics (Suttharattanagul et al., 2022), natural disasters (Rakrachakarn & Kohlbacher, 2020; Sneath et al., 2009), and economic challenges (Moschis et al., 2020). The ability to respond quickly to these crises has become a critical research area. Researchers have begun to develop conceptual frameworks for studying these crises (e.g., Campbell et al., 2020). DeWaard (2016) and Moschis (2021) offer the life course approach as a viable framework for studying global crises. Such frameworks will be needed to help advance research in this area.

Sustainability and Climate Change Research on sustainability and climate change has gained immense prominence. This includes studies on renewable energy, climate modeling, and sustainable agriculture (e.g., Haider et al., 2022). Sustainability entails responsible and forward-thinking decision-making and innovation aimed at minimizing adverse impacts and maintaining equilibrium among ecological resilience, economic well-being, political equity, and cultural vitality, with the goal of ensuring a desirable environment for all species, both now and in the future. Its essence can be encapsulated in three core dimensions: *environmental sustainability*, which involves the ability to sustain renewable resource utilization, curb pollution, and prevent non-renewable resource depletion on an ongoing basis; *economic sus-*

tainability, which relates to the capacity to sustain a defined level of economic productivity indefinitely; and *social sustainability*, encompassing the ability of a social system, such as a nation, to consistently function at a defined level of social well-being over time.

Challenges like sustainability have persisted without resolution for generations. Despite the earnest efforts of countless committed activists, the world's ecological impact continues to rise. There is an urgent need to address sustainability at all three levels, as the three dimensions of sustainability are intricately interconnected and mutually influence one another. However, previous attempts to tackle sustainability problems have often been limited and narrowly focused, creating research opportunities to address sustainability holistically.

15.2.3 Academic Research

Early career researchers should be familiar with trends and recent developments in academic research that are likely not only to create new opportunities for research but also affect the way they will be conducting studies and, consequently, their research productivity. This section highlights several trends and developments in academic research.

Increase in Global Collaborations The Internet has made it easier for researchers from around the world to collaborate on projects. International partnerships and research networks are growing, enabling the pooling of expertise and resources. International collaborations are becoming more common. Researchers are working across borders, sharing resources and expertise to tackle a wide variety of research questions. Collaborative research often yields innovative and impactful results. Building professional relationships can lead to collaborations, mentorship, and new opportunities.

Interdisciplinary Research The boundaries between academic disciplines are becoming increasingly blurred. Many of the most exciting developments are happening at the intersection of different fields, such as bioinformatics (biology and computer science) and neuroeconomics (neuroscience and economics). Researchers are collaborating across disciplines to address complex, multifaceted problems. This approach requires adapting and blending research methodologies from various fields. These technological advancements have not only accelerated the pace of academic research but have also expanded the possibilities for interdisciplinary collaborations and the exploration of new research questions. However, they also present challenges related to data security, ethics, and the need for ongoing skill development among researchers to effectively leverage these tools.

Multi-theoretical Models Increasing interdisciplinary collaboration among researchers promotes the use of multi-theoretical approaches to research and facilitates the development of multi-theoretical conceptual frameworks. This trend can be seen in several areas of behavioral and social sciences; and it has been spilling over into applied fields, affecting the way researchers conduct research for theory development, policy, and practice. For example, the life course paradigm (LCP) (e.g., Elder et al., 2003), which has been called, "one of the most important achievements in social sciences in the second half of the 20th century" (Colby, 1998, p. *x*), has grown in popularity in recent decades as an over-arching multi-theoretical research framework that spans conceptual and theoretical boundaries of behavioral and social sciences (e.g., Billari, 2009; Moschis, 2019). The LCP has seen applications in the applied fields of gerontology and business (e.g., Billari, 2009; Mathur et al., 2008; Moschis et al., 2020; Rowe & Kahn, 2015). And it has served as the basis for the development of the life course conceptual model (Moschis, 2007, 2019), which has been applied to the study of a wide variety of topics in the fields of marketing, healthcare, and personal finance (e.g., Mathur, 2019, 2020; Moschis, 2021). Early career researchers should become familiar with such developments because they are likely to be increasingly employing, developing, and revising multi-theoretical conceptual frameworks that are likely to become even more popular in the future.

Literature Reviews Academic research has exponentially increased in recent decades (Thelwall & Sud, 2022), creating demands for reviewing an increasingly larger number of published research. New software programs make it easier for researchers to conduct more literature reviews, such as bibliometric studies, systematic reviews, and meta-analyses; and they help researchers synthesize existing research, identify trends, and provide evidence-based insights. For example, the use of bibliometrics is gradually expanding to all fields of science, and new software are contributing to its rapid expansion (Aria & Cuccurulo, 2017; Jimma, 2023). Similarly, researchers are conducting more systematic reviews, as additional methods for such reviews become known to researchers, helping them fine-tune their searches and analyses (Xiao & Watson, 2019). These developments are crucial in evidence-based decision-making in fields like medicine, business, and social sciences. Although these trends are likely to continue in the future, the researcher's skills and experiences will continue to play a key role in analyzing and synthesizing previous works and building theories and models.

Early career researchers will be increasingly contacting literature reviews as they will be expected to publish in outlets that are also increasing in numbers. To contact effectual reviews, they will have to evaluate larger numbers of relevant publications that will require extra time and affect their productivity. Consequently, researchers will be forced to develop strategies for reviewing large number of materials relevant to their reviews; and they should stay informed on developments in software programs that would help them become more efficient (for some examples, see Chap. 2, Sect. 2.5).

Open Access and Open Science There is a growing push for open access to research publications and data. This trend promotes transparency, accessibility, and collaboration in academia. Researchers are increasingly sharing their work openly to promote innovation and knowledge dissemination. There is a growing emphasis on ensuring the reproducibility of research. This involves sharing data, codes, and methods openly to allow others to verify and build upon research findings.

Mixed Methods and Multiple Studies Combining qualitative and quantitative research methods is gaining popularity. Researchers are using both approaches to gain a more comprehensive understanding of complex phenomena. In a similar vein, journals are increasingly looking for articles that contain credible research results that are more likely to be achieved with multiple methods and multiple studies, which require extra resources, research skills, and journal space. These trends are likely to foster greater collaboration among researchers, in the interest of efficiency and diverse skills required; and they are likely to force researchers to develop skills at condensing manuscripts.

Remote and Online Research The COVID-19 pandemic accelerated the adoption of remote and online research methods, including virtual interviews, surveys, and experiments. New technologies are likely to enable researchers to obtain information from individuals and household from databases where information about people's activities will be stored and used for commercial and research purposes. Such information will be more accurate and would give researchers additional tools and methods to better accomplish research objectives; and they could help overcome limitations inherent in present methods of data collection. For example, researchers will be able to replace methods of obtaining information retrospectively with data that was accurately collected and stored in databases, reducing errors and improving data quality. These methods are likely to become increasingly popular in the future, placing greater demands on early career researchers to develop skills at not only collecting data remotely but also keeping well-informed of technological developments and learning to effectively employ the new methods. And early career researchers will need to continuously learn about these technological developments and know how to employ these platforms to increase their research efficiency and productivity.

Citizen Science Citizen science, also known as community science or public participation in scientific research, is an approach in which members of the general public, who may not have formal scientific training, actively participate in scientific research projects. These volunteers, often referred to as "citizen scientists," collaborate with professional scientists to collect and analyze data, make observations, and contribute to various scientific studies. The involvement of citizen scientists can significantly expand the scale and scope of research efforts, enabling scientists to collect data from a larger geographical area or over an extended period of time. Online platforms and mobile apps have made it easier for people to participate in these projects and share their observations and data with the scientific community.

Research Ethics and Responsible Conduct There is a renewed focus on research ethics and responsible conduct, including issues related to consent, privacy, and the ethical use of data, especially in light of increased data collection and sharing. With the increasing reliance on data-driven research, issues related to data ethics, privacy, and security have become more critical. Researchers are working on solutions to protect individuals' data while advancing epidemic scientific knowledge. And they will be forced to be more transparent in conducting and reporting their research, as well as sensitive to ethical issues (see Chap. 12).

The Role of Metrics The journal impact factor has become an "epidemic" in academics, along with other similar impact factors such as author citations (h-index). Editors now expect authors to cite in their manuscripts articles that have appeared in their journal as suggestion or requirement for manuscript publication. While editors used to be discrete in their requests years ago, they are now openly admitting to the reason for asking authors to do so. For example, I have been advised by numerous journal editors in recent years to cite articles that appeared in their journals as a condition (stated as "a strong suggestion") for accepting my manuscript; and even to cite articles had no clear relevance to my manuscript! Apparently, this is a widespread practice, because a recent survey of researchers, which I was also asked to complete, attempted to investigate this "phenomenon." Such factors tend to affect the evaluations of journals and faculty who publish in them, although it is increasingly recognized in academia that reported sizes of impact scores cannot be completely accurate because of such practices.

15.3 Personal Insights

15.3.1 Effects of Technology

Technology is likely to affect the way researchers conduct and publish studies. It is likely to affect academic research because of two major changes it has been creating: (a) changes in people's lives and (b) changes in the ways academic researchers conduct and publish studies.

Changes in People's Lives Artificial Intelligence (AI) is already influencing people's behavior in various ways, and its impact is expected to grow in the coming years. The following are ways in which AI has been affecting or likely to affect individuals:

- Enabling businesses to analyze large amounts of data about individual consumer preferences and behaviors. This information is then used to tailor products, services, and recommendations to meet the specific needs and preferences of each consumer. Personalized recommendations on e-commerce platforms, streaming services, and social media are common examples of AI-driven personalization.

- Chatbots and virtual assistants powered by AI are becoming increasingly sophisticated. They can provide instant and personalized customer support, answer queries, and assist with purchasing decisions. Consumers may interact with chatbots on websites, through messaging apps, or even through voice-activated virtual assistants like Amazon's Alexa or Google Assistant.
- Contributing to improved user experiences by predicting user preferences and streamlining interactions. For example, AI algorithms may optimize website layouts, suggest relevant content, or customize app interfaces based on user behavior. Natural language processing (NLP) allows for more intuitive interactions with technology, enabling voice commands and conversational interfaces.
- Businesses use AI-driven predictive analytics to anticipate consumer trends and behavior. This allows companies to adapt their strategies, optimize inventory, and better meet consumer demands. Consumers may experience more accurate product recommendations, timely promotions, and a better availability of products and services.
- Increasingly more efficient and streamlined processes in various industries are driven by AI automation. This efficiency can result in cost savings for businesses, which may, in turn, influence pricing and value propositions for consumers. For example, in retail, automated inventory management and supply chain optimization can contribute to more competitive pricing and improved product availability.
- The same technology is playing a crucial role in enhancing cybersecurity by detecting patterns indicative of fraudulent activities. This helps protect consumers from identity theft, financial fraud, and other security threats. Consumers may experience increased security measures, such as biometric authentication and advanced fraud detection mechanisms.
- Tracking and analyzing health-related data via wearable devices and health apps. This can provide consumers with personalized insights into their well-being and offer suggestions for healthier lifestyles, with AI-driven health monitoring leading to more informed and proactive healthcare decisions.

While AI offers numerous benefits, it also raises ethical considerations, including privacy concerns, algorithmic bias, and job displacement. As AI continues to evolve, it will be crucial to strike a balance between leveraging its capabilities for consumer benefits and addressing associated challenges. Additionally, regulations and ethical guidelines will play a significant role in shaping the impact of AI on consumers' behavior.

The Future of Academic Research These trends reflect the dynamic and evolving nature of academic research, as it adapts to the opportunities and challenges of our modern world. Researchers are continually seeking innovative approaches to answer complex questions and contribute to the advancement of knowledge. The future practice of academic research, including the skills required and the manner in which researchers conduct studies, will be largely influenced by changes in people's lives and the available technologies. Most likely, we will see:

- Greater use of databases that contain information about individuals and households, coupled with decreasing emphasis on collecting the same type of information using surveys.
- Development of skills that help researchers integrate information about individuals from different databases, synthesize, and analyze information from these sources to address research questions.
- Because of the continuous increase in the number of published studies on every topic and availability of data collected via nontraditional methods, researchers will be increasingly relying on existing information rather than collecting new data to address research questions. Reliance on existing databases for addressing research questions will likely increase the importance of literature reviews.
- Increase in the use of emerging technologies for data collection and analysis (e.g., generative AI).
- Researchers likely will need to have diverse research skills, including skills at conducting online interviews, analyzing, and synthesizing data from different sources and databases.
- Advanced sensors, data analytics tools, and machine learning algorithms will significantly enhance the efficiency and accuracy of data collection and analysis. Researchers will be able to process large datasets more quickly and uncover patterns that might be challenging to identify manually.
- The availability of high-performance computing resources will enable researchers to tackle even more complex computational problems and simulations. This is particularly beneficial in fields where simulations are crucial for understanding phenomena.
- Technology will continue to facilitate collaboration among researchers, regardless of geographical locations. Virtual collaboration tools, video conferencing, and collaborative platforms make it easier for researchers to work together, share findings, and engage in real-time discussions.
- Technology will keep playing a key role in the rise of open-access publishing and open science initiatives. Online platforms and repositories make it easier for researchers to share their work with a global audience, fostering transparency and collaboration within the scientific community.
- Laboratory automation and robotics have been contributing to more efficient and reproducible experiments. Automated systems can handle repetitive tasks, freeing up researchers to focus on more complex and creative aspects of their work.
- Digital libraries and archives will keep on providing researchers with increasingly easy access to a wealth of scholarly resources. Online databases, e-journals, and repositories make it simpler to discover and retrieve relevant literature, saving time and expanding the breadth of research.
- Social and professional networking platforms designed for researchers have been helping to increase visibility, collaboration, and networking. Researchers can connect with peers, share their work, and stay informed about the latest developments in their field.
- Artificial Intelligence (AI) and machine learning techniques will continue to assist researchers in pattern recognition, data interpretation, and hypothesis gen-

eration. These technologies have the potential to revolutionize fields ranging from biology and medicine to social sciences.
- Technology has been increasingly facilitating citizen science projects and crowdsourcing initiatives, allowing researchers to engage a broader audience in data collection and analysis. This can lead to large-scale and innovative research projects with diverse contributions.
- Advanced visualization tools, including virtual reality (VR) and augmented reality (AR), will increasingly aid in data representation and interpretation.

While these advancements offer tremendous opportunities, it is important for researchers to stay mindful of potential challenges, such as the digital divide, ethical concerns, and the need for ongoing education to adapt to evolving technologies. Additionally, interdisciplinary collaboration between researchers and technology experts is increasingly valuable in navigating the integration of new technologies into academic research effectively.

15.3.2 Emerging Opportunities for Programmatic Research

My personal recommendations for future research rely heavily on criteria outlined earlier in this chapter and illuminated in greater detail in Chap. 4. They have been formed by integrating recent trends and developments, and subsequent demand for information, with recent developments in life course methodologies in social and behavioral sciences. As mentioned in this book, the life course approach, which is briefly discussed in Chap. 13, is an interdisciplinary framework that examines the ways in which various social, historical, and cultural factors influence individuals' lives from birth to death. It emphasizes the importance of considering the interconnectedness of different life stages and the impact of social structures on individual development. Thus, I recommend areas for programmatic research, which in my opinion are likely to be in great demand, by suggesting the employment of the life course approach for addressing issues in these areas.

Sustainability and Mindful Consumption Sustainability typically refers to actions that meet "the needs of the present without compromising the ability of future generations to meet their own needs" (Purvis et al., 2019: 684); and mindful consumption means "having consciousness in thought and behavior about consequences of consumption" (Sheth et al., 2011: 27), with consciousness reflected in mindful mindset and mindful behavior. The former refers to an underlying sense of caring for all (self, community, and the environment), while mindful behavior is a motive of temperance in various forms of acquisitive consumption (e.g., not buying beyond one's needs). Such acquisitive behaviors have implications for sustainability because they relate to minimizing waste, pollution, and environmental degradation and conserving natural resources (Mathur & Moschis, 2023). Thus, mindful consumption leads to sustainable consumption.

In a recent article (Moschis et al., 2020), we suggest one major approach to sustainable consumption lies in managing demand that would require changes in people's present consumption habits that are excessive. We further maintain that in order to change consumption habits, one must understand the factors to lead to their onset and change; and we explain how the life course paradigm can be employed as a research framework for studying the onset and change in consumption habits. A more recent study suggests the value of using the life course approach for studying mindful consumption (Mathur & Moschis, 2023). The study results highlight the mechanisms responsible for the development of mindful consumption habits that promote sustainability.

Sustainability in consumer behavior is a multifaceted area that intersects with environmental science, economics, psychology, and public policy. Using the life course conceptual framework and data analysis methods suitable to life course research (e.g., Moschis, 2019), researchers could investigate several topics:

- Study the reason(s) people engage in excessive consumption.
- Examine the onset of mindful buying practices. Understand the reason(s) people begin engaging in mindful buying and sustainable consumption.
- Examine the factors that influence consumers to make sustainable choices. This includes studying the role of values, beliefs, attitudes, and personal motivations in driving eco-friendly and socially responsible purchasing behavior.
- Investigate the factors that promote continuity and discontinuity in mindful buying.
- Study the role of various socialization agents in shaping attitudes toward excessive and mindful buying.
- Explore how different sources of information (e.g., advertising, peer recommendations, certification labels) impact consumers' perceptions of sustainability and their purchasing decisions. Analyze the credibility and effectiveness of various information channels.
- Examine the role of packaging in consumers' perception of sustainability. Investigate the impact of eco-friendly packaging, labeling practices, and the potential for reducing waste in product packaging.
- Examine the economic implications of a shift toward mindful buying and sustainable consumption. Analyze the potential benefits for businesses adopting sustainable practices and the role of government policies in incentivizing sustainable production.
- Explore the effectiveness of behavioral interventions in promoting sustainable consumption. This may include the design of nudges, incentives, and gamification strategies to encourage eco-friendly choices.
- Investigate psychological barriers that hinder consumers from adopting sustainable behaviors. This may include studying perceived inconvenience and the psychological distance between consumers and the environmental consequences of their actions.

- Investigate cultural differences in attitudes toward sustainability and mindful buying. Explore how cultural factors shape consumer behaviors, values, and priorities related to environmental and social responsibility.
- Explore technological solutions for sustainable shopping. Examine how technology, such as mobile apps, blockchain, and augmented reality, can facilitate and enhance sustainable shopping experiences.
- Investigate the level of awareness among consumers regarding sustainability issues. Explore effective strategies for educating consumers about the environmental and social impacts of their purchasing decisions.
- Investigate the factors influencing consumers' preferences for sustainable brands. Explore the impact of brand reputation, corporate social responsibility initiatives, and transparency in shaping consumer loyalty.
- Explore consumers' understanding and acceptance of circular economy practices, such as recycling, upcycling, and product lifecycle considerations. Investigate ways to encourage circular consumption patterns.
- Examine the role of social influence and social norms in promoting sustainable behavior. Investigate how peer pressure, social networks, and community engagement can drive mindful buying practices.
- Investigate the long-term impact of sustainable consumption on environmental conservation, social equity, and global well-being. Assess the potential for a shift in consumer behavior to contribute to broader sustainability goals.

By delving into these aspects, researchers can contribute to the understanding of sustainable consumption patterns, provide insights for policymakers and businesses, and guide the development of interventions that promote more mindful and eco-conscious consumer behavior.

Individuals' Interface with New Technologies In looking at individuals' interface with new technologies, several aspects merit investigation. These aspects span various disciplines, including human-computer interaction, psychology, sociology, and ethics. It is evident that new technologies have a profound impact on people's behaviors. Below are several ways in which emerging technologies are changing the way individuals behave, helping create a research agenda:

- Investigate factors influencing the adoption and acceptance of new technologies within the life course conceptual model. This should involve the study of not the mere adoption of the new technology by the person but the *timing* of its adoption since (a) its introduction and (b) one's awareness of the particular technology using hazard models (e.g., Moschis, 2019).
- Evaluate how individuals interact with new technologies in terms of usability and user experience. This includes assessing the efficiency, effectiveness, and satisfaction of users as they navigate and utilize different interfaces and platforms.
- Examine how individuals process information and build mental models when interacting with new technologies. Understanding cognitive load and mental

models can inform the design of interfaces that align with users' cognitive capacities.
- Investigate the accessibility of new technologies for individuals with diverse abilities and needs. This includes studying how interfaces can be designed to be inclusive, accommodating users with disabilities and ensuring equitable access for all.
- Explore individuals' perceptions of privacy and security in relation to new technologies. Investigate how users navigate privacy settings, their awareness of data collection practices, and the impact of privacy and security features on trust and adoption.
- Study the emotional and affective responses of individuals when interacting with new technologies. This includes exploring how interfaces evoke emotions, the impact of design elements on user mood, and the role of emotional engagement in technology use.
- Investigate the impact of technology use on individuals' well-being. This could involve studying screen time, the effects of social media, and strategies for promoting a healthy balance between technology use and other aspects of life.
- Examine how individuals learn to use new technologies and acquire digital skills. This may include studying the effectiveness of training programs, the role of feedback mechanisms, and the impact of interface design on skill development.
- Investigate how cultural and social factors influence individuals' interactions with new technologies. Explore cultural variations in technology adoption, the role of social norms, and how technology interfaces align with different cultural expectations.
- Study the long-term effects of technology use on individuals' behavior, cognition, and social relationships. This may involve longitudinal studies to understand how technology interfaces contribute to changes in lifestyle and societal dynamics over time.
- Investigate how rise of mobile devices and messaging apps has changed the way people communicate. Instant messaging, social media, and video calls have become integral parts of daily interactions, influencing the speed and frequency of communication.
- Examine how social media platforms have been shaping people's behaviors, from influencing opinions and preferences to impacting lifestyle choices. The pursuit of likes, shares, and comments can influence self-presentation and social validation.
- Study how the accessibility of information through the Internet and digital devices has transformed the way people consume news, entertainment, and educational content.
- The convenience of online shopping has changed consumer behavior, with more people opting for digital transactions. The study of this shift has implications for traditional brick-and-mortar retail, influencing purchasing habits and expectations.

- Wearable devices and health apps encourage individuals to monitor their health and fitness actively. This includes tracking physical activity, sleep patterns, and nutritional intake, fostering a more health-conscious lifestyle.
- Examine how streaming services, online gaming, and virtual reality have transformed how people access and engage with entertainment. Traditional TV watching has been supplemented, and sometimes replaced, by on-demand, personalized digital content.
- The adoption of remote work technologies has changed work behaviors, with more people working from different locations. Virtual collaboration tools influence team dynamics, communication practices, and work-life balance.
- The integration of smart home devices and automation technologies has changed how people manage their homes. From smart thermostats to voice-activated assistants, these technologies influence daily routines and home management behaviors.
- AR and VR technologies create immersive experiences that can influence behavior in areas like education, training, and entertainment. These technologies have the potential to redefine how individuals interact with their environment and virtual spaces.
- Examine how the increasing prevalence of cyber threats has changed individuals' behaviors concerning online security. Study people's awareness of the importance of securing personal data and use of strong authentication measures.
- The constant connectivity facilitated by smartphones and other devices has led to concerns about tech addiction. Study individuals who actively seek digital detox strategies to balance their online and offline lives.

Understanding these changes in behavior is essential for computer science researchers, developers, and policymakers. It helps ensure the responsible development of technologies, considering their impact on society and individuals' well-being. Additionally, addressing ethical considerations and promoting digital literacy are crucial aspects of adapting to and shaping these evolving behaviors.

Well-Being in Later Life Although many authors have stressed the significance of leading a fulfilling life in the later years, relatively less attention has been devoted to examining the existing and emerging factors influencing the well-being of older adults. The prevalent model used for studying the well-being of older adults has been the successful aging perspective (SAP), which concentrates on three components—functional capacity, health, and active engagement with life. This model can be considered within the broader life course paradigm (LCP). Social scientists (e.g., Stowe & Cooney, 2014), the creators of the successful aging model (Rowe & Kahn, 2015), and others (e.g., Prakitsuwan & Moschis, 2020; Prakitsuwan et al., 2022) have suggested the LCP as an overarching research framework that contextualizes the SAP. In a recent article, we provide updates on previously identified domains of older adults' well-being—namely, health, activity, and engagement—and underscore the significance of three additional domains: financial comfort, consumption efficiency, and technological competency (Moschis & Mathur, forthcoming).

While past approaches to studying older adults' life satisfaction have been integrated into and superseded by the life course paradigm (LCP), till recently this paradigm had yet to be operationalized as a conceptual research framework that researchers can utilize as a guide. Drawing from the revised conceptualization of older adult well-being, the recently developed life course-based conceptual framework and recent supporting research (discussed in Chap. 13), recommendations for policy and further research are presented to deepen our understanding and improve the quality of life for older individuals. There are numerous aspects of elderly well-being that are worth investigating by applying LCP tenets and paradigmatic principles to help understand the aging process and improve the quality of life for older adults. The following are several suggested areas of research:

- Investigate factors influencing physical health in older adults, including chronic conditions, mobility issues, and functional limitations. Explore interventions and lifestyle factors that contribute to maintaining or improving functional independence and overall well-being.
- Research mental health challenges such as depression, anxiety, and cognitive decline in older adults. Examine protective factors, intervention strategies, and the impact of social engagement, cognitive stimulation, and physical activity on cognitive function.
- Explore the importance of social connections, family relationships, and social support networks for the well-being of older adults. Investigate how social interactions contribute to mental health, emotional well-being, and overall life satisfaction.
- Examine subjective well-being in older adults, considering factors such as life satisfaction, happiness, and fulfillment. Investigate the role of personal attitudes, resilience, and adaptive coping strategies in promoting a positive quality of life.
- Investigate the economic aspects of well-being, including financial security, retirement planning, and the impact of socioeconomic factors on the overall well-being of older adults.
- Explore the influence of housing choices and living arrangements on the well-being of older adults. Investigate the impact of aging in place, assisted living, and other housing options on physical and mental health.
- Examine issues related to end-of-life care, including advance care planning, palliative care, and the role of healthcare decision-making in promoting dignity and autonomy for older adults.
- Investigate the role of nutrition and physical activity in promoting health and well-being among older adults. Explore the impact of dietary choices, exercise programs, and preventive health measures on physical and mental health outcomes.
- Explore how cultural backgrounds, ethnicities, and diverse life experiences influence the well-being of older adults. Investigate culturally sensitive approaches to aging, healthcare, and support services.

- Research the impact of technology on the well-being of older adults. Explore how technology can enhance social connections, provide healthcare solutions, and support independent living.
- Investigate the dynamics of intergenerational relationships and their impact on the well-being of older adults. Explore the role of family support, caregiving responsibilities, and the reciprocal benefits of intergenerational interactions.
- Explore the benefits of community engagement, volunteerism, and lifelong learning for older adults. Investigate how involvement in social and educational activities contributes to a sense of purpose and well-being.
- Research the importance of creating age-friendly communities and environments. Investigate how urban planning, accessibility, and community design can positively impact the well-being and inclusivity of older adults.

By investigating these aspects of elderly well-being, researchers and practitioners can contribute to the development of evidence-based interventions, policies, and practices that enhance the overall quality of life for older adults and promote successful aging.

Cross-Cultural Research Opportunities in cross-cultural research exist by using the life course approach to examine relatively unexplored and under-researched areas. This approach has been increasingly used in cross-cultural research to understand how individuals' lives unfold over time in diverse cultural contexts (e.g., Mathur, 2019, 2020; Moschis, 2019, 2021). Scholars can apply the life course approach to investigate how cultural norms, societal expectations, and historical contexts shape individuals' consumption orientations and trajectories across various cultures. Some key areas where the life course approach could be employed in cross-cultural studies include the following:

- The study of aging processes and intergenerational relationships, examining how cultural norms shape expectations and experiences related to aging, caregiving, and the role of older adults in society. Examine cultural variations in attitudes toward aging, family roles, and elder care.
- Examination of how cultural norms and values influence family structures, roles, and transitions across different societies. This may include studying the impact of cultural expectations on marriage, parenthood, and intergenerational relationships.
- Exploration of how cultural identity develops and evolves across the life course. This can involve studying the impact of cultural heritage, language, and socialization practices on the formation of individual and collective identities.
- Exploration of cultural variations in health beliefs, healthcare-seeking behavior, and perceptions of well-being. Investigation of the impact of cultural factors on coping mechanisms, and individuals' physical and mental health over time.
- Examination of how cultural factors influence the adoption and use of technology. Investigation of differences in attitudes toward digital privacy, preferences

for user interfaces, and the integration of technology into daily life across cultures.
- Researching how cultural values and norms shape consumer preferences, purchasing behavior, and brand loyalty. Exploration of the impact of cultural factors on advertising effectiveness and marketing strategies.
- Exploration of cultural variations in attitudes toward the environment, sustainability practices, and climate change awareness. Investigation of how cultural factors shape environmental policies and behaviors.

15.4 Last Thoughts and Reflections

15.4.1 The Value of Academic Research

Research projects usually begin either with a research question pertinent to practice that begs answer or with the development of a model or theory that seeks applications to practice. Each of these types has greatest relevance to practitioners and academics, respectively. Research that has high value in academics may not show clear relevance to practitioners, as the Stremersch et al.'s (2007) study suggests. Practitioners are likely to be looking for answers to context-specific empirical questions that would suggest a course of action. For example, in response legislators' interest in knowing if social media platforms such as Google and Facebook disseminate information that violates Section 230 of Communications Act, which gives social platforms immunity from liability for partisan disinformation, our recent research helps answer their question (Mathur & Moschis, 2022). It suggests repealing this section and treating these platforms as publishers or speakers of content provided by their users to help reduce the dissemination of political disinformation.

In contrast, academic researchers are interested in producing knowledge that is context-irrelevant; they are interested in generalizing their findings and understanding a phenomenon by addressing theoretical questions. With regard to our findings in the above-mentioned study, they would be interested in understanding the reason(s) social media are effective in dispensing partisan information; and they would employ theories of mass communication, or develop new ones, to provide explanation. This is not to say that legislators are not interested in understanding the reasons social media disseminate partisan information. Rather, they (and practitioners in general) are more interested in answering empirical questions than theoretical ones. I had such an experience during my lengthy tenure as the director of the Center for Mature Consumer Studies (CMCS). As I would talk to executives of various companies, government agencies, and nonprofit organizations in various forums and settings, I would hear them ask questions requiring empirical research, such as "how effective" a promotion stimulus is rather than "why is it effective." They wanted information that would suggest the action they should take to achieve certain results, not the reason(s) their actions would produce results.

Although academics have continuously attempted to produce high-quality research, much of their research appears to have had little value for practitioners. A comprehensible analysis of articles that had appeared in the top 5 marketing journal over a period of 12 years concludes: "Authors visible to academics are not necessarily visible to practitioners; and it remains questionable whether articles that academics assess to be of high quality are also managerially relevant" (Stremersch et al., 2007: 171). The primary factor contributing to the doubtful significance of academic research appears to be its limited perceived value among practitioners. This is partly attributed to the lack of clear relevance between much of academic research and the practical issues and decisions faced by practitioners.

Many topics in some fields of business and social sciences have become rather esoteric, because their findings are intended for, or understood by, only a small number of people with specialized knowledge or interests (Stremersch et al., 2007). Research that does not address business and social problems remains largely esoteric. And esotericism tends to be promoted even by some prestigious journals in these fields. The more prestigious the journal is, the more likely it invites research on topics that involve complex concepts and methods that are not easily accessible or comprehensible to practitioners and community that can benefit from research results. The analysis of the high impact research articles in the top marketing journals by Stremersch and associates (2007: 184) suggests that "articles that aim to have a high impact in marketing science may be different from articles that aim to have a high impact on marketing practice." Academics continue to research and write largely for academics. And although articles often report "implications" of research findings for practice, a main motivation for this is to enhance the article's value and "salability" by implying its relevance to practice.

To summarize, quality of academic research may not be of equal value to practitioners. It is of greater value to academics and their institutions because of the metrics they often are used to evaluate research quality of their faculty. And academic researchers are interested in performing in line with the expectations of their employers rather than those of potential users of their research findings. Although universities acknowledge that research performance is a complex multifaceted endeavor that cannot be assessed adequately by means of a single indicator (e.g., Martin, 1996), they continue to use performance metrics that motivate their faculty members to produce research that creates knowledge, although such knowledge may not have practical value.

15.4.2 The Tyranny of H-Index

There are obvious benefits and risks associated with research strategies as they relate to the h-index. Programmatic researchers are likely to downplay the importance of the index, emphasizing quality over quantity, while those who are driven by numbers that are promoted by an ad hoc research style are likely to favor this research metric. And regardless one's research philosophy and opinion of the validity of the h-index, every researcher is likely to consider the index as long as it is used in decisions concerning faculty hiring and promotion, as well as awards and allocation of resources.

I have learned from reading research related to the h-index that many Nobel Prize winners and esteemed professors had relatively low h-index scores—many in the 20 s and 30 s (Spicer, 2015). Einstein's score as of 2019 was 56 (Gingras & Khelfaoui, 2020). And many individuals with high h-index score may not have made impactful contribution to their discipline. The index increases as a function of the number of years a person has been publishing, the quantity of one's publications, the number of topics researched, and number of co-authors. One can maximize his or her h-index by increasing his or her research output, which can be facilitated by making efficient use of one's resources. This can be accomplished by using the following strategies:

- Publish in lower-tier journals, where it easier and less time consuming to publish.
- Co-author articles with as many researchers as possible, as the number of researchers is inversely related to each co-author's resources devote to the article.
- Look for opportunities to network with different groups of researchers to work on any topic than can lead to a co-authored publication.
- Use self-citations and ask your close friends and collaborates you to cite each other's work.
- Write more literature review articles for low-tier journals, as such articles tend to be easier to publish in these journals that are trying to increase their impact factor.
- Consult with editors of low-level journals and offer to do bibliometric reviews of articles published in those journals, helping raise their journal impact factor.
- Target low-tier and open-access journals that give short review times

There are obvious the potential negative consequences and limitations associated with the use and overemphasis of the h-index in academic and research contexts. While the h-index can provide a quick numerical summary of a researcher's output and influence, its overreliance can lead to several issues. For example, researchers might be incentivized to prioritize quantity over the quality of their work, as increasing the number of publications can boost the h-index. This may lead to a focus on producing more papers rather than ensuring each publication contributes meaningfully to the field. An overemphasis on this metric can lead to distorted incentives and hinder the diverse and nuanced aspects of academic and research contributions.

Researchers and institutions are encouraged to consider a broader set of indicators when evaluating scholarly impact (Martin, 1996). They should be placing less emphasis on h-index as the continuous employment of this metric can have negative effects on academics and science. If this approach to research continues to gain popularity, ambitious academics may increasingly view themselves as "h-index entrepreneurs" (Spicer, 2015). In such a scenario, universities would shift from being creators of knowledge to prioritizing the optimization of metrics. However, recent evidence suggests that the effectiveness of h-index as a measure of scientific reputation may be declining. Koltun and Hafner (2021) describe a recent comprehensive investigation utilizing scientometric measures, which involves the analysis of millions of articles and hundreds of millions of citations spanning four scientific disciplines on two data platforms. Their study reveals a significant decrease in the correlation between the h-index and awards indicating recognition within the scientific community. These changes are linked to shifts in authorship patterns in scientific community, including the rise of hyper-authorship.

As long as universities continue using the available objective metrics to assess research performance, researchers are likely to continue to prioritize maximizing citations, as is often the prevailing trend in numerous leading business schools. And there is limited optimism regarding the possible future change of academic research focus and accessibility of journals for practitioners. Despite the shared responsibility of journals and scholars to establish stronger connections with practical research applications, it raises doubts about whether universities and top journals will continue to offer accessible and comprehensible sources of new knowledge for practitioners (Stremersch et al., 2007).

15.4.3 What Are Your Research Aspirations?

Early in your career, you have to decide what you want to accomplish with your research, your goals and aspirations. Do you want to be known as "specialist" or "expert" on a particular topic, or do you want to be known as a "crackerjack of all kinds?" Do you want to be widely known as a researcher without any focus, not known for anything in particular but enjoy high visibility in the academic community? Or do you want to be known for something in particular? Because your decision is likely to affect your choice of research strategies that are effectual in accomplishing your research career goals and your research trajectory throughout much of your academic career. Each type of decision comes with different strategies that have rewards and inherent risks.

Early career researchers who wish to be known as specialists or experts on a particular topic would need to implement a strategy that promotes programmatic research. This means that they should try to do research exclusively in a particular area or on specific topic. And they should avoid publishing on other topics, when they have the opportunity to do so, because frequent publications outside their areas of expertise are likely to delude the researcher's image or identity in the eyes of one's colleagues and academic community. The programmatic researcher's networks and opportunities for collaboration would need to be confined to research that focus on his or her chosen topic(s). The limited number of networks and opportunities for collaboration are likely to also limit the number of articles you will produce, which would have adverse effects on your h-index of citations.

In addition, as a specialist, the concentration of your publications would be on the selected topic(s); most likely you will have relatively more sole- and senior-authored than junior-authored publications. And you may get relatively more citations per published article, which will not benefit your h-index beyond a certain number (Gingras & Khelfaoui, 2020). But as an expert on a particular topic, you may enjoy benefits such as invitations for speaking engagements at other universities and in business and community forums, and serving as an expert witness on litigation cases (one-way attorneys chose expert witnesses is by getting referrals from editorial offices of journals in your field).

In contrast, if your research aspirations are to be visible and achieve the highest possible h-index, your research strategies should be opposite to those employed by programmatic researchers. Specifically, you should try to increase your research productivity by employing the strategies outlined in the previous section of this chapter. These strategies are not likely to yield the benefits produced by a programmatic research strategy. In addition, you would run the risk of creating perceptions that you are not competent enough to do or lead research independently, without help from others, which can undermine your promotion and tenure if you are employed at a research-oriented institution.

In my view, each of these approaches to research has place in academics. However, it depends a great deal on the researcher's aspirations and their university's research expectations of its faculty. If one wants to be known for his or her research contribution to a particular area, develop the image of an authority on a topic, and secure positions in prestigious universities throughout his or her academic career, then emphasis should be placed on research quality over quantity via programmatic research. I can only advocate for the second approach under two different conditions. First, it could be more suitable to researchers who are early in their careers at less prestigious universities; it could help them demonstrate interest and ability to publish and have potential for impactful research, helping them to secure promotion and tenure. Second, it could be appropriate for researchers in institutions that do not have high or stringent research expectations of their faculties; and it could be most appropriate for universities which are trying to motivate their faculties to publish more in order to support new academic initiatives, such as doctoral programs, and increase their visibility globally.

15.4.4 Achieving Greatness in Academic Research

Early career researches should be keeping up with major developments that affect academic research by attending conferences, reading articles from various disciplines using online searchers, reviewing research papers of peers, and serving as journal reviewers of manuscripts related to their areas of interest. In addition, they should:

- Implement research strategies and tactics most suitable to their academic life stage, as suggested throughout this book.
- Continuously try to improve their article-writing skills.
- Incorporate new technological developments into their research for improving the efficiency and quality of their research.
- Seek opportunities for programmatic research.
- Become familiar with the various types and methods of literature reviews, including their purpose and objectives.

- Network and collaborate with other researchers. Use platforms such as CLSG (https://research.cm.mahidol.ac.th/research/index.php/clsg-home) that promote and facilitate cross-country collaborations.
- Work with researchers in other disciplines; and they should use multi-theoretical conceptual frameworks as foundations for their research.
- Use mixed methods, to the extent their research question or problem lends itself to these methods.
- Maintain the highest ethical standards in their research. Ethical conduct builds trust and credibility in their work.
- Show transparency, especially in their collaborative studies.

Achieving greatness in academic research is a long and challenging journey that requires dedication, perseverance, and a commitment to contributing meaningful knowledge to your field. It is hoped that this book has provided you with some tips and strategies that can help you on your path to becoming an accomplished academic researcher. And, above all, keep in mind the path that would guarantee you achieving excellence in academic research is loving and having passion for what you do.

References

Aria, M., & Cuccurulo, C. (2017). *Bibliometrix:* An R-tool for comprehensive science mapping analysis. *Journal of Infometrics, 11*(4), 959–975.

Baron, R., & Kenny, D. (1986). The moderator-mediator variable distinction in social psychological research. *Journal of Personality and Social Psychology, 51*, 1173–1182.

Billari, F. C. (2009). The life course is becoming of age. *Advances in Life Course Research, 14*(3), 83–86.

Campbell, M. C., Inman, J. J., Kirmani, A., & Price, L. L. (2020). In times of trouble: A framework for understanding consumers' responses to threats. *Journal of Consumer Research, 47*(3), 311–326. https://doi.org/10.1093/jcr/ucaa036

Clement, L. M., & Bradley-Garcia, M. (2022). A step-by-step tutorial for performing a moderated mediation analysis using process. *The Quantitative Methods for Psychology, 18*(3), 258–271. https://doi.org/10.20982/tqmp.18.3.p258

Colby, A. (1998). Foreword: Crafting life course studies. In J. A. Giele & G. H. Elder (Eds.), *Methods of life course research: Qualitative and quantitative approaches* (p. 540). Sage.

DeWaard, J. (2016). Disaster and life course processes. In M. Shanahan, J. T. Mortimer, & K. M. Johnson (Eds.), *Handbook of life course* (Vol. 2, pp. 321–340). Springer.

Easterby-Smith, M., Jaspersen, L. J., Thorpe, R., & Valizade, D. (2021). *Management and business research*. Sage.

Elder, G. H., Johnson, M. K., & Crosnoe, R. (2003). The emergence and development of life course theory. In J. T. Mortimer & M. J. Shanahan (Eds.), *Handbook of the life course* (pp. 3–19). Plenum Publishers.

Gingras, Y., & Khelfaoui, M. (2020). Why the h-index is a bogus measure of academic impact. The conversation published: July 8, 2020 7.52pm BST updated: July 10, 2020 3.17pm BST.

Goodman, J. K., & Paolacci, G. (2017). Crowdsourcing consumer research. *Journal of Consumer Research, 44*(1), 196–210. https://doi.org/10.1093/jcr/ucx047

Haider, M., Shannon, R., & Moschis, G. P. (2022). Sustainable consumption research and the role of marketing: A review of the literature (1976–2021). *Sustainability, 14*(7). https://doi.org/10.3390/su14073999

Hayes, A. F. (2018). *Introduction to mediation, moderation, and conditional process analysis: A regression-based approach* (2nd ed.). Guilford Press.
Javidan, A. P., Li, A., . Lee, M. H., Forbes, T. L. & Naji, F. (2022) A systematic review and bibliometric analysis of applications of Artificial Intelligence and machine learning in vascular surgery. Annals of Vascular Surgery, 85, 395-405. https://doi.org/10.1016/j.avsg.2022.03.019.
Jimma, B. L. (2023, March). Artificial intelligence in healthcare: A bibliometric analysis. *Telematics and Informatics Reports, 9*, 100041. https://doi.org/10.1016/j.teler.2023.100041
Koltun, V. & Hafne, D. (2021). The h-index is no longer an effective correlate of scientific reputation. *PLoS One, 16*(6):e0253397. https://doi.org/10.1371/journal.pone.0253397. PMID: 34181681.
Martin, B. R. (1996). The use of multiple indicators in the assessment of basic research. *Scientometrics, 36*(3), 343–362.
Mathur, A. (2019). George P. Moschis tribute special issue: His philosophy and contributions—Part I. *Journal of Global Scholars of Marketing Science, 29*(4), 359–371.
Mathur, A. (2020). George P. Moschis tribute special issue: His philosophy and contributions—Part II. *Journal of Global Scholars of Marketing Science, 30*(1), 1–3.
Mathur, A., & Moschis, G. P. (2022). The value of information sources in shaping political views: A comparative study of party supporters and undecided potential voters. *Journal of Advertising Research, 62*(2), 176–195.
Mathur, A., & Moschis, G. P. (2023). Antecedents and outcome of mindful buying. *Journal of Consumer Affairs*. https://doi.org/10.1111/joca.12565
Mathur, A., Moschis, G. P., & Lee, E. (2008). A longitudinal study of the effects of life status changes on changes in consumer preferences. *Journal of the Academy of Marketing Science, 36*(2), 234–246.
Mollick, E. R., & Mollick, L. (2023). *Using AI to implement effective teaching strategies in classrooms: Five strategies, including prompts*. Retrieved from https://doi.org/10.2139/ssrn.4391243
Moschis, G. P. (2007). Life course perspectives on consumer behavior. *Journal of the Academy of Marketing Science, 35*(2), 295–397.
Moschis, G. P. (2019). *Consumer behavior over the life course*. Springer.
Moschis, G. P. (2021). The life course paradigm and consumer behavior: Research frontiers and future directions. *Psychology & Marketing, 38*(11), 2034–2050. https://doi.org/10.1002/mar.21586
Moschis, G. P. (2022). *Marketing to the aging population*. Springer.
Moschis, G. P., & Mathur, A. (in print). Seeking profits by enhancing consumer well-being; A life course perspective. In F. Sonmez (Ed.), *Consumer psychological wellbeing*. Springer.
Moschis, G. P., Mathur, A., & Shannon, R. (2020). Toward achieving sustainable food consumption: Insights from the life course paradigm. *Sustainability, 12*(13), 1–18.
Prakitsuwan, P., & Moschis, G. P. (2020). Well-being in later life: A life course perspective. *Journal of Services Marketing, 14*(2), 152–167.
Prakitsuwan, P., Moschis, G. P., & Shannon, R. (2022). Using the life course paradigm to study financial well-being in late life. *Asia Pacific Journal of Marketing and Logistics, 34*(1), 60–74.
Purvis, B., Mao, Y., & Robinson, D. (2019). Three pillars of sustainability: In search of conceptual origins. *Sustainability Science, 14*, 681–695. https://doi.org/10.1007/s11625-018-0627-5
Rakrachakarn, R., & Kohlbacher, F. (2020). Natural disasters and the life course paradigm: The case of 2011 Japanese triple disaster. *Journal of Global Scholars of Marketing Science, 30*(1), 76–87. https://doi.org/10.1080/21639159.2019.1613910
Rowe, J. W., & Kahn, R. L. (2015). Successful aging 2.0: Conceptual expansions for the 21st century. *The Journals of Gerontology Series B: Psychological Sciences and Social Sciences, 70*(4), 593–596.
Sheth, J. N., Sethia, N. K., & Srinivas, S. (2011). Mindful consumption: A customer-centric approach to sustainability. *Journal of the Academy of Marketing Science, 39*(1), 21–39.
Sneath, J., Lacey, R. & Kennett-Hansel, P. (2009). Coping with a natural disaster: Losses, emotions, and impulsive and compulsive buying. *Marketing Letters, 20*(1), 45–60.

Spicer, A. (2015, May 21). Explainer: What is an h-index and how is it calculated? *The Conversation*. https://theconversation.com/explainer-what-is-an-h-index-and-how-is-it-calculated-41162

Stowe, J. D., & Cooney, T. M. (2014). Examining Rowe and Kahn's concept of successful aging: Importance of taking a life course perspective, *The Gerontologist, 55*(1), 43–50.

Stremersch, S., Verniers, I., & Verhoef, P. C. (2007). The quest for citations: Drivers of article impact. *Journal of Marketing, 71*(3), 171–193. https://doi.org/10.1509/jmkg.71.3.171

Suttharattanagul, S. L., Cai, Y., & Moschis, G. P. (2022). Life course explanations of consumer responses to threats: The case of COVID-19. *Cogent Business & Management, 9*, 1. https://doi.org/10.1080/23311975.2022.2151193

Thelwall, M., & Sud, P. (2022). Scopus 1900–2020: Growth in articles, abstracts, countries, fields, and journals. *Quantitative Science Studies, 3*(1), 37–50.

Xiao, Y., & Watson, M. (2019). Guidance on conducting a systematic literature review. *Journal of Planning Education and Research, 39*(1), 93–112. https://doi.org/10.1177/0739456X1772397

Index

G. P. Moschis, *Academic Research in Business and the Social Sciences*,
https://doi.org/10.1007/978-3-031-56548-9

SPRINGER NATURE

GPSR Compliance

The European Union's (EU) General Product Safety Regulation (GPSR) is a set of rules that requires consumer products to be safe and our obligations to ensure this.

If you have any concerns about our products, you can contact us on ProductSafety@springernature.com

In case Publisher is established outside the EU, the EU authorized representative is:

Springer Nature Customer Service Center GmbH
Europaplatz 3
69115 Heidelberg, Germany

The manufacturer's authorised representative in the EU is Springer Nature Customer Service Centre GmbH, Europaplatz 3, 69115 Heidelberg, Germany. If you have any concerns regarding our products, please contact ProductSafety@springernature.com

Printed and bound by CPI Group (UK) Ltd, Croydon, CR0 4YY
01/10/2026
02225849-0012